JUVENILE
JUSTICE
IN
AMERICA

GLENCOE CRIMINAL JUSTICE TEXTS

Allen/Simonsen: **Corrections in America: An Introduction (Second Edition)**
Bloomquist: **Marijuana: The Second Trip**
*Brandstatter/Hyman: **Fundamentals of Law Enforcement**
*Coffey/Eldefonso: **Process and Impact of Justice**
*DeAngelis: **Criminalistics for the Investigator**
Eldefonso: **Issues in Corrections**
Eldefonso: **Readings in Criminal Justice**
*Eldefonso/Coffey: **Process and Impact of the Juvenile Justice System**
*Eldefonso/Hartinger: **Control, Treatment, and Rehabilitation of Juvenile Offenders**
*Engel/DeGreen/Rebo: **The Justice Game: A Simulation**
*Gourley: **Effective Municipal Police Organization**
*Kamm/Hunt/Fleming: **Juvenile Law and Procedures in California (Revised Edition)**
LeGrande: **The Basic Processes of Criminal Justice**
*Lentini: **Vice and Narcotics Control**
*Melnicoe/Mennig: **Elements of Police Supervision (Second Edition)**
Murrell/Lester: **Introduction to Juvenile Delinquency**
*Nelson: **Preliminary Investigation and Police Reporting: A Complete Guide to Police Written Communication**
*Pursley: **Introduction to Criminal Justice**
*Radelet: **The Police and the Community (Second Edition)**
*Radelet/Reed: **The Police and the Community: Studies**
*Roberts/Bristow: **An Introduction to Modern Police Firearms**
*Simonsen/Gordon: **Juvenile Justice in America**
*Waddington: **Arrest, Search, and Seizure**
*Waddington: **Criminal Evidence**
Walton: **Laboratory Manual for Introductory Forensic Science**
*Wicks/Platt: **Drug Abuse: A Criminal Justice Primer**

*GLENCOE CRIMINAL JUSTICE SERIES

G. Douglas Gourley, General Editor
Professor Emeritus and Former Chairman
Department of Criminal Justice
California State University, Los Angeles

About the Authors

Clifford E. Simonsen received a Bachelor of Science in Law Enforcement and Corrections from the University of Nebraska at Omaha while an officer in the Army Military Police Corps. He later finished graduate studies at Florida State University, earning a Master of Science degree in Criminology. After leaving the Army, he was a Research Associate at the Center for the Study of Crime and Delinquency at the Ohio State University, where he received a Master's degree in Public Administration and a Ph.D. in Public Administration of Criminal Justice.

Dr. Simonsen was employed in the Office of Research, Department of Social and Health Services, state of Washington, as primary Research Director in adult and juvenile corrections. He is presently the Chairman of the Law and Justice Program at City College, an accredited private college in Seattle, Washington. He has authored, or co-authored, three texts in criminal justice, including *Corrections in America: An Introduction.*

Marshall S. Gordon III is a graduate of West Virginia University, where he majored in Political Science and Sociology, and of The Ohio State University, where he received a Master of Social Work degree, majoring in Research, Corrections, and Welfare Policy. Mr. Gordon began his professional career as a caseworker in Columbus, Ohio. He was a policy analyst for the Ohio Department of Public Welfare and, most recently, was the Research Project Director for a federally funded project regarding the diagnosis and treatment of adjudicated delinquents in the state of Washington. Mr. Gordon is presently living in New England where he is working as a free-lance writer.

JUVENILE JUSTICE IN AMERICA

CLIFFORD E. SIMONSEN
Chairman, Law and Justice Program
City College
Seattle, Washington

MARSHALL S. GORDON III
Office of Research
Department of Social and Health Services
State of Washington

GLENCOE PUBLISHING CO., INC.
Encino, California

Collier Macmillan Publishers
London

THIS BOOK IS DEDICATED TO OUR CHILDREN:
To Rick and Sheri, who got through childhood
without the juvenile justice system.
And to Jason and Sara, who we know will do the same.

Copyright © 1979 by Clifford E. Simonsen and Marshall S. Gordon III

Printed in the United States of America

Glencoe Publishing Co., Inc.
17337 Ventura Boulevard
Encino, California 91316
Collier Macmillan Canada, Ltd.

Library of Congress Catalog Card Number: 77-73253

1 2 3 4 5 6 7 8 9   83 82 81 80 79

ISBN 0-02-478350-1

Contents

Foreword

This introductory text to juvenile justice in America is both welcome and timely. It examines in considerable detail how the juvenile justice process has evolved and expanded as society has sought to understand, to control, and to influence change in the delinquent behavior of children and youth below the age of majority. Not long before this text was written that age limit was 21 years. Today, the eighteenth birthday is the upper limit of what some consider the protections of juvenile justice—and what others consider its threats and dangers.

Authors Simonsen and Gordon offer a comprehensive and historical review of juvenile justice with candid insights into the progress and regression, the successes and failures which have been part of the efforts to respond effectively to the increasing social problem of delinquency. Progress is measured in terms of broad public commitment to treat violations of law by children more humanely and with more understanding and concern. Regression is found in a juvenile justice system that still and often illegally detains hundreds of thousands of children annually in common jails. Successes are realized from the intervention of juvenile justice services whereby many youngsters often gain the help and self-esteem essential to avoid further involvement in crime. Failures continue because the greatest inequities of juvenile justice still are disproportionately visited upon the poor and minority children in American society.

Despite public commitment to the policy of treating juvenile law violators differently, the juvenile justice system has not been understood by the public. While basically a reactive system, the public today expects that it serve as a preventative or proactive system. Like all public institutions, juvenile justice has responded to its perception of public expectation by concentrating most of its time and resources upon the child as noncriminal offender, that is, as a runaway, a truant, or a rebel against parental authority. As the authors cite, the juvenile court was originally established to deal with crimes of children. Increasingly, however, juvenile "criminals" are being certified from the juvenile to the criminal justice system. Indeed the U.S. Supreme Court in the *Kent* and *Gault* cases has pointed out the failures of the juvenile justice system based on the principle of *parens patriae* or the state as substitute parent.

In the view of many of its critics the best way to prevent children becoming adult criminals is to divert as many as possible from the juvenile justice system. Thus, along with the current debate about whether status (noncriminal) offenders should be removed totally from juvenile justice jurisdiction by statute, the text introduces the student to what is developing as a new system of diversion services. Some of these services are adjuncts to police and probation services; others are operated by the juvenile court itself. A theory is evolving, however, that if children are to be truly diverted the alternative services had best be operated outside the juvenile justice system.

The 1940s and 1950s were years of increased centralization of juvenile justice services. The American Law Institute's Model Youth Correction Authority Act influenced the expansion of state leadership and administration for juvenile justice. The immediate and unfortunate impact of this era was the dramatic increase in the institutionalization of children. Most large cities, often with state subsidy and technical assistance, built juvenile detention homes in order to separate children from adult jails. The great size of the detention homes, however, assured the incarceration of far more children than when only the jail was available. State diagnostic centers were set up to diagnose the mental and emotional ills of delinquents and old and new institutions were given new names implying but seldom rendering various levels of treatment for those ills. Ironically, parole or aftercare for the child released from an institution lagged far behind concomitant developments in the criminal justice field.

In the 1960s and 1970s the appellate courts could no longer ignore the inequities of the juvenile justice system. The long-standing denial of procedural rights was addressed and corrected. But today substantive rights of children still await legal recognition. "Children must be controlled," states our highest court, and strangers with the mantle of authority—the teacher or guard—may still beat them if necessary to punish and to control. Long-awaited federal leadership and legislation in behalf of justice for children could, in America's Bicentennial Year, do no more than provide financial grants to states which would agree to stop locking up children (status offenders) who had not committed offenses that would be crimes if they were adults. After two years of federal funding only nine states were complying with the mandate.

Juvenile Justice in America is a significant and important text because it reveals a juvenile justice system teeming with conflicts and controversy indicative of major changes yet to come. The student who wishes will find opportunity to participate in reshaping the basic principles of juvenile justice and testing new theories of juvenile delinquency causation and treatment. More important will be the student who is motivated to study further in preparation for leadership to help guide the future evolution of a juvenile justice system which will enhance the rights of all children in America.

Milton G. Rector, President
National Council on Crime
and Delinquency

Preface

Juvenile Justice in America is written for the student who is beginning to develop an interest in the juvenile area of the criminal justice system. It focuses on the system itself, the processes within the system, and the young people who become involved in those processes. In addition, the reader is made familiar with the history and background of juvenile justice and its impact on the entire criminal justice system.

This text is based on a specific model emphasizing short chapters that logically build upon each other. The text is designed to keep the reader's attention and interest by presenting each chapter in self-contained yet interrelated parts that can be easily read in short sessions without excessive effort. References are contained at the end of the chapters.

Besides covering the practical and theoretical elements of the juvenile justice system and process, the text makes extensive use of quotes from current literature. Both authors are actively involved in researching the juvenile justice system and both have relied upon these experiences as well as those of colleagues and friends. Relevant and noteworthy excerpts have also been extracted from governmental publications, state research projects, and works by major authors in the juvenile justice field.

Organization of This Text

This text is divided into four major sections and seventeen chapters. Part I, "History and Development of Juvenile Justice," examines the past and present status of the handling of juvenile offenders and the emergence of the juvenile justice system. Chapter 1 examines historical antecedents and present-day application of concepts such as *parens patriae*. This chapter traces the history of juvenile justice from Babylon to America in 1925. Chapter 2 traces changes since 1925 and raises some questions whether the system adopted since that time is substantively different from the earlier attempts at juvenile justice.

Part II, ''The Delinquent: An Enigma,'' looks at the ''clients'' of the juvenile justice system and past attempts to classify and categorize them into manageable groups. Chapter 3 is a review of the major social, physiological, and psychological theories of the causes of delinquency. This chapter also proposes some alternative definitions for the term *delinquency*. Chapter 4 examines the attempts that have been made to classify juveniles for treatment and custody purposes. Prior probability approaches to classification in administrative decision making and in evaluating methods to obtain desired ends are examined as a tool of the classifier. Chapter 5 describes the types of juveniles who fall outside standard classification systems, such as the deviant, disabled, and defective delinquents, and explores possible treatment programs for each type. Chapter 6 explores general diagnostic procedures and the methods or settings used by individual states in treating delinquent youths. This chapter also explores the problems inherent in the implementation of meaningful diagnosis.

Part III, ''The System,'' shows how parts of the larger, adult criminal justice system are simply duplicated in the juvenile system. Chapter 7 examines the relationship that exists between the juvenile in trouble and the police, and the historical and organizational development of police juvenile units. Chapter 8 describes the unique development of the juvenile courts and the processes and participants in them. Juvenile probation is explained in detail in Chapter 9 and shown to be a major force in juvenile justice. Group homes, foster homes, and adoption as processes for handling juveniles and as functions of juvenile justice are explored in Chapter 10. Chapter 11 looks at the history and current status of juvenile institutions, as well as their development and ability to function as a part of the system. Chapter 12 deals with the less than fulfilled promise of juvenile parole and its current status. The last chapter in Part II examines the fragmentation of each subsection of juvenile justice system and the impact of fragmentation upon the administration of juvenile justice, including the exacerbation of the problems of the juvenile justice administrator.

Part IV, ''Change in the System,'' presents an overview of juvenile rights and explores the future developments of the juvenile system. Chapter 14 is devoted to the Supreme Court cases that have slowly provided rights to juveniles in trouble, particularly as they reflect changes in attitudes toward the rights of adults as well. Chapter 15 investigates the most important and much-discussed subject of the 1970s: prevention of delinquency. Diversion is the focal point of Chapter 16 and several successful diversion programs are examined in depth. The concluding chapter is a review of the previously covered subjects, with an effort to integrate the whole into an analysis of the present and future juvenile justice system.

Outstanding Features

The purpose of any textbook is to transmit and instill ideas and information in the minds of the readers. It is essential therefore that the writing be clear and understandable. *Readability* is a major feature of this text. It makes it easier for the instructor to use and it makes it pleasant for the student to read.

Along with and related to readability is the systematic manner in which the text has been organized and how the subject matter is developed for the reader. The subject matter develops in a logical and planned fashion to present the system and process as a whole.

An instructor's manual, with examination questions and objective outlines for each chapter, is another feature for the instructor. The instructor's manual also presents a detailed annotated bibliography for the instructor who wishes to add greater depth to the curriculum. Also included is an extensive glossary of terms as used in juvenile justice from the most current materials available.

C.E.S.
M.S.G.

Acknowledgments

The authors owe a great debt to many people who encouraged this project and who gave us inspiration. First, because both of us received much of our training under his brilliant mentorship, we thank Harry Allen, who has helped so many times in this effort. We thank Milton Rector, for his comments on the manuscript and his laudatory foreword. We also thank him for his continuing efforts to improve the treatment of children in trouble. Doug Vinzant and many others in Washington's Bureau of Juvenile Rehabilitation are thanked for their support and the many unpublished papers that they allowed us to use in our research.

We express our gratitude to all our colleagues around the country for their comments and support. We cannot name them individually, for we would surely miss someone who has helped. Nevertheless, you know who you are, and you also know how thankful we are.

A project of this magnitude takes one away from home and family more than is reasonable or fair. Thus thanks are due to our lovely wives and children, who sacrificed their claims on us in the hope that other children might benefit from our effort.

PART I

History and Development of Juvenile Justice

1 A Historical Look at Children in Trouble

Here by the labouring highway
With empty hands I stroll . . .

A.E. HOUSMAN
from A Shropshire Lad

Is the concept of a juvenile justice system new? Have juveniles traditionally received more lenient treatment from the law and those who enforce it than adults? How did early society handle the child who got out of line? In this brief overview, these and other questions will be examined. We will look at the antecedents of the juvenile justice system, from early history through the 1900s. Although this text is not intended to be a history, it is important for the student of today's juvenile justice system in America to be familiar with the origins of that system.

Early History (2000 B.C. to 600 A.D.)—Primitive Laws

According to Allen and Simonsen, in their recent text *Corrections in America*, behaviors can be viewed as points on a continuum, as shown in Figure 1–1.

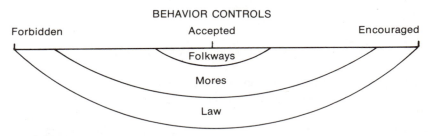

BEHAVIOR CONTROLS

Forbidden   Accepted   Encouraged

Folkways

Mores

Law

FIGURE 1–1. Continuum of behavior.

From the earliest times, certain acts have been universally forbidden or *proscribed*. Some examples are rape, incest, murder, treason, kidnapping, and rebellion. These acts fall at one end of the continuum. Approved or *prescribed* acts, such as having children, getting married, or having a job, fall at the opposite end. Most socially acceptable behavior falls somewhere near the middle. Mores were generally enforced through the use of strong social *disapproval*, such as ostracism, exile, punishment, and even death, or through the use of equally strong social *approval,* such as money and lands, dowries, and fertility rites.

As societies progressed, their loosely structured sanctions became codified laws. The enforcement function was gradually taken out of the hands of the general citizenry and given to special law enforcement groups ranging from witch hunters to the Magistrates Court of England.

The Old Testament concept of an "eye for an eye" (Exodus 21:24) best describes how ancient humans dealt with wrongs committed against themselves or their property. While this ancient concept of revenge cannot be considered to have been law, it has had a strong influence on the development of most legal systems throughout history.

> The practice of retaliation usually begins to develop into a system of criminal law when it becomes customary for the victim of the wrongdoing to accept pecuniary satisfaction in place of blood vengeance. This custom, when established, is usually dictated by tribal tradition and the relative strengths of the injured party and the wrongdoer. Custom has always exerted great force among primitive societies. The acceptance of vengeance in the form of a payment (e.g., cattle, food, personal services) was usually not compulsory and the victim was still free to take whatever vengeance he wished.[1]

As early societies developed language and writing skills, they began to record their laws. The Hammurabic Code, which dates from c. 2270 B.C., is considered by most historians to be the first comprehensive attempt at codifying such laws. This code recorded the laws of Babylon. It attempted to regulate business transactions, property rights, rights of master and slave, and family relationships.[2]

In the period of the Code of Hammurabi, the husband and father was decidedly in charge of the family:

> If a son strike his father, one shall cut off his hands.[3]

Compared to such early sanguine punishment of children by their parents, today's practice of referring the juvenile to court for rebellion or misconduct seems rather mild.

The code also provided for the adoption of children. However, in return for a home, adopted children were expected to be loyal to their adoptive parents. If such an adopted child were to deny the parentage of his adoptive family, he could have his tongue cut out; and if he were to return to his natural father's or mother's home, he could have an eye plucked out.[4]

The code also had many regulations regarding the care of children by parents and marital arrangements. However, these laws were concerned with behavior within the family unit; public offenses were not mentioned. This would lead one to believe that the family was the primary agent in supervision or punishment of its youth. It could also be surmised that outside the home, children suffered the same punishments as adults.

In *A Father and His Perverse Son,* Samuel Kramer quotes from Sumerian tablets dating back to 1750 B.C. These tablets further testify that the problems of parents with their children are as old as humanity.

In those days, boys attended school 12 hours a day all year long from the time they were very young through early manhood. Liberal use of corporal punishment helped to encourage their industriousness. The translation tells of an essay written by a professor at a Sumerian academy to his shiftless son. The father wants the son to stay in school, do his homework, respect his elders, and use his spare time constructively. In other words, the father admonishes his son to do just what most parents still tell their children—get a good education. The son rebels and the father is forced to shout and plead with him.

Peoples influenced by ancient Chinese civilizations had effective methods of dealing with families in which the children—and even the parents— became troublesome. For example, if a man murdered six members of another family, then he and five of his male children (irrespective of age) were executed to atone for the murders. Likewise, if a son were to commit a crime, the father could be flogged one hundred times or more in punishment, even if he knew nothing of the crime committed by his child. In the Old Testament, such acts were described as "visiting the sins of the fathers upon the children" and vice versa. However, the Hebrew Codes sought to change this approach and make each person (or child) punishable for only his or her *own* offenses.

The Babylonian and the Sumerian codes are just two examples of numerous codes of justice developed prior to Anglo-Saxon times. Another example is the sixth-century Byzantine Code of Justinian, which attempted to balance the punishment received with the crime committed. Thus there evolved the concept and symbol of the scales of justice.[5]

Eventually societies attempted to get away from vengeance and blood feuds in dealing with criminal behavior. The public good and the protection of the social order became more important than personal injury or revenge. For example, the Code of Draco, the criminal code of ancient Greece, although extremely harsh, was the first to allow *any citizen* to prosecute an offender in the name of the injured party. The word *Draconian* still means a very severe form of punishment.

Gradually, the severe punishments of the early laws were ameliorated, first in practice and later in amended and/or new laws. Among the Hebrews, for example, punishment by death was replaced by warnings and floggings. Finally, youth were divided into three groups; infant, prebescent, and adolescent, with penalties increasing in severity as the degree of maturity increased.[6]

Little has been recorded about crime and youth in early history. Our knowledge of the time consists of examples of some of the punishments. What types of court systems existed, what jails or prisons were like, and how the policing of juveniles was conducted remain historical mysteries.

Discipline and control of children was the responsibility of parents. Juveniles, when dealt with outside of the family, were probably handled by a royal court or local magistrate. No special juvenile courts existed. Persons, including children, were not generally imprisoned in early times as a form of punishment. They were normally only detained until their punishment was determined and applied. More recent and modern concepts, such as the workhouse or reform school, were unknown in earlier times.

The English Experience (600 A.D. to 1825)

In the Middle Ages, social disorder was widespread throughout the world. The Christian church exercised vast influence in Europe, and acted as the focal point of justice. Those who transgressed civil or canon law were forced to pay debts to both society and God. To determine innocence or guilt, the ordeal was the church's method of trial. The *ordeal* consisted of subjecting a person to painful and sometimes fatal tests. One such ordeal consisted of binding a person's arms and legs and throwing the person into a lake. If the person eventually floated to the surface, the verdict was innocent. If the person remained submerged, the verdict was guilty. In either case, the person was usually dead. Needless to say, the brutality of most of these ordeals ensured a high rate of conviction.

Sexual activities also came under the purview of the church, with those convicted of public or unnatural sexual acts receiving horrible punishments. Extreme punishment was meted out for crimes involving witchcraft or heresy. Often the mere suspicion of such acts resulted in death after severe punishment.

Laws for Juvenile Offenses During the Middle Ages

Just like today, there was delinquency in Medieval Europe, and laws provided specific penalties for offenses committed by children. Below are typical examples of English versions of a "juvenile justice system" in the Middle Ages.

THE LAWS OF KING INE, 688 A.D.–725 A.D.

Of Stealing

If any one steal, so that his wife and his children know it not, let him pay LX. shillings as "wite" [punishment]. But if he steal with the knowledge of all his household, let them all go into slavery. A boy of X. years may be privy to a theft. . . .[7]

THE LAWS OF KING AETHELSTAN, 924 A.D.

Of Thieves

First: that no thief be spared who may be taken "handhaebbende" [ie., with the goods in his hand] above XII. years, and above eight pence. And if any one so do, let him pay for the thief according to his "wēr" [*pretium nativitatis*], and let it not be the more settled for the thief, or that he clear himself thereby. But if he will defend himself, or flees away, then let him not be spared.[8]

The City of London Chamberlain's Court, or the City Custom of Apprenticeship, 1299

. . . The City Chamberlain's Court for dealing with offences of masters and apprentices was in existence in 1299. . . .

Next year the procedure was regulated, two Aldermen being associated with the Chamberlain for the purpose of ensuring that all indentures were registered at Guildhall, and for taking fines from apprentices. More serious cases were brought before the Mayor's Court by bill or petition.[9]

As noted above, by 1300 there was a considerable body of law regulating apprenticeships, laws which affected many free-born English children of the time. An apprentice had to be at least 12 years old; he was expected to be obedient, industrious, orderly, and not wasteful of the goods of his master. If an apprentice got out of line, the child could be sued in the Mayor's Court.[10]

The following is an illustrative example of the case of a delinquent child in sixteenth-century England:

This yeare, the 29 of Januarie [1537/8] was arreigned at Westminster in the afternoone a boye of Mr. Culpepers, Gentleman of the King's Privie Chamber, which had stolne his maisters purse and £11 of money, with a jewell of the Kinges which was in the same purse, and there condemned to death; but the morrowe after when he was brought to the place of execution, which was at the ende of the tylt yeard afore the Kinges Pallace at Westminster, and that the hangman was takinge the ladder from the gallowes, the Kinge sent his pardon for the sayde boye, and so he was saved from death, to the great comforte of all the people there present, &c. . . .[11]

The Chamberlain's Court (Gentlemen of the King's Prince Chamber) is considered to be the forerunner of our modern juvenile courts. This court handled matters between a master and an apprentice only, however. Offenses committed by an apprentice outside the purview of his master were handled by other courts.

Examples of Penalties for Juvenile Crime

The Christian church continued to play an important role in regulating the behavior of children; for example, John Calvin's Catechism (1556) describes punishment for disobedient children as follows:

> *The Minister*
>
> And what is to be sayd of them that be disobedient unto father and mother?
>
> *The Childe*
>
> God will not onely punish them with everlasting payne in the day of judgement, but he will execute also punishmente on theyr bodyes here in thys worlde; eyther by shortnynge their life, eyther by procuring them a shameful death, either at the least a life most miserable.[12]

Children could also be punished for heresy in those days. A blind boy was burned alive for such a crime in Gloucester in 1556, and a 12-year-old boy from Worcester spent several months in chains, narrowly escaping a similar death.

Many readers of Dickens' *Oliver Twist* will recall the gang of pickpockets with whom Oliver becomes involved. In *The Early History of the Guild of Merchant Taylors of London,* the author tells of an actual school of crime in London in 1585:

> Amongst our travells this one matter tumbled out by the waye, that one Wotton, a gentilman borne, and sometime a merchantmane of good crydit, who falling by time with decay kepte an alehouse at Smart's Key, near Billingsgate, and for some misdemeanour put downe. He reared up a new trade in lyfe and in the same house he procured all the cut-purses about this city to repair to the same house. There was a school house set up to learn young boys to cut purses. There were hung up two devyses, the one was a pocket and the other was a purse. The pocket had in it certain counters and was hung about, with hawks bells, and over the top did hang a little sacring bell, and he that could take out the counters without any noyse was allowed to be a public foyster, and he that could take a piece of sylver out of the purse without the noyse of any of the bells he was adjudged a judicial nypper.[13]

Frequently as not, punishment for crimes in the Middle Ages was the same for children as for adults. For example, children convicted of "petie treason" or willful murder could be either drowned, hanged, or burned alive, depending on their background. However, there were exceptions.

Burglary

It is not Burglary in an Infant of fourteene years of age; nor in poore persons that upon hunger shall enter a house for victuall under the value of twelve pence; nor in naturall fooles, or other persons that bee *non compos mentis* . . .[14]

Homicide

An infant of eight yeares of age, or above, may commit Homicide, and shall be hanged for it. . . .

And yet Sir *Edw. Coke* saith, that it is of an Infant, untill he be of the age of 14 yeares (which in law is accounted the age of discretion) as it is with a man *Non compos mentis;* and that in criminal causes (as felon &c.) his act and wrong shall not be imputed to him, for that *Actus non facit reum, nisi mens sit rea,* &c.[15]

Imprisonment

An Infant (through of yeeres of discretion, yet he shall suffer no imprisonment, nor other corporall paine, for any offence committed or done by him against any statute, except that an infant be expressed by name, in the statute.[16]

Murder of Another

. . . Whether an Infant within the age of Nine Years can be guilty of Murder?

And the Judges held, that he ought to be hanged. But *Fairefax* said, that the words of Fortescue were, viz. That the Reason why a person is executed for Murder, is, for example, that others may fear to offend; But such punishment can be no example to such an Infant or to a person that hath not discretion.[17]

Larceny

Whether an Infant, that is under the age of discretion, can commit Larceny?

An Infant, until he be of the age of 14, which in Law is accounted the age of discretion cannot commit Larceny, or other felony; for the principal end of punishment is, that others by his example may fear to offend: But such punishment can be no example to Infants, that are not of the age of Discretion.[18]

Under the laws of King Asthelstan (924–939 A.D.), any thief over 12 years old received pence. However, with the passage of time, the law was eased for children and no one under 16 years could be put to death unless he resisted or ran away.[19]

In addition to the Chamberlain's Court already mentioned, children were also tried in the central court in London, which was commonly called the Old Bailey. Court records reveal that the number of children tried in this court was very small compared to the number of adults. And although court records indicate that many children were sentenced to death, it cannot be ascertained whether these death penalties were ever carried out. Many sentences were commuted or the offender was pardoned by the judge, and such events often went unrecorded. The following transcripts, taken from seventeenth- and nineteenth-century court records, will give the reader an idea of the types of delinquent cases heard in those periods.

1681
July 6, 7, 8, 9.

William Buckley, a Youth, charged with murdering a Bailiff's follower who tried to arrest his master, was found guilty and was condemned to death.

. . .

Dec. 7, 8.

Lydia Arlington, a Girl of about ten years of Age, was Indicted with three more supposed to be her Accomplices, for picking two several Pockets, and Stealing Money to the value of six pounds, but the former taking it upon her Self, having (past doubt) received her Instructions in *Newgate* she was only found Guilty, and the rest acquitted. [This child's name was not listed among the six condemned to death, nor does it occur elsewhere in the sentences.]

1683/4
Feb. 27, 28.

Charles Atlee, a little Boy, Indicted for stealing out of the Shop of Obadiah Bennet, in the Parish of Stepney, 28 s. and 11 d. on the 26th of *January* last: a Maid proved, she saw him run into the Shop, and that it was taken out of the Money-Box, but upon a quick pursuit, he was apprehended, and the Money taken out of his Pocket: He was found Guilty of the said Felony. [Sentenced to be transported.][20]

. . .

1684
November.

Three boys, aged 12, 12, and 13, convicted of stealing, were sentenced to seven days imprisonment. Another boy, aged 12, for stealing a pocket-handkerchief was sentenced to seven years transportation.

   Thomas Fisher, aged 11, for breaking into the dwelling-house of John Ennies, shoe-maker, of Whitechapel, and stealing a bag and 10s. was condemned to death.

. . .

1836
January

James Lynch, aged 9, for stealing a handkerchief from the person of Mr. Henry Harris, in Farringdon Street—7 years transportation.

   John Johnson, aged 9, who had been tried before, was convicted of stealing a till, containing upwards of £1 . . . 7 years transportation.[21]

The examples of punishment of children in this period are many. In 1682, Quaker children in Bristol were put in the stocks and whipped for misbehavior. In Halifax in 1691, children were thrown into debtors prison; to avoid their rotting in jail and dying of starvation, these children were compelled to work for their creditors until the debt was paid. Many were less than 14 years of age. In 1716, in England, a mother and her 11-year-old daughter were executed for witchcraft.

Other Aspects of the Juvenile Problem in the Eighteenth and Nineteenth Centuries

Besides punishment, there were other aspects of juvenile delinquency in the European experience which are relevant. Around the early 1700s, people began to express concern about a growing population of vagrant, destitute, and often delinquent children.

> *The Mayor of London Orders Constables to Take Up Vagrant Children, 1732.*
>
> Mayors Proclamation, November 28, 1732.
>
> This Court taking Notice, that divers Poor Vagrant Children are suffered to skulk in the Night-time, and lie upon Bulks, Stalls, and other Places in the Public Streets of this City, whereby many of them perish by the Extremity of the Weather, and other Inconveniences ensue. Therefore to prevent the same for the Future, This Court doth desire the several Aldermen of this City to call before them the several Constables and Beadles within their respective Wards, and to give them strictly in charge, that if they or any of them shall find any poor Vagrant-Child, or Children, or others, lurking in the Publick Streets of this City in the Night-time, that they immediately apprehend such, and secure him, her or them, in their Watch-house, or some other convenient Place, until they convey them before some Justice of the Peace for this City and Liberty thereof, that they may be examined and sent to the Places of their Legal Settlements, or otherwise disposed of according to Law. And if any Constable, Beadle, or other Officer, shall be found negligent or remiss in his Duty, and shall suffer such poor Child, or Children, or others, to be vagrant, or lie in the said Streets, without obeying this Order as aforesaid, such Constable, Beadle, or other Officer, shall be punished for such his or their Neglect with the utmost Severity of the Law. . . .[22]

Later in the same century, other methods of dealing with delinquent or vagrant youth were tried. One of them, as explained below, could well be an early forerunner for our present trade or industrial school.

> *The Marine Society Apprentices Vagrant and Delinquent Boys to Sea Service on Warships, 1756*
>
> Jonas Hanway, *An Account of the Marine Society . . .*
> *from the Commencement of July 1756, to September 30, 1759.*
>
> One of the earliest private agencies in London to become interested in reclaiming delinquent boys was the Marine Society, established in 1756. No single individual can claim the undisputed honor of founding this Society, but Jonas Hanway, an eccentric London philanthropist, and Sir John Fielding,

blind magistrate, both contributed substantially of their services in getting the infant Society started and in smooth working order.

England at this time was at war with France and Spain, and needed greatly to increase its naval forces. At this juncture the Marine Society was organized with the primary object of encouraging recruits for the Royal Navy, first by outfitting landmen with suitable clothing for sea service (the navy had no regular uniform at this time), and second, by sending stout, active boys, properly clothed, between the ages of thirteen and fifteen, to serve on board the King's ships, as servants to the captains and the other officers. It was expected that these boys after getting a taste of sea life would remain in the service as active sailors. The Society announced it would take no runaway apprentices, nor boys running away from home without their parents' knowledge. Since three thousand boys were needed however, the Society could not be too rigid in its requirements, as regards social status and conduct record. Young vagabonds from the city streets, who were not "defective in *sight, or lame, dwarfish*, or laboring under any *chronical* distemper" were regarded as fair subjects for recruiting. Magistrates were encouraged also to commit delinquent boys to the Marine Society, rather than send them to prison. Even after boys were committed to prison they sometimes were released to the Society, which was proud to claim that by checking these young vagabonds *"in the dawnings of iniquity, Tyburn* might be left a *desert."* [23]

In 1758, there was begun in London a prototype of what has come to be known as a group home; it was established by Sir John Fielding and was called a House of Refuge for Orphan Girls. The purpose of this home was to rescue vagrant girls from almost certain lives of prostitution.

Public asylums for the children of convicts and other destitute or neglected children, such as that founded by the Philanthropic Society in London, were proposed in 1786. In the late 1700s, records from the *Report of the Select Committee Appointed by the House of Commons*, concerned with establishing a new police in the metropolis, show that between 1787 and 1797, 93 delinquent children were transported for crimes from England to Australia. This practice continued into the early 1800s. During transportation, the children were kept in confinement upon the various decrepit ships which took them from their native land.

Boys on Board the Hulks

On board the *Leviathan* [out of a total of 500 convicts] were 35 convicts under 20 years of age, a boy of 13 was the youngest. . . .

On board the *Retribution*, the wards were better ventilated than in the other ships,—they contained in the whole 552 prisoners, and the following is a list of their respective ages and sentences:

Boys under 15 years of age for life . . . . 8 ⎫
Ditto, for 14 years . . . . 6 ⎬ Total 37
Ditto, for 7 years . . . . 23 ⎭

On board this ship were 37 boys confined . . . and not working on shore [with the men]:—they are employed as tailors, shoemakers, coopers, carpenters, bookbinders, etc. . . . Among these boys were two little infants from Newgate of nine years of age. . . .[24]

By 1829, transportation for life was recommended for the growing number of juvenile delinquents.

Imprisonment of children, while frowned upon by early social reformers, did exist. The infamous Newgate Prison in London was one example.

> The keeper of Newgate never attended divine service; and the ordinary did not consider the morals of even the children, who were in Prison, as being under his care and attention. *No care was taken to inform him of the sick, till he got a warning to perform a funeral.* There was no separation of the young from the old, the children of either sex from the hardened criminal. Boys of the tenderest years, and girls of the ages of ten, twelve, and thirteen were exposed to the vicious contagion, that predominated in all parts of the Prison; and drunkenness prevailed to such an extent, and was so common, that, unaccompanied with riot, it attracted no notice.
>
> . . . from the 1st of January, 1816, to the same day, 1817, eighty-five girls, and four hundred and twenty-nine boys, under twenty years of age, were confined in that Prison; and thus were more than five hundred young persons exposed last year to the contamination of the Prison System of the metropolis, and by much the greater proportion of them were associated with old offenders, and hardened delinquents.[25]

The social reformers did have a hand in changing some of the more deplorable conditions of the time, including the treatment and confinement of young criminals. The Warwick County Asylum, instituted in 1818, was the result of the united endeavors and generous contributions of concerned, benevolent citizens. The proposed object of the asylum was to make available to the criminal boy a place where he could escape the ways of vice and corruption. As is the case today, early efforts at reform suffered from the lack of sufficient funds. The public soon lost interest in the asylum, and the only way it survived was to show the franchised public that it could save them money.

Classifying Juvenile Delinquents During the Eighteenth and Nineteenth Centuries

The age at which a child should be held responsible for his or her actions has been debated for centuries. Sir William Blackstone stated that no child under the age of discretion should be punished for any crime.[26] However, just what the age of discretion was seemed unclear; it varied from nation to nation. Today it still varies from state to state.

Early attempts were made at a classification system for delinquent children. Civil law separated minors (those persons under the age of 25) into three classes: (1) *infants*, from birth to 7 years, (2) *pueritia*, from 7 to 14, and (3) *puberta*, from 14 to 25.

The period of pueritia, or childhood, was further divided into two subcategories: (1) *aetas pueritia proxima,* ages 7 to 10½, and (2) *aetas pubertati proxima,* ages 10½ to 14. Generally, children in the first stage of life and the first half of the second stage, or from birth through 10½ years, were not punishable for any crime. Delinquent children from 10½ to 14 years of age were punishable only if the prosecution could prove intent, and persons 14 to 25 could receive capital and other punishments as readily as adults.

By 1815 juvenile crime in London had reached very serious proportions, to the extent that inquiries were conducted to discover the causes. One of the earliest recorded surveys of juvenile delinquency took place in London between 1815 and 1816. According to the survey, juvenile delinquency in metropolitan London was epidemic. Organized gangs of homeless boys survived life on the streets by picking pockets and stealing.

Actual figures on the number of delinquents in metropolitan London at the time of the survey are not available. However, the committee had reason to believe that there were thousands of boys under the age of 17 who daily engaged in criminal activities.

The group formed to conduct the survey realized that inquiry alone would serve no purpose, so they also set out to find ways of providing help so that these wayward youths might turn their paths from vice to virtue. In this effort, they often ran into problems similar to those encountered today. They had to find funding sources for suggested reforms. They had to convince the parents or guardians of a delinquent youth that the best interests of the juvenile might be served in the community and not in prison.[27]

Causal Theories of Delinquency in Nineteenth-Century England

At the time there were several popular theories about the causes of delinquency. Not too surprisingly, causal theories of delinquency have changed little over the centuries. The following passage, taken from *A Treatise on the Police and Crimes of the Metropolis* by John Wade is an example of one such theory.

> There are, probably, 70,000 persons in the Metropolis [London] who regularly live by theft and fraud; most of these have women, with whom they cohabit, and their offspring, as a matter of course, follow the example of their parents, and recruit the general mass of mendicancy, prostitution, and delinquency. This is the chief source of juvenile delinquents, who are also augmented by children, abandoned by the profligate among the working classes, by those of poor debtors confined, of paupers without settlement, and by a few wayward spirits from reputable families, who leave their homes without cause, either from the neglect or misfortune of their natural protectors. Children of this description are found in every part of the metropolis, especially in the vicinity of the theatres, the marketplaces, the parks, fields, and outskirts of the town.

Many of them belong to organized gangs of depredators, and are in the regular employ and training of older thieves; others obtain a precarious subsistence by begging, running errands, selling playbills, picking pockets, and pilfering from shops and stalls. Some of them never knew what it is to be in a bed, taking refuge in sheds, under stalls, piazzas, and about brick-kilns; they have no homes; others have homes, either with their parents, or in obscure lodging-houses, but to which they cannot return unless the day's industry of crime has produced a stipulated sum.[28]

According to this report, some chief causes, if not *the* chief causes, of delinquency were poverty, lack of education, and poor parental guidance. Reliable statistics today show that children from low-income families who do not get an education are much more likely to get into trouble with the law by the age of 18 than youths from middle- or high-income families.

Television, pool halls, and even comic books, have been singled out as the cause of juvenile delinquency in the twentieth century. However, to prove that nothing is really new, the reader should note the following:

Lewd Ballads and Prints Corrupt the Young, 1778

> William Smith (M.D.), *Mild Punishments Sound Policy; or*
> *Observations on the Laws Relative to Debtors and Felons . . .*
> (London, 1778).

Even the ballad singers and street musicians are useful in their spheres to promote vice. . . .

Observe who listen to and buy those lewd ballads, and you will find that young people of both sexes, particularly apprentice boys, servant maids, and gentlemen's servants, are the purchasers. They read them with the greatest avidity, and thereby poison their morals, by affording fuel to their turbulent passions. . . .[29]

and

Harmful Effect of Indecent Publications, 1790–1792

> *Memoirs of an Unfortunate Young Lady; . . .* published in
> *The Bristol Mercury . . .* (Bristol, 1790).

[This touching and convincing autobiography is dated "Bristol, May 11, 1790" and is signed "A Female Penitent." "The public may be certified that this is a true account of an unhappy young woman—though somewhat corrected and improved." She attributes her downfall to two older girl companions.]

. . . [My companions] were great readers—and procured for themselves, and lent to me several books that were TOO BAD indeed and had the most ruinous tendency. To mention their titles is needless, and might be injurious to any who may see this account.[30]

In addition to the above-mentioned causes, the "public" was also blamed for the failure of the Poor Laws of the time to provide adequate homes and care for destitute children.

However, poor children did not make up the entire population of England's delinquents. As has been our own experience in recent years, reforms are made and public interest aroused only when the problem of crime and delinquency creeps out of the slums and begins to affect the rich or well-to-do.

Discipline of English Children of the Upper Middle Classes, 1753

> James Nelson, *An Essay on the Government of Children, Under Three General Heads: Viz. Health, Manners and Education* (London, 1753).

[A rambling, discursive essay by an apothecary whose ideas of child discipline are conditioned by the difficulties he has experienced in getting the pampered, spoiled children of the well-to-do classes to take disagreeable medicine when they are sick.]

In the Government of Children Parents should be obstinately good; that is, set out upon right Principles, and then pursue them with Spirit and Resolution: otherwise their Children will soon grow too cunning for them, and take the Advantage of their Weakness.

Severe and frequent Whipping is I think a very bad Practice; it inflames the Skin, it puts the Blood into a Ferment, and there is besides, a Meanness, a Degree of Ignominy attending it, which makes it very unbecoming: still there may be Occasions which will render it necessary; but I earnestly advise that all the milder Methods be first try'd. A coarse clamorous manner of enforcing Obedience is also to be avoided; it is vulgar, and nothing vulgar should be seen in the Behaviour of Parents to their Children, because through the Eyes and Ears it taints their tender Minds: still, let Parents make their Children later see and feel the Power they have over them.[31]

Early American Experience: From Colonial Times to 1825

Thus far, the beginnings of juvenile justice systems have been described as they existed in Europe, particularly in England. This brief history gives the reader a background to better understand the source of America's juvenile justice system and the major influences on that system.

Colonial youth did not escape the wrath of secular law or of strict Puritan preachings, nor was their treatment much different from that of youth in "jolly old England." Punishment of delinquent children in early New England colonies (1641–1672) is described in the following passages:[32]

Tryals

Also Children, Ideots, Distracted persons, and all that are Strangers or new comers to our Plantation, shall have such allowances, and dispensations in any case, whether Criminal or others, as Religion and Reason require [1641].

> *The Laws and Liberties of Massachusetts*, reprinted from the copy of the 1648 Edition.

Burglarie and Theft

For the prevention of Pilfring and Theft, it is ordered by this Court and Authoritie therof; that if any person shal be taken or known to rob any orchard or garden, that shall hurt, or steal away any grafts or fruit trees, fruits, linnen, woollen, or any other goods left out in orchards, gardens, backsides; or any other place in house or fields: or shall steal any wood or other goods from the water-side, from mens doors, or yards; he shall forfeit treble damage to the owners therof. And if they be children, or servants that shall trespasse heerin, if their parents or masters will not pay the penaltie before expressed, they shal be openly whipped. . . .

Capital Lawes

If any child, or children, above sixteen years old, and of sufficient understanding, shall CURSE, or SMITE their natural FATHER, or MOTHER; he or they shall be put to death: unles it can be sufficiently testified that the Parents have been very unchristianly negligent in the education of such children; or so provoked them by extream, and cruel correction; that they have been forced therunto to preserve themselves from death or maiming. *Exod.* 21. 17. *Lev.* 20. 9 *Exod.* 21. 15.

. . .

Children

[The selectmen of every town are required to keep a vigilant eye on the inhabitants to the end that the fathers shall teach their children knowledge of the English tongue and of the capital laws, and knowledge of the catechism, and shall instruct them in some honest lawful calling, labor or employment. If parents do not do this, the children shall be taken away and placed (boys until twenty-one, girls until eighteen) with masters who will so teach and instruct them.]

The Code of 1650, Being a Compilation of the Earliest Laws and Orders of the General Court of Connecticut . . .
(Hartford, 1822).

The Christian church continued, even in the New World, to have a major influence over the laws of the day. The Connecticut Code of 1650, for example, had as its first dozen capital crimes the following, all supported by biblical references: idolatry, witchcraft, blasphemy, willful murder, slaying through deceit, bestiality, sodomy, adultery, rape, man-stealing, giving false testimony, and rebellion against the commonwealth.

Although most children were given lesser penalties or punishments than adults, many were not. For example:

A Twelve-Year-Old Pequot Indian Girl Hanged for the Murder of a Six-Year-Old White Girl, 1786

Henry Channing, *God Admonishing his People of their Duty, as Parents and Masters. A Sermon, Preached at New-London, December 20th, 1786.*

As the public may wish to be informed more particularly respecting the criminal, Hannah Ocuish, than they have yet been: we have collected the following particulars, which it may not be improper to annex as an appendix of the preceding discourse.

She was born at *Groton*. Early in life she discovered the maliciousness and cruelty of her disposition.

When she was brought to the bar to receive sentence of death, her stupidity and unconcern astonished everyone. While that benevolent tenderness which distinguishes his honor the Chief Justice, almost prevented utterance, and the spectators could not refrain from tears; the prisoner alone appeared scarcely to attend.

About a fortnight before her execution she appeared to realize her danger, and was more concerned for herself. She continued nearly in the same state until the Monday night before her execution: when she appeared greatly affected; saying, that she was distressed for her soul. She continued in tears most of Tuesday, and Wednesday which was the day of execution. At the place of execution she said very little, appeared greatly afraid, and seemed to want somebody to help her. After a prayer adapted to her unhappy situation, was offered to Heaven, she thanked the sheriff for his kindness to her, and then passed into that state which *never* ends.

Negro Slave Boy, Fourteen, Mutilated, Branded, and Whipped with One Hundred Lashes for Aiding in the Murder of His Master, While His Older Brother Was Burned at the Stake, March, 1787.

Duplin County (N.C.) Records, Court Minutes, 1784–1791.

At a Special Court begun and held at the Court House in Duplin County on Thursday, the 15th day of March in the Year of our Lord 1787, for the immediate Tryal of Darby and Peter, two Negroe slaves, the Property of the late William Taylor Esq. now committed and to be tryed for the Murder of the said William Taylor, their Master, which Court being Summoned and Convened by the Sheriff of the said County and being duly Qualified according to law—were Present to wit

        Thomas Routledge
        Joseph Dickson   Esquires Justices[33]
        James Gillespie

The American colonies were quick to catch up with and even surpass the English at incarcerating criminals, including juveniles. The Quakers were instrumental in founding the nation's first true correctional institution, the Walnut Street Jail, in Philadelphia in 1790.

Three Boston Boys Sentenced to the Charlestown State Prison for Stealing, 1813

Boston Municipal Court.

On Saturday, Dec. 11, 1813, three boys, the oldest of whom was about sixteen years of age and the youngest about thirteen, were sentenced in the Municipal Court to five days' solitary imprisonment and five years hard labour in the State Prison, for breaking into a store in the night-time, and stealing a pocketbook, containing, with other articles, about nine hundred dollars in bank bills.[34]

Although the present method of using a separate court for juveniles had not yet been implemented, juvenile delinquents did come before colonial courts and early American courts. It seems that court judges faced the problem of what to do with these children then as now.

Children before the Criminal Courts in New York and in Baltimore, c. 1820

The Second Annual Report of the Managers of the Society for the Prevention of Pauperism in the City of New York . . .
December 29, 1819.

[Statement of Mayor C. D. Colden of New York City]

At every court of sessions, young culprits, from twelve to eighteen years of age, are presented. *The court is utterly at a loss how to dispose of these children.* [emphasis added] If they are sent for a short time to the penitentiary, they are no sooner liberated, then they again appear at the bar. Since I have been on the bench, I have in many instances, sentenced the same child several times. They are seduced by old and experienced rogues, to assist in their depredations. It will not do to let them go unpunished; but it seems useless and endless, to inflict punishments which produce no reformation. . . .[35]

America, too, had its reform movements. Several citizen groups tried to deal with the problem of the rising number of juvenile delinquents. *Dunlap's American Daily Advertiser,* August 5, 1791, carried the following editorial concerning teenage gangs in Philadelphia:

The custom of permitting boys to ramble about the streets by night, is productive of the most serious and alarming consequences to their morals. Assembled in corners, and concealed from every eye, they can securely indulge themselves in mischief of every kind. The older ones train up the younger, in the same path, which they themselves pursue; and here produce in miniature, that mischief, which is produced, on a larger scale, by permitting prisoners to associate together in crowds within the walls of a jail. What avails it to spend the public money in erecting solitary cells to keep a *few* prisoners from being corrupted by evil communication, whilst we hourly expose *hundreds* of our children to corruption from the same cause; and this too, at an age, when the mind is much more susceptible of every impression, whether good or evil? But, tell it not in New-York, neither publish it in the streets of Baltimore, that the citizens of Philadelphia thus strain at gnats, while they swallow camels,—as it were hurtle-berries!

. . .

A few nights ago, a number of boys assembled in Fifth-street, between Market and Chestnut-streets, to divert themselves with firing squibs. A gentleman on horse-back, and a servant driving a carriage, with a pair of horses, happened to pass by at the same instant; and also several persons on foot, who might have had their limbs shattered, if the horses had broken loose. The boys thought this a fine opportunity for sport and mischief, and eagerly seized the moment, to light a squib, and fling it towards the horses. Luckily, indeed, the beasts were in good hands, and, though frighted, were yet, by dextrous management, prevented from taking head. Had not this been the case, the newspapers might, before now, have given us a list of five or six persons killed or wounded. This may be sport to *boys*, but 'tis death to *us* men.[36]

It is obvious that the editor of this early American newspaper was not at all happy about the differential treatment afforded youths, even in 1791.

In 1823, a House of Refuge for juvenile delinquents was proposed by the New York Society for the Prevention of Pauperism. To plea for their cause, the society obtained statistics on persons brought before the Police Magistrates during 1822. There were 450 persons, all under the age of 25, and a considerable percentage of these were both boys and girls from ages 9 to 16. None of these children had actually been charged with a crime other than vagrancy; they had no homes and were forced to fend for themselves.

Age of Reform and Reform Schools: 1825 to the Early 1900s

As the Industrial Revolution began, many secular and puritanical laws against truancy and vagrancy were conveniently forgotten in order to take advantage of cheap child labor and to make way for the urban sweatshops which lay just around the corner. Unfortunately for adults as well as for children, the expanding, exploitative economy of young America provided less protection for the individual. In an attempt to keep pace with the newly emerging economy and its needs, the prison movement's search for the causes of delinquency soon gave way to merely dealing with the physical manifestations of delinquency and to exploiting the child labor potential.

By 1828 the first institution for juvenile delinquents in the United States came into existence. It had taken over five years of careful planning and maneuvering for public support on the part of the Society for the Prevention of Pauperism, which went on to become the Society for the Reformation of Juvenile Delinquents in the City of New York.

The concept of this early institution was sound; it provided juveniles with a place of imprisonment or punishment which separated them from adults. However, what it did *not* provide was separate kinds of punishments. Children were still bound and fettered as adults with such things as handcuffs, the ball and chain, leg irons, and the ''barrel.''[37]

A routine day in the House of Refuge in 1828 was not unlike a child's routine day in one of our modern institutions.

> The Refuge movement spread north to Boston and south to Baltimore and became the public-private merger solution to the growing number of homeless and troublesome street kids. As it spread, cruel and archaic practices spread with it. What started as a good idea based on real and pressing needs became, in the hands of people interested more in their jobs and an image of order, very much like what it was designed to replace.[38]

Sporadic attempts were made from time to time to expose the deplorable conditions in those "houses of refuge" to the public and the press. Some reforms were brought about by the efforts of such men as Elijah Devoe, the assistant superintendent of the New York House of Refuge, William Sawyer, a magistrate in Massachusetts who decried sending children to places which turned them out in worse condition than they were when put in; and Edward Everett Hale, whose 1855 essays on juvenile delinquency offered the suggestion of guilt and stigma-free alternatives to the "criminal rules" of the day.

The depression of 1837 rekindled the flame of "nativism." Again, foreign-born paupers were victims of abuse and neglect at the hands of the politicians—and victims of worse at the hands of Refuge house managers. Refuge houses went so far as to publish the names and native citizenship of juveniles and their parents. In the beginning, blacks were barred from admittance to houses of refuge or, if admitted, were treated badly. Philadelphia's House of Refuge chief stated that it would be degrading to the white children to associate them with "the offending offspring of the poorest, most ignorant, most degraded and suffering members of our community." Eventually separate houses were opened for black youths.

The goal of Refuge managers was to indoctrinate the poor unfortunates who passed through their doors with "good solid middle-class values." Those who were slow to get the point in the beginning soon learned to play the game. The transformation of institutionalized young people into game-wise youth is nothing new.

Offending juveniles were often apprenticed to farmers or to others offering an honest trade in return for hard work and, of course, a generous gift from those to whom they apprenticed to the Refuge house. The idea then, just as it remains today, was to get a child a job and keep him busy; after all, "idle hands are the devil's workshop." In fact, about 90 percent of the children released from houses of refuge each year entered into apprenticeships.

By the mid-1800s, houses of refuge were enthusiastically declared a great success. Managers even advertised their houses in juvenile magazines such as the *Youths Casket* (1851). Managers took great pride in seemingly turning total misfits into productive, hard-working members of society. Redeemed children even wrote managers letters of testimony: "I seem plucked as a brand from the burning. I am a guilty rebel, saved by grace,"[39] stated one lad.

However, these exaggerated claims of success were not undisputed. There were attacks from both without and within. Managers and administrators often disagreed over methods of discipline. By the 1850s, there was a proliferation of reform schools in most Eastern seaboard states. The houses of refuge had failed to prevent the growth of juvenile delinquency by reforming delinquents, and there arose a need to identify certain children as a special class of deviants known as *juvenile delinquents*.

Preventive Agencies and Reform Schools

In 1849, George Matsell, the New York City police chief, publicly warned that the numbers of vicious and vagrant youth were increasing and that something must be done. And done it was. America moved from a time of houses of refuge into a time of preventive agencies and reform schools.

The causes of delinquency were viewed differently by philanthropists and others behind this new movement. Refuge house managers had viewed children as inherently wicked and sought to change them. In the new system, children were thought to be corrupted by their environments. Reformers of the day wanted to give children a break, a fresh start, and not condemn them for coming from the "wrong side of the tracks."

The church also took a strong hand in trying to deal with the problem of delinquency. The Methodist Episcopal Church, for example, opened a mission in New York City (called the Five Points Mission) to give vagrant and destitute children a basic education. The mission's director, Reverend Lewis Pease, even moved his wife and family into Five Points, which was in one of the poorest areas of New York City, and gave out clothing, food, and jobs to the poor.

> Although the new philanthropists were afraid of urban lower-class disorder, their awareness of its pervasiveness made them suspicious of plans for institutions resembling houses of refuge, which they believed, overemphasized the period of incarceration required to teach children how to behave. . . . Philanthropists of the new child-saving organization were inspired by the quite traditional belief that the family, not the institution, was the best reform school. They thought that delinquency would largely disappear if their societies collected vagrant and destitute slum children and placed them out with farm families on the expanding and developing middle border. ["Placing-out" was similar to our present day practice of informal probation.][40]

Child-saving societies employed agents to take groups of delinquent or vagrant children west by train. The children were then parcelled out in towns along the way. Unlike the apprenticeships associated with the houses of refuge, there were no binding agreements between the child or the child placers and the families with whom they were to begin new lives.[41]

Thus the agrarian work ethic emerges as the panacea of delinquency. Reformers sought to empty the streets of the slum children and put them all on farms. No one epitomized this movement more than Charles Loring Brace (1826–1890), the founder of the Children's Aid Society in 1853. In one of his many speeches, Brace told of the speech of one of his "western-ized" newsboys to fellow "newsies": "Do you want to be newsboys always, and shoe blacks, and timber merchants in a small way selling matches? If ye do you'll stay in New York, but if you don't you'll go out West, and begin to be farmers, for the beginning of a farmer, my boys, is the making of a Congressman, and a President."[42]

Placing-out encountered strong opposition, even though, as Brace claimed, a survey of western prisons and almshouses in 1875 proved that his "children" had gotten into very little trouble in their new environments. The opposition came from institutions deprived of the labor of children in training before being placed out. Others argued that it was senseless to send a child all the way out West when there were adequate facilities for them in the East.

Beginning in the mid-nineteenth century, municipal and state governments became interested in founding and administering juvenile institutions. They were called reform schools, and they emphasized formal training.

States and municipalities initially sought *private* support for their reform schools, but eventually the majority of the costs were paid out of state or city revenues.

Today, many juvenile institutions are divided into cottages. In the mid-1800s, Cottage Reform Schools became popular. They divided children into classes based on their criminal profiles. However, the majority of school operators did not use this method, stating for example, "You may divide these boys into classes, and the vicious will grow more vicious, . . . but when mixed with the rest, and when they see a public opinion in favor of reform, they will reflect, improve, and in the end be reformed."[43] The proponents of the Cottage Reform Schools contended that mixing different classes of delinquents would simply multiply the crime problem and not solve it.

During the Civil War, penitentiaries and jails were practically empty, while reform schools were filled beyond capacity. The latter was attributable to the absence of parental authority when fathers were called into the service. Many of the reform schools made room for younger boys by releasing the older ones to the military.

Post–Civil War economic conditions forced institutions for juvenile delinquents to curb many of their nonbasic activities. During the late nineteenth and early twentieth centuries, governments of western and northern states were given the responsibility for the control and care of many additional categories of indigent persons, including children in orphanages, almshouses, insane asylums and mental hospitals. This shift in responsibility forced the juvenile institutions into competition with these other agencies for the funds they needed. As a result, many of the juvenile correctional facilities were forced to operate on deficit budgets which reduced them to nothing more than delinquent warehouses.

Although the number and the variety of institutions for delinquents did recover from this economic setback and resumed their growth, the severity of the problems which they faced also grew. As a result of poor management and lack of adequate resources both during and following institution-alization, the state institutions founded after the turn of the twentieth century offered very little in the way of adequate treatment and subsequent planned re-entry for youths into the community once it was determined that they were ready to be discharged. All too often, youths were forced out of institutions for lack of any other alternative than to turn them loose unsupervised and back on the streets.

Explanations for Delinquent Behavior: Late 1800s to Early 1900s

The years preceding and following the turn of the century did see some basic though often crude attempts to explain delinquency and the emergence of various treatments for changing human behavior patterns. These attempts accompanied the introduction of the social science approach in the field of juvenile corrections. Granville Stanley Hall (1846–1924), for example, developed an evolutionary explanation of delinquent behavior based on the notion that childhood years are a period of savagery in which the forces of good and evil constantly do battle with one another for the possession of the child's soul. Hall categorized juveniles in trouble as victims of circum-stances who deserved pity, understanding, and love. When forces of good had won the child, he was considered to have been born again. Thus, this theory came to be known as the "recapitulation theory": i.e., through proper guidance and influence, social reformers could transform evil youths into "angels of virtue."

Jane Addams (1860–1935), a noted child saver and founder of a famous social settlement in Chicago known as Hull House, was also influenced by this "recapitulation theory." Addams believed that juveniles had naturally free spirits in quest of joy and happiness. She theorized that this quest was stifled by an urban environment which placed commercial interests above creative fun and recreation. Unfortunately, Jane Addams's view—that delinquents were actually good children turned bad by the modern, urban environment and its resultant economic conditions—could not explain why some juveniles were incarcerated and why others from similar backgrounds were not. Those dissatisfied with the beliefs of Addams sought other explanations for the occurrence of delinquent behavior. One of Addams's contemporaries, William Forbush, believed that juveniles who were strug-gling with the forces of good and evil became stuck in what he called a *psychic arrest*. Psychic arrests were considered periods of continued tenden-cies toward crime; a person was considered to be permanently locked into a life of crime if the period of his or her psychic arrest did not pass. However, this theory, like those before it, lacked empirical verification and was based almost entirely upon theoretical speculation.

Scientific explanations advanced very little during this period. There were some attempts to apply scientific principles of study to delinquents, but these were conducted more as laboratory experimentation than as attempts to scientifically explain delinquent behavior. For example, in the early 1900s special institutions for defective delinquents offered scientists and behavioralists a captive population for their experimental use. In Indiana, in 1907, the first sterilization statute in America was passed; other states followed suit, and by 1936, 25 states had similar laws allowing for the sterilization of defective delinquents.

Sound scientific explanations for delinquent behavior failed to permeate the institutional atmospheres of the day. According to Mennel,

> The difficulty remained learning how to teach morality—the supposed foundation of social and individual lawfulness. Organized care of juvenile delinquents continued to be challenged by crises and changes most of which originated quite apart from the constructs of scientists and pedagogues. Similarly, proposed solutions to institutional problems were often derived from nonscientific ideas and attitudes.[44]

These nonscientific ideas and attitudes, which often were the result of economic pressures, contemporary views on morality, and political manipulations, brought the advancement of significant scientifically based causal theories on delinquency to a standstill. In *The Child Savers,* Anthony Platt states that "studies of delinquency in the early 1900s have been parochial, inadequately descriptive and show little appreciation of underlying political and social conditions."[45]

The Juvenile Court Movement Begins

Institutions, Houses of Refuge, and reform schools had attempted to provide juvenile delinquents with secure custody and a climate of reform which separated them from adults. However, not until 1899 did the courts decide to provide the juvenile with differential treatment. In 1899, the Illinois legislature unanimously passed an act to regulate the treatment and control of dependent, neglected, and delinquent children, otherwise known as the Juvenile Court Act. By 1917, juvenile court legislation was a reality in all but three states, and by 1932 there were estimated to be over 600 independent juvenile courts in the United States. By 1945, there were juvenile courts in every state in the country.

The early juvenile court system was part of a general movement toward the separation of juvenile offenders from adult felons. It was regarded as one of the greatest advances in the crusade to protect children's welfare and to revolutionize the treatment of delinquent and neglected youths. But the juvenile court system, while revolutionary in theory, was not the hoped-for panacea which it was at first thought to be.

For an in-depth discussion of the juvenile court from its beginnings to the present, the reader is referred to chapter 9, "The Juvenile Court."

Summary

Prior to the start of the modern era, several circumstances molded the future of the juvenile justice system in America. Among them was the practice of dealing with delinquent and dependent youth which has come to be known as the *mother image,* in which women crusaded for children's rights and for treatment of children different from that accorded adult criminals. These social activists became known as "the child savers." Modern practices of social work with neglected and dependent youths owe much to this movement, which, even according to anti-feminists, was strictly a female domain. These women, including Jane Addams, Louise Bower, Ellen Herotin, and Julia Lathrop, were usually well traveled and well educated, and they had access to financial and political resources.

Another practice which began prior to the start of the modern era but has carried over into our present-day juvenile justice system was the practice of providing alternatives (resources and conditions permitting) to institutionalization for dependent and neglected juveniles. However, despite the existence of Houses of Refuge, reform schools, special institutions, and the practice of placing-out children into apprenticeships, children were still jailed or imprisoned with little or no consideration of whether they had committed a crime. The incarceration of dependent and neglected youths (status offenders) today is comparable to the practice in the late 1800s and early 1900s. Bicentennial U.S.A. required the Federal Juvenile Justice Act to discourage states from locking up juveniles who commit no crimes.

County jails, especially in nonmetropolitan areas remote from the pressure of public opinion, were used to brutalize children into strict obedience to their parents and to terrorize them into admission of a crime. This practice too, continues in today's treatment of incarcerated youths. The following excerpt, which describes an incident that took place in the 1970s, is illustrative of this point:

Eddie Sanchez became a ward of the state of California when he was four and took the all-too-familiar route of bounding in and out of foster homes, ending up in prison. He was chosen for a trial Behavior Mod program called START, which he helped to sabotage by destructive behavior. From then on, he was labeled a serious troublemaker. A letter from Sanchez describes what followed.

I was supposedly misbehaving. At first I was put on Prolixin in pill form. I had to take it three times a day. The effect was I'd suffer muscle spasms that felt like cramps, and I seemed to have lost a lot of my coordination, as my arms would not swing when I walked.

But the officials did not think this helped me as I still got in trouble. So one day several guards came to my cage and escorted me to the shock-treatment floor.

I was put on a bed and my sleeve was rolled up on my right arm and this doctor got this needle. . . . He hits me and I right away feel a tingling sensation in my whole body, sort of like when your foot goes to sleep, then like somebody pushed a 200 lb. weight on my chest. All my air is driven from my body, then my muscles all relax, even my eyes until I can't move nothing.

After a while, the shot wears off and I am led back into the hole. This was done several times. I never consented to it or signed a permission slip as I was seventeen.[46]

In the 1920s and 1930s, there was mounting frustration on the part of academicians, behavioralists, and social reformers as to what the future of juvenile justice should be. Healy and Bromner in *Delinquents and Criminals: Their Making and Unmaking,* for example, were highly critical of reform schools and of the juvenile courts for their failure to understand and to meet the needs of the individual delinquent. Juvenile justice in America was slowly moving from an age of reform and punishment to an age of rehabilitation and understanding. What is of interest here is that the juvenile justice system's attitude toward delinquent youths today is slowly slipping from emphasis on rehabilitation and understanding back toward stress on reform and punishment.

In closing this chapter on the early history of juvenile delinquency and juvenile justice, we would like to offer the following observation by Ruth Cavan. In reviewing the history of delinquency, Cavan states,

Undoubtedly the most disturbing fact about this recital of delinquency and crime on the part of children is that no society has mastered the technique of successfully initiating children into the expectations and demands of their society and thus avoiding the problem of delinquency. Today each society still struggles with the twin problems of the socialization of its children and the rehabilitation of the deviants.[47]

REVIEW QUESTIONS

1. What is juvenile delinquency? What were some of the historical explanations of its causes, as discussed in this chapter?

2. Explain the following terms:
   a. House of Refuge
   b. Reform school
   c. Placing-out
   d. Recapitulation theory
   e. Mother image

3. As shown in this chapter, juvenile delinquency has a long history. Were the problems of delinquency which early societies faced different from those of today? Explain.

4. Who were some of the social reformers of the nineteenth and early twentieth centuries? What do you think motivated these early reformers to seek changes in the juvenile justice system?

5. Describe the concept of the "continuum of behavior" and tell how it would be applicable to the theories of delinquency for periods of time discussed in this chapter.

NOTES

1. Harry E. Allen and Clifford E. Simonsen, *Corrections in America: An Introduction* (Encino, Calif.: Glencoe Press, 1975), pp. 4–5.

2. For a thorough and comprehensive look at the Code of Hammurabi and other early laws, see Albert Kocaurek and John H. Wigmore, *Source of Ancient and Primitive Law, Evolution of Law, Select Readings on the Origin and Development of Legal Institutions,* vol. 1 (Boston: Little, Brown, 1951).

3. Code of Hammurabi, item 195. Richard R. Cherry, Barrister-at-law. Reid Professor of Constitutional and Criminal Law in the University of Dublin. Reprinted from *Lectures: Growth of Criminal Law in Ancient Communities* (London: Macmillan and Co., 1890).

4. Cherry, ibid., items 192, 193.

5. Although the code of Emperor Justinian of the Byzantine empire did not survive the empire's fall, it did form the basis of most of the Western world's laws.

6. Ruth Shonle Cavan, *Juvenile Delinquency* (Philadelphia: Lippincott, 1969), p. 6.

7. Allen and Simonsen, *Corrections in America: An Introduction,* p. 8.

8. Benjamin Thorpe, ed., *Ancient Laws and Institutes of England* (London, 1840), pp. 47, 85, 103.

9. A. H. Thomas, ed., *Calendar of Plea and Memoranda Rolls, Preserved Among the Archives of the Corporation of the City of London at the Guild-hall, A.D. 1364–1381* (Cambridge: Cambridge University Press, 1929), pp. 16, xl, xlvi.

10. For further discussion on the subject of apprenticeships the reader is referred to Evans Austin, *The Law Relating to Apprentices, Including Those Bound According to the Custom of the City of London* (London, 1890), pp. 110–11.

11. Charles Wriothesley (Windsor Herald), *A Chronicle of England During the Reigns of the Tudors, from A.D. 1485 to 1559,* William Doulas Hamilton, ed. (Printed for the Camden Society), vol. I, M.S. 11 (1875), pp. 73, 134–35; vol. II, p. 129.

12. John Calvin, *The Catechisme or Manner to teache children the Christian religion, wherein the Minister demandeth the question, and the childe maketh answere.* Made by the Doctor and Pastor in Christes Churche, John Calvin ([Pub.] By John Crespin, 1556), p. 74.

13. Charles M. Clode, *The Early History of the Guild of Merchant Taylors of . . . London,* part II (London, 1888), p. 294.

14. Wiley B. Sanders, ed., *Juvenile Offenders for a Thousand Years* (Chapel Hill: University of North Carolina Press, 1970), p. 11.

15. Ibid., p. 11.

16. Ibid., p. 13.

17. Ibid., p. 13.

18. Ibid., p. 14.

19. Cavan, *Juvenile Delinquency*, p. 6.

20. Sanders, *Juvenile Offenders for a Thousand Years*, p. 22.

21. Ibid., p. 36.

22. Ibid., p. 40.

23. Ibid., pp. 52–53.

24. Ibid., p. 70.

25. Ibid., p. 99.

26. Sir William Blackstone, *Commentaries on the Laws of England*, ed. Thomas M. Cooley, vol. 1 (Chicago: Callaghan, 1899) p. 1230.

27. Having a child or children in jail was cheaper, so many parents would then have extra money for alcohol or gambling.

28. Sanders, *Juvenile Offenders for a Thousand Years*, p. 135.

29. Ibid., p. 63.

30. Ibid., p. 91.

31. Ibid., p. 46.

32. Ibid., pp. 317–18.

33. Ibid., pp. 320–23.

34. Ibid., p. 328.

35. Ibid., p. 330.

36. Ibid., 330–31.

37. The child was tied with his or her arms and legs around a barrel, thus exposing his or her backside quite handily to the whip.

38. Larry Cole, *Our Children's Keepers* (New York: Grossman, 1972), p. xviii.

39. Robert M. Mennel, *Thorns and Thistles* (Hanover: University of New Hampshire, 1973), p. 24.

40. Ibid., p. 35.

41. Compare this practice with present programs of getting slum children out to summer camps once a year.

42. Mennel, *Thorns and Thistles*, pp. 37–38.

43. Ibid., pp. 56–57.

44. Ibid., p. 101.

45. Anthony Platt, *The Child Savers* (Chicago: The University of Chicago Press, 1969), pp. 10–11.

46. Kenneth Wooden, *Weeping in the Playtime of Others* (New York: McGraw-Hill, 1976).

47. Cavan, *Juvenile Delinquency*, p. 7.

2 The Modern Era

I can't send him back to his whore of a mother. His school has thrown him out. He has done nothing more than try to run away from his miserable home. All I can offer this child is jail.

MAGISTRATE DAVID S. SCHAFFER

By 1925, special juvenile courts had been created by state legislatures throughout the United States. Thus, the delinquent child joined the dependent and neglected child as a ward of the state (*parens patriae*).

Since the 1920s the emphasis in dealing with juvenile delinquents has, for the most part, shifted from punishment and imprisonment to an attempt to understand the delinquent as an individual member of society. A more positive direction has been taken in that efforts have been made to socialize and rehabilitate the delinquent. A staff psychologist of the Whittier State School claimed:

> The basic philosophy of correctional education has changed from the concept of punishment to that of adjustment through the understanding of individual differences.[1]

Juvenile Justice During the Depression: A Bleak Era

But the 1930s—the period of the Great Depression—brought a disruption in the progress and development of the juvenile justice system. As a result of the depression, institutional and reform school budgets were cut back and skilled and knowledgeable administrators were let go when staffs were reduced. Once again the philosophy of control and repression, accompanied at times by cruel and unnecessary punishment, became dominant.

During the Great Depression, new explanations of juvenile delinquency were proposed. One of these was the causal theory championed by Virginia

P. Robinson and Jesse Taft, two maverick social workers. They believed that delinquency was the result of family disintegration and conflicts. Because of conflict and maladaptation within the family unit, the child doesn't develop the ability to differentiate between right and wrong and exhibits unacceptable social behavior. Psychiatric treatment became the cure of the day. From this approach, many forms of psychoanalytic treatments, including those developed by Freud, were used.

Yet, it was still a generally accepted belief that the family alone was responsible for delinquency, and this led to demands that parents of delinquents be punished for failure to control the behavior of their children. For about ten years (1937–1946) the systematic punishment of parents was tried. Parents were fined heavily and even jailed for the acts of their offspring. However, the social effects of punishing parents were often disastrous.

> When the mother is imprisoned, the home is broken up and her children must be placed in institutions or foster homes or left to care for themselves. Typically when she was released, she receives no help in reassembling her children and reestablishing her home. Meanwhile, the respect for her by neighbors and children declines. Older children are given a crutch on which to lean in shifting responsibility for their conduct to their mother. If the father is the one imprisoned, the mother must go to work or the entire family must be supported by relief agencies.[2]

It was also found that judges began to rely on punishing the parents instead of attempting to deal with the rehabilitation of the children. It became evident that blaming delinquency entirely on the family and punishing the parents for the "sins" of their children was not the answer to the problem. It was simply one of the many serious attempts to find a single, simple cause of delinquency.

Courts did continue a tendency toward treatment of children which was lenient compared to the punishment of adults for similar offenses. Unfortunately, courts and law enforcement agencies across the country varied widely in their treatment or punishment of juveniles who had committed like offenses. Punishment ranged from horsewhipping to prison terms.

Boy Burglar Is Sentenced

With his mother standing at his side, Eugene Wheeler, 19-year-old burglar, was sentenced yesterday to serve from one to four years at Monroe reformatory by Superior Judge Malcolm Douglas.

Wheeler, with three other youths, broke into the plant of the Currin-Green Shoe Manufacturing Company, 2715 Western Avenue, December 1.

Arthur King, one of the gang, was sentenced last month to the Monroe reformatory. The other two were turned over to the juvenile court.[3]

This article appeared on December 24, 1930, concerning a case in Lapeer, Michigan.

Fathers Thrash Sons by Order

By order of the court, seven boys were severely horsewhipped by their fathers today as their mothers looked on approvingly. Circuit Judge Henry H. Smith prescribed the unusual sentence after the youths had pleaded guilty to a store theft.[4]

The depression era was also plagued by many of our current problems. For example, a very large number of juveniles are arrested today on drug charges. In the 1930s, juveniles were arrested with equal zeal for drinking—a violation of the prohibition of alcoholic beverages.[5] Not unlike the casualties of today's drug culture, Prohibition had its own casualties. This account, from the *Seattle Post Intelligencer* of December 14, 1930, is a graphic example:

A Prohibition Party

Early in this month of December some young people in Gary, Ind., got together and held the kind of party which is unfortunately not unusual in these prohibition days.

These young people—unwisely—but young people are frequently unwise—wanted to have drink at their party. There were no comparatively harmless light wines or beer available, so the young people brought bootleg whisky.

As a result of drinking this vile, maddening poison, one young girl, 18 years old, is dead; and to quote from the press dispatches, "five young men from good Gary families are held on charges of first degree murder."

The young woman, whose portrait is printed herewith, has a sweet, innocent, bright, girlish face. Undoubtedly, she would have done no wrong if she had been in possession of her senses.

But she was not in possession of her faculties, nor were the young men who are held as criminals. Their minds were maddened, their bodies soddened by bootleg whisky. The press dispatches add that:

> Several parents of the young people involved, shocked by the tragedy, place the blame for it on conditions which they say exist throughout Gary's younger set. The party at which Arlene died, they said, was not an isolated instance of drinking.

"It was just like any other party," said Mrs. Mary Shirk, whose son Harry was one of the five young men held for the grand jury on charges of murdering Arlene.

Just like any other prohibition party!

Mrs. Mary Shirk should have said: Just like any other party where vile, bootleg whisky is drunk by inexperienced young people who cannot get innocuous light wines and beer.

Mrs. Mary Shirk, continuing, says:

> I worried, of course, as all others of this generation have; but nobody guessed the tragedy that would come of this party.
> There is liquor now everywhere. Nobody can escape it.

Mrs. Shirk speaks truly—there is prohibition everywhere, and bootleg liquor everywhere, and drunkenness everywhere, even among the youth of the land, and general demoralization everywhere; and crime and law-defiance almost everywhere.

That is the penalty of prohibition.[6]

It is interesting to note that the parents of the juveniles involved bemoaned the fact that their children could not acquire "innocuous light wines and beer" instead of the "vile bootleg whiskey." One wonders how many parents of juveniles spaced out on acid today would bemoan the fact that their children could not legally acquire "innocuous supplies of marijuana" instead of vile and potentially fatal doses of the "hard" drugs.

The Post-Depression Era

Although the Illinois Court Act of 1899 did much to lead the way toward individualized treatment of the juvenile delinquent and dependent child, its practicality and efficacy came into question in the post-depression era of the 1940s and 1950s. It became apparent that the juvenile was in a "Catch 22" situation.[7] For, while the youth's treatment was in fact given separate attention by the courts, the informality of proceedings under *parens patriae* deprived the juvenile of the same legal rights provided to adults who committed similar acts.

Deprived of equal protection under the constitution, juveniles were subject to the discretionary authority of the courts, the police, and child service agencies. The courts, therefore, did what they could to process the ever-increasing number of juvenile cases (see Figure 2–1) coming before them.

The post-depression era also spawned large detention facilities for juvenile offenders. The Youth House, a "kid Big House for big and little kids" in New York City, was typical of large juvenile detention facilities of this era. It soon acquired the reputation of being a poorly equipped, understaffed dumping ground for delinquent and dependent children. All the cruelties and brutalities which could be imagined in a "kid prison" took place in the original Youth House and its equally notorious successor. It has been claimed that Youth House (with its current per-child cost of $50 per day or $18,250 per year) and detention facilities and institutions like it destroy more children each year than any known disease. Youth House processes approximately 10,000 children in New York each year, and although conditions there periodically become a public issue, it continues to operate with the same destructive force as in the past.

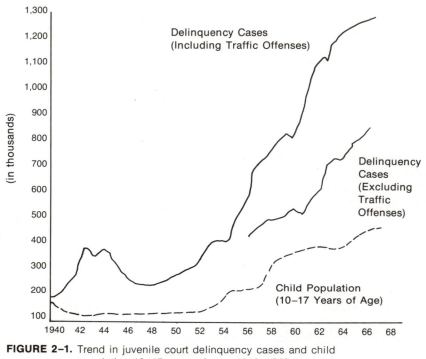

FIGURE 2–1. Trend in juvenile court delinquency cases and child
population 10–17 years of age, 1940–1968.

Source: *Juvenile Court Statistics, 1966* (Washington, D.C.: U.S. Government Printing Office,
1966), p. 11.

In the 1940s and 1950s, with a growing number of crimes committed by
juveniles, police forces began to set up specialized juvenile units made up of
specially assigned officers. For example, in 1944 the Chicago Police
Department's Crime Prevention Bureau provided increased educational opportunities for juvenile officers. Juvenile personnel, especially policewomen,
were given a special 12-week course of instruction on the treatment of
juveniles, including the subject of their referral to social agencies.[8]

The growing number of crimes committed by juveniles in this period
meant a growing institutional population. Although an effort was made to
provide juveniles with facilities to keep them separated from adult criminals,
in most large cities these new juvenile detention facilities became little more
than juvenile jails. And, when they became filled, dependent delinquents
and status offenders were often moved to adult jails, which defeated the
purpose of separate facilities.

In the post-depression era, belief that the disintegration of the family was
the prime cause of delinquency faded, and environmental factors and

individual personalities were seen as its main cause. Many authorities of the day believed that "official" delinquency was primarily a lower-class phenomenon.

However, the findings of several studies conducted during the 1950s indicated that there was not a universal, causal relationship between social class and law-violating behavior. For example, the theory was tested in one study as follows:

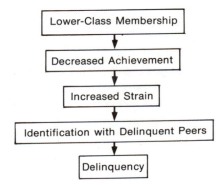

A purposive sample of 482 serious delinquents (249 in Utah and 233 in Los Angeles), and 185 nondelinquents (100 in Utah and 85 in Los Angeles). While the overall sample was well distributed over the class structure—more than one-half from lower levels, about one-third from lower middle and middle levels, and less than one-fifth from upper levels—it may have been deficient in terms of minority representation. In Utah, there were virtually no minorities included, since few reside there; in Los Angeles, only about one-quarter were of minority status, mostly black.

The Findings. Perhaps the most significant finding was the fact that, in neither location, was social class of much explanatory value. It did not help to explain any of the major concepts of the theory: lack of achievement, a high degree of strain, identification with peers, or official delinquency itself. These factors were related as much to membership in other class levels as to lower-class membership.

This result tends to support the findings of recent studies using self-reported, and thus nonofficial delinquency. These studies seriously question the existence of a universal, causal relationship between social class and law-violating behavior (Nye, Short, et al., 1958; Clark and Wenninger, 1962; Dentler and Monroe, 1961; Porterfield, 1946; Reiss and Rhodes, 1961; Empey, 1967; Empey and Erickson, 1966; Gold, 1966). They suggest that middle- as well as lower-class adolescents are involved in a large amount of illegal behavior.[9]

Some current attempts to cope with and/or prevent delinquency aren't all that different in scope and design from those of the 1940s and 1950s. For example, the concept of a Youth Authority such as practiced in California and several other states had its beginnings in 1940 with the development of the American Law Institute's Model Youth Correction Authority Act. This model for youth authorities was devised after careful study and consideration by many of the most outstanding criminologists, law professors, social welfare specialists, and judges in the country. Their major concern was for the treatment of those juvenile offenders who fell outside the age of most juvenile court jurisdictions and who, as a result, were often tried in adult criminal courts and sentenced to adult prisons. The model act developed by the American Law Institute was published in an attempt to urge various states to adopt a similar body of procedures and guidelines:

1. Name: Youth Correction Authority.

2. Administrative organization: board of three persons with staggered nine-year terms, appointed by the governor; the board to select its chairman.

3. Age of jurisdiction; sixteen to twenty-one, from criminal or juvenile court.

4. Type of commitment: mandatory commitment to the Youth Authority by the court for all persons under twenty-one at the time of apprehension, convicted of a crime punishable by imprisonment for less than life; children aged sixteen and over might be committed by the juvenile court. The Authority, not the judge, would make the decision whether to grant probation or commit to an institution.

5. Type of commitment: the commitment to the Authority would be for an indeterminate period; the Authority would make the decision when to terminate commitment, release on parole, and so on; however, persons might not be held after age twenty-five and those under eighteen committed by the juvenile courts not after age twenty-one. If release would be dangerous, the court might approve of continued control.

6. Administration of facilities for diagnosis and retraining: the function of the Authority was to be mainly diagnostic, but it was also permitted to administer training schools and similar facilities. [10]

California adopted this concept both for adults and juveniles; Wisconsin and Minnesota followed suit, as did a number of other states, making several modifications. To date, although many such modifications have been made, states have been reluctant to implement the full provisions of the youth authority movement; however, the concept of parole release and aftercare supervision of children (see chapter 13, Parole) did get a tremendous boost in the 1940s and 1950s from the Youth Authority Model.

Other similarities between present trends and the 1940s and 1950s are reflected in the following description of an unusual project in 1946 to prevent youths' troubles; this description was made by the chairperson of a special subcommittee of the District Health Committee of New York City.

The committee confronted two questions. First, can we identify at an early stage symptomatic difficulty that later may develop into serious behavior trouble? Secondly, in these cases, by mustering and coordinating the skills of the psychiatrist, psychologist, social worker, physician, vocation worker, and others, can we successfully diagnose the underlying difficulty in the child and his family, and offer a planned treatment service which will remove or modify that difficulty? The answer to both was an emphatic *yes*.

The committee has a six-step procedure which consists of, first, the principal of the school selecting those students whose personality deviations indicate serious social or health problems. The case was then cleared with the social services exchange. Data about the student was gathered by either a committee member or a social worker and assembled and presented for clinical discussion. The fifth step is the formulation of a plan of action for the student and finally periodic reports were made to the committee on the child's progress. Basically the plan was an attempt to manipulate the environment of a child under stress, or stated in somewhat different terminology, to bring together all the resources of the *community* to aid the child.[11]

It is often assumed that the idea of community-based treatment, diagnosis, and planning in the field of juvenile delinquency is the brainchild of the 1960s and early 1970s. As the passage above indicates, community involvement in juvenile justice is far from new.

The post-depression era gave rise to many studies and causal theories, including a book by Sheldon and Eleanor Glueck, *Unraveling Juvenile Delinquency*, a review of which is excerpted below.

The book is the result of a 10-year study by the Gluecks and others on their team to ascertain the causes of youthful criminality. It appears that up to this time most people were in agreement that something should be done about the youthful offender but no one had identified the problems except to state that they in fact did exist. The Gluecks found three factors prevalent among their 500 delinquents studied:

— The boys generally had poor family relations. Their fathers were needlessly harsh or completely lax in maintaining discipline, seldom firm but kindly. They received little parental love.
— They clashed with other people; were highly assertive, defiant, suspicious, destructive, and impulsive.
— They had turbulent personalities, were adventurous, extroverted, suggestible, stubborn, and emotionally unstable.

Two conclusions were made in the article. First, that detecting delinquency in its earliest stages is a job for specialists. It cannot be done, the Gluecks admit, by any simple, easily interpreted pencil and paper test. Secondly, the husband and wife team felt that in delinquency, society is faced not with predestination, but with destination. And probably destination can often be modified by intelligent early *intervention*.[12]

The literature of the late 1940s and early 1950s was filled with reports of *intervention strategy*, in which there was introduced into the life of a juvenile some outside intervening factor, such as intensive counseling. The influence of this intervening factor on the juvenile's future delinquency behavior was then evaluated. Dr. Edwin Powers, in the *Annals of the American Academy,* described an experiment which utilized one such intervention strategy in an attempt to prevent delinquent behavior among a population of 650 boys.

> This particular 10-year study called for 650 boys to be divided among 10 counselors. (The essence of the relationship between the boy and his counselor was personal intimacy and friendship.) Treatment consisted of the application of whatever skills each counselor was capable of supplying. Dr. Powers states, "In brief, it can be said that the treatment program, utilizing some of the best professional advice obtainable, comprised an unusually wide diversity of special services to boys and their families, from removing nits from boys' heads to preparing them for higher education."
>
> The conclusion of the study was somewhat vague in that the counselors were unable to stop the rapid advance of young boys into delinquency with any greater success than the usual deterrent forces in the community. Some of the boys were evidently deflected from delinquent careers which, without the counselors' help, might have resulted in continued or more serious violations. The researchers felt that although they were not completely successful in the first stage of delinquency prevention that in working with boys ages 8–11 later and more serious stages were to some degree curtailed.[13]

In the 1950s, a number of intervention strategy programs for youth were set up, providing job training and creating jobs. In 1956, for example, the Citizens Union of New York for the Prevention and Cure of Delinquency recommended the establishment of work camps for delinquent boys. The basic idea behind these camps and similar programs was to divert juveniles from exhibiting delinquent behavior by providing them opportunities for good jobs. This idea was expanded upon in the early 1960s and thereafter through the establishment of such programs as (1) the Job Corps under Title 1-A of the Federal Poverty Program, (2) the Neighborhood Youth Corps under Title 1-B of the same program, and (3) the work-study program for college students under the same program. Through these programs, underprivileged youths are given an opportunity to upgrade their education and to learn a trade or a skill which might lead to a decent, steady job. It should be noted that while the primary goal of these programs is to provide opportunities to juveniles in need, the prevention of delinquency is often a secondary objective and result. This differs somewhat from the concept of the work camps of the 1950s, whose primary objective was the prevention of recurrent delinquent behavior in juveniles who had already exhibited such behavior prior to coming into the programs.

Portrait of the Delinquent in the 1940s and 1950s

What kind of children were the delinquents of the Gas House era? They were children and young adults from every corner of America. During and shortly after World War II, they were wearing jeans, T-shirts, white socks, pedal pushers, bobby socks, and white blouses. They were called "hoods" and "punks," and were members of gangs. Mexican youth gang members on the West Coast, called Pachucos, drove hot rods or rode the large motorcycles of that era.

During the 1950s, delinquents, called "greasers" and "hoodlums," were characterized by the slicked-back "D.A." haircuts, argyle socks, pegged pants, and black leather jackets. In metropolitan areas, they formed territories or "turfs" and fought "rumbles" or wars with opposing gangs. They were examined, studied, and discussed by everyone from the local police to speakers at ladies clubs. They were often on the receiving end of new tactics of cure and prevention.

The 1960s and 1970s: Chaos and Construction

In the 1960s and 1970s there have been revolutionary legal, social, and procedural changes in the development and scope of the juvenile justice system. In the past two decades the United States has engaged in the unpopular war in Vietnam, seen confrontations, riots, and killings on college campuses, witnessed political assassinations, and gone through radical changes in all areas of social intercourse and activity.

During this era, men have been put on the moon, planes have been perfected that travel faster than the speed of sound, surgeons have transplanted human organs and performed unbelievable feats in medicine. Humanity has advanced technically and scientifically beyond our great-grandparent's wildest dreams.

But have these technical and social advances solved the problem of juvenile delinquency in this country? Have present-day scholars, writers, and researchers found any revolutionary new theories regarding the cause, cure, or prevention of this major problem? Unfortunately, the answer to both questions is *no*.

The FBI's *Uniform Crime Reports* reveals that over *one half* of all arrests for property offenses in the United States involve persons under 18.[14] More than *one million* juveniles, accused of delinquent or criminal behavior, appear in juvenile court each year. A fourth of all persons charged with rape, a third of all persons charged with robbery, half of all persons charged with burglary and larceny, and more than half of all persons charged with auto theft are under 18 years of age. Given these statistics, it seems the struggle against the twin problems of socialization of our children and rehabilitation of our deviants is being lost.

Statistics indicate that almost one in every 30 school-age youths has appeared, or will appear, at some time in juvenile court. In some neighborhoods, the figure is significantly higher. Translated into percentages, this means that between 3 percent and 20 percent of the youthful population are exhibiting behavior that might lead to their appearing in court for some charge. And, if one accepts Martin Gold's and others' studies of self-reported delinquency, up to 95 percent of all youths exhibit behavior that could lead to court appearances.[15] However, Gold found that the most serious and persistent offenders were from lower socioeconomic backgrounds, and that the juveniles most often apprehended by the police and referred to the juvenile courts were also the most persistent offenders. One has to wonder whether the juvenile justice system is programmed to arrest and to process primarily the poor and minority youths, while the middle- and upper-income juveniles escape arrest because of their accessibility to all kinds of diversions and because the police departments and the courts are more tolerant of these juveniles and more likely to allow them to remain in their homes and neighborhoods after violating the law rather than subjecting them to incarceration.

A comparison between the rates of commitment for adults and for children in the 1960s appeared in a National Council on Crime and Delinquency publication. The article is quoted here in part.

> Since there is some awareness of the unfairness of these improper commitments, one would hope that the situation would get better, that is, that commitments would decrease. That is true of commitments of adults to prisons; since 1962, the prison population in most of the states has been decreasing. After the end of World War II the number of people in the prisons rose to a high in 1961 of 220,149. That number gradually came down to 194,896 in 1967, the latest year for which I have information.[16]
>
> But the opposite has been happening with respect to the population of the training schools for juveniles. According to the U.S. Children Bureau, in 1958 there were 36,000 children in state training schools. In 1962 the figure was 3000 higher; in 1964 it was 5000 higher, the total being 44,000. In 1968 there were 54,000 children in training schools, camps, reception, and diagnostic centers. There are additional large numbers of children held in detention homes, jails, reformatories, and prisons.
>
> This trend is wrong; it is bad for children, and it is needless. A community that undertakes to build larger institutions for children is doing a disservice to children and to the community.
>
> The concept that juvenile courts and training schools are good for children is evidently still strongly believed, and presumably is behind the continuously rising commitment rate. But is this a true concept? A recent study suggests that it is not. Martin Gold and J. R. Williams studied 847 children 13 through 16 years old in 48 states who had been apprehended for delinquency and processed through the courts. Thirty-five of them were matched with others of similar characteristics who had committed delinquencies but had not been caught. In 20 of the 35 comparisons, the apprehended member of the pair subsequently committed more offenses than his unapprehended control. In 10 of the 35, the unapprehended control committed more offenses. Five pairs committed an equal number.
>
> The authors concluded that "apprehension itself encourages rather than deters further delinquency."[17] The study is not one of training schools

particularly. Only 4 percent of those apprehended were committed to training schools. The cases of 59 percent were disposed of by the police without involving the courts.[18] But the high rate of recidivism among those released from training schools—higher than for adults—indicates that training schools share whatever is operative here.[19]

More current figures, incidentally, indicate that 43,447 juveniles were in state institutions, ranches, and camps in 1969; 42,202 in 1970; 36,801 in 1971; 26,724 in 1973; and 28,001 in 1974.[20]

We have previously indicated that adults are getting more protection under the law than are juveniles. In recent years, the courts have attempted to rectify this situation by concentrating on bringing about reforms in the treatment given to both delinquent and nondelinquent juveniles. It should be pointed out, however, that the question of children's rights is multidimensional and complex. It involves not just procedural rights in juvenile courts and the applicability of constitutional rights to juveniles, but extends to the complex issues of the political, economic, and social position of minors in our society. This subject is made even more complex by the ever-changing status of youth and the resulting confusion reflected in adult attitudes toward children and youths.

When juvenile courts were first established at the turn of the century, they were seen as a positive response to the demand for social justice. The objective was ''not so much to punish as to reform, not to degrade but to uplift, not to crush but to develop, not to make him a criminal but a worthy citizen.[21] The doctrine of *parens patriae* was used to justify the relaxation of traditional criminal law procedures. While this doctrine allowed the courts to assume parental responsibility for the child and thus to look out for his or her welfare, it had unforeseen consequences. Because the state was proceeding in the ''best'' interests of the child, some courts believed that rights such as entitlement to bail, indictment by grand jury, speedy trial, trial by jury, immunity against self-incrimination, confrontation of accusers, and the right to counsel could be denied.

In an attempt to bridge the gap between the ideal and reality in juvenile court proceedings, the U.S. Supreme Court heard several cases involving the rights of juveniles charged with criminal or delinquent acts.[22] These cases, ranging from the trend-setting decision in *Gideon* v. *Wainwright* to that of *In re Gault*,[23,24] dealt with establishing the same right to legal counsel for juveniles as for adults. A detailed discussion of these and other cases will be found in chapter 15, A Juvenile's Legal Rights.

The road from no legal rights to full protection for juveniles under the Constitution is a long one, and the journey is by no means finished. As future operational or administrative members of the juvenile justice system, our readers will hopefully take an active part in making sure the rest of the journey is both smooth and rewarding.

Institutions in the 1960s and 1970s

As in the past, institutionalization of delinquent children continued unabated in the 1960s and 1970s. Were these institutions any more effective in treating delinquency or rehabilitating juvenile delinquents than in the past? Did locking these youths away solve any of the delinquency problems which society must face? Charles Mangel, in an article entitled "How to Make a Criminal Out of a Child," offers some sobering answers to these questions.

> As I write this, some 100,000 children are sitting in jails and jaillike institutions throughout the country. They are as young as six. Most, perhaps 60 percent, are not delinquents. They have committed *no criminal acts*.
>
>   . . .
>
> Yet we pass all this by as if it does not exist. "Why are we so willing to give up on the child in trouble?" asks Lois Forer in *No One Will Listen*. "There are two possible reasons. The first is that we don't want to help; the second, that we don't believe we can help. We know that the children who suffer from lack of facilities are primarily poor children—black, Puerto Rican, Indian, deprived—in short, *not our children*."
>
> Few people feel any sense of outrage. I met in Chicago with a group of lawyers, judges, and social workers who spend their days working with children in court. They impressed me as decent men and women. They uttered all the right words. But they spoke with a curious hollowness of feeling. As the evening wore on, I found myself being grateful that the future of my children did not depend on their concern.
>
> "The way things are now, it is probably better for all concerned if young delinquents were not detected," says Milton Luger, former director of the New York State Division for Youth. "Too many of them get worse in our care." Not one state in this country, adds the National Council, is doing a proper job of rehabilitating kids in trouble.
>
> We are a slipshod people. We tend to do nothing unless a crisis is at hand, and then we seek simplistic, temporary measures. We wrap ourselves in our comforts, tend to think the universe is where we are and blink at those who are cold, hungry, sick, in trouble. It appears the time of slippage may be ending. The time may be beginning when, compassion and purity of purpose aside, we are going to be hurt significantly if we don't reach out to those aliens who dare not to be self-sufficient. "If you are among brigands and you are silent, you are a brigand yourself," a folk saying goes. Civilization is not a matter of museums and global communications. It derives from a quality of mind and of concern. And by that definition, we, of course, are not a civilized nation at all, rather a self-centered, stupid one. And the soothing words of all our politicians, all our churchmen, all our "important" people matter not. We are incompetent.[25]

Only exerpted here, the entire article is a harsh criticism of the way in which juveniles are treated in this country by the courts, the institutions, or whomever. While there *are* fine programs and many good staff people doing excellent work throughout the country with delinquents, they are only dealing with a small percentage of our youth. For the majority, what Mr. Mangel has described is reality.

Recent Changes

In 1969, Dr. Jerome Miller took over as youth commissioner for Massachusetts and made some revolutionary changes in that state's juvenile justice system. Juvenile corrections in the United States hasn't been the same since.

One of the more radical actions was closing the Lyman School for Boys in January, 1972. The Lyman School for Boys was opened in 1846 and was the first institution of its kind in the nation.

> The closing of Lyman School was the finale of an intense drama that had been going on in Massachusetts for more than two years. The era of confining children in large correctional institutions was dead, declared Dr. Jerome Miller, commissioner of the Department of Youth Services (DYS), and a new age of decent, humane, community-based care for delinquent youngsters was beginning.
>
> The idealistic young reformers who had worked so hard to close down the institutions cheered. But juvenile justice professionals, both in Massachusetts and other states, were stunned, and in many cases, horrified, at what Jerome Miller had done.
>
> Since 1972, Miller and his supporters have been crisscrossing the nation, trying to persuade other administrators that institutions for juveniles are both destructive and unnecessary, and telling and retelling the story of what Miller calls his great "crusade" in Massachusetts.[26]

What were the results of this "crusade" in Massachusetts? Did closing down the large juvenile correctional institutions make a difference? Miller had contended that training schools were not only ineffective at reforming juvenile lawbreakers, but that they were profoundly destructive, and that those children who went through them were more likely to commit new crimes when they left than when they were admitted.[27]

At the present time, noted criminologist Dr. Lloyd Ohlin and his two co-researchers, Drs. Robert Coates and Alden Miller, are conducting a study of the effects of the new totally community-based system compared to the institution-based system which had been in effect in Massachusetts. The study is being conducted at the Center for Criminal Justice of the Howard University Law School.

After analyzing some of the preliminary findings of this study, one gets the feeling that the new community-based corrections system thus far is no better ("better" meaning reduced rates of recidivism) than the previous system of institutional training schools. However, it must be noted that the new system is no *worse* than the old one, and would appear to be far more humane. There are still many questions to be answered and much more data to be gathered and analyzed.

What seems important about this innovation in Massachusetts is its radically new and nontraditional approach to solving old problems. If the final results of the study are positive, or at least not negative, such a system might well be worth an attempt on a national basis. However, juvenile corrections administrators outside Massachusetts have generally taken a negative stand on the closing of institutions.

> Very few believe, as do Dr. Jerome Miller and his successors, that institutions are inherently destructive and should be eliminated. And even those few who agree with Miller say that it would be politically impossible to do away with all institutions.
>
> In preparation for an article in a previous issue, *Corrections Magazine* asked every top juvenile corrections administrator in the nation for his views on whether institutions should be closed and replaced by a community-based corrections system. . . . [For example,] Allen Breed of the California Youth Authority said that he has a ''good deal of respect for Jerry Miller,'' but that what he did in Massachusetts was ''very tragic and I'd hate to see other states imitate it.''[28]

Yet, there are those in the field of juvenile corrections who feel that simply closing an institution is not enough. They feel that as institutions are closed, they should also be torn down. For example, there are many old prisons which have been ''abandoned'' for new ones, only to be reopened again in a short while. Americans are great at finding a use for vacant buildings. If not used as prisons, they are used as facilities for the mentally ill or other social misfits.

Portrait of the Delinquent in the 1960s and 1970s

The police faced a different breed of young person during the period of the 1960s and 1970s. A generation of children known as ''flower children'' and ''children of love'' in the sixties and ''hippies'' and ''freaks'' in the seventies confronted and confused the police. These were juveniles who began smoking marijuana in the seventh and eighth grades, and moved on to taking ''sopors,'' ''uppers,'' ''downers,'' ''bennies,'' ''reds,'' or even ''coke'' or LSD in high school.

Young people today seem inundated with a new ethos in American society which is sometimes called ''the hang-loose ethic.'' It is cool and irreverent, and it reflects a good deal of disaffection toward many of our more traditional values. For this reason, it is perhaps understandable that it is more worrisome to parents, educators, police, and others than the mere wildness or deviant flirtations of young people of the past.[29]

The police face juveniles today who may call them ''pigs'' or far worse. From past dealings with the courts, many juveniles feel that nothing will happen to them because authorities are usually lenient. The sixties and seventies have brought with them a new concern for young people in trouble, possibly because there are so many of them and their numbers are increasing. Community-based corrections, diagnostic centers, and treatment centers, along with group homes, foster homes, and rehabilitation centers reflect this period, but so do the traditional reform and training schools and "kid prisons."

Summary

From the era of the Depression and Prohibition, through the post-depression era and into the sixties and seventies, the United States has been faced with social, moral, and economic problems caused by juveniles. They commit crimes, run away from home, or simply refuse to be treated as children any longer. Typologies and treatment modalities are continuously debated by researchers and experts in the field of juvenile corrections. Institutions and prisons for juveniles are seen as ineffective by such as Jerry Miller and his followers. Still, they are seen as worthwhile and appropriate by some and as necessary evils by others. Police forces have become "specialized" in attempting to deal with delinquents. Some are attempting to prevent juvenile crime before it happens by working closely with the community in developing diversions for children who might otherwise get into trouble.

Supreme Court decisions such as *In re Gault* have brought some constitutional protection and redress from legal wrongs to our young people, but many other court actions are still in progress.

It seems that the definition of *delinquency* and standardization of semantic meanings for other terms commonly used in the field of juvenile justice still need to be resolved. Often, the procedures of a juvenile court in one county in a state may differ significantly from those of a neighboring county in the same state.

Much has been written about juvenile corrections and the juvenile justice system. The authors of this text offer no panacea for the problems of delinquency but propose only to explore with the reader the various aspects of juvenile justice in an attempt to familiarize the student with these problems and challenges. Juvenile delinquency affects all of our lives, whether we are aware of it or not. The solution to this problem cannot be passed off as someone else's responsibility. As members of the same society, it is a problem which belongs to each of us. This brief history of the development of juvenile justice in America sets the stage for the following investigation of the programs, processes, systems, and people that are dealing with the problems today.

REVIEW QUESTIONS

1. In what ways is the delinquent of today different from the delinquent of 50 years ago?

2. How have attitudes of personnel within the juvenile justice system changed since the 1930s?

3. Is closing juvenile institutions, such as was done in Massachusetts, a solution to problems within the system?

4. Relate an experience you have had as a juvenile with the police, whether good or bad, and tell how you feel it affected your life.

NOTES

1. Robert M. Mennel, *Thorns and Thistles* (Hanover, N.H.: University Press of New England, 1973), p. 167.

2. Ruth Shonle Cavan, *Juvenile Delinquency* (Philadelphia: Lippincott, 1969), p. 15.

3. *Seattle Post Intelligencer*, Seattle, Washington, January 8, 1930.

4. Ibid., December 24, 1930.

5. The Prohibition Act, or the Eighteenth Amendment (ratified January 16, 1920), banned the sale of alcoholic beverages. U.S. Statutes at Large, vol. 41; p. 305.

6. *Seattle Post Intelligencer*, Seattle, Washington, December 14, 1930.

7. "Catch 22" means that you can escape from an unpleasant situation only by meeting certain conditions. But if you meet those conditions, you cannot escape. This expression was popularized by Joseph Heller's novel of the same name. The novel is about an army pilot constantly required to fly suicide missions. He knew it was crazy to fly the missions, but according to the army, because he knew it was crazy, he was perfectly sane. And since he was sane, he could continue to fly the missions.

8. Eliot Ness of Chicago's Police Department Crime Prevention Bureau, and later of television fame, advocated that instead of apprehending young delinquents as offenders, police or juvenile officers should be trained to make referrals to proper social agencies for guidance and treatment. See Eliot Ness, "New Role of the Police," *Survey* (March 1944), p. 77.

9. Gary B. Adams, ed., *Juvenile Justice Management* (Springfield, Ill.: Thomas, 1973), pp. 275–276.

10. See Clifford Shaw and Henry D. McKay, *Juvenile Delinquency in Urban Areas* (Chicago: University of Chicago Press, 1942); Cletus Dirksen, *Economic Factors in Delinquency* (Milwaukee: Bruce, 1948); William W. Wattenburg and J. J. Balistrieri, "Gang Membership and Juvenile Delinquency," *American Sociological Review* 18 (1950): 631–635; Ernest W. Burgess, "The Economic Factor in Juvenile Delinquency," *Journal of Criminal Law, Criminology, and Police Science* 43 (May–June, 1952): 29–42; A. K. Cohen, *Delinquent Boys: The Culture of the Delinquent Gang* (New York: Free Press, 1955); and Sol Rubin, "Changing Youth Correction Authority Concepts," *Focus* 29 (1950): 77–82.

11. Elizabeth Fajen, "Curing Delinquency at the Source," *Survey*, October 1946, pp. 261–262.

12. Gary B. Adams, ed., *Juvenile Justice Management* (Springfield, Ill.: Thomas, 1973), pp. 323–324.

13. Edwin Powers, "An Experiment in the Prevention of Delinquency," *The Annals of the American Academy,* January 1949, p. 81.

14. William J. Kirk, Jr., "Juvenile Justice and Delinquency," *Phi Delta Kappan,* February 1976, p. 395.

15. Martin Gold, "Undetected Delinquent Behavior," *Journal of Research in Crime and Delinquency* 3 (January 1966): 27–46; Martin Gold, *Delinquent Behavior in an American City* (Belmont, Calif.: Brooks/Cole, 1970); Maynard L. Erickson and LaMar T. Empey, "Court Records, Undetected Delinquency, and Decision Making," *Journal of Criminal Law, Criminology and Police Science* 14 (December 1963): 456–69.

16. *National Prisoner Statistics, Prisoners in State and Federal Institutions for Adult Felons,* no. 44 (Washington, D.C.: U.S. Bureau of Prisons, 1969).

17. Martin Gold and Jay R. Williams, "The Effect of 'Getting Caught': Apprehension of the Juvenile Offender as a Cause of Subsequent Delinquencies." With responses by Richard B. Stuart, Judge John P. Steketee, Robert F. Drinan, *Prospectus,* u., 3, 1, 1970.

18. Martin Gold, *Delinquent Behavior in an American City* (Belmont, Calif.: Brooks/Cole, 1970).

19. Sol Rubin, "Children as Victims of Institutionalization," (Hackensack, N.J.: National Council on Crime and Delinquency, 1974), pp. 11–12.

20. Robert D. Vinter, et al., "Juvenile Corrections in the States: Residential Programs and Deinstitutionalization. A Preliminary Report" (Ann Arbor: National Assessment of Juvenile Corrections Project, University of Michigan, 1975), p. 13.

21. Mildred L. Midonick, *Children, Parents, and the Courts: Juvenile Delinquency, Ungovernability, and Neglect* (New York: Practicing Law Institute, 1972), p. 1.

22. Ibid., p. 2.

23. *Gideon* v. *Wainwright* (372 U.S. 335); 1963.

24. *In re Gault* (387 U.S. 1); 1967.

25. Charles Mangel, "How to Make a Criminal Out of a Child," *Look,* June 29, 1971.

26. "Moving the Kids Out: A Unique Experiment," *Corrections Magazine,* November–December, 1975, p. 29.

27. This theory is backed up in part by the findings of Martin Gold and J. R. Williams (see footnote 20) in which they concluded that "apprehension itself encourages rather than defers further delinquency."

28. "Juvenile Corrections in Massachusetts," *Corrections Magazine,* November–December, 1975, p. 7.

29. James A. Gazell and Thomas G. Gitchoff, *Youth, Crime and Society* (Boston: Holbrook Press, 1973), p. 17.

PART II

The Delinquent:
An Enigma

3 Causal Theories of Delinquency

Delinquency is neither an entity nor a disease, nor is it even analogous to a disease: delinquents are not necessarily sick people, either literally or figuratively.

EDWARD ELDEFONSO
ALAN R. COFFEY

What is the cause of the condition called delinquency? Historically, the traditional literature on crime and delinquency has approached answering this question by examining behavior patterns, sociological influence, and economic factors which might lead a child to be labeled as delinquent.

Despite many theories—and consequent programs developed to test those theories—little headway has been made in eradicating one of America's most costly problems.[1] Milton G. Rector, in an article for the *Encyclopedia of Social Work,* states that there exists no comprehensive, internally consistent, verifiable theory of delinquency from which to establish guidelines for action or treatment programs that are effective in dealing with the problem of delinquency.[2] The absence of a conclusive theory and the resulting ineffectiveness of practical solutions should challenge the student to become an active participant in the effort to find answers to delinquency.

One might ask whether or not it might be easier to enumerate those factors which are common to America's *nondelinquent* juvenile population. In other words, what are the social, cultural, environmental, and hereditary factors which are not linked to delinquency? If one were to select statements about the causes of delinquency and examine their obverse side, what would one find? To establish such an approach, let us first examine a list of factors contributing to delinquency as noted by the Gluecks. Among other things, they found that delinquency appeared to start in homes which were characterized as follows:

- Six out of every ten juvenile delinquents have fathers who drink to excess.
- Three out of four are permitted by parents to come and go as they please.

- Three out of five are from homes where there is discord between parents.
- Seven out of ten are from homes where there is no group or family recreation.
- Four out of five have parents who take no interest in the children's friends.
- Four out of five delinquent boys say their mothers were indifferent to them.
- Three out of five delinquent boys say their fathers were indifferent to them.
- Many have mothers who drink to excess.
- Many come from broken homes.
- Few get religious training of any kind.[3]

It would, of course, be a gross oversimplification to suppose that delinquency would be reduced if these characteristics were reversed—to suppose, for example, that if a child were *not* permitted to come and go as he or she pleased, or if both parents *did* get along, and so forth, that the child wouldn't be delinquent. Many who are not familiar with delinquents assume that there is an easily defined difference between delinquents and nondelinquents. In fact, some studies indicate that there are no significant differences between delinquents and nondelinquents.[4] For instance, R. R. Korn's training aid prepared for the Santa Clara County Juvenile Probation Department in California points out:

> There is no valid basis for assuming that the behavior of officially adjudicated delinquents. What strikingly differentiates the officially processed delinquents population of children, committing similar acts, but not formally processed as delinquents. What strikingly differentiates the officially processed delinquents from those whose behavior is either not detected, or not officially acted upon, is a chain of social-like processes ranging from the (a) arrest, (b) formal adjudication as delinquent, (c) official supervision and restriction within the open community, (d) brief or prolonged incarceration in the enforced company of similarly processed children in correctional institutions. . . .
>
> . . . the most physical and demonstrable difference derives not from the nature of the delinquent behavior itself, but rather from the nature and extent of community reactions to this behavior—actions ranging from tolerance to indifference, or indifference to prolonged correctional incarceration. We have, in effect, implied a major difference, whether or not juvenile misbehavior is tolerated and ignored ("Don't worry, he'll grow out of it") and formally dealt with in the family setting ("He'll get what's coming to him when Dad comes home"), or formally punished by the impersonal law enforcement agents of society ("We hereby commit you during the period of your minority to the New York State Training School at Otis Ville.")[5]

However, the student will find that there are many books on library shelves which declare that there *are* observable and predictable differences between delinquents and nondelinquents. These books contain theories from many disciplines, ranging from those based on the so-called medical model[6] to those embracing the so-called process model[7] and everything in between. The authors feel that the most valid difference between delinquents and nondelinquents is a mere matter of who gets caught and who does not. Apart from this, we do not hold that there is any cut-and-dried difference between the two groups. If such a discernible difference did exist, it would make predicting who might become a delinquent and who might not far easier, and would thus assist the juvenile justice system in achieving its most sought-after goal: preventing juvenile delinquency in the first place.

This chapter will examine some well-known definitions of delinquency and will further pursue the theoretical bases of causality.

Definition

Before attempting to discuss conditions or circumstances that appear to cause delinquency, it is important for us to clearly define juvenile delinquency. The difficulty of this task has been recognized by knowledgeable experts in the field:

> In the area of juvenile justice, semantic meaning has been and continues to be a problem. Terms have different meanings to different people and agencies, and attempts at universal standardization have fallen short of their goal. . . . It is interesting to note that many of our states apparently do not agree on how to describe a juvenile delinquent in precise terms. In virtually all states, the behavior which can bring a child before the juvenile court may only be constructed in terms of certain moral judgments of the community, which are derived from the older laws of chancery of the British common law courts. Thus, children may be adjudicated not only for violations of state statutes or municipal ordinances, but also for noncriminal behavior (i.e., incorrigibility, truancy, the habitual use of obscene language, absenting themselves from their homes or associating themselves with vicious persons) which are fundamentally matters of community taste, standards, and discretion.[8]

In *Process and Impact of the Juvenile Justice System,* the authors discuss the ambiguous use of the term *juvenile delinquent.*

> In general, juvenile delinquency is a catchall term; it means different things to different people. To some the manner of attire—for example, wearing mod clothes or having long hair—is sufficient to label a child a delinquent; to the suburban homeowner, a delinquent may mean a youth who rides his bicycle across the lawn; and to one accustomed to reading sensationalistic newspaper headlines about teenagers, the term delinquent conjures up images of a youthful hoodlum who spends his time engaged in committing robbery, rape, and murder.[9]

However, even the clearly identified delinquent is difficult to categorize. Take the following case as an example:

Two boys who have nothing in common but the fact that each violated a law, one caught in an armed robbery and the other caught stealing a sodapop from a grocery store, may both fit into the same legal pigeonhole, but obviously, they do not share a common psychological category. We have found that the label *delinquent* cannot be used without qualification as though it denoted a common set of facts or a specific kind of person. We cannot assume that because a boy was in court he was ipso facto a member of some subspecies of human beings.[10]

To simplify the process of definition, juvenile delinquency can be divided into two separate areas—legal and social.

Legal Definition

Juveniles in the United States must obey and are subject to the same ordinances and criminal statutes governing adults. In addition, they are also governed by a second set of rules which are applicable because of the special status of juveniles. Currently, about one-fourth of all youths brought before our juvenile courts are involved in offenses which, if committed by an adult, would not be a crime. For example, Washington's Substitute House Bill No. 371 lists the following conditions which characterize a child as dependent and therefore subject to the jurisdiction of the juvenile courts. A dependent child is one:

1. Who has been abandoned; that is, left by his or her parents, guardian, or other custodian without parental care and support; or
2. Who is abused or neglected . . . or
3. Who has no parent, guardian, or custodian; or
4. Any child:
   a. Who is in conflict with his or her parent, guardian, or custodian;
   b. Who refuses to remain in any nonsecure residential placement ordered by a court . . . ;
   c. Whose conduct evidences a substantial likelihood of degenerating into serious delinquent behavior if not corrected; and
   d. Who is in need of custodial treatment in a diagnostic and treatment facility.[11]

The Children's Bureau, a federal agency, gives the legal definition of delinquency as follows:

Juvenile delinquency cases are those referred to courts for acts defined in the statutes of the state as the violation of a state law or municipal ordinance by children or youth of juvenile court age, or for conduct so seriously antisocial as to interfere with the rights of others or to menace the welfare of the delinquent or of the community.[12]

Washington has a similar but more concise legal definition:

> The words *delinquent child* mean any child under the age of eighteen years who violates any law of this state, or any ordinance of any town, city, or county of this state defining a crime or who has violated any federal law or law of another state defining a crime, and whose case has been referred to the juvenile court by any jurisdiction whatsoever.[13]

The 18-year-old age limit mentioned in the Washington code is typical of approximately two-thirds of the United States. Some states include youth up to age 21 in their delinquency statutes.

Ruth Cavan, in *Juvenile Delinquency*, describes the legal, or, as she put it, "official," definition of delinquency:

> Officially, juvenile delinquency consists of misbehavior by children and adolescents that leads to referral to the juvenile court. In some states the specifics of such misbehavior are rather explicitly stated in the law; in other states the definition of delinquency is so vague and general that the dividing line between delinquency and normal misbehavior is the verdict of public opinion, the opinion of the policeman who arrests the child, or the judgment of the juvenile court. This lack of exactness and uniformity has led some cynics to say that juvenile delinquency is whatever the law says it is. It would be more exact to say that it is behavior which the people of a state and their leaders believe to be a threat to public safety or a hindrance to the best development of the child, and whose prohibition they have incorporated into law.
>
> Specifically, juvenile delinquency in different states ranges from the most serious crimes such as murder, burglary, or robbery, to irritating but trivial acts such as playing ball in the street, building a tree house in a public park, or obstructing traffic on a sidewalk. Fortunately, most delinquent acts are of the less serious variety. But there is always the fear on the part of adults that the trivial acts, if continued, may somehow lead to long-lasting or serious misconduct.[14]

Obviously there are many legal definitions of delinquency. Depending on the source, whether state laws, social commentators, or textbooks, the definition will vary. The authors feel, however, that the definition given above, that of Ruth Cavan, is the most comprehensive, and we shall, therefore, select it above the others and use it as our reference throughout this book. We now turn to a discussion involving the *social* impact of delinquency.

Social Definition

The social definition of delinquency primarily involves the views of the family, friends, and community regarding a child's behavior.

For example, the child may be barred from certain groups, may be labeled delinquent, and may thus be considered unacceptable in some circles. He may elicit disapproval from the community and be forced to associate with groups and persons who are less conductive to the transmitting of socially accepted norms.[15]

The social definition, therefore, is a reflection of how the delinquent's parents, friends, neighbors, and community view him or her as a person. This is often quite different from the way courts, parole or probation officers, or other official agencies might see the person.

The legal definition of delinquency, therefore, may be viewed as providing only a partial insight into the delinquency problem. To this extent, a knowledge of the sociological factors surrounding delinquency becomes important in the quest for a solution to the definition problem. Cavan, for example, states that the legal definition of delinquency is inadequate for the understanding of the juvenile's position in society, for the public's approval or disapproval of that child, or for understanding the factors contributing to the juvenile's becoming labeled as a delinquent.

Three Factors in Determining Delinquency

In an attempt to establish whether a youth should be placed in that category of juveniles labeled as delinquent, one should keep in mind both the legal and social aspects of the defining process. In the determination of who is to be labeled a delinquent there are three basic factors of behavior which should be observed and considered: (1) the frequency of the act; (2) the seriousness of the act; and (3) the attitude of the juvenile committing the act.

The frequency of an act indicates whether an antisocial pattern of behavior exists, even in the face of the dual stigma of legal and social labeling as delinquent. For example, if a youth repeatedly steals automobiles for joy-riding, the pattern of behavior exists and it is antisocial and delinquent in nature. The seriousness of an act tends to indicate how the community involved might view the youth. For example, rape is a serious antisocial offense, whereas getting intoxicated is not. While *seriousness* is a subjective term, what is done about a specific act is an objective indicator of how a community's juvenile justice system is operating. For example, in the case of a rape, the community (i.e., the people in that community) may bring strong pressure upon the law enforcement officials and the courts to have the juvenile involved arrested and removed from their community, whereas the same community may view intoxication as good-natured fun, part of growing up, and may do no more than publicly censure the youth with a slap on the hand. Finally, the attitude of the child must be evaluated in the context of the act. Normally, a child's attitude toward authority is indicative of his or her likelihood of breaking the law. But an impulsive act of window smashing is quite different and separate from chronic auto theft. The child that constantly rebels against authority and displays hostile attitudes toward parents, teachers, and other authority figures probably will at some time or other come into conflict with the law.

Summary

Although we have adopted Cavan's definition of juvenile delinquency, it is important to keep in mind that there are many other legal and social definitions of the term. Definitions, even legal ones, may change from state to state, from city to city, and even from community to community. Attempting to arrive at an all-purpose definition that covers all the collective and diverse categories of behavior that are designated as delinquent is impossible. Delinquency can be, and often is, spoken of in broad generalities. But, when examining a specific case, one must consult local statutes or state codes in effect where the juvenile committed the crime, where he or she was arrested, and where he or she legally resides.

Theories of Causation

"Nothing is so practical as a good theory" is an often-quoted comment of Kurt Lewin.[16] Good theories are excellent guides for both practitioners and researchers.

Has the field of juvenile delinquency had the advantage of a number of "good" theories? There are many theories of causation, ranging from those concerned with chemical imbalances of the brain to those which examine environmental deprivation. Most leading authorities in the field have presented their own theories as to why children become delinquents. Unfortunately, many of these theorists have neglected to offer action programs that realistically test their concepts. Others, though they have provided testing, have seldom followed up thoroughly enough.

Theories of causation are *necessary,* but practical programs which can empirically test the theories are *imperative*. In judging various theories which the reader may encounter in books on juvenile delinquency, one must keep in mind certain criteria. Milton Rector has outlined the criteria of a "good" theory and defined its relationship to the problem of delinquency.

> If rigorous criteria of a "good" theory are employed, existing theories of delinquency and crime do not hold up well. Minimum requirements for a theory are that (1) the theory of knowledge accepted as its basis be described; (2) assumptions underlying the theory—the basic postulates the theorist takes on faith—be stated; (3) constructs used in the theory be identified, with their means of definition; (4) hypotheses derived be stated in testable terms; (5) pertinent empirical evidence be examined; (6) limitations or boundaries to the

theory be made explicit; (7) implications for delinquency and crime prevention, treatment, and control programs be set forth; and (8) implications for research be assessed.

No available delinquency and crime theories satisfy all these requirements; no comprehensive, internally consistent theoretical framework is available to impose order and guide research and practice in this area. Precursors to antisocial conduct are known, but the needed comprehensive system, building upon presently available knowledge and earlier theory, has yet to emerge.[17]

It is important for the student of the juvenile justice system to have a basic awareness and knowledge of early criminological theory. However, this subject will be discussed only briefly here. References are supplied for the interested reader who wishes to pursue this subject further.

The classical school of criminology was founded in the 1700s by Cesare Beccaria. Its emphasis was on the crime committed by the person, and its basic tenet was that humans are rational beings who seek the *good* things in life (that is, they are pleasure-oriented) and avoid the *bad* (or pain-oriented). Assuming, therefore, that people prefer pleasure to pain, Beccaria contended that no one would commit a criminal act unless it could be anticipated that the pleasurable consequences would outweigh the painful ones. The purpose of society was to secure the happiness of the majority. Early laws were quite simple, with punishments administered publicly and aimed primarily at deterrence.

Beccaria and his contemporaries embraced the doctrine of free will and its correlative that each person is morally responsible for his or her own acts. In keeping with this doctrine, Beccaria's principles about punishment are summarized as follows:

> Beccaria put the problem of punishments on a new plane, stating that the purpose of penalties is not retribution, but prevention; justice requires a right proportion between crimes and punishments, but the purpose of penalties is to prevent a criminal from doing more harm and to deter others from doing similar damage. . . . Beccaria wanted a society of kind and civilized people and he believed that the abolition of cruel punishments, including the death penalty, would contribute to the formation of such a society.[18]

The next step toward causal theories was taken by members of the neoclassical school of criminology, among whom Cesare Lombroso (1836–1909) and Charles Goring (1870–1919) are the best known. Lombroso, an Italian army physician, was influenced by the increasing emphasis on physiological, sociological, and anthropological approaches to understanding individual behavior. He shifted the emphasis away from the criminal act to the criminal. Unlike the classical school, which regarded the criminal as a free agent, the neoclassical teachings considered the criminal to be the product of hereditary social forces, some of which were beyond his or her control.

Lombroso turned his search for explanations of crime to the physiological characteristics of the criminal himself. He believed that the criminal was a less developed human being with a brain capacity much the same as our primitive ancestors: The criminal was an evolutionary throwback (atavistic). Criminals, according to Lombroso, supposedly differed physiologically from others because of abnormal brain development and physical characteristics, or *stigma*, such as low foreheads, protruding ears, and narrow, deep-set eyes.

Lombroso's efforts stimulated other research; in fact, some of his followers went further than he did, maintaining not only that there was a criminal type but that that type could be divided into subgroups, with different physical stigma for thieves, murderers, and so forth.

Charles Goring, an English criminologist, tested the hypothesis that physical stigma play an important role in crime and its prediction. He measured approximately 3,000 recidivist English convicts for 37 of Lombroso's stigma. When Goring discovered that the postulated anatomical differences did not hold true, he began to suggest that perhaps another factor, intelligence, might be more significant. Goring (1913), in speaking of the results of his studies, concluded:

> We have exhaustively compared . . . different kinds of criminals with each other, and criminals as a class with the law-abiding public. From these comparisons no evidence has emerged confirming the existence of a physical criminal type such as Lombroso and his disciples have described. . . . Our results nowhere confirm evidence nor justify the allegations of criminal anthropologists. They challenge their evidence at almost every point. In fact, both with regard to measurement and physical anomalies in criminals, our statistics present a startling conformity with similar statistics of the law-abiding classes. The final conclusion we are bound to accept . . . must be that there is no such thing as a physical criminal type.[19]

In early writings it is not uncommon to find that the mentally retarded or feeble-minded people were wrongfully labeled as inherently criminal types.[20] However, American thought on the theory of crime and delinquency has been traditionally unreceptive to the notion that organic factors cause some people to commit criminal acts. Harry Allen, a noted researcher in this field, has expressed this attitude:

> "The extravagant claims, meager empirical evidence, naiveté, gross inadequacy, and stated or implied concepts of racial and ethnic inferiority" in the work of earlier theorists constitute a "disreputable history" which thoroughly discredited the few important empirical findings of biological investigations of criminal behavior.[21]

It appears that the proponents of the physiological criminal type and the phrenologists (those who attempt to interpret the bumps on a person's head in a manner similar to palm reading) have usually fallen short of substantiating their theories with irrefutable, empirical data. Indeed, it is probable that they were even mistaken to try. In any case the early concept of a physical criminal type is generally not considered as a relevant or realistic theory today.

Contemporary Theories

Among the more important contemporary causal theories are the social, psychological, physiological, phenomenological, constitutional, and economic theories. The discussion of these theories of crime causation begins with the *social* theories.

Major Social Theories

The social theories of juvenile delinquency are grounded in present-day sociological thought and focus strictly on the *collective* behavior of the individual rather than the individual behavior. Discussion of social theories has caused sociologists to address themselves primarily to two basic questions: How does the juvenile in society acquire criminality? How does society acquire or produce crime?

The "process model," of which social theory is considered to be a part, is meaningful to a present-day discussion of causality. The "process-model" is in direct conflict with the "medical model," which contends that criminal behavior is the fault of the individual, caused by some flaw in the individual's psychological, biological, or physiological makeup. The process mold holds that criminal behavior is caused by factors external to the individual: economic class, environmental surroundings, delinquent subcultures, lower-class structure, and so forth. The process model, therefore, contends that, as the result of various cultural, economic, sociological, racial, and ethnic conditions or influences, criminal behavior is produced, and that changes in these conditions have the potential to influence the incidence of criminal or delinquent behavior.

Social theories state that a child's individuality cannot be separated from his or her interactions in a group. Of special importance in group interaction is motivation. However, social theory concerns itself with those things that determine motivation in societal interactions that are *external* to the juvenile. Internal or psychological motivation are not given as much emphasis. In *Explaining Crime*, Gwynn Nettler emphasizes this point:

> A strictly sociological explanation is concerned with how the *structure* of a society or its *institutional practices* or its *persisting cultural themes* affect the conduct of its members. Individual differences are denied or ignored, and the explanation of collective behavior is sought in the patterning of social arrangements that is considered to be both "outside" the actor and "prior" to

him. That is, the social patterns of power or of institutions which are held to be determinative of human action are also seen as having been in existence *before* any particular actor came on the scene. They are "external" to him in the sense that they will persist with or without him. In lay language, *sociological explanations of crime place the blame on something social that is prior to, external to, and compelling of a particular person.* [22]

Nettler identifies two types of sociological explanations of criminality and delinquency: (1) the structural and (2) the subcultural. In both instances, culture conflict is assumed to be the primary causal factor of juvenile crime.

The Structural Approach   The French sociologist Emile Durkheim (1853–1917) was one of the first writers to discuss the effect that a particular social structure and its scheme of organization has on social deviancy. Durkheim debunked the early theories that sought the causes of crime in anthropological factors. He disagreed with those who attempt to discover the cause of crime in the external characteristics of life, such as economic conditions, population densities, climate, or ecological circumstances. For Durkheim, crime is a normal fact of life resulting from various degrees of social interaction, and it is in the very nature of society that "it is necessary to look for an explanation. . . . Crime is normal because a society exempt from it is utterly impossible. . . . [The] fundamental conditions of social organization logically imply it." [23] No societal or human defect, therefore, causes crime; it cannot be considered abnormal or pathological. "A society exempt from [crime] would necessitate a standardization of the moral concept of all individuals which is neither possible nor desirable." [24]

Durkheim's theory of anomie was a major contribution to the understanding of deviant behavior. *Anomie* is a state in which structured social norms no longer control a person's actions. Durkheim attempted to show, for example, how suicide is linked to an individual's failure or inability to successfully integrate into a stable, organized social group. Because this is so, the person experiences the absence of meaningful rules and life has no purpose. As a result, this person, having entered a state of anomie, is prone to commit suicide.

The theory of anomie as an explanation of deviant behavior was refined by Robert E. Merton, an American sociologist. [25] Merton argued that people live by two sets of goals, one which governs the *means* by which they seek something and the other which governs the *ends* that they desire. Thus one set of values specifies socially accepted means and the other socially accepted ends. Most members of a stable society will tend to accept and pursue value orientations of both means and goals, and will thus conform to accepted ends. Most members of a stable society will tend to accept and pursue value orientations of both means and goals, and will thus conform to accepted standards. Anomie is experienced when either or both of these

value orientations are rejected. Often, in dealing with delinquent populations, a discrepancy is discovered between the institutionalized means available within a juvenile's particular environment and the goals to which the
child has learned to aspire. This discrepancy is usually made apparent to the
dominant, normal, rule-making society by an act of the delinquent—by
definition—behavior. It is, after all, not what a child does or does not do
which makes an act delinquent, but rather society's reaction to that act. For
instance, one would assume that a gathering of angelic-looking choir boys
would produce no deviant behavior. However, if one of the boys were
constantly to sing much louder than the rest, his actions could be deemed as
deviant by the choirmaster.

Merton's central hypothesis states that deviant behavior may be regarded
sociologically as a breakdown between culturally prescribed aspirations and
the socially structured means for realizing these aspirations. American
society, Merton points out, places too much emphasis on achieving "the
Great American Dream" while showing less concern about how this dream
is achieved (i.e., "dirty" money can be spent just as easily as "honest,"
hard-earned money). Consequently, juveniles from lower-class backgrounds
experience great pressures to achieve under less favorable circumstances
than children of other classes. And they are therefore more likely to exhibit
deviant behavior.

In *Delinquency and Opportunity*, Richard Cloward and Lloyd Ohlin
expanded and applied the theory that delinquent behavior is more likely to
be experienced among lower-class juveniles to explain urban gang behavior.
Their hypothesis is stated as follows:

> The disparity between what lower-class youth are led to want and what is
> actually available to them is the source of a major problem of adjustment.
> Adolescents who form delinquent subcultures, we suggest, have internalized
> an emphasis upon conventional goals. Faced with limitations on legitimate
> avenues of access to these goals, and unable to revise their aspirations
> downward, they experience intense frustrations; the exploration of noncon-
> formist alternatives may be the result.[26]

According to Nettler, this explanation characterizes delinquency as being
both adaptive and reactive in nature.[27] It is adaptive insofar as it is
instrumental in the attainment of goals which most youth generally share,
and reactive because it is partly prompted by the resentment of juveniles at
being deprived of things which they either believe they should have or have
been advised or told they should have.

The Subcultural Approach   "Subculture is a term devised by social
scientists to refer conveniently to variations within a society on its cultural
themes, patterns, artifacts, and traditional ideas, as these are incorporated
and expressed within various groups."[28] It is the nature of a community's

integration of legitimate and illegitimate means which will normally determine the nature of the subcultural accommodations to goal-achieving criteria. Cloward and Ohlin have identified three types of delinquent subculture: (1) the criminal subculture, (2) the conflict subculture, and (3) the retreatist subculture.[29]

The criminal subculture, and criminal gangs, "will develop where there is cross age integration of offenders plus close relations between the carriers of criminal and conventional values."[30] For example, a young boy who grows up in a family where the father and brothers and their associates are all involved in criminal activities may himself be either intrigued or coerced into similar displays of delinquent or criminal behavior. The criminal subculture is comprised of juveniles who are thought to have become delinquent as a result of associations or contacts with persons who are outside the law. Many parole and probation authorities state, as a condition of parole or probation, that the juvenile shall not associate with known felons or persons whose influence may have a negative potential.

Albert Cohen, in *Delinquent Boys*,[31] indicates that the basis of delinquency lies in the variables of social class structure. He theorized that the delinquent from a lower-class environment lacks self-respect, and in his frustration with his class or social position, he strikes out against middle-class values (called a *reaction formation*) and adopts opposite values. As a result, a delinquent subculture is formed which emerges as a collective attempt to contend with and to solve class-based frustrations and angers.

Walter B. Miller,[32] a principal advocate of the conflict subculture explanation of delinquency, rejects Cohen's contention that delinquency is produced by lower-class conflict with or reaction formation to a larger dominant society. Instead, he contends that the violation of middle class norms "is a 'by-product of action' primarily oriented to the lower-class culture, and the standards of lower-class culture cannot be seen as merely a reverse function of middle-class culture—as middle-class standards 'turned upside down'; lower-class culture is a distinctive tradition many centuries old with an integrity of its own."[33]

Miller uses the concept of focal concerns in explaining his interpretation of the conflict subculture approach. Focal concerns are areas or issues which command widespread and persistent attention and a high degree of emotional involvement, and which Miller feels tend to characterize a lower-class culture. Some of these focal concerns are trouble, toughness, smartness, excitement, fate, and autonomy. Miller prefers to speak of these focal concerns within a conflict subculture rather than of values, because focal concerns can more readily be observed and examined in direct field investigation.

Lower-class delinquency resulting from a conflict subculture cannot be classified as deviant or aberrant in Miller's view. Rather, it is part of the lower-class culture and, within the group, is highly functional and necessary in preparing youngsters for an adult life which will probably be lived within the confines of that subculture. Therefore, delinquent behavior among lower-class youth can be considered as *normal* behavior within that class. What causes a lower-class youth's behavior to be considered delinquent is that the youth's focal concerns come in *conflict* with those rules and norms which comprise the traditional and institutional values of the middle class.

The final type of delinquent subculture to be discussed is the retreatist subculture. "A retreatist subculture, and retreatist gangs, will develop among boys locked out of the above two avenues [criminal and conflict subcultures] because of the lack of means integration and because of 'internalized prohibitions' or 'socially structured barriers' to the use of violence. This 'double failure' leaves only retreat, most specifically through drugs and alcohol."[34]

A retreatist subculture can occur, therefore, almost by default. Youth barred from participation in the criminal or conflict subcultural gangs often find themselves banding together out of commonality, and thus, as their numbers increase, a gang comes into being. Juveniles comprising a retreatist gang are often typified as being "odd-balls," misfits, or loners in relationship with the larger delinquent subculture around them. Because of rejection by their peers, parents, or others, they may seek out or simply happen to find themselves hanging around with other youth "outsiders." They replace violent or criminal behavior with retreatist behavior, such as drinking, smoking pot, or other activities which, while they may cause trouble with the law, are generally either nonviolent or low-key.[35]

Other Social Theories   In addition to these social theories already reviewed, there are a few others which deserve brief mention. One of these is Edwin Sutherland's theory of differential association, which, according to Trojanowicz, "is probably one of the most systematic and complete theories of delinquency causation that has yet been constructed."[36] Sutherland hypothesized that a person becomes a delinquent as a result of experiencing an excess of definitions (influences or role aspirations) encouraging law-violating behavior as opposed to those encouraging law-abiding behavior. Furthermore, these definitions are provided to juveniles through their most intimate personal groups, such as peers and family.

The theory of differential association holds that (1) delinquent behavior is learned behavior, (2) delinquent behavior is acquired by interacting and communicating with other people, (3) the primary experience of learning criminal or delinquent behavior occurs within intimate personal groups, (4) learned behavior includes both the techniques for committing crime and explaining the motivation for such acts, (5) the motives are learned from various definitions found in legal codes which may be interpreted as either favorable and unfavorable,[37] (6) a person's excess of definitions (role aspirations or goal achievements) favorable to law violation cause delinquent behavior, (7) the differential association is not stagnant but varies in duration, frequency, and intensity, (8) the process of learning criminal and anti- or noncriminal patterns involves all of the mechanisms of any other learning process, and (9) although delinquent behavior may be seen as an expression of needs and values, it is not explained by those needs or values because nondelinquent behavior is an expression of the same needs and values.[38]

In empirical testing, the differential association theory has, in general, been relatively unsuccessful. Despite this drawback, it has been a prolific source of ideas and suggestions for practical steps to be taken in reducing the delinquency rate. Malcolm Klein has summarized these steps as follows:

1. Group treatment for offenders should be employed in circumstances when the dominant values and behaviors are lawful (and the group is meaningful to the offender).

2. Reward systems should be promulgated for the encouragement of prosocial endeavors of offenders.

3. Role-playing of prosocial roles in essentially lawful situations should be employed as a treatment technique.

4. Because the criminal label tends to cut a person off from association with the law-abiding citizen and force him to fall back upon criminal associations, attempts should be made to avoid stigmatization as criminal, convict, delinquent, and the like.

5. Factors conducive to the continuance of criminal associations should be attacked directly.

6. Incarceration of offenders should be avoided, and periods of incarceration decreased as much as possible.

7. Encouragement should be given to civic programs that would break down the integration of criminal systems.

8. Encouragement should be given to programs designed to ''de-isolate'' or reintegrate individuals removed from the mainstream of community life.

9. Neighborhood programs . . . should be attempted as a means of integrating the various elements of a neighborhood into self-activation against well-entrenched criminal systems.[39]

Summary of Social Theories   In Durkheim's anomie and Merton's subsequent elaboration of this theory, the discrepancy between the institutional means available to juveniles and the goals desired by them has been identified as a source of frustration and stress. This stress is especially evident among members of the lower class, and it often leads to delinquency. Sutherland's work emphasizes the importance of environment in determining delinquent behavior. And Cloward, Ohlin, and Cohen have explained delinquent behavior as a reaction against the dominant middle-class system and social institutions.

Psychological Theories

Unlike the sociological or group interaction theories, psychological theories are concerned with determinants of *individual* motivation. These theories emphasize the relationship between personality, or psychological functioning, and the development of delinquent behavior.

"At present there is no single psychological theory . . . that has been tested empirically and totally explains, in all circumstances, juvenile delinquency and criminality."[40] Psychological research has contributed much to understanding the causes of crime. These contributions have primarily consisted of knowledge concerning deprivations in human needs and desires, and individual deviations in personality.

Psychoanalytic Theories   August Aichhorn and other proponents of psychoanalytic theory have held that all delinquents are emotionally ill.[41] However, while it may be generally recognized that many delinquents do have emotional conflicts, Aichhorn's theory is not supported by factual evidence. Attempts have been made to adapt the Freudian (psychoanalytic) viewpoint in investigating the causes of crime and criminality; however, most of these studies have been unsuccessful in pinpointing variables or causal factors. This discussion will be limited to those aspects of psychoanalysis which are relevant to the determinants of delinquent behavior.

From the psychoanalytic point of view, behavior may be seen as essentially functional. It exists in order to fulfill certain needs and drives and it has consequences beyond its immediate purposes. Every child possesses a reserve of antisocial impulses (the id), and as a result of reality contact, he or she develops controls (ego) and regulators (superego) which influence and direct impulses. With juvenile delinquents, the controls are looked upon as having failed to function effectively. The dominance of the id over the ego and superego is explained in terms of faulty early training or parental neglect.

Delinquency may be thought of as a symptomatic method of coping with a basic problem of individual adjustment. The delinquent differs from the nondelinquent because his or her conflicts, anxieties, and frustrations are unlike those of nondelinquent youth in both type and degree. In a study based on psychoanalytical methods, the Gluecks investigated personality differences between delinquent and nondelinquent youth. They made the following conclusions:

1. Delinquents are more extroverted, vivacious, impulsive, and less self-controlled than the nondelinquents. They are less fearful of failure or defeat than the nondelinquents.

2. Delinquents are less concerned about meeting conventional expectations and are more ambivalent toward or far less submissive to authority. They are, as a group, more socially assertive.

3. To a greater extent than the control group, the delinquents expressed feelings of not being recognized or appreciated.[42]

Typically, psychoanalytic theories stress the importance of dysfunctional development, poor family relationships, inadequate impulse control, and so forth, as indices of delinquency. The resultant defenses against anxiety—which may occur often—include the desire to get caught and/or be punished, the need to seek revenge, or any of a number of self-protecting tactics which may result in a delinquent act. Because delinquency is viewed in psychoanalytic methods as being caused by personality disturbances, its control and reduction depends on successful treatment or remediation of emotional conflicts or disturbances. When dealing with delinquents, it is emphasized that the early formative years are crucial to later personality development. Consequently, early diagnosis and treatment of emotional disturbances is imperative.

Psychoanalysts assume that childhood experiences take precedence over most, if not all, cultural and social experiences. They believe that behavior can be explained by analyzing the child's unconscious mind and its underlying conflicts.

Although the specific reasons for a delinquent or criminal act must be sought in the juvenile's life history, the causative factor in the psychoanalytic approach to criminology is that delinquent behavior is an attempt to bring a disturbed psychic state of mind back into balance. However, this approach suffers from disagreement among theorists as to why the person actually seeks this balanced state of mind. Difficulties arise in naming the specific factors in a child's socialization which render that child likely to commit delinquent acts. In an article entitled "Psychoanalysis and Crime," D. Feldman has identified five variations of the basic *balance* formula:

1. Criminality as neurosis
2. The antisocial individual as an instance of defective socialization
3. Criminal behavior as compensation for frustration of conventional psychic needs
4. Criminal behavior as a function of defective superego
5. Criminal behavior as anomie[43]

The reliability and credibility of this causative formula is questionable at best. Psychoanalytic theory tends to be too general and all-inclusive. It is full of extraneous meanings, and is seldom concerned with or based on observable facts.

The student of the juvenile justice system should have a basic knowledge of psychoanalytic theory. However, this subject is far too complex and esoteric to be covered thoroughly in a single, introductory chapter. The best general introduction to psychoanalysis is still Freud's own work, which should be read together with the 1933 continuation and revision, *New Introductory Lectures in Psychoanalysis.*[44]

For the student interested in research in the juvenile justice system, the following statement by Vetter and Simonsen should be helpful in evaluating how well research generated by psychoanalytic theory has fared.

> Most of the research generated by psychoanalytic theory does not seem to be directed toward the subsequent modification of the theory in the light of newly acquired information but rather toward demonstrating the essential validity of the basic postulates and assumptions of the theory. Because of the ambiguity and lack of operational specificity of the constructs in the system, no hypothesis derived from psychoanalytic theory can be either clearly confirmed or clearly refuted. For these and other reasons, critics of psychoanalysis have charged that the theory and its proponents do not conform to the widely accepted canons of empirical verification and refutation implicit to the scientific method.[45]

Containment Theory   The containment theory, whose chief theorist is Walter Reckless,[46] is a combination of both social theory and psychological theory. In other words, it is a sociopsychological theory. Containment theory emphasizes the concept of self. Reckless feels that there are two important aspects of individual control—*inner* control and *outer* control. When there is a balance between these controls, the child will be a conformist. When there is a disbalance, the child will be a deviant. Reckless hypothesizes that persons with a good *self-concept* will engage in less criminal activity than persons with a poor self-concept.

In "A New Theory of Delinquency and Crime," the author of this theory, Walter Reckless, describes the concept of containment as follows:

> In a vertical order, the pressures and pulls of the environment are at the top or the side of the containing structure, while the pushes are below the inner containment. If the individual has a weak outer containment, the pressures and pulls will then have to be handled by the inner control system. If the outer buffer of the individual is relatively strong and effective, the individual's inner defense does not have to play such a critical role. Likewise, if the person's inner controls are not equal to the ordinary pushes, effective outer defense may help hold him within bounds. If the inner defenses are of good working order, the outer structure does not have to come to the rescue of the person.[47]

Effective control of delinquent behavior as well as its possible elimination or reduction involves, then, both internal and external variables, the internal being the conscience and the external the environment. One should complement the other and often each has to exert influence and control for the other. When these variables are working properly, the person has a satisfactory self-concept and is less likely to commit a delinquent or criminal act. However, this does not explain why some persons with a poor self-concept do not engage in criminal activities. Also, critics of the containment theory have observed that the relationship between self-concept and delinquency is quite speculative. Indeed, several questions remain to be answered regarding this theory. For example, is a poor self-concept the *cause* or the *result* of delinquency and why should a poor self-concept make a child more vulnerable to delinquency than a good self-concept?

Reality Theory   The reality theory is based on the premise that all persons have certain basic needs which must be met. Accordingly, a child will act irresponsibly or unruly when these needs are not or cannot be met. Reality *therapy* seeks to encourage a young person to act responsibly and thus refrain from antisocial or delinquent behavior. The chief proponent of this theory, Dr. William Glasser, contends that reality therapy can be utilized by all members of the juvenile justice system. It has such general applicability because it does not emphasize ambiguous psychiatric terminology, extensive testing, or even exhaustive record keeping of case histories.

Reality therapy sharply contrasts with psychoanalytical methods because it emphasizes the present, not the past behavior of a child. Because of its less sophisticated methodology, reality therapy has a widespread, popular appeal to many people working in corrections. However, as a scientific explanation, the concept that delinquent behavior is caused by a youth acting in an irresponsible manner—one which deprives others of the ability to fulfill their own needs—is untested and, perhaps, untestable.[48]

William Isaac Thomas (1863–1947), a psychologist, formulated a theory which supports Glasser's idea of fulfilling basic needs. This theory contends that the individual requires an adequate and wholesome outlet for the expression and/or attainment of basic needs and psychic drives. The individual also has to satisfy and find outlets for social needs. If these needs are frustrated, a person may seek fulfillment in law-violating behavior. Furthermore, the absence of affection and security can easily lead to sexual delinquency, theft, and incorrigibility in children.[49]

Summary of Psychological Theories   Like the social theories, the psychological-psychoanalytical theories have contributed to knowledge and speculative thought about delinquent and deviant behavior. Psychological theories, and more especially the psychoanalytical theories, have traditionally assumed that certain *universal* uniformities of human behavior exist. Because these theories are based on generalized assumptions, it should keep in mind that they are not applicable to all classes or types of delinquent behavior.

Physiological Approaches

The physiological approach attempts to explain criminal behavior by finding its cause in certain biological characteristics. Antisocial behavior in either psychopathic or sociopathic personalities is believed to be caused by physiological makeup. Psychopaths and sociopaths have a tendency to be impulsive, to lack tolerance for sameness, and to show an inability to judge right from wrong. Other traits or characteristics of the psychopathic personality are emotional immaturity, instability, reckless behavior, unruly acts, excessively self-centered attitudes, lack of self-discipline, inability to learn from experiences, and a marked deficiency of moral sense and/or control.[50]

H. C. Quay, in his article "Psychopathic Personality as Pathological Stimulation-Seeking," sought an explanation for the behavioral characteristics of the psychopath. Quay hypothesized that the psychopath's "primary abnormality lies in the realm of basic reactivity and/or adaption to sensory inputs of all types."[51] In other words, delinquent behavior in children with psychopathic personalities may be explained as an extreme form of stimulation-seeking behavior. The psychopathic personality requires sensory inputs of a much great intensity and variety than does the normal person. In attaining or attempting to attain these inputs, the psychopath engages in thrill-seeking or impulsive behavior, a circumstance not unnormal for this personality type.

Quay observes that there are two possible ways to explain this personality condition: (1) basal reactivity (a measure of galvanic skin response) which is less than that of an average person and (2) an adaptation rate which is greater than the average rate.

> The first is that basal reactivity to stimulation is lowered so that more sensory input is needed to produce efficient and subjectively pleasant cortical functioning. A second possibility is that there is a more rapid adaptation to stimulation which causes the need for stimulus variation to occur more rapidly and with greater intensity.[52]

Vetter and Simonsen have supported Quay's theories on psychopathic personalities, and have made the following observations concerning the underlying causes:

> In general, increased activity in the sympathetic division of the autonomic nervous system appears to have an excitatory or facilitative effect upon cortical activity in the brain. Lacey, however, has suggested that this apparently does not hold true for increases in heart rate and blood pressure. Evidence is

available that indicates that increased heart rate and blood pressure may actually lead to an inhibition of cortical activity.

Changes in heart rate or blood pressure become stimuli to internal receptors, whose activation may lead reflexively to changes in the relationship of the organism to the environment, in terms of the accessibility of the organism to environmental stimulus inputs. An individual with *cardiac lability* (a consistently exaggerated or hyperactive cardiovascular response pattern) might be described as a person who requires a higher level of intensity and broader range of stimuli than the nonlabile individual in order to reach some response threshold. It is as though he is "several stimulus degrees under par."

In a series of studies beginning with the work of Funkenstein, Greenblatt, and Solomon, and culminating in the Ohio Penitentiary study of Lindner and his associates, the presence of such cardiac lability has been confirmed in a population of psychiatrically identified antisocial offenders. This research is in basic agreement with Quay's proposal that the antisocial (psychopathic) individual is characterized by pathological stimulation-seeking and that it is possible "to view much of the impulsivity of the psychopath, his need to create excitement and adventure, his thrill-seeking behavior, and his inability to tolerate routine and boredom as a manifestation of an inordinate need for increases or changes in the pattern of stimulation.[53]

While most studies of the psychopathic personality have been concerned with adult populations, their findings may be generalized to include the psychopathic juvenile delinquent. This is especially true if one accepts the notion that personality is formed in the early years of a person's life. Unless one were to undergo a complete change in one's biological systems in later life, the personality of a child (if indeed it is biologically influenced) is the personality of the adult.

Recent theoretical formulations such as Quay's pathological stimulation seeking, for example, encompass a sophistication and clarity that is notably absent in earlier works. In fact, there is a vast contrast between the earlier (Beccaria and Lombroso) and contemporary biological and genetic (physiological) hypotheses concerning criminality. To illustrate this point, it should be noted that since its discovery in 1961, the XYY chromosome has been linked with hereditary biological abnormalities among men and the possible causation of consequent criminal behavior, something that earlier theorists had not yet even envisioned, and, while research on the XYY syndrome is subject to the criticism that findings to date are more provocative than conclusive, the XYY researchers are capable of specifying the relevant variables in their investigation in a way that was not at all possible for Lombroso in his studies regarding stigma. Contemporary physiological researchers have at their disposal more highly sophisticated and technically advanced tools with which to test their hypotheses than did their earlier counterparts; one would, therefore, expect their findings to be more valid and accurate.[54]

Phenomenological Theories

Phenomenological theories concentrate on the development or lack of development of interpersonal motivity, cognition, or adolescent striving. The crux of these theories is that behavior, including delinquent behavior, is a product of an individual's perceptions of self with the person's environment.

Theorists Douglas Grant, M. Grant, and Clyde Sullivan have developed a concept of personality maturity levels by which delinquent youth may be classified. They are:

1. With discrimination only between self and nonself, the infant behaves as if he is the whole world.
2. With a conception of people as givers and withholders, and without the ability to predict, explain, or understand the behavior of others, the person is apt to blow up and run away when thwarted.
3. The person attempts to manipulate the environment to get what he wants. He is "rules oriented," and may adopt either a conforming or manipulating style.
4. The person has internalized a set of standards and is aware of expectations of others. He is susceptible to feelings of inadequacy and guilt; defensive actions may result in delinquency.
5. Recognizing patterns of behavior in self and others, the person notes their consistency.
6. The individual realizes his own different social roles and differentiates between the self and the temporary role.
7. The person perceives integrative processes in self and others.
   Persons integrated at levels 6 and 7 are rarely delinquent.[55]

Most, if not all, of these seven levels of integration are common to most people sometime in their lives. When perception of one's surroundings and oneself fail to change with the removal of the condition which initiated those perceptions, one is likely to have problems functioning in a "normal" society. This misperception, therefore, may cause a person to act in a delinquent or unruly manner.

The theory offered by Sullivan and the Grants simply put, states that different kinds of juvenile delinquents require different kinds of treatment to deal with the various levels of their misperceptions (there is evidence which supports this approach). The placement of youth into the various levels of classification is intended to facilitate this treatment.

According to Rector the adolescent period of a child's life is the one to watch most carefully for a breakdown or confusion of a child's perceptual abilities.

Adolescent striving is a central concept in the writings of Erik H. Erikson, S. N. Eisenstadt, and Herbert Bloch and Arthur Niederhoffer. Adolescence as a critical period of development provides in its natural processes clues to delinquent behavior. The transition from the dependence of childhood to the autonomy of adulthood makes great demands on youth. The youngster strives to achieve identity, principally by experimenting with new roles and behaviors. He is often supported in this experimentation by an adult audience which expects and condones it but frequently fails to teach its limits.

Delinquent behavior is a normal part of the normal acts of youngsters seeking to find themselves in an ambiguous role structure. The delinquent gang is a collective response to the age-transition problem, wherein the individual finds peer support for his temporary strivings.[56]

Constitutional Theories

Constitutional theories have nothing to do with legal codes or the Constitution of the United States. They refer, instead, to the constitutional makeup of one's body. They emphasize the role of physique and temperament as the causative factors associated with delinquent behavior.

Sheldon and Eleanor Glueck are perhaps best known for their research concerning this approach to delinquent actions. In *Physique and Delinquency,* they compare nondelinquents and delinquents in terms of four somatotypical classes (i.e., mesomorphic (athletic), ectomorphic (thin), endomorphic (heavy), and balanced body types. Their initial analysis deals with the question of whether boys of one body build are influenced by certain personality traits or characteristics which may cause them to exhibit delinquent behavior either to a greater or lesser extent than boys of another body build. The Gluecks conclude, from their studies, that variations of body type alone do not indicate the existence of a predisposition for delinquency. However, while they feel that there is no delinquent personality or stable combination of personality traits that determine whether a given juvenile will become delinquent, they do suggest that body types, when combined with the influence of other factors, often cultural or social in nature, in addition to personality traits that are assumed to be innate, may have significance in identifying potential delinquent behavior.[57]

Economic Theories

The connection between poverty and crime or delinquency was established a long time ago. Through the years, various economic remedies have been tried to cure delinquency through monetary means. In 1961, for example, ten million dollars was appropriated under the Juvenile Delinquency and Youth Offenses Control Act for grants to youth development projects for the prevention and treatment of juvenile delinquency in inner city neighborhoods. During this time of the "Great Society," the problems of delinquency and poverty received much attention as the crime rate increased in poor neighborhoods and began to creep into the suburbs. In fact, many of the community-action programs of the 1960s began as programs to treat juvenile delinquency and ended up as antipoverty programs.[58]

Economic remedies such as the Juvenile Delinquency Act are based on the hypothesis that delinquency rates and rates of poverty are related. There are those like Jackson Toby,[59] however, who feel that delinquency is caused more by a resentment of poverty within an affluent society than by the fact of poverty. In others words, it is not *being* poor that hurts but rather *knowing* that you are poor. For the youth in a ghetto, delinquent acts become a way of fulfilling expectations that cannot otherwise be satisfied.

At one time, it might have been possible to say that most delinquents came from slums or ghettos, had little or no education, and were raised in poverty-stricken homes. However, delinquents today cannot be so conveniently categorized. A new phenomenon in the form of middle- and upper-class delinquency now faces the juvenile justice system.

The rapid urbanization of American society from the late nineteenth century to the present has had many repercussions. Not the least of these is the growth of "suburbia." In recent decades, the suburbs have become the "escape" environment of the middle and upper classes.

Although suburbia has not shared many of the problems of the urban slums and ghettos, it has produced many unforeseen problems of its own. Suburbia may be described as a place where individuality is lost or absorbed, and the modern nuclear family and its traditional functions are disintegrating. Middle-class children in many instances have daily schedules as busy and demanding as those of their parents. Their activities range from clubs, social events, and sports to school, church, and organizations.

> Although family life is "important," and love and constant association are expected, the dreams for holding the family together are obscure. The commuter father is no longer a figure of authority. Rearing the child and running the suburb are left to the mother and the schools and the experts on whom both rely. The desires and demands of children—their play space, their training, their future careers, their happiness—become the predominant forces in suburbia.[60]

Americans, especially those in the suburbs, are becoming alienated and frustrated. This is not only true of the "lower classes" but of the talented, the rich, the gifted, and the average, adjusted affluent American. Crime and delinquency in suburban areas is increasing at an alarming rate. In 1964, for instance, the FBI noted that suburban crime rates had risen by 17 percent over 1963, and that persons under the age of 18 accounted for over one-half of all serious crimes in suburban communities. In 1965, the FBI reported an additional increase of 8 percent over 1964 and a 13 percent increase in 1966 over 1965. Juvenile crime continued to account for over half of all crime.

One study conducted in California with middle- and upper-class youth has shown two significant patterns. First, the rate of "unofficial" delinquency is far greater than that of "official" delinquency, or delinquency that is recognized as such. Second, much of the delinquency among upper- and middle-class suburban youth appears to be a by-product of their powerful social systems; that is, much adolescent behavior, both delinquent and nondelinquent, is influenced, if not controlled, by peers and peer pressure. For example, data from the California study indicate that 75 percent of the official cases of suburban delinquency were committed by two or more youths.[61]

> The specific patterns of delinquency are interesting and provocative. For example, we have found that the majority of delinquent acts are against property—such as theft, burglary, and larceny. What can account for attacks on property by well-groomed, well-dressed youths, with money in their pockets, who more often than not drive to the scene of their delinquency in the family car? We have observed time-sequence patterns of delinquency which may be a reflection of suburban life. In general delinquency is at a time during the school day, when the school provides a form of baby-sitting for adolescents. Delinquency increases substantially after classes and remains high until dinner time. It disappears almost completely as the father returns home and is joined by his children for the dinner ritual. Delinquency rises again after dinner and remains high until late in the evening when, by mutual agreement of youth and adults, it is time to return home to ensure a good night's sleep for tomorrow's identical pattern.[62]

Juvenile delinquency among strictly upper-class youth remains hidden behind a dark veil of mystery. Knowledge about criminal behavior in this group is extremely limited. In fact, a public profile or image of the upper-class delinquent is virtually nonexistent; they seem above suspicion regarding delinquent acts.[63]

In any event, delinquency is not limited to one socioeconomic class of youth. Most of the traditional theories of delinquency causation have used lower-class youths as subjects of their research. It is not surprising, therefore, that these theories are not easily adapted to middle- and upper-class delinquents.

Summary

There are many theories regarding delinquency which are not mentioned in this chapter. Only those most generally accepted have been examined. It is clear that no single theory offers a panacea for what causes a young person to become a delinquent. Many of these theories could be more useful and verifiable if there existed action programs designed to adequately test and prove them. Theory without practice based on sound research does little to solve the problem of juvenile crime.

REVIEW QUESTIONS

1. Define the following terms:
   a. Juvenile
   b. Juvenile delinquency
   c. Delinquent.

2. How many instances can you think of in which you have personally observed several different "legal definitions" of delinquency within geographical areas in close proximity to one another? Describe them.

3. What are "differential association" and "reality therapy" and how do they relate to the basic tenets of psychoanalysis? If they do not, state why not.

4. State how the theories presented in this chapter might apply to middle- or upper-class youth, keeping in mind the environmental differences between them and lower-class youth.

5. Explain why someone you either know personally or know of may have committed a delinquent act.

NOTES

1. For example, the daily per capita institutional cost for a juvenile in the State of Washington for 1976–1977 is estimated at $50; this equals $18,250 per year [*State of Washington, Comprehensive Plan Supplement for Juvenile Justice & Delinquency Prevention,* 1976; p. 33].

2. Milton Rector, "Crime and Delinquency," *Encyclopedia of Social Work,* 16th ed., vol. 1 (New York: National Association of Social Workers, 1971), p. 162.

3. "What Every Parent Should Know". *Newsweek,* December 11, 1953, p. 37.

4. G. Udd, and A. L. Porterfield, *Youth in Trouble* (Austin, Tex.: The Leo Potishman Foundation, 1946).

5. R. R. Korn, "The Counseling of Delinquents," Training Aid No. 1 (San Jose, Calif.: Santa Clara County Juvenile Probation Department, 1968), p. 4.

6. The so-called medical model refers to theories of the causation of delinquency which are biological in nature. Examples of these theories are the anthropological/morphological approach (Lombroso, Gluecks, and others), the hereditary approach (Digamber Gorgaonkaar), and the physiological approach (Quay).

7. The so-called process model is nonbiological in nature. It refers to theories of causation of delinquency which are sociological in nature. The structural approach (Durkheim and Merton), the subcultural approach (Coffey et al.) are representative of this model.

8. Edward Eldefonso, *Law Enforcement and the Youthful Offender,* 2nd ed. (New York: Wiley, 1973), p. 21.

9. Edward Edelfonso and Alan R. Coffey, *Process and Impact of the Juvenile Justice System* (Beverly Hills, Calif.: Glencoe Press, 1976), p. 2.

10. Ibid.

11. Engrossed Third Substitute House Bill No. 371, State of Washington, 45th Legislature, 1st Extraordinary Session, April 11, 1977, The Committee on Institutions, pp. 18–19.

12. Juvenile Court Statistics, 1966 Children's Bureau, Statistical Series, 90 (Washington, D.C.: Children's Bureau, 1967), p. 7.

13. Title 13, Juvenile Courts and Juvenile Delinquents, Chapter 13.04, Section 13.04010, Washington State Revised Code, p. 2.

14. Ruth S. Cavan, *Juvenile Delinquency: Development, Treatment, Control,* 2nd ed. (Philadelphia: Lippincott, 1969), p. 4.

15. Robert C. Trojanowicz, *Juvenile Delinquency: Concepts and Controls* (Englewood Cliffs, N.J.: Prentice-Hall, 1973), p. 20.

16. Kurt Lewin, *Field Theory in Social Science,* ed. Dorwin Cartwright (New York: Harper & Row, 1951).

17. Rector, *Encyclopedia of Social Work,* p. 162.

18. Marcello Maestro, *Cesare Beccaria and the Origins of Penal Reform* (Philadelphia: Temple University Press, 1973), pp. 158–59.

19. D. G. Hardman, ''The Case for Eclecticism,'' *Crime and Delinquency* 10 (1964), p. 202.

20. The classic works on this topic are R. Dugdale's *The Jukes* and Henry H. Goddard's *The Kallekaks*. For good reviews of these and other early theoretical viewpoints, see Harry E. Barnes and Negley K. Teeters's *New Horizons in Criminology* (1951), Richard R. Korn and Lloyd W. McCorkle's *Criminology and Penology* (1967), and Paul W. Tappan's *Crime, Justice and Correction* (1960).

21. Harry E. Allen, ''A Biological Model of Antisocial Personality,'' a paper presented at the Ohio Valley Sociological Society Meeting, Akron, Ohio, May 1, 1970, p. 2.

22. Gwynn Nettler, *Explaining Crime* (New York: McGraw-Hill, 1974), p. 138.

23. Walter A. Lunden, ''Emile Durkheim: 1858–1917'' in *Pioneers in Criminology,* Hermann Mannheim, ed. (New Jersey: Patterson Smith, 1973), p. 390.

24. Emile Durkheim, *The Rules of Sociological Method* (Catlin, 1938), p. xxxviii.

25. Sophia M. Robison, *Juvenile Delinquency* (New York: Holt, Rinehart and Winston, 1960), pp. 181–82.

26. Richard A. Cloward and Lloyd E. Ohlin, *Delinquency and Opportunity* (Glencoe, Ill.: Free Press, 1960), p. 86.

27. Nettler; *Explaining Crime.*

28. Vetter and Simonsen, *Criminal Justice in America,* p. 68.

29. Cloward and Ohlin, *Delinquency and Opportunity,* p. 86.

30. Rector, *Encyclopedia of Social Work,* p. 169.

31. Albert A. Cohen, *Delinquent Boys* (New York: Free Press, 1955).

32. Walter B. Miller, ''Lower Class Structure and Generating Milieu of Gang Delinquency,'' *Journal of Social Issues* 14 (1958), p. 19.

33. Rector, *Encyclopedia of Social Work*, p. 169.

34. Ibid.

35. For a further discussion of this theory, see Clarence Schrag; "Delinquency and Opportunity: Analysis of a Theory," *Sociology and Social Research* 46 (January 1962), pp. 167–75.

36. Trojanowicz, *Juvenile Delinquency*, p. 38.

37. In the United States, these legal definitions are often mixed, and as a result there is culture conflict in relation to the legal codes.

38. Edwin Sutherland, *The Sutherland Papers*, ed. Albert Cohen, Alfred Lindesmith, and Karl Schuessler (Bloomington, Ill.: University Free Press, 1956), pp. 8–10.

39. Malcolm W. Klein, "Criminological Theories as Seen by Criminologists: An Evaluative Review of Approaches to the Causation of Crime and Delinquency." Unpublished manuscript, Youth Studies Center, University of California, Los Angeles, December, 1967.

40. Trojanowicz, *Juvenile Delinquency*, p. 47.

41. August Archhorn, *Wayward Youth* (New York: Viking, 1953), p. 3.

42. Eleanor Glueck, and Sheldon Glueck, *Unraveling Juvenile Delinquency* (New York: Commonwealth Fund, 1950), p. 102.

43. D. Feldman, "Psychoanalysis and Crime," in *Delinquency, Crime and Social Process*, eds. D. R. Cressey and D. Ward (New York: Harper & Row, 1969), p. 434.

44. For further resource material on psychoanalytical theory, the reader is referred to Calvin S. Hall's *A Primer of Freudian Psychology* (1954), Clara Thompson's *Psychoanalysis* (1950), G. S. Blum's *Psychoanalytic Theories of Personality* (1953), or in such introductory texts in abnormal psychology as Robert W. White's *The Abnormal Personality* (1964) or James C. Coleman's *Abnormal Psychology in Modern Life* (1956).

45. Vetter and Simonsen, *Criminal Justice in America*, p. 72.

46. Walter C. Reckless, "A New Theory of Delinquency and Crime," in *Juvenile Delinquency: A Book of Readings*, ed. Rose Giallombardo (New York: Wiley, 1966), p. 223.

47. Ibid.

48. William Glasser and Norman Iversen, *Reality Therapy in Large Group Counseling* (Los Angeles: Reality Press, 1966).

49. William I. Thomas, ed., *Source Book for Social Origins* (Chicago: University of Chicago Press, 1907).

50. M. Gordon, C. Simonsen, and H. Allen, *A Case Closeup: The Unrelated Crime and the Acherman Act* (Monograph, The Ohio State University, 1973).

51. H. C. Quay, "Psychopathic Personality as Pathological Stimulation-Seeking," *American Journal of Psychiatry* 122 (1965), pp. 180–83.

52. Ibid., p. 181.

53. Vetter and Simonsen, *Criminal Justice in America*, pp. 64–65.

54. Patricia A. Jacobs, M. Brienton, and M. Melville, *Nature*, December 25, 1965, pp. 1351–52.

55. Douglas Grant and M. Q. Grant, "A Group Dynamics Approach to the Treatment of Non-Conformists in the Navy," *Annals of American Academy of Political and Social Science* 322 (March 1954), pp. 135–36.

56. Rector, *Encyclopedia of Social Work*, p. 166.

57. Sheldon Glueck and Eleanor Glueck, *Physique and Delinquency* (New York: Harper & Row, 1956), pp. 27–31.

58. Frances Fox Piven and Richard A. Cloward, *Regulating the Poor* (New York: Pantheon Books, 1971), p. 270.

59. Jackson Toby, "Affluence and Adolescent Crime," in President's Commission on Law Enforcement and Administration of Justice, *The Challenge of Crime in a Free Society* (Washington, D.C.: U.S. Government Printing Office, 1967).

60. Robert M. Carter, "Delinquency in the Upper and Middle Classes," Reading 15, *Youth, Crime and Society*, eds. James Gasell and G. Gitchoff (Boston: Holbrook Press, 1973), p. 262.

61. Ibid., pp. 265–66.

62. Ibid., p. 267.

63. See Nye, Short, Jr., and Olson, "Socioeconomic Status and Delinquent Behavior, *American Journal of Sociology* 63 (1950), p. 381; Vaz, "Self-Reported Juvenile Delinquency and Socioeconomic Status," *Canadian Journal of Corrections* 8 (1966), p. 20; and Richard A. Cloward, "Illegitimate Means, Anomie, and Deviant Behavior," *American Sociological Review* 24 (April 1959), pp. 164–76.

4 Classification: The Wheel of Fortune

Classes do not exist in nature . . . but they are a necessary instrument by which the human mind can better understand the multiform reality of things. In daily life, criminals would often not appear so well defined as the classification suggested.

ENRICO FERRI

Webster's New World Dictionary defines *classification* as "an arrangement according to some systematic division into classes or groups." In classifying individuals, one separates a group of people into smaller groups, each with something in common. Consider, for example, a situation involving four juveniles—Browne, Greene, Anderson, and Johnson—who are to be classified. Assume that Browne and Greene are in one group (or set) and that Anderson and Johnson are in another. This division of four persons into two groups may be called classification only if you can say something about Browne and Greene that you *cannot* say about Anderson and Johnson. For example, Browne and Greene are both males, while Anderson and Johnson are both females.

This is the simplest form of classification based on obvious facts. The student should keep in mind that almost anything suitable for scientific observation is also suitable for classification, and the possibilities of classification are almost limitless. It should be noted that although Browne and Greene in the above example may be alike for some classification purposes (e.g., sex), they may also be totally unalike in other categories (e.g., age, crime committed, and so forth). To help illustrate this point further, consider that boats may be classified as "floating objects." But the classification "floating objects" might also include ducks, logs, barges, and other things. Boats may also be classified as a means of transportation, a classification that could include such otherwise unrelated objects such as airplanes, motorcycles, and trucks.

Classification, according to P. MacNaughton-Smith in a Home Office Research Unit Report, depends on both the available data and the definition of likeness or lack of likeness chosen for the given purpose.[1]

When individuals are classified, they are invariably defined or described by their classification. When the group being observed is comprised of juvenile delinquents, the group is a set of delinquents. This set is called the *initial set*. If one wishes to classify these juveniles, then one divides this initial set into a number of *final sets* or *taxa*. Observations of differences as the basis of classification must be used cautiously. They must be accurate and objective. If they are not, the grouping in the same final set will not be *proof* of likeness, but rather the result of *observed* likeness. For instance, it might appear to a homeowner that two boys seen running from her house were juvenile thieves, when in fact one of them was actually chasing the other in an attempt to recover the woman's property. Mentally, the woman has placed both boys in the same class—thieves—based on what she thought she observed. Observation in this case would wrongly label or classify one of the boys as a delinquent.

Classification versus Labeling

At this point, it is appropriate to introduce a subject which often confuses people, the difference between classification and labeling. Labeling may be seen as a much less sophisticated exercise than classification. *Webster's New World Dictionary* defines *label* as "a descriptive word or phrase applied to a person, group, theory, and so forth, as a convenient generalized classification." Labeling, therefore, may be seen as a consequence of classification. One typical example of the labeling process often occurs when people misinterpret causal relationships. For example, many people associate the reading of comic books, especially violent ones, with crime and delinquency. Therefore, they may conclude that comic books cause delinquency and may label a juvenile reading a comic book as a delinquent. Classification, on the other hand, would require a *comparison* or *contrasting* of individuals. Labeling does not involve any such process.[2]

Classification in the Past

In the past, most attempts at classifying offenders were devoted to adult groups, with some recognition given to the fact that children, because of their age, constituted a separate group. Common correctional practices separated adult and juvenile offenders, and there was some experimentation, on a limited basis, with reeducation or retraining of youthful offenders. By separating and assigning prison populations by age, sex, and potential for salvation, correctional administrators in the past were initiating a system of classification which has remained, in large part, with us today.

Ever since the practice of putting people into prisons or jails has existed, there have been various means of separating one type of prisoner from another. Thus separation (i.e., simply physically isolating one offender group from another) has become identified with classification.

Most early forms of classification were primarily based on superficial characteristics. For example, men were housed separately from women in Spanish prisons as early as 1518. In the early eighteenth century the Society of St. Vincent de Paul, which cared for orphans and the poor, realized the necessity of segregating children from adults, and instituted separate so-called Houses of Refuge for children. One of the first houses of refuge for delinquent children was started in Germany in 1824, and a similar refuge was established in New York in 1825.

In the Walnut Street Jail, built in Philadelphia, in 1790, a rudimentary classification of prisoners was practiced. Men were separated from women, and children from adults. In 1797, "the management of the Walnut Street Jail actually began a classification that may be regarded as the first attempt to separate prisoners by type."[3]

The first such major institution for juveniles was the New York Reformatory at Elmira (1876). The founders of the New York Reformatory and others patterned after it reasoned that the separation of young offenders from the adult criminals would allow the correctional personnel to more successfully facilitate the treatment of their young charges. These juvenile institutions offered educational programs for their population of young offenders, as opposed to the industrial programs offered in the adult prisons.

The notion that a system of classification of offenders might lead to better, more effective treatment programs spread to other institutions, juvenile and adult alike. Warden Cassidy of the Eastern Penitentiary (1833) remarked on this new type of prison administration called classification:

> . . . after hearing so much of herding and grading, congregation and classification, I am the more fully convinced that the individual treatment for the people that have to be cared for in prisons for punishment of crime, is the simplest and most philosophical and is productive of better results.[4]

During the latter part of the nineteenth century, a slow but discernible trend toward treatment programs was evident. These programs affected both classification and administrative systems. However, progress in treatment was hindered by a lack of money to underwrite such programs.[5]

In the twentieth century, classification of prisoners has moved from the obvious differences among prisoners, such as age and sex, to those related to personality characteristics and to various types of crime. In 1917, for example, New Jersey implemented the first formalized prison classification system in the United States, a system that was the result of the Prison Inquiry Commission of the same year. The commission, among other things, brought clinical experts inside the prison walls to prepare and implement classification systems. Classification in New Jersey prisons was identified as follows:

1. The difficult class who were hostile to society and require close custody.
2. The better class who are good prisoners with reasonably good prognosis but are serving for long terms and require close custody.
3. The simply feeble-minded whose condition is not complicated by psychopathic traits.
4. The senile and incapacitated class.
5. The psychotic and epileptic class who should be transferred to the hospitals for the mentally ill.
6. The defective delinquent class whose low intelligence is combined with high emotional instability and may need long periods of custody and training under an indeterminate sentence.[6]

A congressional act of 1930 provided a program for the classification of federal prisoners. The federal system was similar to New Jersey's and was quickly adopted by other eastern metropolitan states.[7]

In "Changing Classification Organizational Patterns: 1870–1970," Vernon Fox also examines the influence of the advent of classification schemes as they relate to the treatment needs of prisoners.

> Classification, in its modern sense, is an administrative vehicle by which treatment resources get to an inmate. Conversely, classification, in its older sense, was a way of getting inmates to the program that would benefit them most and/or hurt them least. A modern classification system serves both functions.[8]

And Milton Burdman, in discussing better uses of classification in the planning of a treatment program, states:

> On a state-wide basis, the inmates are sent to the programs by sending them to different institutions to achieve some homogeneous grouping and to protect some younger from older inmates. Within the institution, classification becomes a delivery system by which treatment resources are brought to the inmates. Classification has been referred to as (1) the nerve center for assignment of inmate personnel, (2) a referral system for formal education, counseling, therapy, and other forms of treatment, and (3) a process for evaluating and reporting on case progress.[9]

In Washington, juveniles are assigned to an institution on the basis of their age, sex, and risk potential. One of the shortcomings of such a system is that juveniles, regardless of diagnostic evaluations, are made to fit the institution's needs and limited treatment capabilities and not the other way around.

While classification by management needs has had some good effects at juvenile institutions, it has been implemented at the risk of tailoring the treatment needs of juveniles to fit the institutions, whether or not those needs are in concert with the institution's treatment philosophy. Diagnostic practitioners are often frustrated by this course of events. They see their treatment recommendations being accommodated to a managerial classification system and wonder why they should bother with the diagnostic process in the first place.

Classification Today

The National Advisory Commission of Criminal Justice Standards and Goals in its *Task Force on Corrections Report* comments as follows on classification today.

> Most correctional classification schemes in use today are referred to as classification systems for treatment purposes, but even a cursory analysis of these schemes and the ways in which they are used reveals that they would more properly be called classification systems for management purposes. This judgment does not imply that classification for management purposes is undesirable. In fact, that may be the only useful system today, given the current state of knowledge about crime and offenders. It is important, however, that corrections begin to acknowledge the bases and purposes of classification systems that are in use.
>
> There is another problem with trying to answer the question: Classification for what? While it is often conceded that no generally valid and useful system of classification for treatment now exists, there seems to be broad agreement within the corrections field on the desirability of finding such a system. It is also pointed out that a number of serious and dedicated social science researchers have been working for years on developing "treatment-relevant typologies" of offenders, and there is a possibility that they will reach a consensus on the basic components of a classification system and types of offenders fairly soon. It is one of the ironies of progress that just as the development of "treatment-relevant typologies" at last appears likely, there is growing disenchantment with the entire concept of the treatment model.[10]

In dealing with juvenile correctional populations, classification systems can be useful and beneficial in several ways. One is as an effective managerial tool for institutional administrators. "Managerial" in this sense means effective control to prevent the juveniles from returning to delinquency while the agency or institution is still responsible for them. But not all classification systems today are aimed at easing the management of the offenders or at assessing the risks of recurrent delinquent or criminal behavior. For example, classification for treatment purposes has proven effective. One must consider, however, that the true function of treatment in an institution or other correctional setting is to modify undesirable personality traits of offenders or the aspects of their environment which are in part responsible for their delinquent behavior. This being the case, it becomes paramount that offenders be assigned to treatment programs which will accomplish these goals. Unfortunately, until the matter of overall classification of juvenile offenders is handled in a generally accepted way, it is impossible to compare individual treatment programs being conducted throughout the United States, let alone systems of classification for treatment purposes.

The two major purposes for offender typologies—classification for management purposes and classification for treatment purposes—will now be examined in greater detail.

Classification for Management

It has already been stated that, for purposes of this text, the term *management* means the efficient and effective control of the behavior of the offender in order to curtail further law violations while the offender is the responsibility of a correctional agency. In an institutional setting, for example, efficient and effective management involves such things as (1) protecting the weak delinquent from the strong, (2) separating the hard-core offender from the person with nondelinquent attitudes or background, (3) keeping instigators from those who are easily instigated, (4) separating those who are homosexual from those who are nonhomosexual, and so forth.

Classification for management purposes is intended not only to protect or separate one kind of delinquent from another. It is intended to protect the community from the offender too. Delinquents with high escape or "run" potential, for example, must be identified and placed in the more secure facilities. The classification of delinquents in an institutional setting has a direct bearing on other management decisions. Open or closed settings, single or dormitory rooms, types of job assignment, time in the institution, types of punishment, time spent in isolation, custody security levels, and the use of tranquilizing drugs are among the more common examples.

Management classification systems have taken on a new responsibility today. That responsibility entails the accurate assessment of the offender's potential risk in terms of danger to both self and the community, and the subsequent placement of the offender in a facility capable of assuming that risk and protecting the offender from both himself or herself and other inmates and the community from the offender.[11]

It is generally accepted that classification for the purpose of managerial decisions takes place in one of three locales or organizational arrangements:
(1) classification units within an existing institution,
(2) those within a reception and/or diagnostic center, and
(3) those within the community itself. The superiority of any of these locales over the others is a widely debated topic.

All three types may be found within most state systems. However, with the emphasis on community-based corrections, the community classification center, which often entails a much wider range of personnel and resources than previously supposed, is most favored and potentially effective.

Institutional Classification   The first locale, that is, classification within an existing juvenile institution, is prevalent in many state correctional systems. Of this setting, the National Advisory Commission on Criminal Justice Standards and Goals has said:

> The classification unit system suffers from a number of defects that virtually deprive it of usefulness. Reports typically are submitted to administrative authorities, who may or may not follow the recommendations. Even when high-quality diagnostic work is produced, the results may not be applied, because diagnosis has not been linked directly or operationally with available programs. The system also becomes the victim of institutionalization. Procedures usually are rigid. Too many inmates are kept too long in the reception unit and process. The procedures take on the character of an assembly line, with little selectivity in adapting the process to the individual inmate. Invariably the research component is completely lacking, and there is no check on whether the process really is fulfilling its purpose.[12]

Questions about the effectiveness of classification inside the institution are more applicable to adult systems than to juvenile systems. Nevertheless, juveniles are subjected to the same classification procedure. When one considers that it is commonly agreed that the less contact juveniles have with the general juvenile justice system (let alone with actual institutions), the greater are the chances of their not repeating their delinquent behavior, one can build a good case for seeking alternatives to classifying them within the institution.

Diagnostic Center Classification   Reception-diagnostic centers, such as the Training Institute of Columbus, Ohio (TICO), and Cascadia Juvenile Reception and Diagnostic Center in Washington, offer a classification setting somewhere between the institution and the community. The reception center setting for the classification of youth emerged in the early 1940s. It grew out of the youth correction authority concept first enacted in California, Minnesota, Wisconsin, and Texas. The youth correction authority movement offered responsible supervision and programming of juveniles in trouble from their entrance into the reception center until their release from aftercare supervision.

Under the system of classifying juveniles in the reception-diagnostic centers, all juveniles in a state who are so ordered are sent to one central facility for study, classification, and recommendations for treatment. This classification process presupposes a plan and a theory which are consistent throughout the system. It places the major responsibility for collecting needed information on one centralized facility.

The *Task Force on Corrections Report* comments thus on the classification of offenders at a reception center:

> While the reception center concept was progressive for its time, it has become obsolete. The system is administratively convenient and efficient in that a limited staff can provide services for a large number of offenders. However, this very administrative efficiency is largely accountable for its obsolescence.
>
> Traditionally, the reception and diagnostic center has provided summary reports including information on social background, criminal history, initial adjustment to custody, medical examination, psychological assessment, vocational skills, educational level, religious background and attitudes, recreational interests and abilities, and psychiatric evaluation. Today, it is not necessary that any of these components of the diagnostic report be completed in a diagnostic or reception center. A number of the items usually are produced by probation and parole officers in the community. Although medical examinations and psychological and psychiatric evaluations require professional services, these services also are available in the local community through both contract and public agency programs.
>
> The reception center, because of the ceaseless repetition in the nature of its work, becomes even more institutionalized than other forms of the classification process. Schedules are adhered to rigidly, and offenders are kept too long in the centers waiting for the diagnostic skills or services of a limited number of persons. The process itself is uniformly extensive and thorough for most offenders, and more information is produced than can be used effectively for classification purposes, considering the current lack of correctional knowledge and resources.
>
> The futility of much of this work is evident in the separation of the study and diagnostic process from operational units. Independent institutions usually do not rely on information developed at the diagnostic center and may repeat clinical evaluations and studies.[13]

Community Classification   Current interest in developing and programming correctional efforts in the community directly conflicts with the role of the reception center. Classification in the community can be just as effective as reception center classifying because the community has more resources than previously considered possible. In fact, one major disadvantage of the centralized reception center is overcome by the community approach; it is distance. The distance of a central facility from most communities often prevents local individuals who know a youngster and his or her problems from becoming involved. This, of course, is unfortunate and can result in the inappropriate placement of a juvenile. The community is, naturally, more aware of and responsive to its own needs and can readily develop resources to deal with its young offenders. Community settings make it possible to develop outpatient services for most youth. Thus many youths not requiring detention can remain at home while being studied for classification. The community approach can also reduce the state's cost in handling juvenile cases.

Various Ways to Classify Juveniles

Not all offenders should be or can be managed in the same manner. Just as there is no single theory to explain all criminal or delinquent behavior, so there is no single management technique to deal with delinquents. This is a main reason why juvenile justice systems are relying more and more on typologies in handling their offender populations. Some of the more common approaches used have been the prior probability approaches.

Prior Probability

Prior probability or *base expectancy* approaches are founded on knowledge of violation probability.[14] Prior probability classification systems are useful in administrative decision making and in evaluating methods to obtain a particular desired effect. Not all juvenile offenders respond properly in a community-based setting. Because they take into account the risk of recidivism, prior probability approaches are especially helpful in deciding which offenders can and which cannot be managed locally.

Prior probability classification systems are found in a number of studies, among them are the Borstal studies, the California Youth Authority, the California Department of Corrections Base Expectancy studies, the Glueck prediction tables, and others.

The Borstal studies are examples of English research intended to test the different responses of selected offenders who were exposed to different correctional settings. The Borstals, designed to care for offenders between the ages of 17 and 21, take their name from the Borstal Prison in Rochester, England, where experiments with separate treatment for juveniles was conducted. The goal of the Borstal is the total development of the youth—body, mind, character, and attitude toward self and society.

> Using the criteria of freedom from rearrest and imprisonment in the five years following release from the Borstals, the Home Secretary's reports show seldom less than 60 percent success. In the Healy and Alper study the Borstals attained as much as 84 percent success. By contrast, the Gluecks' study of 500 criminal careers chalked up less than 12 percent for the Massachusetts reformatory inmates following their release.[15]

In 1961 the California Youth Authority developed a variation of the Maturity Level Classification (I-Level),[16] which measures rational control procedures for different types of delinquents. The classification was to be used in its community treatment programs. The I-Level classification system involves seven graduated steps in the development of the perceptual frame of

reference by which a youth integrates experiences. These levels are num-
bered I-1 to I-7. Studies show that most juveniles are placed at levels I-2
through I-4. Level I-2 includes juveniles who perceive the world in an
egocentric way and who are concerned primarily with their own needs
satisfaction. Level I-3 comprises juveniles who attempt to manipulate their
environment. They know that the way they behave will determine whether
they obtain their desired results. Level I-4 includes delinquents who have an
internalized set of learned standards (i.e., from peers, family, environment,
and so forth) with which to evaluate their own and other people's behavior.

The I-Level classification system has been used extensively in California
and has been tried in several other states with varying degrees of success. It
has some major drawbacks, however. For example, as much as two full
years are needed to train a fully qualified I-Level technician. As a result, few
technicians are available for corrections work. The preclassification interview can take up to two hours for only one of the subject areas. Several
additional hours are needed by another I-Level staff member to interpret the
data obtained in the interview. It is obvious that this system is both
expensive and time-consuming. Its possible use as a predictive management
tool must be evaluated accordingly.

The California Department of Corrections has done studies which linked
base expectancy scores with the juvenile's success or failure on parole.[17]
Those juveniles who showed a low risk of parole failure were assigned to
parole officers with minimum supervision caseloads (*minimum supervision*
means one contact with the parole officer every three months). It was found
that violation rates during the 12-month experimental period were no greater
for those who received minimal supervision than for those who received
regular supervision. Regular supervision involved one-third more office
contacts, twice as many field contacts, and more than twice as many
collateral contacts. Thus, by using base expectancy scores for management
classification purposes, the California Department of Corrections could make
accurate assignments of offenders and could determine the degree of supervision that they required. Not only was this beneficial to the offenders
involved, but it also gave the parole office sound information with which to
arrange staff scheduling and caseload sizes and assignments.

In their studies the Gluecks have developed varying tables from which the
prior probability of delinquent behavior may be predicted. In searching for a
typology which would reflect the interaction between nature and nurture in
delinquency, the Gluecks have stated:

> In pursuing our interest in further refining the predictive devices, we were
> experimenting at about this stage with a method for identifying potential
> delinquents at two to three years of age, and discovered that two of the traits
> of basic character structure (derived from the Rorschach Test), *destructiveness*
> and *nonsubmissiveness to authority*, were highly discriminative in identifying
> potential delinquents among very young children. Although other traits might

have been chosen (such as *defiance, emotional lability*), the two mentioned appeared to offer the greatest likelihood of usability, because child psychologists whom we consulted agreed that these could be determined at three years of age and sometimes even earlier.[18]

In *Unraveling Juvenile Delinquency,* the Gluecks have shown that their three predictive tables (one based on family interpersonal factors, one based on characteristics derived from the Rorschach test, and one based on information gathered in psychiatric interviews) correctly identified the subject boys as either delinquent or nondelinquent in 49 percent of the cases. Two of the three tables also correctly identified delinquents in another 37.8 percent of the cases studied. Therefore in a total of 86.8 percent of the cases, there appeared to be agreement between two or three of the selective measures used.[19]

Aside from the prior probability approaches there are several other classification systems which may be useful in classification of juveniles for management purposes. These will be mentioned here by name only, with references to the particular works that would be helpful in doing further research.

These classification systems include (1) the reference group typologies represented by Schrag[20] and Sykes[21] and the social class typologies represented by Miller,[22] (2) behavior classifications from offense types to conformity-nonconformity dichotomies as represetned by Roebuck,[23] McCord, McCord, and Zola,[24] Ohlin,[25] and Reckless,[26] (3) the psychiatric-oriented approaches represented by such people as Jenkins and Hewitt,[27] Aichoan,[28] and Argyle,[29] and (4) the social perception and interaction classifications of Peterson, Quay, and Cameron,[30] Hunt and Hardt[31] and Russon.[32]

The prior probability studies and the classification systems listed above are useful prediction tools for the efficient management of juvenile offenders. Prediction is an essential criterion of science; it is also the basic condition of most rational action. Predictive instruments, such as classification systems or typology studies, can be important tools, especially when used in conjunction with clinical judgments for making administrative decisions regarding the management of offender populations (i.e., parole, risk, security, and so forth).

Comprehensive Classification

In discussing comprehensive classification systems, the National Advisory Commission on Criminal Justice Standards and Goals has stated:

> Each correctional agency, whether community-based or institutional, should immediately reexamine its classification system and reorganize it along the following principles:

1. Recognizing that corrections is now characterized by a lack of knowledge and deficient resources, and that classification systems therefore are more useful for assessing risk and facilitating the efficient management of offenders than for diagnosis of causation and prescriptions for remedial treatment, classification should be designed to operate on a practicable level and for realistic purposes, guided by the principle that:
   a. No offender should receive more surveillance or "help" than he requires; and
   b. No offender should be kept in a more secure condition or status than his potential risk dictates.

2. The classification system should be developed under the management concepts discussed in chapter 10 [of this report] and issued in written form so that it can be made public and shared. It should specify:
   a. The objectives of the system based on a hypothesis for the social reintegration of offenders, detailed methods for achieving the objectives, and a monitoring and evaluation mechanism to determine whether the objectives are being met.
   b. The critical variables of the typology to be used.
   c. Detailed indicators of the components of the classification categories.
   d. The structure (committee, unit, team, etc.) and the procedures for balancing the decisions that must be made in relation to programming, custody, personal security, and resource allocation.

3. The system should provide full coverage of the offender population, clearly delineated categories, internally consistent groupings, simplicity, and a common language.

4. The system should be consistent with individual dignity and basic concepts of fairness (based on objective judgments rather than personal prejudices).

5. The system should provide for maximum involvement of the individual in determining the nature and direction of his own goals, and mechanisms for appealing administrative decisions affecting him.

6. The system should be adequately staffed, and the agency staff should be trained in its use.

7. The system should be sufficiently objective and quantifiable to facilitate research, demonstration, model building, intrasystem comparisons, and administrative decisionmaking.

8. The correctional agency should participate in or be receptive to cross-classification research toward the development of a classification system that can be used by all correctional agencies.[33]

The development of a method to accurately identify juvenile offenders with a high potential of recidivism or who might be dangerous to themselves or others would greatly benefit corrections today. Such a system could be applied at the time of disposition or sentencing in making the right choice in each case, increasing the cost-effectiveness of correctional programs, and looking after the potential safety to the community. Worth mentioning, however, is the fact that sentencing decisions are not based on risk factors alone or even the desire to protect others from the offender. For courts are also expected to maintain civil liberties, act as deterrent forces to others, maintain a sense of fair play, and punish those who transgress the law. Many of these goals are not altogether compatible with protecting the interests of society and reducing recidivism.

> An institutional response to crime is a necessity; incarceration is not. This may be a major challenge to classification in the future—to find alternatives to incarceration for various types of offenders which will better serve to punish, to deter, to express disapproval, or to reduce the probability of recidivism.[34]

Summary

Classification schemes were devised to serve particular purposes. Some have direct application to the management of offender populations; others have direct applications to their treatment; and still others are useful in deducing hypotheses that can be tested. Classification systems are needed for the control of delinquents, for demonstrating treatment effectiveness, and for enumerating possible etiologies. "The New Testament stresses the uniqueness of each creature," state Wenk and Halatyn.[35] This teaching is based upon the Judaic tradition of recognizing a human as a whole person. With this thought in mind, it should be noted that any classification tends to dehumanize those who are classified. They lose their individuality, and their wholeness is distorted. Unless the problem is realized and faced, "the advantage gained through classification may not outweigh the loss to the individual."[36]

Indeed, there are those in the field of corrections who would argue that classification schemes are not justified at all. They point out that inherent in any classification is the danger of labeling and stigmatizing the person being considered for study. Szazs and Menninger have criticized the supposed need to classify individuals in general.[37, 38] The issue, in their opinion, is that science cannot presently identify enough data to adequately classify individual offenders. Their criticism is not as much a disclaimer of the method of *deriving* at typologies. It is, rather, a comment on their potential *misuse*.

It is possible to decrease the chances of labeling, stimatizing, or ignoring the person's individuality by involving the offender in the classification process. The offender, who is almost always excluded from this process, can be very helpful in assessing his or her specific needs and in selecting programs for resolving delinquency problems.

> Even superficial analysis of most current classification programs in correctional services would indicate that decisions regarding offenders' needs are made on the basis of court policy, agency policy, and management convenience. So much emphasis is placed on the attitude of the committing court, the public relations of the agency, bedspace requirements, and release quotas that correctional staff seldom involve the offender in determining what might meet

his needs for growth and development. These practices completely frustrate and nullify the purposes of classification and turn the entire process into an exercise concerned with form rather than substance.[39]

Professionals who are responsible for the classification process should also be concerned about eliminating discriminatory decisions: that is, decisions that are made on the basis of sex, race, education, offense pattern, ancestry, or, simply, whether the staff just happens to dislike the offender. If this kind of subjectivism is the only rationale for treatment of the offender, it should be recognized as such and replaced with factual, verified knowledge.

What, then, should a good classification system do? It should be able to answer three basic questions: (1) What caused the juvenile to become a delinquent? (2) What kind of help does the offender need to prevent further law violations? And (3) where can the juvenile obtain the help needed? Most classification systems have ignored the first two questions while concentrating on the third. As yet, it would appear that the knowledge or techniques to answer the first two are lacking.

Until more reliable knowledge is acquired, correctional administrators must proceed on the basis that the only obtainable objectives within present knowledge are those of predicting risk and evaluating the juvenile for efficient management. In the meantime they must await a truly scientific typology and contribute what they can toward such a development.

Standard 611 of the *Task Force on Corrections Report* describes the approach to the classification procedure that exemplifies the most effective use of the system as it now exists.

The same intellectual honesty should be used to acknowledge that involving the offender with the corrections system actually is experienced by him as a form of punishment, despite the most sincere motives of correctional personnel to offer "rehabilitative treatment." And "rehabilitative treatment" too often is an exercise in semantics lacking in substance. Therefore, to subject the offender to more surveillance or security than he requires, and to coerce him into subjecting himself to "treatment" that he does not want, and perhaps does not need, may produce results counter to those intended by the classification system.

The correctional agency should develop its classification system with the assistance of all possible advice—from lawyers, offenders, community representatives, professionals, etc. The result should be issued in written form, so that everyone concerned will know its objectives, its assumptions, and its policies and procedures. The critical variables should be identified because the logic represented by selection of these variables is derived from certain behavioral assumptions. Detailed, specific indicators of the components of the classification categories also should be presented, so that the system's utility can be verified by empirical evaluation.

Furthermore, a contemporary classification scheme must have a clear hypothesis (a reasoned guess) concerning what is needed to achieve the social reintegration of the offender, along with a plan of care, custody, and programs that should be checked or reexamined continuously to determine the scheme's effectiveness and appropriateness.

Finally, the system should be sufficiently objective and quantifiable as to facilitate research and decisionmaking. It also should be flexible enough to contribute and be adaptable to cross-classification research that will enable corrections eventually to adopt a common classification system. Until offender classification is handled in some generally acceptable way, it is impossible to compare programs used in various parts of the country. Cross-classification agreements by leading typologists will open the path for sufficient advances in correctional programming. They can become a means by which the community-based program is encouraged and central diagnostic facilities, institutions, and procedures deemphasized.[40]

Classification of offenders can be many things to many people. It has been looked at here in a general way—its definition, the physical settings of classification systems, and its dual capacity of management and as treatment purposes. In addition, areas of concern have been pointed out for those interested in the future of classification as a useful tool in both the efficient handling of offenders and for their impartial and humane treatment.

REVIEW QUESTIONS

1. Define what is meant by *classification*. Give examples of how you personally have seen a classification system used.

2. What is meant by (1) *management classification* and (2) *treatment classification?*

3. What are the essential parts of a "good" classification scheme or system?

4. Of the purposes of classification discussed in this chapter, which is the more realistic, given present-day knowledge? Why?

5. Do you feel that the juvenile should have a say in how the classification will affect his or her life? Why or why not?

6. How can the classification needs of the offender and of the correctional field be best met in each of the following: an institution, a reception center, or in the community?

NOTES

1. P. Smith-MacNaughton, "Some Statistical and Other Numerical Techniques for Classifying Individuals," A Home Office Research Unit Report (London: H.M. Stationery Office, 1964).

2. See the works of Edwin Lemert on labeling theory.

3. H. E. Barnes and N. K. Teeters, *New Horizons in Criminology,* 3rd. ed. (Englewood Cliffs, N.J.: Prentice-Hall, 1959), p. 466.

4. Annual Report of the Eastern Penitentiary, 1968, p. 80.

5. Vernon B. Fox, "Changing Classification Organizational Patterns: 1870–1900," *Correctional Classification and Treatment* (Anderson, Ohio: 1975), p. 8. The reader is referred to the "Proceedings of the National Prison Association from the Nashville Meeting of 1889" for a discussion on the status of classification from 1870 to 1900.

6. W. J. Ellis, "Classification as the Basis for Rehabilitation of Prisoners," *News Bulletin of the National Society for Penal Information* 2, no. 1 (February 1931).

7. Congressional Act of 1930 (C, 339, Section 7, 46 Stat. 390).

8. Fox, "Changing Classification Organizational Patterns," p. 9.

9. Milton Burdman, "Better Uses of Classification in Planning a Treatment Program," *Proceedings of the American Correctional Association* (New York: A.C.A., 1959, 1960), pp. 129–130.

10. National Advisory Commission on Criminal Justice Standards and Goals, *Task Force on Corrections Report* (Washington, D.C.: G.P.O., 1973), p. 197.

11. Ibid., p. 207.

12. Ibid., pp. 205–206.

13. Ibid., pp. 206–207.

14. Base expectancy concerns the probable success prediction device used to aid in parole decisions.

15. Sophia M. Robison, *Juvenile Delinquency* (New York: Holt, Rinehart and Winston, 1960), p. 429.

16. See Marguerite O. Warren, *Interpersonal Maturity Level Classification: Juvenile Diagnosis and Treatment of Low-, Middle-, and High-Maturity Delinquents* (Sacramento: California Youth Authority, 1966).

17. J. Havel, "Special Intensive Parole Unit IV: The High-Base Expectancy Study," Research Report No. 10 (Sacramento: Department of Corrections, 1963).

18. Sheldon Glueck and Eleanor Glueck, *Toward a Typology of Juvenile Offenders* (New York: Grune and Stratton, 1970), p. 46.

19. For further discussion of the Glueck prediction tables, see Sheldon and Eleanor Glueck, *Unraveling Juvenile Delinquency* (Cambridge: Harvard University Press, 1950).

20. C. A. Schrag, "A Preliminary Criminal Typology," *Pacific Sociological Review* 4(1961): pp. 11–16.

21. G. M. Sykes, *The Society of Captives* (Princeton: Princeton University Press, 1958).

22. W. Miller, "Some Characteristics of Present-Day Delinquency of Relevance to Educators." (Unpublished paper presented at the 1959 meetings of the American Association of School Administrators.)

23. J. B. Roebuck and J. Caldwallader, "The Negro Armed Robber as a Criminal Type: The Construction and Application of a Typology," *Pacific Sociological Review* 4(1961): pp. 21–26.

24. W. McCord, J. McCord, and I. Zola, *Origins of Crime* (New York: Columbia University Press, 1959).

25. L. Ohlin, *Selection for Parole* (New York: Russell Sage Foundation, 1951).

26. W. Reckless, *The Crime Problem* (New York: Appleton-Century-Crofts, 1950).

27. R. L. Jenkins and L. Hewitt, "Types of Personality Structure Encountered in Child Guidance Clinics," *American Journal of Orthopsychiatry* 14(1944): pp. 84–94.

28. A. Aichorn, *Wayward Youth* (New York: Viking, 1935).

29. M. Argyle, "A New Approach to the Classification of Delinquents with Implications for Treatment" (Sacramento: Department of Corrections, 1961), pp. 15–26.

30. D. R. Peterson, H. C. Quay, and G. R. Cameron, "Personality and Background Factors in Juvenile Delinquency as Inferred from Questionnaire Responses," *Journal of Consulting Psychology* 23(1959): pp. 395–399.

31. D. E. Hunt and R. H. Hardt, "Developmental Stage, Delinquency, and Differential Treatment," *Journal of Research in Crime and Delinquency* 2 (1965): pp. 20–31.

32. A Russon, "A Design for Clinical Classification of Offenders," *Canadian Journal of Corrections* 4(1962): pp. 179–188.

33. National Advisory Commission, *Task Force on Corrections Report*, pp. 210–211.

34. Ibid., p. 204.

35. E. Wenk and T. Halatyn, *An Analysis of Classification Factors for Young Adult Offenders*, vol. 1 (Davis, Calif.: Research Center, National Council on Crime and Delinquency, 1974), pp. 65–66.

36. Ibid., p. 66.

37. T. Szasz, *The Myth of Mental Illness* (New York: Harper & Row, 1961).

38. K Menniger, M. Hayman, and P. Pruyser, *The Vital Balance* (New York: Viking Press, 1963).

39. National Advisory Commission, *Task Force on Corrections Report*, p. 200.

40. Ibid., p. 211.

5 Deviants, Defectives, and the Disabled

At one time or another almost every human condition and social factor has been put forward as the cause of deviance. . . . Everything from a tainting of the gene pool to a basic illness of society itself has been blamed for contemporary "waywardness"—the coddling of youth and the neglect of youth, poverty and affluence, authoritarianism and permissiveness, the growth of secular rationality and the decline of secular rationality, too much freedom and too many pressures to conform.

J. L. SIMMONS

It is a difficult enough task for those in the juvenile justice system to cope with the problem of "normal" juvenile delinquents. (As the term is used here, a "normal" delinquent is one who does not fall within the definitions of deviancy, disability, or defectiveness which will be found in this chapter.) Today, however, the juvenile justice system is forced to cope with juveniles who are delinquent *and* who have emotional, physical, or mental problems. As a result, the system barely keeps up with its responsibilities.

An increasing number of children who become involved in the juvenile justice system do not fit the stereotypes of the misunderstood child who is culturally, economically, and socially deprived. More and more, mentally ill and retarded children and children with physical disabilities such as blindness and deafness are committing delinquent acts and being referred to juvenile authorities for supervision and treatment. And, as the Vietnam era showed, there were, and continue to be, groups of juveniles outside the political, social, and moral patterns of middle-class America. Such youths may be labeled as deviant.

These youths do not all fit easily into the scheme of diagnosis, treatment planning, and actual treatment programs designed for "normal" youths. Consider, for example, the low level of success that juvenile treatment programs usually have with their target groups. Just think how much worse the situation would be if mentally and physically disabled youths are added to these groups. Very few of the effective juvenile programs in this country are prepared to deal with less-than-"normal" delinquents; the ineffective programs, of course, are not capable of dealing with them at all.

Traditionally, if a mentally retarded youngster commits an illegal act, reaction has taken one of two forms. On the one hand, the child might be placed in a "special school" or state institution. On the other hand, the child might be returned home to its parents to be punished or watched more closely. In either case, nothing is done about the child's disability or the child's environment, both of which probably had something to do with the act of delinquency in the first place.

Even if a treatment program were available, it would most likely not be able to absorb the disabled delinquent. Most treatment programs are operated with homogeneous groupings. The management and treatment classification systems examined in earlier chapters are good examples. State correctional authorities and delinquency planners are, therefore, extremely reluctant, and are often unable to allocate funds for treatment facilities for the less-than-"normal" juvenile delinquents. In most cases, their needs are either totally unmet or are inadequately met.

Let us now examine this problem more closely. Who are the deviant, defective, and disabled juvenile delinquents? What effect are they having on the juvenile justice system, and what effect is the system having on them?

Deviant Delinquents

To deviate, according to *Webster's New World Dictionary*, is "to turn aside from a course, direction, standard, doctrine." The word *deviant*, derived from the verb form, simply means a person who deviates from the accepted norm of behavior. By definition, all juvenile delinquents could be considered deviant—they have broken the law or breached a social doctrine. Their actions have caused them to become involved with the juvenile justice authorities because they strayed from legally or socially accepted behavior.

Generally, however, the word *deviant* does not have such a broad connotation; it is used in a narrower sense. A deviant juvenile delinquent is one whose behavior, actions, and life-style offend or are abhorrent to the sensitivities of the majority of Americans. Included in this group are radicals, hippies, homosexuals, prostitutes, pimps, and drug users. Most people are less offended by a delinquent who robs a store than by a young person who sells marijuana to schoolmates or by a youth with long hair who clashes with police in a political demonstration.

Once applied, the deviant label is hard to throw off. For some children the mere association with deviants is enough to stigmatize them to the point where they engage in active deviancy where none had previously existed.

> Since the majority of deviants engage in illicit activities only sporadically, their traces are fairly widespread over space and time, making them hard to build into condemning evidence. Whether this is a deliberate ploy or merely necessitated by nondeviant commitments and involvements, it serves to minimize risks. . . .

> . . . Large numbers of people can thus occasionally deviate with relative
> impunity. But if discovered, a temporary deviant may be put in such a position
> that he can hardly refrain from deviance in the future. Identified as a deviant,
> nondeviant opportunities frequently become less available to him. If officially
> punished or treated, he often finds that the only place he can now go is back
> into the milieu which nurtured his deviance in the first place.[1]

This point of view is exemplified by the social theories of Durkheim and
Merton concerning delinquent subcultures and opportunity structure. (See
chapter 3 for a further discussion of causality and deviant behavior.)

Deviant youth often find that they are outsiders whose path has been
chosen for them. Merely living in the culture or subculture in which one is
raised may cause a child to be thought of as having a deviant life-style.
Take, for example, the case of a 12-year-old girl whose mother and sister
are both prostitutes. To that girl the life-style of her parent and sister are a
strong influence on what she may perceive as a meaningful social norm.
Unless she is removed from her environment or unless she comes into
contact with or accepts a set of values totally foreign to her experience, one
could rightly assume that she, too, may become a prostitute. To this girl, her
family, and peers, the choice of a life of prostitution would probably be
considered perfectly normal and far from deviant. However, to the dominant
middle-class culture, this girl would certainly be labeled both delinquent and
deviant.

> Miller regards lower-class delinquency as not deviant or aberrant behavior
> except from a narrow, middle-class viewpoint. Delinquent behaviors are part
> of lower-class culture and highly functional to preparing youngsters for adult
> life within that culture. Thus the delinquent behaviors exhibited by lower-class
> youth are normal. This behavior is antisocial only in the sense that it runs
> counter to the moral expectations of the institutional carriers of middle-class
> mores.[2]

Deviancy, in the sense that it is more than an incidental straying from the
straight and narrow path, may be viewed as a continuous circle, especially if
deviancy involves class-based norms of what is and what is not acceptable.

Not all deviant children are members of a potentially deviant group at
birth.[3] Drug users and teenage alcoholics from middle- and upper-income
classes are typical examples. Their deviance may be viewed as their
rejection of the value system in which they were brought up. Conversely,
children from the lower classes are considered deviant because of their
acceptance of the value systems in which they grew up.

The degree to which a youth's deviant behavior affects his or her contact
with the juvenile justice system depends primarily on two major factors:
discrimination and accommodation. The first factor is exemplified by the star
fullback on the high school football team who is smoking "pot" and who is

more likely to avoid contact with the justice system than his nonathletic, nonscholastic counterpart.

It is the authors' opinion that deviancy and the labeling of those who are deviant is discriminately controlled by any given segment of the population in a position to influence definitions and outcomes of certain behaviors.

Many such accommodations are made for deviant juvenile behavior. It is when the situation changes that this heretofore accommodated deviance becomes a problem to be dealt with. For example, the celebration of our nation's Bicentennial brought with it many infractions of fireworks laws which, although tolerated during that celebration, would not be tolerated afterwards.

To some extent the concept of deviance is a flexible or variable one. It changes when and as people change their attitudes toward certain behaviors and acts. Acts or behaviors that were labeled deviant a few years ago may not be considered so now. For example, in the mid-1960s, the so-called flower children were described as deviant. Today, most people would not designate them as such; indeed, they are looked on now as innocents and viewed with a marked sense of nostalgia.

But there are limits on the degree to which people will alter their attitudes. It is highly unlikely that robbery, for example, will ever get a legal green light. When a youth is accused of robbery and is brought before the court, the law that the youth has violated is clearly defined and the case can be disposed of in the prescribed manner. However, consider a case where the use and/or possession of a small quantity of marijuana is the "crime." In many cities and states, there is a growing trend to decriminalize marijuana use. Alaska, Oregon, and other states have already taken steps to loosen the legal restrictions concerning marijuana. In this case the court is confronted with the problem of what to do with a youth whose only "crime" or deviant act is possessing or using marijuana. According to the law, the youth must be punished for violating an enforceable statute. But attitudes toward this law are changing, and, in fact, the law may be substantially revised to allow the legal use of marijuana. The problem for the court is multiple: Has the youth actually committed a crime? Should the court punish the youth? What kind of judgment can the court hand down in such a case? Obviously, there is a dilemma when today's legal sanction may be tomorrow's standard of conduct.

Deviancy is defined by the society in which it exists. How that society defines deviancy affects the numbers of youth who are sent to institutions, group homes, or other custodial facilities. Fewer youths would be institutionalized if society redefined more liberally what it considers deviant. Washington's Senate Bill 3116 (July 1, 1977), for example, requires the release of dependent/incorrigible children from all state institutions. In effect this move serves to remove previously held social and legal sanctions against dependent/incorrigible youth which made their behavior punishable by institutionalization.

Defective Delinquents

Unlike deviancy, which is largely a socially or culturally defined phenomenon, defectiveness results from something lacking in a juvenile's mental or emotional makeup. A defective delinquent is:

> an individual who, by the demonstration of persistent aggravated antisocial or criminal behavior, evidences a propensity toward criminal activity, and who is found to have either such intellectual deficiency or emotional unbalance, or both, as to clearly demonstrate an actual danger to society so as to require such confinement and treatment, when appropriate, as may make it reasonably safe for society to terminate the confinement and treatment.[4]

The Maryland Act from which this definition comes states that under certain conditions, a request may be made to examine a juvenile for possible defective delinquency. The youth must have been convicted and sentenced in a court of the state for a crime or offense committed on or after June 1, 1954. The crime must come under one or more of the following categories: (1) a felony; (2) a misdemeanor punishable by imprisonment in an institution or penitentiary; (3) a crime of violence; (4) a sex crime involving physical force or violence, a difference of age between a youth and an adult, or a sexual act of an uncontrolled and/or repetitive nature; (5) two or more convictions in a criminal court of the state for any offenses or crimes punishable by imprisonment.[5]

If, after such examination, the juvenile is found to be a defective delinquent:

> the court shall so inform the defendant, and shall order him to be committed or returned to the institution for confinement as a defective delinquent, for an indeterminate period without either maximum or minimum limits. In such event, the sentence for the original criminal conviction, or any unexpired portion thereof, shall be and remain suspended, and the defendant shall no longer be confined for any portion of said original sentence, except as otherwise provided herein. Instead, the defendant shall thenceforth remain in the custody of the institution for defective delinquents, subject to the provisions of this article. (An. Code, 1951, §9; 1951, ch. 476, §9; 1957, ch. 762; 1961, ch. 629, §1.)[6]

It may appear to the reader that the definition of a defective delinquent is vague. However, any attempt to write a precise legal definition of a medical condition runs the risk of over-definition. This definition is not so vague, however, as to violate due-process procedures of law.

Within this definition are included mentally ill offenders and emotionally ill offenders. Also, a check of the requests for examination for defectiveness under the Maryland Act and elsewhere reveals that defectives include sexual offenders and violent offenders.

Mentally or Emotionally Ill Juvenile Delinquents

The mentally or emotionally ill offender is defined as any youth whose behavior is (1) bizarre, self-destructive, or statistically rare (i.e., a juvenile who has delusions or hallucinations) and is not within the "normal range" of behavior given the individual's cultural background and the situation in which the behavior occurred; (2) within the "normal range" but occurs more frequently or intensely than average; (3) "normal" but fails to occur or occurs so infrequently (i.e., a juvenile who withdraws completely or will not speak for long periods of time) as to be statistically rare; and (4) interfering seriously with the individual's ability to adapt to his or her environment appropriately.

It is not uncommon to find that adults who commit crime suffer from mental or emotional illness. But is mental or emotional illness prevalent enough among the juvenile delinquent population to warrant concern? The answer is decidedly *yes*. In a recent year in Washington, 9,600 youngsters referred to the juvenile courts were diagnosed as needing mental health services. Each year, there are approximately 140 children within the Washington State Bureau of Juvenile Rehabilitation system who are in need of psychiatric treatment, and probably 50 of that number should be committed to a psychiatric facility. This is surely ample evidence that there is both a problem regarding mentally and emotionally ill delinquents and a need to help them.[7]

Treatment and Prevention

A detailed and comprehensive study of the mentally ill child is currently being conducted by the Bureau of Juvenile Rehabilitation in Washington. The study is looking into who the mentally ill delinquents are, what is being done to treat them, and how treatment methods can be implemented. This is just one example of recent efforts made by practitioners and corrections staff throughout the country to recognize and handle knowledgeably and realistically the mentally ill or emotionally ill juvenile offender.

Traditionally, the mentally ill juvenile offender has had neither specialized treatment or treatment facilities available to him. In *The Mentally Ill Offender—A Survey of Treatment Programs*, Scheidmandel and Kanno state that they sent a short questionnaire to directors of state mental health programs, asking them to name special institutions for treatment of juvenile mentally ill offenders. "The responses indicated, however, that such special facilities do not exist; it appears that juvenile mentally ill offenders are treated either with juvenile mental patients who are not offenders, or with nonmentally ill juvenile offenders."[8]

Causes of Mental Illness Among Juveniles

The probable causes of poor mental health or mental illness among juvenile offenders are similar to the causes of mental illness among the general child population. Among these factors are poor diet, brain damage, lead poisoning, failure to thrive, infantile autism, life crises, physical abuse, and child-training practices.[9]

The age-old argument of heredity versus environment still dominates most discussions of the causative factors of mental illness. But modern medical research has shed some new light on this subject. For example, research on phenylketonuria—a genetic disorder of phenylalanine metabolism which, if untreated, causes severe mental retardation in infants through the accumulation of metabolic products—has led to the discovery that a modified diet can save children from this fate. Other dietary changes suggested by the results of animal studies have helped eliminate possible brain damage to children.

Perceptual handicaps which have been caused by brain damage or impairment can be treated medically. Children with such problems can make remarkable progress if they have a stable, loving home environment and special educational programs.

Lead poisoning from eating paint or putty can cause mental damage or death to children. Lead poisoning is prevalent in ghettos, slums, and poor neighborhoods where landlords use the cheapest products in painting, building repairs, and maintenance.

Failure to thrive describes a condition of deficient physical development in infants. Its symptoms include problems in feeding, loss of or failure to gain weight, vomiting, diarrhea, problems in sleeping, listlessness, excessive crying, and general irritability. Failure to thrive has been related to poor child-parent relationships such as lack of stimulation, harsh discipline, emotional deprivation, and caloric deprivation. Professionals should seek to make parents aware of their own emotional problems before attempting to help the child. Especially important is altering parental attitudes toward the child.

Infantile autism, though rare, is a very serious condition unique to infancy and early childhood whose causes are not known. It is characterized by the lack of human contact. Evidence of infantile autism occurs in the first few months and is four times as common in boys as in girls. An autistic child disregards anything outside of his or her own existence, usually by trying to ignore it. The prognosis for autistic children is not good, despite stimulation programs developed for use by parents and siblings.

Life crises such as accidents, prolonged illnesses, the birth of a sibling, or the death of a parent or relative are also emotionally disturbing to a child, sometimes to the point of impairing the child's emotional development. The reasons why some children do not survive these life crises situations unimpaired are as yet unknown. This is a question for researchers in the field to answer.

Physical abuse of children is usually experienced at the hands of their own parents. Abusing parents come from all social strata and ranges on the socioeconomic scale, intelligence, race, and religion. Although there is no composite portrait or stereotype of the abusing parent, statistics indicate that white parents of lower socioeconomic and educational background comprise the largest number of abusers.

Of all potential causes of mental and emotional illness, child abuse is one of the most devastating. The abused child seems to carry life-long psychological scars and is likely to abuse his or her own child. Without professional advice and counsel, child abuse is certain to be self-perpetuating.

"Beating, scapegoating, terrorizing, berating, rejecting, or otherwise deliberately injuring a child destroys or seriously distorts the developing personality. In one study, only 30 percent of abused children were found to be within normal limits on follow-up examinations; 42 percent suffered mental retardation, and 28 percent showed significant emotional disturbances. A child psychiatrist judged only 10 percent of 22 abused children she reevaluated to be free of physical, intellectual, and emotional problems; 15 percent of her cases were dead [by the time of reevaluation]. Another recent review alludes to an 88 percent morbidity rate, including speech problems and emotional disorders. In a series of 52 abuse cases, 57 percent had followup IQ assessments of less than 80."[10]

Child abuse is a major problem. While the victim is the child, the act of child-beating is often a signal that a suffering parent is reaching out for help. Only through working with the entire family can there be hope of lessening the frequency of child abuse. The parents are not to be condemned but rather helped. There are many organizations, including child advocacy programs, which have been set up to give guidance and counseling in such cases.

Separation and placement of a child outside the home have also been suggested as potential causes of problems for young children. Prolonged absences from the home because of hospitalization or placement in an impersonal institution create special mental health problems for the young child. Placement outside the home can occur when the child's parents are unable to provide proper care for the child. A parent may have a mental breakdown or be imprisoned or be in some other circumstance which prevents adequate parenting of the child. Foster homes are the preferred method of handling a child in such situations. However, rigid discipline of foster parents, lack of continued care and affection, and an ever-changing array of parent-figures only adds further confusion and distress to the child's life. Adoption at infancy seems to present the least serious type of separation, but even adopted children have been stereotyped as having a tendency toward serious behavior problems.

The important factor to remember when substitute care becomes necessary is that its purpose is best served in the child's own community or neighborhood or better still in the intensive development of services for children right in their own homes.

Causes of Mental Illness in Older Children

The causes looked at thus far are those encountered in the early development of the child. Poverty, racism, and human deprivation are factors that relate to problems encountered in the child's later development.

"Poverty and racism are interrelated factors that cannot be ignored. Their consequences for mental health are alienation, frustration, and a lowered ceiling on achievement."[11]

The U.S. Department of Labor has indicated that the lower income level for an urban family of four should be at least $10,041. But according to a joint commission studying poverty, a family of four requires at least $15,000 annually to adequately meet its needs. On the basis of these figures, about one-half of the families in America are impoverished. In *Growing Up Poor*, Catherine S. Chilman has identified eight factors that are usually found to coexist among them. They are low income, large families, broken families, poor housing, little education, chronic unemployment, cultural patterns influenced by poverty, and, most importantly, poor physical and mental health.[12]

Racism affects the children of minority groups by making them think of themselves not only as different but also as inferior. Coupled with poverty and the problems created by being poor, the effects of racism can cause strong mental and emotional problems to surface in a child's life.

Human deprivation has a decided effect on the mental or emotional health of a child. It takes the form of poverty and racism but certainly is not limited to them. The National Institute of Child Health and Human Development, in an article entitled "Perspectives on Human Deprivation," states that there are five areas in which poverty, racism, and other aspects of disadvantage apparently affect development:

1. Imaginative capacity—The lack of the child to engage in daydreaming [which is thought] to be the result of poor parent-child interaction.
2. Achievement—The middle-class children score higher on tests than do their lower-class counterparts. This leads to anxiety and a sense of worthlessness.
3. Affection—A weak affectional system in children may be traced to parental neglect or the lack of appropriate stimulation.
4. Social roles—Disadvantaged people often do not have access to the socially accepted adult roles such as worker, marriage partner, or parent. This causes poor self-image and the desire to be accepted in roles (i.e., prostitution, gambler, and so forth).

5. Self-esteem—Parents who are absent, apathetic, or rejecting do not provide good examples or models of how a child should grow or succeed. Much to the disadvantaged child's detriment, when he or she is accepted, it is more likely to be with uncritical approval or infantile nurturance rather than with limits or respect.[13]

Treating Mentally Ill Juveniles

Having acquainted the reader with some of the more prevalent causes of mental or emotional illness among children, we now focus our attention to another area. How should mentally ill juvenile offenders be treated? Should they be treated as "criminally insane" or merely as other mentally ill persons in hospitals? Do juvenile offenders who are mentally or emotionally ill have a right to treatment?

"Authorities are divided on the question of whether juvenile proceedings should be equated with criminal proceedings or with civil commitment proceedings.[14] The answer seems to depend upon the provisions of the particular juvenile court act. Some statutes provide that if, as the result of a mental examination, the juvenile is found to be incompetent by reason of mental illness or retardation, the juvenile court proceedings are to be suspended and civil commitment proceedings instituted.[15] However, under other statutory schemes, the juvenile's incompetence is no bar to an adjudication of delinquency.[16]

It seems, therefore, that there is no uniform rule or statute which states that a juvenile who is mentally or emotionally ill should be handled either civilly or criminally. However, defense attorneys for such juveniles should be extremely cautious in asking for a dismissal of charges because of the juvenile's mental condition.

> Most other motions to dismiss, if successful, end societal intervention into the life of the accused. A successful motion to dismiss because of insanity or incompetency may result in commitment to a mental facility for a period of years while the result of the original delinquency or ungovernability charges would likely be probation or a short placement in a state training school.[17]
>
> In deciding whether or not to move to dismiss on the grounds of insanity or incompetency, counsel must carefully gauge the likely consequences of his motion. He must consider whether a longer period of commitment in a mental facility will be in his client's best interests. Some suggest that avoiding an adjudication of delinquency or ungovernability prevents the stigmatization of the juvenile. However, there is strong authority that mental commitment is itself stigmatizing.[18] Furthermore, the conditions in most state mental facilities often are worse than those in state training schools, which at least tend to be more open settings.[19]

The question of a mentally ill or mentally retarded person's right to treatment has recently received attention in such cases as *Rouse* v. *Cameron* (373 F. 2d 451 (D.C.C.R. 1966) and others.

Right to treatment is a legalistic doctrine which was first raised in relation to the involuntary commitment of mentally ill persons who are not dangerous to themselves or others and who have not committed any criminal acts. Many of these people, including juveniles, have been simply institutionalized and forgotten by the outside world. When the right-to-treatment question was raised it also called into question whether patients were in fact getting suitable treatment. If they are not getting adequate treatment, some courts have held that they must be released.[20] Right to treatment, however, has been limited to patients in mental institutions and other similar facilities. As yet, no court has ruled that an adult offender sentenced to a prison or other correctional facility has a right to treatment.[21]

Besharov contends that, "There are greater grounds for asserting a juvenile's right to treatment because of the juvenile courts rehabilitative purpose. As the juvenile court's desperate lack of treatment capability becomes more painfully apparent, the question of a juvenile's right to treatment will become the subject of judicial and legislative concern."[22] A further discussion of a juvenile's right to treatment, whether that juvenile is mentally ill or otherwise, will be found in chapter 15.

Juvenile Sexual Offenders

In this text, the juvenile sexual offender is considered to be a defective delinquent. An argument can be made for placing the sexual offender in the deviant category, for many sexual offenders are in fact deviant. However, the sexual juvenile offender's behavior and potential threat to society is primarily that of a defective personality because of a deficiency in the juvenile's makeup.

For most states, the definition of a juvenile sexual offender is similar to that used by Washington. A juvenile sexual offender is a person who has a record of any of these sexual offenses, as defined by the Criminal Code: rape, statutory rape, indecent liberties, public indecency, incest, or obscene phone calls. These offenses may have been committed either in the juvenile's community or in a juvenile institution or youth camp. In Washington, as in so many other states, there is no consistency between how the juvenile justice system defines juvenile sexual offenses and how the community-at-large defines them. The need of a sanctioned definition of sexual offensive behavior in juveniles, and the establishment of standard procedures for handling these cases, is acute and immediate.

Treatment services designed for the juvenile sexual offender do not exist. The reasons are deeply rooted in American attitudes toward such crimes. The idea of rehabilitation stops with the sexual defective. Society has considered these people to be morally defective, and in need of being locked up, physically punished, or even killed. In the past sexual offenses were thought of as acts committed only by persons possessed by the devil. Today, sexual defectiveness is viewed as a serious psychological problem for which the offender should be medically treated and not simply punished.

However, the seriousness of the offense determines how strong a sanction society will insist upon. The stronger the sanction, the more likely it will punish rather than treat the offense. Strong sanctions *are* imposed against persons committing such offenses as rape, indecent liberties, and incest. Other sexual offenses, such as petting, masturbation, pornography, premarital sex and extramarital sex, are seen as forms of deviant behavior. Sanctions against these acts are less frequently invoked than in the past. Unlike the other forms of sexual defectiveness, their repugnance to society is dependent upon defined behavioral standards. For example, while rape by a teenager is never likely to be condoned in this country, premarital sex may be tacitly, or even openly, condoned depending on society's mood at the time. The present so-called sexual revolution reflects this generation's attitudes.

In a study entitled "Report on the Male Sexual Offender," published by the Department of Social and Health Services of Washington, the subject of treatment for the juvenile sexual delinquent was thoroughly examined. The study found that the staffs interviewed generally agreed that there was a need for treatment for sexual offenders. They also commented, however, that one specific program just for sexual offenders would not be the answer or even desirable.

In the questionnaire for the study, the staffs were asked to explain what they had done with juveniles whom they had treated in the past. The answers ranged from a common-sense approach (e.g., "Used a *Playboy* magazine to find out what turned him on" or "Taught him masturbation") to a set of interventions of a more sophisticated nature (e.g., "Worked with sexual fantasies" or "Outlined alternative sources of gratification"). Overall, it was discovered that the treatment techniques were similar to those commonly practiced in treating people (not specifically juveniles) who have committed sexual offenses. There was, however, no continuity or bridge in the treatment of juvenile sexual offenders between treatment plans. And only a few of the known methods were used in treating any one youth. The individualizing of treatment was in part deliberate and in part the result of what was immediately available to them at the time, without the benefit of being able to evaluate the vast number of alternatives.

In summary, the Washington study reported that no systematic approach to treatment existed and no definite procedures for handling juvenile sexual offenders had been set up. Also, evidence indicated that current practices, while well-intentioned, could reinforce the pattern of denial of wrongdoing in the sexual offender. The study recommended establishing a task force to investigate the problem of juvenile sexual offenses. The goals of the task force should be:

1. To define what a sexual offense is, to identify who the sexual offender is, and to specify treatment programs for helping the sexual offender.

2. An in-depth examination of the sexual offender program at the state mental hospital to discover the aspects of their program which may be relevant to the development of programs in the Bureau of Juvenile Rehabilitation; for example, which offenders are helped by group treatment, which are not.

3. A search of the professional literature; identification of programs in progress and individual therapists treating juvenile sexual offenders.

4. Utilization of existing research in developing systematic methods for noticing, diagnosing, and treating juvenile sexual offenders, possibly in the form of pilot projects.

5. The development of criteria for eligibility for acceptance in programs for sexual offenders; methods of treatment; and criteria for successful discharge from programs.

6. A research design which would provide for ongoing program evaluation and directed change.

7. A consideration of the ethical and political problems involved in having (or not having) special programs for sexual offenders.

8. A search for additional funding for sexual offender pilot projects through Law and Justice, National Institute of Mental Health, or other sources.[23]

A recent nationwide survey has shown that many states do not have the resources required to fund and staff specialized programs for sexual offenders, who usually comprise only a small percentage of their total juvenile population.

In some states, like Washington, juvenile sexual offenders whose I.Q. is below a certain level (69 in Washington) are often never even involved in a criminal proceeding. Instead, they are tried civilly and are remanded to the state's mental health department for disposition, placement, and treatment.

Violent Offenders

The violent juvenile offender is one who threatens or actually physically assaults a person or a person's property, causing direct injury or harm to the victim, to others, or damage to property. In this text, a violent offender is considered to be a defective delinquent.

The arrest rate for violent crimes in the United States has more than doubled since 1963. FBI statistics show that suspects under the age of 18 account for 23 percent of all arrests for violent crimes.[24] As with sex crimes, public attention increases in direct proportion to the incidence of violent crimes. Because violent crimes arouse stronger public feeling than do nonviolent crimes (i.e., economic crimes), the criminal justice system spends more time and energy trying to reach proper placement and parole decisions regarding the violent offender. The percentage of youths who have committed violent crimes has been gradually increasing over the past several years, and therefore efforts to rehabilitate these youngsters have increased.

As more public attention is focused on the violent delinquent offender there is more pressure exerted on the juvenile justice system to do something to "solve" the problem. Most pressure is in the form of stepped-up criticism of the system's mishandling of the violent offender.

What contributes to or causes violence among young people? Many young people point out to authorities that this is an "age of violence" or simply that this is a violent country. Violence is not viewed, however, as a monopoly of the state. Rather, it is a logical solution to problems when all else fails. During the last two decades, this country has experienced an almost uninterrupted level of domestic violence. The assassinations of John and Robert Kennedy and of Martin Luther King, the Vietnam antiwar riots, the Charles Manson case, politically inspired terrorism, and mass sniper killings have all occurred in these years. Most people have come to tolerate and even accept a certain degree of violence in society as an unavoidable side effect of stress. "Eons ago man crept from his cave as he overcame his fear of his environment. Now, it appears, the violence of our world is forcing him back inside. If you think this a metaphor, I suggest you visit the nearest 'total security' apartment complex, 'total security' retirement community, or 'total security' vacation spa."[25]

Violence on television, just like violence in comic books and in other sources available to children, does have an impact. Just what that impact is depends on several factors: (1) the age of the child, (2) his or her previous exposure to violence, (3) peer group ideas about violent behavior, (4) parental or home training concerning violent acts, and (5) the child's own character which may or may not be susceptible to television's influence. One thing is certain, however, "the second TV generation is upon us, and neither the worst fears nor the rosiest hopes for television have been fulfilled. But we know now that TV's impact is tremendous. Decisions made by concerned adults can make that impact either positive or negative."[26]

Marshall McLuhan, the prophet of the electronic media, has also spoken on the subject of violence on television. He suggests that television "alters the image that people have of themselves. It changes their relation to others. The gap so created can only be filled by violence. Such violence has no goal except the need to form a new image, to create a new meaning for the individual or the group."[27]

Treatment and Prevention

Treatment of violent offenders has taken many forms, from strict punishment to tender love and care to, more recently, brain surgery. Sociology has contributed, thus far, more to the study of violence than other disciplines. Sociologists attempt to identify the conditions in society which tend to produce violent persons. Once the conditions are understood and eliminated, it is thought that the violent person will no longer be a societal problem. The usefulness of this approach is limited, however, because it offers no means for dealing with those who have already been subjected to harmful social conditions. The neurophysiological approach to the subject of violence does not have the same limitation. Its advocates suggest that violence may be related to brain damage which can be corrected and prevented through brain surgery. Very complex surgical techniques, recently developed, have made this approach more feasible. However usable this technique may now be, it is still a subject of major controversy. Its opponents argue that violent offenders who are treated thus are left incapable of normal functioning. For further discussion of this treatment approach the reader is referred to the book published in 1970, written by Doctors Vernon Mark and Frank Ervin, entitled *Violence and the Brain*.[28]

Despite the juvenile justice system's efforts in treating delinquency, it may be said that today's youth tend to take delinquent acts too lightly. For example, Melitta Schmidenberg, in the article "Juvenile Murderers," quotes the following:

> "Children soon learn that . . . being a minor puts them in control of incredible power, that of excuse and toleration of juvenile delinquency. Delinquency provides excitement, and even in the event he is caught, the delinquent knows that the punishment will not be harsh, and often he considers punishment just another excitement. Children consider childhood their 'first life' distinctly separate from their 'second life,' adulthood, and they find it hard to believe that juvenile delinquency will affect their future life." This passage was written by Danny who, reports Schmideberg, at age 13, after careful preparation, killed his sister in cold blood.
>
> The more humane treatment of young offenders and the tendency to lean over backwards in sympathizing with the "agony" of the murderer and forgetting the victim, has the undesirable effect on the offender that it helps him to take his offense too lightly.[29]

It has been suggested that the key to curbing violent offenses and other delinquent acts among juveniles is contained in the familiar adage "An ounce of prevention is worth a pound of cure." Prevention, however, presupposes that one can predict with accuracy which juveniles are prone to violent behavior and which are not.[45] This simply isn't possible, at least at the present time. No reliable, accurate methods exist for predicting who the violent person might be. The methods that have been tried, such as classification schemes and violent offender indexes, have not been effective and have not produced a workable predictive model.

But even supposing the juvenile offender could be identified, would this capability make any difference in the long run? The answer to this question is clearly given in an article from *Crime and Delinquency*.

> Currently, violence prevention and treatment of known violent persons remain rather primitive, consisting largely of more secure confinement and the administration of calming drugs or counseling. . . . Confidence in the ability to predict violence serves to legitimate intrusive types of social control. Our demonstration of the futility of such prediction should have consequences as great for the protection of individual liberty as a demonstration of the utility of violence prediction would have for the protection of society.[30]

As in the case of the sexual offender, most states do not have a policy regarding the care, custody, and treatment of violent offenders. In Washington, for example, one study showed that of 25 youths who were rated as the most severe violent offenders, less than half (12) were placed in a security program. The ranking of these youths by the severity of their violent behavior (highest to lowest violent offender index score) revealed no relationship between placement in the security program and the severity of violent behavior. In fact, many youths identified by the study group as violent offenders were not viewed as such by the treatment staff. Those youths that were considered violent by the staff were classified as such primarily because of behavior and attitudes shown *while in the institution*, not because of behavior prior to commitment.

Stanley Cohen suggests four problems for future research and theory development connected with violent juvenile offenders. They are:

1. The convergences, both in terms of societal reactions and actual behavior, between traditional delinquency and various types of ideological violence.
2. The nature of public folklore and fantasy about adolescent violence and the processes by which such images are created and transmitted.
3. The effect of societal definitions, particularly in the mass media and the official control culture on the cause and development of certain forms of violence.
4. The need to supplement traditional causal explanations with more faithful accounts of the contexts and structures in which the action takes place and its meaning to the individuals involved.[31]

Disabled Delinquents

The terms *disabled, handicapped,* and *impaired* will be used interchangeably in this chapter. Physical handicaps and impairments come within the scope of the definition of disability which follows.

> Disability may be defined as a reduction in personal coping and adaptive function, which causes significant limitations in overall performances of daily living. It may include disturbances of homeostatic and adaptive processes that ordinarily provide for reasonably stable and healthy behavior of a person in response to the physical, psychosocial, and economic demands of life.[32]

In 1968, the Bureau of Education for the Handicapped reported that of the 58 million children between the ages of 5 and 19 years in the United States, nearly 6 million were handicapped in some way. More than 3.7 million were physically handicapped (i.e., hard of hearing, deaf, speech impaired, blind or partially blind, or crippled).

The handicapped juvenile delinquent is a special problem for the juvenile justice system. Because of the cost of proper treatment and rehabilitation for a physically handicapped child, many communities are forced to deal with the child as a delinquent only.

> Actual cost studies and review of reimbursement practices of purchasers of rehabilitative services have been conducted at the Texas Institute for Rehabilitation and Research on a thousand consecutive patient admissions for comprehensive rehabilitation. These studies showed that the average cost per patient was $4,376 and that each patient had an average of 2.3 sponsors for institutional service alone. . . . Of this group of 1,000, 70 percent were able to meet only 36 percent of the cost of care from personal resources.[33]

A child with a physical handicap may totally disrupt a family. The parents either dote on the child, thereby ignoring the rest of their children and contributing to the child's problem, or they pretend the child does not have a handicap at all. In either case the parents' normal relationship to and training of a child are distorted, usually at the expense of that child as he or she grows older.

Departments of pediatrics and psychiatry have conducted studies of the effects of early physical defects that impair certain physical activities essential to normal personality development. Their data suggest that there is, in fact, a causal relationship between certain kinds of physical handicap and personality development.[34]

In adolescence, the physically disabled child experiences fears of being different. These fears only add to the difficulty of coping with an already confusing and difficult period in the child's life. Some of these children withdraw completely or exhibit strong acting out behavior. In either case, reaching that child is more of a challenge than even specially trained doctors, therapists, or nurses are able to handle, let alone an institutional correctional staff person or other member of the juvenile justice system.

Juveniles with physical disabilities who commit delinquent acts are reacted to in much the same way as are nondisabled delinquents. There may be more sympathy, and the police may be more apt to be lenient with the disabled, but otherwise they are treated as delinquents.

Prescriptive treatment plans for the physically disabled generally do not exist or are extremely limited when they do. There are currently no major programs for rehabilitating disabled juvenile delinquents. As with violent and sexual offenders, the disabled are not separated for special treatment within the juvenile justice system.

While there are virtually hundreds of various programs designed to help the handicapped, such as the Bureau of Vocational Rehabilitation, the Salvation Army, Sheltered Workshops, Developmental Disability Bureaus, and Goodwill Industries just to name a few, there are still too many physically disabled persons, including juveniles, whose needs go unmet year after year.

Even with the advancements in medical knowledge, it seems that a person's financial status alone determines whether or not he or she will get the much needed help to learn to function normally in a normal society in spite of a handicap or impairment.

Physical examinations in detention facilities and other diagnostic settings have uncovered medical problems ranging in severity from heart disease and kidney and endocrine defects to hernias requiring surgery. The majority of these defects, if caught at an earlier age, could have been corrected surgically at much less cost to both patient and society. In some cases, these defects may have actually contributed to the youngster's delinquent behavior, such as truancy from school, and may have been a factor in their difficulty with the law.

The disabled delinquent is, however, still a delinquent, a youth who for one reason or another has broken the law. If this segment of our delinquent population is to be properly attended to, their special problem must be realized and some form of treatment or rehabilitation must be available for them even if the disability has absolutely no connection with their becoming a delinquent or committing a delinquent act. And if their disability does appear to be related to their behavior, then both the delinquent behavior and the child's disability must be considered simultaneously in arriving at proper treatment.

While it is known that juveniles with disabilities do become delinquent, the exact causal relationship between a child's disability and his or her potential to commit delinquent acts is not known. Prevention of mental and physical disabilities to youth, therefore, may or may not have a significant enough impact upon the delinquency problem to warrant the juvenile justice system's whole-hearted efforts toward preventing these disabilities in the first place. Furthermore, many disabilities occur as the result of accidents, injuries, and violence, factors which would have to be accurately predicted in order to be prevented. There are, however, many disabilities which are the direct result of such things as birth defects, improper early childhood diet, or environment. Prevention of these disabilities is possible.

Summary

The simple classification of delinquent youths into a homogenous, single group is not realistic. In this chapter, it has been shown that three major categories—*deviant, defective,* and *disabled*—are handy categorizations for further classification of delinquent children. The juvenile justice system has a difficult enough time treating so-called normal delinquents. How much more inadequate it is to cope with these special-category delinquents should be obvious to the reader. It is imperative for anyone in the juvenile justice system to become better aware of these special problem cases and attempt to meet them with special solutions.

Social and cultural problems for *deviant* juveniles are not always solved by incarceration or punishment. Many of the behaviors that are defined as deviant at one time may not be labeled as such at another time. The transitory nature of the deviant labeling process makes the planning and allocation of resources and facilities in the system difficult, if not impossible. Simply deciding that a behavior that was previously "normal" is now delinquent—and deviant—can have an immediate impact on every aspect of the system. The move toward the deinstitutionalization of many categories of status offenders has tended to reduce overcrowding of juvenile institutions and lessen the work load of institutional staffs.

The *defective* delinquent, whether mentally or emotionally defective, is often a victim in his or her own right. Sexual offenders usually are products of defective personality development rather than simply deviant behavior, no matter how repugnant it might be. All of these defective categories are shown to be more in need of specialized treatment programs than punitive confinement. The violent juvenile offender is also considered to be a defective type of personality. Most systems are not able to cope with these difficult categories because they lack classification and diagnostic programs that are directed toward caring for their special problem.

While defective and deviant delinquents have long been recognized, only recently has the *disabled* juvenile found his or her way into the system in significant numbers. In general Americans have been protective of youths with physical handicaps and impairments. Physically impaired juveniles were often diverted from the juvenile justice system into other systems when they got into trouble. The previous emphasis seemed to be on the *juvenile's* problem and not as much on the act itself. While this attitude still exists, it seems more and more that the *act* is the determining factor in the disposition of the juvenile's case. Perhaps this is an effect of the *Gault* decision and other recent decisions. It remains to be seen whether this redirection of emphasis will be beneficial or harmful to the juveniles involved.

This chapter has attempted to point out the extremes that are present in the juvenile justice system. Obviously, various solutions and remedies are bound to be offered in the face of so many offenders with such complex social, psychological, and physical problems, in addition to their basic delinquency. As juvenile justice systems become more like the adult system, the danger of overlooking these crucial problems in favor of increased use of custody and process is a real threat. In the case of these youths, it is essential that treatment be made available to help them cope with and recover from their individual handicaps.

REVIEW QUESTIONS

1. Define each of the following:
   a. Deviant delinquent.
   b. Defective delinquent.
   c. Sexual offender.
   d. Violent offender.
   e. Mentally and emotionally ill offender.
   f. Disabled delinquent.

2. How many programs or facilities can you think of which are specifically prepared to handle any of the offender groups mentioned in 1 above?

3. If you were a member of the staff of a juvenile correctional facility, how would you suggest treating a child committed for murder who was suffering from acute paranoia and was totally withdrawn?

4. Do you think that the delinquent types discussed in this chapter would come primarily from a lower socioeconomic background? Explain your answer.

NOTES

1. J. L. Simmons, *Deviants* (Berkeley, Calif.: Glendessary Press, 1969), p. 68.

2. Milton Rector, "Crime and Delinquency," *Encyclopedia of Social Work*, 16th ed., vol. 1 (New York: National Association of Social Workers, 1971), p. 170.

3. M. E. Wolfgang, R. M. Figlio, and T. Sellin, *Delinquency in a Birth Cohort* (Chicago: University of Chicago, 1972).

4. Maryland Revised Code, Article 31B, Defective Delinquents; p. 641. (An. Code, 1951, §5; 1951, ch. 476, §5; 1957, ch. 558; 1961, ch. 629, §1.)

5. Ibid., p. 647.

6. Ibid., p. 669.

7. "The Specialized Information and Program Development for the Male Sexual Offender, Violent Offender, and Mentally Ill Youth in the Bureau of Juvenile Rehabilitation," Department of Social and Health Services (Washington), Office of Research, June, 1976.

8. P. L. Scheidemandel and C. K. Kanno, *The Mentally Ill Offender: A Survey of Treatment Programs* (Washington, D.C.: American Psychiatric Association, 1969), p. 1.

9. Donald Brieland, "Mental Health and Illness in Children," *Encyclopedia of Social Work*, 16th ed., vol. 1 (New York: National Association of Social Workers, 1971), pp. 783–91.

10. Suzanne Ward, "Suffer the Little Children and Their Family" (Washington, D.C.: U.S. Air Force, 1975), p. 8. This article was part of the information packet which the U.S. Air Force put out for the recruitment of social workers.

11. Brieland, "Mental Health and Illness in Children," p. 788.

12. See Catherine S. Chilman, *Growing Up Poor* (Washington, D.C.: U.S. Department of Health, Education, and Welfare, 1966).

13. National Institute of Child Health and Human Development, "Perspectives on Human Deprivation: Biological, Psychological, and Sociological" (Washington, D.C.: U.S. Department of Health, Education, and Welfare, 1969).

14 See *In re Jay S.*, 37 App. Div. 2d 815, 324 N.T.S. 2d 812 (1st Department, 1971), in which the decision was made that an incompetent juvenile may not be tried in juvenile court.

15. For example, D.C. Code Ann E. 16-2315 (c) (1) (1973).

16. D. J. Besharov, *Juvenile Justice Advocacy* (New York: Practicing Law Institute, 1974), pp. 307–308. (See Arizona Revised Statute Ann §8-242 (supp. 1972).

17. Nationwide, the average length of stay in state training schools is 9.9 months.

18. See Erving Goffman, *Stigma* (Englewood Cliffs, N.J.: Prentice-Hall, 1963).

19. Besharov, *Juvenile Justice Advocacy*, p. 306.

20. For example, U.S. ex rel. *Schuster* v. *Herold*, 410 F 2d. 1071, 1087 (2d Cir., 1969).

21. *Director of Patuxent Institution* v. *Daniels*, 253 Md. 16,221 A. 2d 397 (1966).

22. Besharov, *Juvenile Justice Advocacy*, p. 433.

23. T. F. Clark and W. E. Henry, *Report of the Male Juvenile Sexual Offender* (Olympia, Wash., Department of Social and Health Services, Bureau of Juvenile Rehabilitation, 1975), pp. 74–75.

24. *FBI Uniform Crime Report, 1970, 1971, 1972, 1973, 1974* (Washington, D.C.: U.S. Government Printing Office, 1971, 1972, 1973, 1974, 1975).

25. Milton Rector, President, National Council on Crime and Delinquency, in a letter to Clifford E. Simonsen.

26. Rose Mukerji, "T.V.'s Impact on Children: A Checkerboard Scene," *Phi Delta Kappan*, January, 1976, p. 316.

27. Ovid Demaris, *America the Violent* (Baltimore: Penguin, 1970), p. 358.

28. Vernon Mark and Frank Ervin, *Violence and the Brain* (New York: Harper & Row, 1970), pp. 258–59.

29. M. Schmideberg, "Juvenile Murderers," *International Journal of Offender Therapy and Comparative Criminology*, 7, no. 3 (1973): 240.

30. E. A. Wenk, J. O. Robinson, and G. W. Smith, "Can Violence Be Predicted?" *Crime and Delinquency*, October, 1973, p. 402.

31. Stanley Cohen, "Directions for Research on Adolescent Group Violence and Vandalism," *British Journal of Criminology*, 2, no. 4 (October, 1971): 337–38.

32. William A. Spencer and Maurine B. Mitchell, "Disability and Physical Handicap," *Encyclopedia of Social Work*, 16th ed., vol. 1 (New York: National Association of Social Workers, 1971), pp. 204–205.

33. Ibid., p. 209.

34. J. A. Oakland and W. D. Sherman, "An Examination of Erickson's Theory from the Perspective of a Study on Congenitally Paraplegic Children." Paper presented at the 46th Annual Meeting of the American Orthopsychiatric Association, New York, April, 1969.

6 Diagnostic Practices and Trends

Psychiatrists, in their approach to delinquency, have from the very beginning taken it for granted that the mental condition and personality of delinquents must deviate from the normal. It has been seen that this view is at the very foundation of their ideological position. This also accounts for the fact that so many psychiatric facilities for delinquents never diagnose a single patient as normal.

JOSEPH S. ROUCEK

The term *diagnosis* has different meanings for different people. As the term applies to corrections, diagnosis is a process wherein individuals are evaluated in order to determine why they have become what they are, and/or why they have experienced the problems which brought them before the courts, or into contact with the police, or other components of the juvenile justice system. According to Perlman, "Any diagnosis aims to identify and explain the nature of a person's problem, to appraise it within a framework of specific intentions and goals, and to use that appraisal as a guide to action. But the content of a diagnosis—those facts and forces that are placed under the spotlight for examination at any given time in any given case— must be defined by the goal of the helping effort. Diagnosis for what? is the question that must be answered by any worker who seeks to determine what he needs to know and understand about the material he is to influence."[1]

Diagnostic approaches, as they are practiced today, have their beginnings in the early to mid-1930s. They are, in part, built upon the basic principles of the psychosocial approach to casework. This approach stresses both the psychological well-being of the juvenile and the social environment in which he or she lives. It also stresses the importance of the family, that is, the effect of the family relationships upon the development of the child.

Florence Hollis states that, "For many years the psychosocial school was referred to as the 'diagnostic' approach, because its stress on the importance of diagnosis was one of several points of difference with the functional school. It is also sometimes called the Freudian or psychoanalytic school, because it has drawn heavily upon Freudian theory for its understanding of the personality factor in problems of social adjustment."[2]

The functional approach, which emerged as a separate school of thought in the mid-1930s, differs from the psychosocial approach in three ways:

Understanding the Nature of Man

The functional school works from a psychology of growth. It sees the center for change as residing not in the caseworker but in the client, with the worker's method consisting of engaging in a relationship process that releases the client's own power of choice and growth. The functional group emphasizes man as "determining himself from himself" and from the relationships and external conditions of his life and as acting on and using relationships, including a potential relationship with a social caseworker, in the continuing creation of himself. It uses the term "helping" rather than "treatment" in referring to its method.

Understanding the Purpose of Social Casework

The purpose of the social work agency is viewed as a partial or concrete instance of social work's overall purpose and as giving focus, direction, and content to the worker's practice. Casework is not considered a form of psychosocial treatment of individuals or families but a method for administering some specific social service, with such psychological understanding of and skill in the helping process that the agency service has the best possible chance of being used for individual and social welfare.

Understanding the Concept of Process in Social Casework

The functional school developed the concept of social casework as a helping process, through which an agency's services are made available; the principles involved are those having to do with the initiating, sustaining, and terminating of a process in human relationship. This means that the worker enters into the relationship with an avowed lack of knowledge of how it will turn out, since that answer has not yet been written; only client and worker together can discover what can be done with the help offered. The worker's responsibility is for control of his part in the process, not for the achievement of any predetermined end. The use of the social casework "method" (what the worker did) is seen as resulting in the social casework "process" (involving the interaction of worker and client and moving in time from its inception through to its consummation and ending).[3]

Both the psychosocial and functional approaches to casework are still in use, but the psychosocial approach is the basis from which most diagnostic assessments draw their conceptual framework. While Freudian in origin, the diagnostic approach as practiced within today's juvenile justice system is not as detailed or strenuous in its strict *traditional* psychological examination of personality and character as is the psychosocial approach. Rather, it has been more broadly structured to include the drawing of inferences about the nature of the juvenile's problem by examining it from as many perspectives as are helpful, necessary, and possible in order to determine what types of intervention appear suitable for the alleviation of the juvenile's problems.

Whereas the psychosocial approach has relied solely on the caseworker's knowledge and perception of the juvenile's personality, the diagnostic approach has been expanded to include techniques such as role playing, role definition, group interaction, and expectations to provide the diagnostician with additional tools for arriving at a more complete understanding of the individual and his relationship not only with himself, but with society as a whole. The diagnostic approach also goes beyond evaluating the child's environment mainly through the perceived effect of family relationships, to include the effects of peer pressure, school, offense background, psychiatric evaluation, physical and dental examinations, and the youth's attitudes toward authority.

Diagnosis Today

The following definition of diagnosis draws on the experiences and practices within the scope of the juvenile justice system: *Diagnosis is the identification of the problems and the assets of an individual by applicable and/or available means, and the recommendation of the corrective actions that should be taken to solve the problems within the limits of those assets.*

At the present time, the purpose of diagnostic evaluation is to obtain and make available professional, factual, documented, and usable information to the courts, to the training schools and institutions, to treatment personnel, to parole and probation staff, and to aftercare personnel. This information is then used in determining the appropriate treatment that can most adequately meet the needs of the particular child.

What kind of information is needed for an adequate diagnosis of a child? The Bureau of Juvenile Rehabilitation of Washington has formulated the minimum information required for diagnosis. The information comes from eleven areas: (1) court expectations; (2) delinquency history; (3) social, emotional, and mental history; (4) family background and developmental history; (5) educational background; (6) medical information and history; (7) treatment program and previously tried placements; (8) placement resources; (9) what children respond to (stimuli); (10) attitude toward commitment; and (11) vital statistics.[4]

Court Expectations

Courts use both *diagnostic only* and *regular* commitments for many purposes. In choosing between these two forms of commitment, the court must decide what it expects to gain by placing the youth in the diagnostic program.

The correct choice isn't always clear even when reports on the youth are available. In a "diagnosis only" commitment, the diagnostic program is most effective when the following facts are known:

1. The plans being considered by the court
2. The kinds of information useful to the court in deciding upon the proper course.
3. Specific needs the court has in requesting this evaluation (i.e., time for the youth to consider his situation and ways in which to handle it, a chance to obtain an outside opinion on treatment planning, special psychological information).

Delinquency History

The primary purpose of the juvenile justice system is to control and eliminate delinquency and the behavioral problems that cause delinquency. As soon as a youth enters the system behavioral problems should be identified so that the subsequent behavioral changes may be recorded and monitored during the time the juvenile is within the system.

In addition, police reports on serious incidents in a youngster's past (particularly violent crimes) as well as recent referrals (those of the past six months to a year) are helpful. Unless it is an unusual case, copies of every witness's report are not necessary.

Social, Emotional, and Mental History

A history of the social, emotional, and mental background helps in assessing a youth's strengths and weaknesses. Short-term treatment must concentrate on behaviors that can be changed; the emotional and mental strengths of the individual should play a part in this treatment. These strengths should be evaluated early in the youth's stay to ensure sound initial treatment decisions.

A psychiatric evaluation is usually not as useful to the central state facility as a psychological evaluation because it does not provide an intelligence estimate or involve testing.

Family Background and Developmental History

Information about family background and development history is used in predicting the effect of the family on the youth's adjustment in a treatment program, in providing knowledge about significant relationships in the youth's past and problems resulting from these relationships, in identifying crisis points in the youth's life, and in giving important information that will have bearing on understanding the youth's present behavior and reactions.

The Social History Report (Figure 6–1) provides a guide for obtaining useful facts about a youth's family and developmental history.

SOCIAL HISTORY REPORT

Routing Information   **Case Identification**

TO: _____   CASE NAME: _____

FROM: _____ DATE: _____   SERIAL: _____ STATUS: _____

AREA: _____ OFFICE: _____   BIRTH DATE: _____ SEX: ____ RACE: _____

REPORT REQUESTED BY: _____   JPC ASSIGNED CASE: _____

1. IDENTIFYING DATA

   a. Youth's Birthplace: _____
   b. Youth's Birth Status: _____
   c. Other Names Used: _____
   d. Youth's Address at Time of Commitment: _____
   e. With Whom Living at Time of Commitment: _____
   f. Family's Relationship to Youth: _____
   g. Legal Guardian: _____
   h. Social Security Number: Youth: _____ Father: _____ Mother: _____

2. PERSONS AND AGENCIES INTERVIEWED

3. AGENCIES THAT HAVE WORKED WITH YOUTH AND FAMILY

4. DELINQUENCY HISTORY (Use only as supplemental to court report. Identify any particular chronic
   and/or peculiar problems.)

5. DEVELOPMENTAL HISTORY

   a. Early History (Use only when obvious value in detailing youth's problems.)
   b. Medical History (Detail only if pertinent.)
   c. Description of Youth (Use as parents perceive youth, attitudes, and behavior patterns.)

6. FAMILY HISTORY—Revised

   a. Marital History and Youth's Previous Living Situations
   b. Father
   c. Mother
   d. Siblings
   e. Family Income
   f. Parents' Perception of Problem
   g. Impression of Family Functioning
      (1) How parents relate to youth
      (2) Parents' concept of discipline
      (3) Evaluation of parent role (how they should/do perform as parents).
      (4) JPC's impression of performance and evaluation (identify strengths and weaknesses).
      (5) Family's financial resources, including benefits, veterans, social security, welfare, etc.,
          medical/hospital insurance. (Note: Income is reported elsewhere—Pre-Admission History).

7. COMMUNITY INFORMATION

   a. Placement possibilities, including own home. (Note attitudes, family structural compatibility,
      and other placement considerations.)
   b. Community attitudes toward placement
      (1) Neighbors
      (2) School Officials
   c. Community support services available.

8. SCHOOL AND VOCATIONAL HISTORY

   a. School Performance
      (1) Last school attended and grade completed
      (2) Level of scholastic performance
      (3) Attendance and general conduct
   b. Vocational History
      (1) Part-time or full-time jobs held
      (2) Performance evaluation

9. IMPRESSIONS AND RECOMMENDATIONS

   a. Overall evaluation by JPC
   b. Family's willingness to become involved and cooperate
   c. Problem list (JPC's perception of specific problems)
   d. Strengths and assets of family and youth which can be used in dealing with problems

FIGURE 6–1. Social history report.

Source: From Thomas G. Pinnock, *Necessary Information for Diagnosis* (Olympia, Wa.:
Bureau of Juvenile Rehabilitation, Department of Social and Health Sciences, 1976), p. 11.

Educational Background

Information about a youngster's past school experience is necessary to make realistic plans for the future. One should gather knowledge of the youngster's vocational aptitudes, work experience, and academic skills and problems. Results of educational vocational testing, transcripts, and release forms should be included.

Those charged with obtaining educational background information should request the following from the youngster's former school:

1. Transcript
2. Current grade placement
3. Classes enrolled in, credits earned, withdrawal or final grades.

Other information regarding attitude, behavior, personality characteristics, relationships with teacher and other students, accomplishments, and special interests should also be asked for.

Medical Information and History

Medical problems or illnesses will determine which resources can be used, what precautions should be observed, and what arrangements should be immediately made for treatment. A general immunization status should be included in a medical history.

1. If the juvenile has been or is under a doctor's care, the name and address of the doctor are kept on record.
2. A release form signed by the parents is required so that the medical history of the student can be obtained.
3. If the court requests any special medical report, the request should be put in the form of a letter.

Treatment Program and Previously Tried Placements

To avoid wasting time and money on already tried programs and to prevent the possibility of subjecting the child to failures, information on all treatments and placements used up to the present should be known. At the very least, one should obtain a brief synopsis of placements and reasons for termination.

Also useful is a notation of the community programs which have been tried, whether or not they have been successful.

Placement Resources

The choice of placement resources, both within and without the system, and the possibility of placing youngsters outside the system, must be known so that the staff can work toward appropriate placement. Equally important is the community's attitude toward the youth. The community includes law enforcement personnel, court staff, and schools. The community's attitude may directly affect placement planning during the youth's treatment. For example, the community may put forth a greater effort at locating potential placements for a youthful thief with a low crime profile than for a recidivist rapist. For expedient planning, therefore, any known placement possibilities should be turned up and investigated as early as possible.

What Children Respond To

A youth must be involved in planning treatment; his perceptions of what is important must be recognized in order to effect measurable gains and to bring about changes without unnecessary delay and resistance.

A probation officer's report should detail useful information regarding a youth's attitude toward commitment and his perception of problem areas. Suggestions of what goals are perceived as meaningful to the youth should also be included.

Vital Statistics

The vital statistics report or face sheet is needed for proper record keeping, for complying with federal and state regulations, and for selecting placement.

Although the above-mentioned areas apply specifically to uses within Washington's Bureau of Juvenile Rehabilitation, they can be used as guidelines for preparing an adequate diagnosis anywhere within the juvenile justice system.[5] Whatever the format, however, this information must either accompany the child to the diagnostic center or must be gathered while the child is in the center. If gathered while the child is in the facility, the information is usually obtained through the coordinated efforts of a member of the diagnostic staff and outside agencies such as schools and the courts, that are required to obtain it.

Collecting Information

Many times the child's length of stay in the diagnostic facility depends on how much information is to be collected after arrival and how difficult it is to obtain that information. It can happen that a juvenile will arrive at a diagnostic facility with almost no background information. In this event, a full diagnostic evaluation must be postponed until all the information is made available. The juvenile may be forced to unnecessarily endure a long period of detention, especially if the diagnostic facility is centralized and far from the place from which the juvenile came. This keeps him away from home, school, and needed community resources. This unnecessary stay can be shortened or eliminated if the court delays sending the juvenile to the diagnostic facility until the entire dossier of information is completed. This option works better if the diagnostic facility is located in the juvenile's home community. However, if it is located in a centralized state facility, this option becomes less realistic.

For example, the staff from the community-based diagnostic facility, in conjunction with the juvenile court, could gather the necessary information while the child remains at home or in a supervised alternative placement in the community. It would be next to impossible for the staff from a centralized facility to do this without someone taking the responsibility for the child during the information gathering process. In most states, this responsibility falls upon the centralized facility. To carry out this responsibility, the central diagnostic center must transport the child from the community and hold him in custodial detention.

If a youth is a danger to either himself or others, and if detainment is clearly indicated, such detention can better be served in the community where local resources are directly available to the diagnostic staff and to the juvenile.

Once the basic background information is gathered and available to the diagnostic staff, the person(s) in charge of making the diagnostic recommendation may wish to supplement this information with further investigation or testing of the child, depending upon the child's needs and requirements. For example, an EKG, EEG, and/or neurological examination may not be appropriate or even necessary for most juveniles but could prove to be useful for others.

Processing at the Diagnostic Facility

Typically, a diagnostic facility will follow standards in the evaluation process, especially a state central facility. In almost all cases the juvenile will arrive at the diagnostic facility with his or her legal file, which outlines the youth's previous court and police contacts.

When the youth arrives at the diagnostic center he or she is usually assigned a review chairperson who examines and evaluates the available material on the youth and makes recommendations for further study or investigation. The length of time the youth has to spend at the facility may depend upon the availability and schedule of a needed evaluative resource. In many centers, for example, the psychologist needs two or three weeks advance notice prior to doing a psychological evaluation of the youth.

After the youth's needs have been determined the review board meeting is held and a specific diagnostic classification is established for the youth and recommendations for treatment and placement are made. In most instances the juvenile courts will follow recommended treatment, and the juvenile will be processed accordingly.

If the juvenile is diagnosed in a state's central diagnostic or reception classification center, the diagnostic review board meeting will usually be attended by the group life counselor, the social worker, the teacher, the cottage supervisor, and the review board chairperson. The juvenile also has the right to have an attorney present if he or she wishes. The diagnostic facility located at the community level, however, provides a broader based participation in the review board meeting.

The diagnostic meetings provide an opportunity to report, share, and exchange as much information as possible regarding the juvenile who is the subject of the meeting. Information that is collected at these meetings becomes the basis of the recommendations for the disposition of the case.

A good diagnostic facility, a good diagnostic staff, and a well-researched recommendation *do not* assure that the juvenile will actually benefit from the diagnostic process. Unfortunately, in most jurisdictions, once the juvenile enters the institution or group home, or is returned to the community, there is absolutely no guarantee that the diagnostic recommendation will be followed.

This is a major concern to diagnosticians throughout the country. The following excerpt from a letter from North Carolina's Division of Youth Services to the authors illustrates this point.

> . . . others had campaigned constantly to close these diagnostic centers be-
> cause there were essentially *no* treatment personnel in the system's five regular
> training schools capable of implementing the recommendations contained in
> the assessments of children retained in the training school system. . . . North
> Carolina, at the time the diagnostic centers existed, failed to meet two of the
> essential criteria for diagnostics: [1] there were really no differential treatment
> modalities to which committed children could be assigned on the basis of the
> diagnostic results, and [2] related to this there were no people (or programs)
> to implement the recommendations coming out of the assessments being
> written. The diagnostic center personnel were well aware of this situation and
> if they had not used their ability at that time (it does not exist now) to divert
> significant numbers of children inappropriately placed in the system, the
> futility of writing reports to no practical purpose would have made their jobs
> untenable and created horrendously high turnover.[6]

If the philosophy underlying the diagnostic process is to have any relevance or meaning, the juvenile justice system must establish useful and effective treatment facilities to carry out diagnostic recommendations. At the very least, observing the recommendations of a treatment plan would be one way to accomplish this end. Otherwise, the time, money, manpower, and other resources of the diagnostic facilities—especially the community diagnostic centers—are wasted. If the juvenile justice system continues to give mere lip service to diagnostic evaluations and recommendations, it would be far more reasonable to simply close these centers and send the juveniles directly to youth reception or classification facilities where they can be assessed for "risk," labeled, and transferred to an institution.

Diagnostic Settings: Survey of States

In chapter 4, it was said that classification systems are implemented in one of three locations or organizational arrangements; they are:

1. Within an existing institution
2. Within a reception center
3. Within the community itself.

Diagnosis of children also takes place in each of these locations.

Before discussing diagnostic settings and the strengths and weaknesses specific to these settings, however, let's examine the diagnosis methods of various states.

Alaska   Field probation and parole officers prepare the diagnostic studies. These studies are conducted where and when possible, depending on the location of the juvenile.

Arkansas   A centralized diagnostic and reception center utilizes the I-level classification system as a treatment modality.

California   Juveniles are currently diagnosed at reception centers and clinics throughout the state. However, the system has proven to be less than ideal and is gradually being replaced by a program of community-based diagnostic facilities.

Florida   Diagnosis of juveniles is made by experienced youth counselors who attempt to place the child in a program suited to his or her needs. When children are severely maladjusted, emotionally disturbed, or retarded, outside consultation with appropriate professionals is obtained. A primary objective is to keep the child in his or her community if at all possible.

Hawaii   Juveniles at the Hawaii Youth Correctional Facility are treated according to a plan based on diagnostic studies done prior to and after commitment. The treatment plan is spearheaded by the probation officer who had the juvenile committed. It involves as many disciplines as are needed to evolve a realistic treatment plan. The plan is formulated within 30 days after commitment and all diagnostic work-ups have to be completed within that period.

Indiana   The Indiana Youth Authority was one of the first in the nation to initiate a diagnostic procedure strictly for use by the courts with jurisdiction throughout the state. Usually, diagnostic programs were conducted for the sole use by a juvenile institution. Both the Indiana Boys School and the Indiana Girls School have juvenile diagnostic units. Over 1,000 boys have been evaluated in the state's diagnostic program since it began. Of these, only 27 percent have required incarceration. For the other 73 percent, suitable alternatives have been selected.[7]

Kansas   There is no centralized diagnostic service. Provisions are made in the juvenile courts for judges to refer children to state mental hospitals and the evaluation unit of the youth center for evaluation prior to a dispositional hearing.

Kentucky   The Department of Human Resources runs short-term diagnostic treatment facilities at reception centers. A direct-staffing approach is used. Each center has a full complement of residential professional staff responding to the needs of the child. Diagnosis is accomplished by a highly trained staff in the community.

Massachusetts   The state is currently committed to community-based diagnostic services but is experiencing some transitional difficulties. It is felt that diagnosing children at one specific point (e.g., in a reception center) would be easier. However, the problem of how to make timely and accurate diagnosis on a regional basis is proving difficult to solve.

Minnesota   The Department of Corrections provides institutional services for juveniles on a regional basis. Consequently, each of the state's two training schools follow its own diagnostic process.

Missouri   At present, there is no full-fledged diagnostic service for juveniles. Recently, implementation of a regional classification approach was begun. Most classification and diagnosis in the past occurred at the reception cottages at the Training School for Girls and the Training School for Boys.

New Mexico   Diagnostic services are provided for juveniles at the New Mexico Youth Diagnostic Center in Albuquerque. This is a coeducational program which also houses delinquent girls received as regular commitments.

North Carolina   Community-based diagnostic centers have been abolished. Diagnosing children is carried out at state institutions.

Oregon   The approach to the subject of diagnosis is essentially an after-the-fact approach. All juveniles committed to state institutions are remanded by juvenile courts to the Children's Service Division for placement. On-site diagnostic services are provided after receiving the "student" from the community. Information in the form of written reports from the community and contacts with the parole counselor are used in diagnosis. The diagnostic services are for the use of staff in working directly with the "student" in the institution. It is interesting to note that in Oregon *all* boys are admitted to one institution and *all* girls to another.

South Dakota   There is no diagnostic center as such. Instead, delinquent juveniles are handled through the court systems and may be committed directly to an institution by the judge or referred to a staff member of the youth services program for review and recommendations on the most suitable placement.

Tennessee   Diagnostic evaluation is conducted at a central reception and diagnostic center. However, a Law Enforcement Assistance Administration (LEAA) grant permits the state to contract for services at the community level.

Washington   Currently, juvenile diagnosis is conducted at both the state and the community level. In 34 of the state's 39 counties, all juveniles are sent to the Cascadia Juvenile Reception-Diagnostic Center for diagnosis and treatment planning. Youth from the remaining five counties may be diagnosed in their respective communities. Washington is presently receiving a LEAA grant to evaluate the efficacy of diagnosing juveniles in the community as opposed to the state. The major question to be answered in this study is: What is the most effective manner to diagnose and plan treatment for adjudicated juveniles in terms of cost to the state, rate of recidivism, utilization of community resources, management problems to state institutions, and length of institutional stay?

Of the sixteen states mentioned here, Washington is the only one where the *physical* location of a diagnostic facility is found in the child's own community. Other states may incorporate community resources into their diagnostic evaluations and may even have regional rather than centralized diagnostic facilities, but they do not have, or are not at the point of having, actual physical placement in individual communities.

Diagnosis at Community, Region, or State: Which Is Best?

Much has been said about the right location of diagnostic facilities and in which locations the best interests of the juvenile justice system and of the youth may be served. Those who diagnose juveniles on a regular basis can offer informative, realistic, and experienced opinions on this matter. The following statements or comments on the choice of a location of diagnostic facilities will give the reader an idea of opinions on this issue.

Florida   The administrator of Florida's Department of Health and Rehabilitative Services states that the overall aim is to keep the child in the community, because "our community programs are usually cheaper to operate, appear to be as effective in terms of recidivism, and certainly promote more family involvement in the child's treatment plan."[8]

California   California's Department of Youth Authority is currently attempting to fund an assessment of an intake services program to be located in San Francisco for youthful offenders committed to the Youth Authority from that county.

Missouri   A part of the 1976 Missouri State Plan for the Division of Youth Services addresses diagnostic services needs. This plan outlines the following three approaches to diagnostics and classification.
   I. Centralized diagnostic center (Example—Washington State model). Develop functional description of youth and his/her problem with recommendations for treatment.
   II. Regional diagnostic and placement recommendations based on fairly elaborate decisions or criteria.
   III. Regional placement decisions based on relatively limited criteria such as age, offense, and academic achievement. Here, decision would be made as to the need for institutional or community placement. Further classification would occur at the institution, if [youth is] placed there. In this case, the regional "classifier" would be involved extensively in the development of community treatment efforts (for example, the Ohio model).

Kentucky   In Kentucky, the Department of Human Resources conducts diagnostic services on a regional basis, using direct staffing. Direct staffing offers several advantages to these regional centers and to the implementation of proper diagnosis for juveniles in a more localized setting.

Washington   The Diagnostic Coordinator for one of Washington's three experimental community-based diagnostic centers identified fifteen advantages and four disadvantages of the local centers.

The committee also briefly discussed other possibilities, such as using the state's mental health division to do diagnosis, rewriting the juvenile commitment to require certain items as part of the commitment process, and combining some of the above-mentioned ideas. However, as the report says: "After reviewing models used in other states, the committee found that the system currently used in Washington appears to be meeting the needs of youth better than most. It was felt that any alternative should be tried on a pilot basis with careful review, rather than making a major program revision and fiscal investment. . . ."[9]

Diagnostic methods in Florida, California, Missouri, Kentucky, and especially Washington with its wide range of alternatives, are excellent examples of virtually every plausible diagnostic placement alternative and of the advantages and disadvantages of each. The experiences of these five states offer valuable guidelines to anyone interested in the diagnosis of juvenile offenders and where that diagnosis may most appropriately be accomplished.

Overview of Diagnostic Practice

Like their counterparts in other clinical and social agencies, those involved in the diagnostic process at institutional, regional, or local community diagnostic facilities individually and collectively arrive at classification, diagnoses, and placement decisions through a complex process. This process involves the work of the staff in making realistic and knowledgeable decisions after collecting and evaluating a mass of information derived from social histories, from direct behavioral observation and interviews, and from psychological testing procedures. The ability of the staff to make these crucial decisions depends not only on the quality and quantity of information received from committees about children. It also depends on such acquired skills as accurate observation and reporting; techniques for eliciting diagnostic information in both structured and unstructured social situations; a working knowledge of social development and intervention, both of which are principles necessary for proper diagnosis and treatment planning; a working knowledge of available programs; and, very important, an ability to organize and analyze the information logically.

As mentioned earlier in this chapter, the result of the diagnostic process should be a well-thought-out and realistically workable treatment plan for the juvenile and enough relevant information about the juvenile to allow the treatment staff to do its job effectively. If a diagnostic label, such as antisocial personality, schizoid, etc., must be applied at classification centers which double for diagnostic facilities, that label should be of secondary importance to a comprehensive narrative description of the child.

After the juvenile has been diagnosed and has had a treatment plan formulated, it is up to the juvenile court to review the diagnostic material, to agree or disagree with the recommendations made, and to suggest alterations if the court wishes. If the treatment plan requires that the child be placed in an institution or training school, it is normally up to the individual state's Department of Youth Services or Youth Authority to actually commit the child.

In some states, Washington for example, all juveniles who are adjudicated as delinquents by the juvenile courts must be diagnosed at either the state facility or at one of the community diagnostic centers prior to being institutionalized.

It is interesting to note that when Washington began operation of its community-based diagnostic programs, these programs replaced the state facility in every way. However, two of the major drawbacks of diagnosing juveniles in their home community came into play. The community-based facilities found that they still had to send some of their children to the state facility for diagnosis. The reasons were (1) the child's community wanted the child out of the community because of the sensitive or repugnant nature of the crime he or she had committed or (2) the security measures at the local diagnostic centers were not adequate, and the maximum security of the state facility was required.

States considering the use of diagnostic centers at the local level may be able to overcome this second problem with proper planning and improved security measures at the local facilities. As for the people in a community not wanting the child to remain in the community, not even the best-equipped and/or staffed local diagnostic center may be able to overcome this problem. If this is the case, an alternative to the community center is mandatory.

In other states, such as Indiana, juveniles may or may not be referred for diagnostic study once they come in contact with the juvenile justice system. However, in Indiana the courts are free to take advantage of the diagnostic centers, and a referral will normally be made if the courts ask for more thorough information about the child prior to making their final decision.

The majority of states follow these guidelines: (1) all juveniles adjudicated as delinquent or incorrigible are diagnosed; (2) the diagnosis of a child is up to the discretion of the court; or (3) all juveniles actually committed to a state's Youth Services bureau, or its equivalent, after adjudication are diagnosed.

After the juvenile has been diagnosed, juvenile authorities have several alternatives open to them. This is generally true in all states. The juvenile can (1) be committed to a state's institution or training school, (2) be placed on direct parole, (3) be placed on probation, (4) enter a group home, (5) be placed in a foster or adoptive home, (6) be transferred to adult jurisdiction, (7) be required to submit to further evaluation, or (8) be discharged from the juvenile justice system altogether. If the child recidivates or violates parole, for example, that child may have to undergo complete or partial rediagnosis, in which case some of these alternatives will no longer be possible.

Summary

Before leaving this chapter, two basic questions should be addressed: (1) Is the diagnosis of an adjudicated juvenile desirable? and (2) If diagnostic evaluations are to continue, should they take place at a community or state facility?

According to knowledgeable practitioners and current trends, literature, and research, the answer to the first question is a definite *yes*. In order to formulate appropriate, accurate and applicable treatment plans for juveniles in need, the information and evaluations done during the diagnostic process are crucial.

The answer to the second question appears to be "in the community." Arguments both for and against community-based diagnosis have been examined in this chapter. But the authors feel that the arguments *for* diagnosing juveniles in the community far outweigh those *against* such a practice.

Unnecessary processing of a youth by the juvenile justice system does occur when the child is removed from his or her community and transported to a state diagnostic facility, especially if the child is returned to the community immediately after diagnosis. According to Justice Department studies, the experience of being institutionalized, even for the 30- to 60-day diagnostic period, may be harmful to the child and may even increase that child's recidivism potential.

Delinquency in the United States is a problem in which local communities need to take a greater interest. The majority of delinquents or independents who are institutionalized return to the community sooner or later. A community's involvement with its delinquent youth should not wait until this point. It should, instead, begin with the first police report, arrest, or court appearance.

The use of local resources and sources of information most familiar with the juvenile in the process of evaluation, diagnosis, and treatment planning is an excellent way for the community to begin to understand its youthful citizenry.

Preliminary data analysis of Washington's diagnostic project indicates that juveniles diagnosed in the community appear less likely to be institutionalized than juveniles diagnosed at the state's central diagnostic facility. This appears to be due, in part, to the great availability of alternate placements in the community and to the commitment of the local diagnostic staff in helping the juvenile succeed in the community setting.

By lessening the chance of institutionalization, these community-based diagnostic centers are also lessening the unnecessary involvement and processing of juveniles by the juvenile justice system. To have any success in dealing with the increasing delinquency rate and the problems that go with delinquency, the system must strive toward this goal.

REVIEW QUESTIONS

1. Define *diagnosis*. Discuss its importance within the juvenile justice system.

2. What information is necessary in order to diagnose a juvenile?

3. What should the results of a good diagnostic evaluation include? Why?

4. Discuss the advantages and disadvantages of diagnosing a juvenile in (1) the community, (2) a regional center, and (3) in a central state institution or facility.

5. If you were a diagnostician at the local level, how would you make sure that the recommended treatment plan for a particular youth was given fair and proper consideration by the treatment facility?

NOTES

1. Helen Harris Perlman, "Social Casework: The Problem-Solving Approach," *Encyclopedia of Social Work,* 16th ed., vol. 2 (New York: National Association of Social Workers, 1971), p. 1213.

2. Florence Hollis, "Social Casework: The Psychosocial Approach," *Encyclopedia of Social Work,* 16th ed., vol. 2 (New York: National Association of Social Workers, 1971), p. 1217.

3. Ruth E. Smalley, "Social Casework: The Functional Approach," *Encyclopedia of Social Work,* 16th ed., vol. 2 (New York: National Association of Social Workers, 1971), pp. 1195–1196.

4. Thomas G. Pinnock, *Necessary Information for Diagnosis* (Olympia: Bureau of Juvenile Rehabilitation, Department of Social and Health Services, 1976), pp. 1–19.

5. Thomas G. Pinnock, *Necessary Information for Diagnosis*, pp. 1–19.

6. Letter from Dale T. Johnson, Assistant Director, Research and Development, State of North Carolina, Department of Human Resources, Division of Youth Services (Raleigh: September 1, 1976), to Marshall S. Gordon.

7. Peggy A. Brown, *Juvenile Diagnostic Unit, Indiana Boys' School, Finding Alternatives* (Indianapolis: Indiana Department of Correction, Juvenile Diagnostic Unit, 1976), p. 13.

8. Letter from James T. Clark, Administrator, State of Florida, Department of Health and Rehabilitative Services, to Marshall S. Gordon, September 3, 1976.

9. Bureau of Juvenile Rehabilitation, Committee on Intake, Diagnosis, and Placement, *A Report: Department of Social and Health Services* (Olympia: January, 1976), pp. 12–23.

PART III

The System

7 Delinquents and the Police

When a child is handled firmly by the police, but always
kindly and courteously, regardless of his uncouth manner,
such practice cannot fail to command respect in the long run.

SHERWOOD NOWMAN

What do you think of when you hear the word *police*? The friendly man or
woman who stands on the corner in your neighborhood directing traffic? The
patrol officer who you see walking a beat or riding around town in two-tone
cars? Most of us have been brought up to either believe in or to accept this
image of the police. Far too often, however, the police are shown in a
different light, one closer to an abusive reform-school guard than the
friendly person in the blue uniform.

In this country, people are hired, appointed, or elected to wear uniforms,
carry badges and guns, and be, as Grover Cleveland put it, "servants of the
people to execute the laws which *people* have made." These public servants
include city police, sheriffs, state patrol officers, warehouse guards, institutional guards, and truant officers. Each and every one of these control and
law enforcement agents could and often does have contact with children.
One might ask if that contact will be in the role of friendly helper or abusive
bully.

Once our police forces have been given their powers, many citizens turn
their backs and assume that as long as they are not personally being
molested, the police are doing a fine job. Having hired keepers, guards, and
controllers for the poor, the deviant, and the misguided, the attitude is then
"business as usual." But a society's responsibilities run deeper than this.
Our own society has had a hand in producing the problem groups that exist
and it should be aware of the controls being used to handle those groups.
Americans generally react to police matters only when those matters infringe
upon their personal rights. Otherwise, their silence tends to condone actions
of the police against others less able to react. By giving approval to what

happens to children at the hands of the police, the police are led to believe that they are doing a good job. Only when there is reaction to the mistreatment and abuse of others will things change.

Emergence and Growth of Police Departments

Although the United States was settled by people of many European countries, England and English common law have had the most influence on the American system.

The night watch was the prevalent form of policing in the cities of the new colonies. Agricultural areas, especially in the South, were policed by an early form of the present-day sheriff who kept the peace. The night watch, consisting of volunteers, soon became a very distasteful duty. Many Americans shunned this obligation (just as some of their descendants shun jury duty today) because they were too busy or too unconcerned. Those who could afford it hired "shiftless folk" to stand watch for them. Under the night watch system, which was the only form of law enforcement in many American towns until the early 1800s, crime was rampant.

Clearly, untrained and unqualified "police" could not do the job. Many people complained loudly that these hit-and-miss police practices were bringing about social chaos and disorder. After nearly 30 years of discussing reform, Philadelphia became the first city to provide a fully paid and trained, round-the-clock police force. Following Philadelphia's example, many other cities set up their own police forces.

Modern policing in the United States began in 1844 when the New York state legislature authorized funds for day-and-night police forces throughout the state and empowered communities to organize police departments. In 1845 the New York City police forces were consolidated, the old night watch was abolished, and the day-and-night shifts were organized. Chicago followed suit in 1851, New Orleans and Cincinnati in 1852, Baltimore and Newark in 1857, and Providence in 1864. By the 1870s most of the nation's major cities had full-time police departments. At the turn of the century few American cities were without full-time police forces.[1]

Corruption and political interference are not unique to today's police force. In the nineteenth century, salaries for officers were extremely low, and no long lines formed at the recruiting office. Those few who did show up were needed so badly that the recruiting officer often looked the other way in judging their qualifications. "The aim of the police department was merely to keep a city superficially clean and to keep everything quiet that was likely to arouse public ire."[2]

Police forces, although formally recognized and organized, were still ineffectual in crime control. The "spoils system," the brainchild of Andrew Jackson, was one of the primary reasons. Rotation in office enjoyed so much popular favor that police posts of both high and low degree were constantly changing hands, with political fixers determining the price and conditions of each change. The whole question of police corruption simply churned about in the public mind and eventually became identified with the corruption and degradation of city politics and local governments in the period.[3]

The Pendleton Act, which established the Civil Service system in the federal government, was passed in 1883. With it came the end of the ''spoils system,'' and the consequent stability in local government eased many of the problems of the burgeoning police systems.

Juvenile Police and "The Mother Image"

Until the late 1800s and the early 1900s, juveniles were subject to the same laws and punishments and the same treatment by the police as adults. There were no juvenile courts or juvenile laws to regulate the treatment and protection of children. Early courts and correctional systems followed English common law in cases involving juveniles. Children under seven years of age were held to be unaccountable for their acts. Children between 8 and 14, if able to distinguish between right and wrong and understand the consequences of their deeds, were subject to the same laws as adults. Those 14 years and over were considered to be fully accountable for their acts. Among the first to take a stand for differential handling and treatment of juveniles by the police were groups of women. As a result, the early concept of the juvenile officer was heavily endowed with ''the mother image.''

Until the problems of the slums began to affect the lives of the ''refined'' citizenry, not much thought was expended on what should happen to youths in trouble. At the turn of the century, people started urging the police to protect them from delinquents and youthful beggars. The police at that time, however, were only guardians of the peace, not social workers. The concept of special juvenile police units—to patrol neighborhoods and help stop delinquency before it started—had not been accepted, and the somewhat brutal police methods of the time were applied to youths as well.

Protests favoring differential treatment of juveniles caught the public fancy, creating a general clamor for change throughout the nation. As a result of the efforts of the Society for the Prevention of Cruelty to Children (comprised mostly of women), in 1877 the New York state legislature passed the first law in this country which dealt specifically with police treatment of juveniles.[4] It read in part:

> Any child under restraint or conviction, actually or apparently under the age of 16 years, shall not be placed in any prison or place of confinement, or in any courtroom or in any vehicle for transportation in company with adults charged or convicted of crime except in the presence of proper officials.[5]

Additional laws to protect and separate juveniles from adult criminals were passed in the ensuing years. One of the most important, and the cornerstone of the present system, was an 1899 act designed ''to regulate the treatment and control of dependent, neglected, and delinquent children'' which was signed into law in Illinois in April, 1899. This was the first act in the United States that included a definition of juvenile delinquency: ''Any child under the age of 16 who violates any law of this state or any city or village ordinance'' was held to be a juvenile delinquent. The law was designed to avoid treating the child as a *criminal*, placing emphasis on rehabilitation of juvenile offenders rather than on punishment.[6]

With the passage of the Illinois act a policing authority was introduced whose specific duty was to work with delinquents. This authority was the juvenile probation officer, an official position even today. Many modern metropolitan police departments have special units to deal with juveniles exclusively; other police forces cooperate with county probation workers. In most smaller communities the same police who shoot it out with major criminals also investigate vandalism by gangs of roving youths.

If the past can teach something about the problems of juvenile delinquency, then these lessons should be disseminated and heeded. But past events and standards should not hinder progress in trying to make today's juvenile justice system work. As Richard Kobetz put it, ''The role of the juvenile officer in police community relations work will become more important in the 1970s because the only way to ever eliminate juvenile delinquency is to prevent it in the first place. But juvenile delinquency is a problem so great in magnitude that the United States has been unable to eradicate it since the nation's first police constable faced a colonial juvenile delinquent in Boston in 1636.''[7]

Police: The First Contact with the System

The juvenile's first contact with police is, in the authors' estimation, the most important contact he or she may ever have with the juvenile justice system.

The way the youth is treated by the police will have a decided influence on that youth's impression of both the juvenile and adult legal system. In fact, as noted by Allen and Simonsen, ''a juvenile's initial contact with the law is known to affect the likelihood of recidivism.''[8] It is therefore to the benefit of the youth, and to the benefit of the juvenile justice pocketbook, if this initial contact is based on solid training, planning, and staffing.

The police, in their contacts with juveniles, often determine whether or not these youths will become further involved with the juvenile justice system. In many cases, police make what is referred to as ''on-the-spot adjustments.'' These adjustments may take the form of a warning to the youth, a ride home in the police cruiser, or possibly a meeting with parents or guardians. Some readers of this text may have experienced ''on-the-spot adjustments'' first hand when growing up. Consider for a moment whether your life would have been different had the police decided to refer the case to court for an adjudicatory hearing.[9] Such police discretion is a valuable tool when used properly, but it is also open to abuse.

The Role of the Police

Generally, the first role of the police in dealing with the young is that of detection, investigation, and arrest. Each year police departments throughout the country receive thousands upon thousands of complaints from citizens about juveniles. These complaints range from broken windows to vandalism and gang brutality to neglected or abused children. How the police handle complaints or crime reports depends on the individual department and the individual officer.

Detection

Detection of a crime or response to a complaint will normally lead to an investigation by police and may lead to an arrest. Detection is often left to persons or agencies outside the police department. Even today, only the larger or more sophisticated forces have juvenile officers on the streets. When police are assigned to a specific neighborhood and know that neighborhood, its people, its problems, and its resources, they become effective forces in the detection and deterrence of delinquency or abuse. Unfortunately, the police are usually used in the role of *reactors* to a complaint or crime, instead of *preventors* of crime.

Once the police are aware that a delinquent act has been committed, they find themselves in the role of investigators. In *Law Enforcement and the Youthful Offender: Juvenile Procedures,* the author states that, ''The interview is probably the most important means the police officer has for carrying out his investigation.''[10]

Interviewing

During the investigation of a delinquent act the suspects, if any, may be held in detention, released to parents, and so forth. It is therefore extremely important that the police investigate the act thoroughly so that the youth may not be falsely labeled as a delinquent.

In the course of interviewing the suspect, witnesses, and other parties who are involved, the police face a crucial test of their effectiveness in the community. Often they come into a situation already labeled as ''pigs'' and possibly distrusted by all concerned. This attitude is especially true in traditionally high-crime and low-income areas.

The officer has to learn as much about the alleged offense or abuse as possible in the shortest time possible. Interviewing is more art than science and must be learned. The officer must be flexible; for example, interviewing a 16-year-old girl picked up countless times for prostitution and wanted on a drug charge will not be and should not be the same as interviewing a 10-year-old who got caught stealing pop bottles.

In questioning suspects in criminal cases, several restrictions have been placed on the police. Whether these restrictions provide safeguards against "overzealousness," as charged by some critics, or whether they are well-meaning but unrealistic erosion of necessary police authority is questionable. Nonetheless, the practical result is that the effectiveness of interrogations as a police technique is seriously curtailed in many cases, especially with suspects who are in fact guilty. These few suspects have learned to rely upon these restrictions for protection from punishment, knowing full well that if they cannot be interviewed adequately, this manner of proving guilt is denied the police. On the other hand, the innocent are denied opportunity to prove their innocence without being formally charged. The people and not the police are the ultimate victims of these restrictions. The police do not seek the privilege of denying suspects their rights, but they do feel that some balance between rights and cooperative responsibilities must be achieved in the public interest.[11]

If the interview is successful, the police will normally have sufficient proof of a suspect's guilt or innocence. If there was no suspect at the onset of the investigation, interviews often provide one.

While interviewing may be the most important cog in the investigatory wheel, it is not always feasible or successful. Many delinquent acts have no witnesses at all, or at least none that will cooperate. In such cases investigatory techniques (that is, piecing together clues, fingerprints, and so forth) must come into play.

Questioning and Arresting

Assuming that the investigation does turn up a suspect, the next step is confrontation and/or arrest. Here, too, the conduct of the police weighs heavily on the attitudes of the youth, his or her peer group, and the community. Citizen cooperation is extremely important to the police in all their dealings with the young. Many times the police, with citizen consent, are able to waive legal guidelines, such as search warrants. Citizen cooperation saves time and money and should be encouraged. As adults, these citizens have the right to waive legal proceeding because they are considered to be mature persons and to understand what they are doing.

Questioning and arresting juveniles presents special problems to the police. In *Haley* v. *Ohio*, the courts have stated, in considering whether a juvenile's statements are voluntary, that the length of questioning, the child's age, the time of day or night of questioning, whether the child was fed and allowed to rest, whether the child was allowed the counsel of parents or an attorney, and the overall police attitude toward the child's rights are all extremely important factors.[12]

One of the best tests of a child's rights is whether the child has been treated with what Kenney and Pursuit call *fundamental fairness*.[13] Fundamental fairness means "that police officers must decide in each case whether a child is sufficiently mature and sophisticated to really know what he is doing when he gives consent to be taken to the police station to be questioned, or to be searched without being taken into custody or arrested on the basis of probable cause. Factors to be considered by the police in making this decision in addition to the age of the child are his apparent intelligence and all around maturity, his experience or lack of experience in such situations involving the police, the seriousness of the violation. . . , and the extent of the continuing danger to society in the situation. Even when police decide that the child is mature enough to make this decision for himself, every effort should be made to notify his parents.[14]

The concept of fundamental fairness varies in significance and definition according to different jurisdictions. This being the case, the wise police administrator will seek the counsel of legal advisors on what the law is and how it is interpreted in the local jurisdiction before a child is questioned, searched, or arrested.[15]

In *Miranda* v. *Arizona* (384 U.S. 436), the court ruled that a suspect must be advised of his or her rights (for example, the right to remain silent) when in any way deprived of freedom of movement. California, in 1967, incorporated these requirements into its juvenile rules for arresting youths. Several other states have followed suit since then.

However, even the *Miranda* ruling does not guarantee that once read his or her rights, a juvenile knows what they mean. Since many authorities consider a child's problem to be a family problem, one of the best safeguards of a child's rights is to have the parents present at all police proceedings.

Whether or not a child is arrested or taken into custody, another role of the police is brought into play—that of judge, jury, and executioner. As pointed out earlier, many youthful offenders never enter the juvenile justice system. They are released, reprimanded, or punished before the court ever enters into their lives. The old story of a child picked up in a rich neighborhood, driven home to mom and dad, and given a stern warning, while the youth in the inner city is run in and spends the weekend in detention, is not at all unrealistic. Different police practices in different neighborhoods are undeniable and often necessary. Large inner-city police forces often do not have the manpower to deal with youths in any other way than to arrest them and get them off the streets. In smaller or well-to-do communities where crime rates are lower, the police are often more understanding and lenient toward disruptive or delinquent youths. Thus, there is developing need for guidelines for police dispositions.

Guidelines for Police Disposition: The Power of Discretion

In any situation the course of action the police may choose may vary considerably among departments and among individual officers. The course of action is governed to some extent by departmental practice, either explicitly enunciated or tacitly understood. Such policies are difficult to evolve; indeed, in many instances policies could not be specific enough to be helpful without being too rigid to accommodate the vast variety of street situations. Nevertheless, it is important that, wherever possible, guidelines be formulated for the police in their dealings with juveniles. Without specific, standardized, and universal guidelines, it is extremely difficult for both the police and the citizenry to know if an adequate job is being done. What may be more reasonable and practical, and of course more helpful, is that practices be at least standard within each precinct or department.

Guidelines that are formulated must meet the local needs and must be flexible enough to allow for individual treatment of each case. The fact that, in most cases, all laws relating to juveniles are either state or federal laws and that local police departments are therefore bound to guidelines made by the state legislature or the federal courts, does not necessarily mean that any nice, neat, clear guidelines actually exist. For this very reason, police departments have or should develop their own practices for dealing with juveniles.

The International Association of Chiefs of Police and the IACP Professional Standards Division have compiled a list of 30 police guides for police use with juveniles. These guides represent a coordinated effort by an organization which deals with the problem on a daily basis.

The IACP guidelines are a logical and honest approach to operational needs parameters. However, the authors feel that an additional major guideline is needed; it is the disposition of youth. Richard Tuthill, the first judge to sit in the Chicago Juvenile Court (1899), stated in a meeting with his new juvenile probation officers that "kindness and love for children must be used in this work if we would receive the benefits which we should from this court. The burden will rest mainly upon you who will gather the cases for the court . . . the bringing of the child before the court should be only as a last resort."[16]

Judge Tuthill's words are still appropriate today. To avoid using the "last resort" of bringing a child before the court, the police officer has several available dispositions. They range from a verbal reprimand to voluntary police supervision. Our recommended guidelines follow:

Disposition of Youth

- Police should exercise, whenever practical, every alternative at their disposal before applying for a petition to the court. To do this they must know agencies other than the court to which they can and should make referrals.

- If on-the-spot adjustments are used, they should be used equally, regardless of the juvenile's skin color or which part of town he or she comes from or who the parents are.

- While diversion from formal court procedures is desired, police should not withhold evidence or other relevant facts concerning a case from the courts.

- Police should be trained and educated so as to be better able to judge the juveniles they are confronting. They need to be able to evaluate the effect of their disposition decisions. A sad-eyed lad running a long "con" story may require something stronger than a warning, while a youth who ran away from home because his father beat him continuously may not benefit from being driven back to the source of his problem.

- Police should make periodic checks on those they have diverted. Continuous warnings do the youth no more good than do continuous harassment and arrest. The power of helpful discretion must be brought to bear.

These guidelines are presented to give the reader an idea of the specific areas that have to be considered. For every police administrator, flexibility in applying guidelines and policies used by the police will be needed in dealing with juveniles in their specific environment.

Police and the Neglected or Abused Child

Thus far, this discussion has talked mainly of police and delinquent youths. However, as pointed out in chapter 5, there are several types of children who come under the purview of the police.

Childhood is a reasonably happy and secure time for most children; they have parents or relatives who provide for them, protect them, and give them some love. But there are many children whose childhood has been lost or scarred by parents who fail them altogether or who inadequately meet their basic needs. These children are called neglected. They come from all kinds of homes and income strata. Rich children can be as easily neglected as those who are poor.

Police must make sure that neglect or abuse does exist when handling a case of this nature. Their methods of investigation and interview should be much the same as when responding to delinquency cases. An additional tool useful to police is the photograph; it will help substantiate the condition of the child or his home at the time contact is made.

In dependent neglect cases it is usually persons other than the parents who make the complaint. As a result, it can be difficult for the police to gain the cooperation of the parents in their investigation. The investigating officer must be certain to find out if the reported neglect or abuse is an isolated incident or only one event in a history of such occurrences.

The officer should make an immediate assessment of the situation and determine if action to protect the child must be taken. Many answers to complaints from interested parties, school teachers, social workers, and so forth, can be handled with a warning or reprimand to the parents. The officer often simply informs the parents that any further complaints regarding the treatment of their children may result in a court appearance.

Based on the officer's judgment, recommending professional counseling for the family may be advisable. Here, the officer's knowledge of community resources is vital. Many cases of abuse or neglect are a parent's cry for help. With their cooperation and a referral to the appropriate source, the child may be saved the agony of further moral, mental, emotional, or physical punishment at the parents' hands.

Today, there is an alarming increase in the rate of parental abuse and/or neglect of children in this country. The causes, effects, and treatment of neglect cannot possibly be examined thoroughly in this chapter because these subjects would require too much space. However, the reader can get some idea of where the police fit into such cases.

Factors in Police Action

The following are factors which either alone or in combination require immediate police action:

1. Evidence of the "battered child syndrome" and fear of recurring abuse by parents.
2. Lack of appropriate adult supervision, discipline, and/or guidance.
3. Lack of adequate physical care and/or protection from potentially harmful things or events.
4. A parent's sexual exploitation of children, whether incestuous or for money, i.e., child pornography.
5. Failure to provide for the child's basic needs of food, clothing, and shelter appropriate to the climate in which the child lives.

Stories and accounts of abuse of children at the hands of their parents or others are numerous. Police departments, courts, and social agencies have records and photographs on file that would turn anyone's stomach. The ways in which children are abused stand as an indictment of the inventiveness of mankind, ranging from boiling an infant alive on the stove to locking a six-year-old in a box for several years.

Alternatives in Police Action

Assuming that the situation warrants punishment of the parents or removal of the child from the home, what are the alternatives available to the police?

Just as laws dealing with delinquency vary from state to state, so, too, do the laws dealing with parental abuse and neglect. "Mental incapacity of a parent, together with cruelty, immorality, or depravity, are specific reasons for the courts to consider parents unfit to care for their children.''[17] In addition, children who are left in someone's care by their parents without being visited by them or without payment for their support for a year may be considered abandoned children and therefore in need of the state's protection.

These general legal guidelines apply in most states and juvenile court systems. However, they do not even begin to cover the problem. Eldefonso suggests that "With all variations in legal provisions relating to neglect, agencies are in general agreement that the most effective laws place emphasis on the responsibility of the community to act in behalf of the children rather than against the parents.''[18]

Police are normally the ones who will take the child from his or her home. They have the legal responsibility and authority to place an abused or neglected child in protective custody. There are some social agencies which also have this legal power; they are guided by the same laws as are the police.

Whenever possible the police should consult with community social agencies when custody is required. Many communities have "shelters for kids," foster homes, and group homes. All too often, however, a neglected child will spend days or even months in a county jail cell. This latter situation stems from inadequate planning and coordination of community resources on the part of the community leaders.

Unknown to many parents is the fact that they may be financially liable for all or part of the costs incurred for housing, feeding, and clothing their children while in protective custody. In the state of Washington, parents are liable in cases involving both delinquent and dependent neglected children, but the amount paid is normally based on the parent's ability to pay.

The question of the police role in the handling of neglected or abused children is an old and complex one. The police and the child are usually part of the same community (except in the cases of runaways) and the problems of kids in need of help are the problems of the community. Consequently, only when everyone becomes aware of this community problem and understands its nature will the thousands of abused and battered kids have a hope of being heard and helped. The police are the important and crucial first step in this process. Given the money, the resources, and the training, they can become, as an extension of those they serve in the communities, a more effective force.

Police and Delinquents

While not every adult criminal started out as a juvenile delinquent, statistics show that by the time most juveniles, delinquent and nondelinquent alike, are 16 years old, a large percentage have had some contact with the police. One of the best ways to keep juveniles from becoming statistics in the FBI Crime Index is to get them before they become adults. During the past few decades, police departments have begun to place special emphasis on working with young people. More and more police services for juveniles, including special police units, are being established. It has been alleged that the nuclear family unit in America is breaking down and that this breakdown is a source of delinquency. To fill the parental void, police often assume a more central role in containing juvenile acting-out behavior (i.e., rebellious-ness, deviancy, and other actions or attitudes which make juveniles difficult to handle) and delinquent behavior. Whether they like it or not, the police are becoming painfully aware that juvenile delinquency is a social condition which neither they nor this country can longer afford. Simple use of investigation and arrest with a lack of concern for the *why* of delinquent acts is plainly not enough. The police are also finding themselves used as a primary *treatment* tool. Present police tactics seem to be losing out to delinquency. The police are being forced to alter their methods of investiga-tion, detainment, and arrest to fit the problems of the modern delinquent. Generally, the police gather facts regarding persons, things, and places in every criminal case they handle. Traditionally, "the techniques for such processes are not amenable to variations according to the age of the suspect; therefore, in the area of routine crime investigation, few if any differences are noted between cases involving adult suspects and those involving youths."[19] These differences are beginning to exist in many police depart-ments.

One area requiring change is the methods used in housing facilities designed for juvenile delinquents. Delinquents should be separated from PINS (persons in need of supervision) and from MINS (minors in need of supervision). The police, through the use of their discretionary powers, are in a good position to help in this effort. Keeping the runaways from the influence of the teenage thief would benefit them in the long run. To impose this separation, the police must acknowledge that there is a difference between delinquents on one hand and PINS and MINS on the other. To this end, police attitudes and training are more and more being molded.

Specialized knowledge in handling delinquency cases brings about un-wanted and unneeded problems, however. For example, those personnel with no special knowledge in handling delinquency cases will pass along all responsibilities for these cases to the so-called diaper squad. Thus, they gain no experience in this field. Furthermore, better-than-average patrol officers are frequently assigned to the delinquency squad, leaving the patrol division short of needed talent and ability. While specialization has its place, all members of a police force should be trained in handling juveniles, de-linquent or otherwise.

Community relationships and planning are essential parts of the daily routine of policing. It has already been noted that *knowledge* of community resources can be a police officer's best friend. The *wisdom* of when and how to use these resources can be another. Police come in contact with schools, hospitals, welfare agencies, and athletic programs daily. In these daily contacts lie the seeds for effective cooperation and teamwork.

Police charged with maintaining law and order often regard a young vandal and his behavior from the perspective of the offense (symptom) and the letter of the law. Workers in social agencies do not use the same perspective. From these divergent viewpoints, much community friction and misunderstanding exists, where the so-called do-gooders on one side and the so-called "pigs" on the other often clash. Police are not social workers, nor are they meant to be. It is essential, therefore, that the police have access to social agencies when their judgment tells them they should. This point is emphasized because the police cannot rely on social service agencies to do their jobs for them. In *Dynamics of Delinquency*, William C. Kuasaceus explains: "The first or basic step in a community program of prevention and control of juvenile delinquency is not to procure psychiatric, psychological, recreational, or casework services; the basic and initial step is to bring the police services up to their full potential."[20]

While use of community resources is a current and useful trend, the police should develop capabilities of their own. This may seem contradictory, and to some extent it is. The police must develop, collectively, an open and trained mind in their dealings with juveniles. Once they do, they should also be immune from unwarranted interference in performing their duties.

Police Operations

Delinquent children behave differently from their adult counterparts. Therefore, they must receive different handling and treatment. Different handling and treatment does not mean, however, that well-tested, routine police procedures do not apply to operations involving juveniles; they do. Good sound police work is good sound police work whether investigating juvenile vandalism or Mafia killings.

Police operations are based on and have evolved from a few basic concepts pertaining to the problem of crime, whether adult or delinquent. According to Kobetz, they are:

1. In human society, the unrestrained expression of selfish impulses cannot be permitted and *everyone* must learn to accept restrictions for the good of all.
2. In all civilized societies, man has found it necessary to explicitly define certain of these restrictions in a formal code known as the law and to establish machinery for its implementation.
3. In our democratic society it is acknowledged that *everyone* is entitled to equal opportunity and to equal protection under the law.
4. National policy decrees that neither race, color, national origin, sex, nor religion shall in any way modify or limit one's rights to the enjoyment of these blessings.

5. No person and no group may be permitted to disregard the law, for to do so threatens the foundation of the freedoms of all.

6. The law specifies not only certain things people may or may not do, but also specifies many requirements and restrictions relative to its enforcement—requirements and restrictions which apply to the police as well.

7. When violations occur, the job of the police requires that action be taken within the limits imposed by the law.

8. Under some circumstances, police power may be employed in the interest of preserving public order and safety and to prevent unwarranted interference with the liberties of others even though to do so results in curtailing the activities of some.

9. We hold, as a matter of policy in relation to offenders, that the police are not in the punishing business any more than they are in the rehabilitating business. The police job is to prevent crime and to detect and apprehend offenders.

10. The treatment of offenders is not a function of the police.[21]

The degree to which police adhere to basic concepts depends primarily upon the society which gives the police their powers. Normally parents or other appropriate adults teach children principles of right and wrong which are to govern their behavior, and restrictions on this behavior are codified into laws which are enforced by the police. When any person acts in violation of these restrictions, the person and society are at odds.

There are always individuals who feel they are above the law or that certain laws are unjust and may be disobeyed. How many people really drive 55 mph on the freeways and are perfectly honest on their income tax returns? Some groups of young people seem to feel that the position of their parents in the community or the fact that they are "just kids" allows them to violate the law with comparative impunity. Social pressures to control such groups have pushed police into the realm of social work, but the treatment of offenders is *not* a proper function of police operations.

Areas of Controversy and Disagreement in Police Operations

Records, photographs, files, and fingerprints are accepted as facts of life when dealing with adult criminals. These same practices, when applied to juveniles, often cause controversy and heated discussion. Adequate records for juvenile cases must be maintained by police. Records are helpful in defining delinquency, in evaluating delinquency prevention and treatment programs, and in indicating reasons why certain neighborhoods have high or low juvenile crime rates. They also provide the police, the courts, and institutions with accurate background and demographic information for each juvenile.

Records

Records should be brief, accurate, and to the point. Long narratives, reflecting opinions about the child or family situation, should be kept out of primary records and included only in special reports. Care should be taken to protect the identity of the child from those who do not officially have to know it.

Expunging or destroying a juvenile's police record once he or she has been cleared of a complaint or has reached adulthood is a controversial issue. On the one hand, some people believe that the juvenile's future employers, creditors, and so forth, have a right to know about his or her past; on the other, a growing number of people feel that a person's adult life should not be prejudged by acts committed as a juvenile. For example, many job applications today ask the applicant to list any arrests (other than traffic violations) *excluding* those prior to age 18.

Fingerprinting and Photographing

Fingerprinting and photographing juveniles is an additional area for controversy. While some states have laws forbidding such practice, except by order of the juvenile court, this practice is more usually determined by police policy. Some departments routinely fingerprint all children taken into custody, while photographing is less widespread.

Proponents of fingerprinting and photographing argue that if the police are going to keep records on juveniles that they may as well use the most accurate known methods of identification. Opponents contend that these practices publicly associate kids with criminal procedures and that the juvenile should not be so labeled and stigmatized.

Professionals in the field believe that when fingerprinting must be used, the same safeguards applied to other forms of recordkeeping should apply: (1) to lessen the chance of associating kids with criminals, their use should be limited to occasions where law or the courts sanction their use and where no other form of evidence is available; (2) juvenile fingerprints should not be recorded in the criminal section of any fingerprint registry; and (3) juvenile fingerprints should be destroyed after their use has been served.

These guidelines also apply to the use of photographs. This practice should be utilized only when a youth is a suspect in the commission of a serious crime such as rape or murder, when he or she has a long juvenile record of delinquency, and when it can be assumed that this pattern of crime will continue. In a case where a runaway refuses to reveal his or her identity to the police, it may be necessary to take and circulate pictures.

Publicity

Another area of controversy is the release of a juvenile's name to the press in relation to a delinquent or criminal act. Common practice today is to withhold names except in the case of serious or spectacular crimes. Minor delinquency act, dependency cases, and runaways are usually not reported by news media.

The police do not make a practice of contacting the press to gain publicity either for their charges or themselves. It is usually the other way around, but news often leaks to the media from sources other than the police. The decision to release this information to the public is then out of the hands of the police. Responsible journalism, coupled with legal guidelines defining the relationship between the press and the police, will alleviate misunderstandings that might exist between these two groups.

Police and the Law

Police departments must deal with crime and criminals according to the laws of the land. The *Miranda* v. *Arizona* case (384 U.S. 436), for example, has led to the release of many guilty persons because the police failed to follow one of these laws—the law which guarantees a suspect his or her constitutional rights.

Police and the *Parens Patriae* Doctrine

Prior to the U.S. Supreme Court ruling in *Kent* v. *U.S.* (see below) in 1967, both the court system and the police followed the doctrine of *parens patriae* (parents for the state). The courts and police considered taking a juvenile into custody, for example, as exercising its right to custody of the child in the same way that a good parent would claim custody of one of its own children.

Many things which adults can do lawfully, a minor may not do lawfully, at least not without the intervention of the police and courts. *Parens patriae* also excluded juveniles from the protection of the Constitution because the states were supposedly acting in a protective, nonadversary capacity. As a consequence, juvenile court proceedings were civil in nature and noncriminal. The child could claim only the right to ''fair treatment.''

Within the juvenile court system across the United States, there were great differences in the extent of punishment or treatment afforded to juveniles. For example, judges who heard juvenile cases usually dispensed with a jury trial, right to counsel, or other rights guaranteed to adults. While the courts claimed to be acting as *parens patriae*, police treatment of a juvenile offender often fell far short of this concept. The juvenile suspected of committing a criminal act often received the same treatment given an adult counterpart.

Juveniles were, therefore, being treated as children in need of a parent's protection by the court and denied constitutional rights, while at the same time they were treated by police as adults except that adults were at least assured that their constitutional rights were being protected.

Kent v. *U.S.* was the first major ruling to change this double standard for the treatment of juveniles. Essentially, the Supreme Court ruled that a juvenile is entitled to representation by counsel, a hearing, access by counsel to all reports considered by the court in hearing a child's case, and a statement of reasons for the court's decision.

In *In re Gault* (1968), the Court went a step further than the *Kent* decision. It required that the juvenile have the right to counsel (as in *Kent*), but it also provided for advance notice of the adjudication hearing, that a juvenile has the right to confront and to cross examine a prosecution witness, and that he has the right to be protected from self-incrimination.

Miranda v. *Arizona* provides that every agent of law enforcement, before he or she questions any suspect in custody or any person who is in any way being deprived of his freedom of movement and action, must first advise that person of his or her constitutional rights exactly as follows: (1) You have the right to remain silent. (2) If you choose not to remain silent, anything you say or write can and will be used as evidence against you in court. (3) You have a right to consult with a lawyer present with you during any questioning. (4) You not only have a right to consult with a lawyer before any questioning, but if you lack the financial ability to retain a lawyer, a lawyer will be appointed to represent you before any questioning and you may have the appointed lawyer present with you during any questioning.

The Supreme Court has not yet considered the applicability of *Miranda* to juvenile cases, however. Other courts which have considered the issue have determined that these requirements do apply to juveniles,[21] and California has statutorily codified the *Miranda* requirements for juveniles.[22] Just how many young, nervous juvenile offenders are capable of understanding the recitation of these rights is unknown. Nevertheless, if police must categorically advise a juvenile of his or her rights, and if these rights are subsequently violated, the juvenile may become as immune to prosecution as have hundreds of adults since the *Miranda* decision was handed down in 1966.

Until the Uniform Juvenile Court Act of 1968, a child could be taken into custody by police in a situation where an adult would have been exempted by the Fourth Amendment. The Uniform Juvenile Court Act set some limits in nondiscriminatory home removals of children by police. It provides for the taking of a child into custody only if there are reasonable grounds to believe that the child is suffering from illness or injury or is in immediate danger from his or her environment and that the removal is therefore necessary.

Important federal legislation has made it possible for police departments to expand their staff and services in the area of delinquency and delinquency prevention. Two of these laws are the Juvenile Delinquency Prevention and Control Act of 1968 (updated by the Juvenile Justice and Delinquency Prevention Act of 1974) and the Omnibus Crime Control and Safe Streets Act of 1968. Under the Juvenile Delinquency Prevention and Control Act, the states must submit comprehensive plans in order to be eligible for funds to implement delinquency prevention and rehabilitation programs. The Safe Street Act provides that participating states must develop comprehensive law enforcement improvement plans and that juvenile delinquency planning is a mandatory component.

Both of these acts promise financial support to state and local governments and public agencies if these government units and agencies can develop plans which meet federal guidelines. Since these acts became law, most states have received monies for a great many programs, monies which most generally are made available through LEAA (Law Enforcement Assistance Administration).

From *parens patriae* to *In re Gault*, the police have had to change their methods and tactics in handling both delinquents and dependent juveniles. With the passage of time, the gap between police and court handling of juvenile criminals or adult criminals is narrowing. In Washington, there is even talk of lowering the age of criminal responsibility from 16–18 to 12–14 for certain categories of crime.

"By sheer volume, juveniles are now and undoubtedly will continue to be a serious consideration for all police departments. One of the greatest problems facing the police is one of their image with juveniles—the opinions of police formed by juveniles who come in official contact with police will be long-lasting and far-reaching in attitude formation for many years."[23] Thus, the police find themselves becoming full-time partners in the juvenile justice system.

Summary

Juveniles are not exempt from the law and the enforcement of the law. They must answer for their deeds just like anyone else. Immaturity and youth are not excuses for theft, rape, murder, or vandalism. Just as police are not always permitted to use force when arresting someone just because he is an adult does not mean that police may not use force when arresting someone simply because he is a child.

Basically, then, there are no real differences in police philosophy toward adults or juveniles. There are, however, various differences in the adaptations of that philosophy. These differences do not change basic police objectives, but they do affect the procedural methods used in handling a juvenile.

The similarity of police philosophy toward an adult criminal and juvenile criminal should not be misunderstood or misinterpreted. Police departments are genuinely concerned about rehabilitating juveniles who get into trouble with the law. Because of their acceptance of this growing public policy, police departments are more than ready and anxious to cooperate with other community agencies.

Many police departments recognize that the reduction and/or elimination of juvenile delinquency may lead to some reduction or elimination of adult crime. Although not all juvenile delinquents become adult criminals, many adult criminals started as delinquents. Proper handling of even one adult by police when he was a juvenile may have helped him avoid criminal behavior patterns as an adult. For this reason, the police must conduct themselves with the utmost care and diligence in handling juvenile cases.

REVIEW QUESTIONS

1. What should a police officer do with a juvenile he has taken into custody for committing a delinquent act?

2. How should an officer handle a child abuse or neglect case?

3. What role should the police officer play in a community program to prevent and control juvenile delinquency?

4. What are some of the more significant laws or court cases since 1960 which have changed the police departments' handling of delinquent or dependent juveniles?

5. What are the problems for the police in coping with juvenile crime? What suggestions can you make to help the police cope with this task more effectively?

NOTES

1. Richard W. Kobetz, *The Police Role and Juvenile Delinquency* (Gaithersburg, Md.: International Association of Chiefs of Police, 1971), pp. 139–41.

2. Arthur M. Schlesenger and Dixon Ryan Fox, eds., "The Rise of the City, 1878–1898" in a *History of American Life*, vol. 10 (New York: Macmillan, 1934), p. 115.

3. Bruce Smith, *Police Systems in the United States*, 2d. rev. ed. (New York: Harper and Row, 1960), pp. 105–106.

4. Kobetz, *The Police Role and Juvenile Delinquency*, p. 147.

5. Timothy Hurley, *The Origins of the Illinois Juvenile Court Law* (Chicago: Visitation and Aid Society, 1907), p. 14.

6. Kobetz, *The Police Role and Juvenile Delinquency*, p. 148.

7. Ibid., p. 170.

8. Harry E. Allen and Clifford E. Simonsen, *Corrections in America* (Encino, Calif.: Glencoe Press, 1975), p. 337.

9. An adjudicatory hearing is one held to determine whether the allegations of a petition are supported by the evidence beyond a reasonable doubt or by a preponderance of the evidence.

10. Edward Eldefonso, *Law Enforcement and the Youthful Offender* (New York: John Wiley and Sons, 1973), p. 294.

11. Ibid., p. 297.

12. *Haley* v. *Ohio*, 332 U.S. 596 (1948).

13. John P. Kenney and Dan G. Pursuit, *Police Work with Juveniles and the Administration of Justice* (Illinois: Thomas, 1975), p. 62.

14. Ibid., p. 62.

15. Ibid., p. 63.

16. *Chicago Tribune*, July 4, 1899.

17. Eldefonso, *Law Enforcement and the Youthful Offender*, p. 318.

18. Ibid., p. 319.

19. Nelson A. Watson and George W. O'Conner, *Juvenile Delinquency and Youth Crime: The Police Role* (Gaithersburg, Md.: International Association of Chiefs of Police, 1964), p. 288.

20. William C. Kvaraceus, *Dynamics of Delinquency* (Columbus: Charles E. Merrill Books, 1966), p. 196.

21. Kobetz, *The Police Role in Juvenile Delinquency,* p. 127.

22. E.g., *Lopez* v. *United States,* 399 f. 2d. 865 (9th Cir. 1968).

23. Cal. Welf. & Inst'ns Code §625 (West, 1973).

24. Kobetz, *The Police Role and Juvenile Delinquency,* p. 73.

8 The Juvenile Court

Studies of organization, structure, and functioning of the
juvenile courts have shown that, with a few notable
exceptions, most juvenile courts fall short of the
recommendations set forth in the Standard Juvenile Court Act.
New issues faced by the juvenile courts today have been
considered jointly by the National Probation and Parole
Association and the National Council of Juvenile Court
Judges, their recommendations only tend to accentuate how
far most juvenile courts must go if they are to approximate
minimal standards as specialized courts dealing with children
under the happy union of child welfare and the behavioral
sciences.

WILLIAM C. KVARACEUS

A juvenile court is a judicial tribunal established to deal in a special way
with children's cases. Juvenile courts exist in most jurisdictions throughout
the country; they are also known as family courts. Regardless of the name,
the functions and duties of these courts are the same. They only handle cases
involving children up to statutorily defined ages, usually from 16 to 18. The
juvenile court hears cases involving neglect, dependency, child abuse, and
delinquency.

Referrals to the juvenile court generally come from parents, school
agencies, or law enforcement officers. The majority come from the police.

The juvenile court may be a completely separate court with a given
jurisdiction or it may be a functional component of another court. Juvenile
courts established by state constitutions require special legislation to define
the powers which such courts may exercise. The "clout" of the juvenile
court depends on the legislative body and its current attitudes. A state
legislature can also decide to place the duties and functions of the juvenile
court with other courts, granting these courts authority by statute. In
Washington, for example, the superior court in each county functions as a
juvenile court; in New York there is a family court in each county; and in
Ohio a few counties have an independent juvenile court, while other
counties hear juvenile matters in the court of common pleas.

Juvenile courts have been described in a number of ways. "Throughout
the brief history of the juvenile court, the debate on the nature of the court
has often been ambiguous, leading to the conclusion that the juvenile court
is a polymorphous agency which changes its identity like a chameleon,
sometimes assuming the role of a criminal court, at other times serving as a

social welfare agency, and in the interim being the kindly, benevolent father figure for those children who behave in an antisocial manner."[1]

Rulings and pronouncements on the purpose, role, and definition of the juvenile court have been issued over the years; here is a sample:[2]

1. The purpose of the statutes creating juvenile courts was not to provide additional courts for the punishment of crime; rather, the purpose is to establish special tribunals having jurisdiction within prescribed limits, of cases relating to the moral, physical, and mental well-being of children to the end that they may be directed away from paths of crime.[3]

2. A district court's jurisdiction encompasses all criminal offenses and exclusive original jurisdiction over all felonies and of all persons brought therein charged with the commission of crime. The juvenile court is not a separate and distinct court, but the district court with enlarged powers.[4]

3. The juvenile court is not a criminal court, but rather a statutory court having special jurisdiction of a parental nature over delinquent and neglected children, and its purpose and procedure are governed by rules applicable in civil cases.[5]

4. Juvenile courts are generally defined as courts having special jurisdiction of a parental nature over delinquent and dependent children and are frequently referred to as specialized courts.[6]

5. The juvenile court is not designed as a trial court in the ordinary sense. Its purpose is more informative than punitive, and its operating methods differ decidedly from those of a criminal court. Technicalities and formalities are largely done away with, and its simple procedure is designed to gain the confidence of those coming before it, and to enable the judge to best control and guide his wards, with more consideration for the future development than their past shortcomings.[7]

6. The objectives of a statute creating a juvenile court are to provide measures of guidance and rehabilitation for the child and protection of society, not to fix criminal responsibility, guilt, and punishment.[8]

7. In *Gault*, the Supreme Court stated that the extension to children of fundamental constitutional procedural rights . . . does not mean a total substitution of the adult criminal system for the present children's system.[9] The Court further stated: "The problems of preadjudicative treatment of juveniles . . . are unique to the juvenile process; hence what we hold in this opinion with regard to the procedural requirements at the adjudicative stage has no necessary applicability to other steps of the juvenile process."[10]

8. The [District of Columbia] Court of Appeals held that "there is sufficient dissimilarity between juvenile proceedings to deny application of the doctrine (pretrial discovery) to this issue. Criminal trials are comparatively formalistic. But flexible and informal procedures are essential to the *parens patriae* function of the juvenile court, and we have not been made aware that the juvenile court in this jurisdiction departs in practice from that philosophy."[11]

9. In *McKiever* v. *Pennsylvania*, Justice Blackmun, in a separate concurring opinion, stated: "Imposition of trial by jury as a matter of constitutional precept [in juvenile proceedings] would (1) possibly remake the juvenile proceeding into a fully adversary process, (2) put an effective end to the idealistic prospect of an intimate, informal, protective proceeding, (3) not strengthen greatly, if at all, the fact-finding function, (4) provide an attrition of the juvenile court's assumed ability to function in a unique manner, (5) not remedy the defects of the juvenile court system, (6) impede further state experimentation in dealing with the problems of the young, and (7) inject into the juvenile court system the traditional delay, the formality, and the clamor of the adversary system and, possibly, the public trial."[12]

One theme that runs consistently through these nine descriptions of the juvenile court is that the juvenile court is *not* an adult court. It is debatable, however, whether this distinction can be retained for very long. For example, the *Gault* decision, for all practical purposes, destroyed the *parens patriae* concept of the juvenile court. And with *Gault* and other recent Supreme Court decisions, there has been a definite trend away from the informal, paternalistic models of the past in favor of greater formality in the juvenile court process of adjudication and treatment.

This trend, given impetus by the recently imposed requirements of *Kent*, *Gault*, and others, has already created serious stresses in the administration of juvenile justice and juvenile courts. These stresses have led to a growing controversy as to the role of the juvenile court within the United States. There are those who feel that granting the juvenile court the full adversary functions and duties of the adult court would greatly hamper and detract from its informal approach to the cases it hears. Others contend that the IJA-ABA (Institute of Judicial Administration-American Bar Association) Juvenile Justice Standards Project will change the juvenile court to a junior criminal court, a change they consider to be essential if the juvenile court is to survive.[13] Further discussion of the role and the future of the juvenile court will be taken up later in this chapter. But first, let us examine a brief history of the juvenile court and court system.

History of the Juvenile Court

The juvenile court system in America was part of a movement aimed at removing youngsters from the criminal law process (see chapter 1) and creating special programs for delinquent, dependent, and neglected children.

The English common law concept of *parens patriae* was a major influence on the development of American juvenile law and eventually the juvenile court. The development of the juvenile court stemmed from the court of Chancery Jurisdiction of England which provided special consideration for children. Under this jurisdiction, the crown asserted the power of *parens patriae* over children on the assumption that they were wards of the state. Until a special judicial tribunal for children set up in Massachusetts in 1874 and the creation of the first official juvenile court in Cook County, Illinois, in 1899, criminal jurisdiction over juveniles lay with the regular criminal courts.

Increased urbanization, industrialization, immigration, and a growing concern for crime prevention in the nineteenth century led to various reform and welfare movements regarding children. One of these movements—the wave of humanitarian efforts by feminists group (such as the Chicago Women's Club and Hull House), penologists, and philanthropists—led to the founding of the juvenile court in Illinois. Based on a medical model of scientific investigation, the juvenile court's original goals were to investigate, diagnose, and prescribe treatment, not to adjudicate guilt or to fix blame. Lawyers were not seen as necessary since the juvenile courts would not be of an adversary nature. In fact, the traditional juvenile court became part of a juvenile justice system which expressed considerable leniency and tolerance toward youth who engaged in antisocial conduct. Instead of processing children through a formal criminal justice system where they would be stigmatized as criminals and subject to punishment, the state would deal with delinquents in an ex parte civil process, which was to be both benign and paternalistic.

For some, the reforms which preceded the development of the juvenile court and those which followed were not sufficient. Judge Julian Mack, a well-known early juvenile court judge, commented on the juvenile court's development as an outgrowth of the general reform movement in the treatment of children: "What we did not have was the conception that a child that broke the law was to be dealt with by the State as a wise parent would deal with a wayward youth."[14]

Once conceived, the idea of juvenile courts spread with amazing speed. In April 1899, the Illinois legislature passed the Juvenile Court Act, which created the first statewide court for children. The Juvenile Court Act brought dependency, neglect, and delinquency cases under one jurisdiction and created features which have since characterized the juvenile court in the United States.

Within 12 years, 22 states had followed Illinois's example and by 1925 all but two states had juvenile courts.

By 1945, the holdouts—Maine and Wyoming—had joined. In 1970, there were 2,662 juvenile courts in the United States.[15] Today, it is estimated that there are over 2,700 juvenile courts, courts with vast dissimilarities in organization, procedure, staffing, and provision of needed services to youth in trouble.

Much has been written regarding the humanitarian philosophy behind the development of the juvenile court. The more traditional explanations of the child-saving movement have emphasized the noble sentiments and tireless energy of middle-class philanthropists.

> It is widely implied in the literature that the juvenile court . . . represented a progressive effort by concerted reformers to alleviate the miseries of urban life and to solve social problems by rational, enlightened, and scientific methods. With few exceptions, studies of delinquency have been parochial, inadequately descriptive, and show little appreciation of underlying political and cultural conditions. Historical studies, particularly of the juvenile court, are for the most part self-confirming and support an evolutionary view of human progress.[16]

The above quotation, taken from A. M. Platt's *The Child Savers*, serves as a reminder that well-intentioned people who desire to save children were not solely responsible for the acceptance of the juvenile court concept. The development of the court, and of similar reforms in corrections, was born out of the needs of the times. It was looked upon as a solution to the increasing numbers of homeless, wayward, and delinquent youths. If the conditions that helped produce so many delinquent youths (increasing urbanization, immigration, and industrialization) had not occurred, the juvenile court might never have been necessary.

For the reader who wishes to acquire a thorough, accurate, and realistic picture of the history of the juvenile court, beyond the brief account offered here, we recommend reading not only accounts of the early reform movements but of political, economic, and social conditions of the period as well. The reform movements were a direct outgrowth of harsh conditions and the juvenile court system was not the only reform accomplished.

The Juvenile Court Today

The original goals of the juvenile court were based on the concept that children needed the state to act as a kindly parent and protect them from the severity of adult courts and penal institutions. The emphasis was on the child's *need* and not the *deed*. Courts were concerned primarily with rehabilitation and treatment, not guilt or punishment or even innocence. The court's idealistic goals of diagnoses, investigation, and provision of treatment were severely hindered by the absence of social agencies in those times, agencies which today handle a large number of children and their problems.

A U.S. Children's Bureau survey in 1920 indicated that the separation of juveniles from adults was not fully realized, in spite of the intent of the Juvenile Court Act. The survey found that only 16 percent of all juvenile courts had separate hearings for children and probation services with adequate recorded social histories on those brought before the court.[17] A similar survey conducted by the Children's Bureau and the President's Commission on Law Enforcement and Administration of Justice in 1966 revealed significant disparities between desirable and actual court practices. It has been observed that "there is nothing uniform" in the operation of the juvenile courts and that:

> in the analysis of their procedures, confusion has come from a common inclination to picture them as uniform throughout the country and to idealize them, to describe optimium [sic] practices (or, at least, procedures conceived ideal by the analyst) as though they were characteristic.[18]

And

> While Roscoe Pond called the juvenile court one of the "great social inventions" of the nineteenth century, twentieth-century critics have been calling it one of our biggest failures. From the time of their establishment, juvenile courts have been plagued with improperly defined goals, procedures, and jurisdictional boundaries. Thus, they have become the "municipal dumps" for problem children.[19]

What is it that interferes with the function and operation of the juvenile court today? The problem is one basic to most large social institutions. It is that juvenile courts are continually given more duties and responsibilities than resources with which to perform those duties and responsibilities. Oftentimes, social institutions are abused simply because they exist. The juvenile court is a perfect example.

The juvenile court has had to bow to the capricious nature of those who wish to use it. Thus its autonomy has been gravely undermined and it is held in low esteem by judges, lawyers, and other professionals in the corrections field. Robert Vinter of the University of Michigan has written that:

> The petitioner or referring person understandably expects the court to act in a way which will meet his own expectations or those of his organization. Delay, refusal to act, and action contrary to his desires, even if for reasons valid in law or in fact, are often regarded by the petitioner as jeopardizing his legitimate interests, and he is consequently frustrated or antagonized. The police, for example, tend to refer cases when they want vigorous action to reinforce police authority or to increase the severity of sanctions. They may actually have assured the youngster that the court will deal forcefully with him. These cases are not always proper instances for court intervention, yet the police may view the court's refusal to act as uncooperative and jeopardizing law enforcement. Schools, parents, and social agencies impose somewhat similar demands on the court, almost as though they were its customers or patrons and the court's primary purpose were to fulfill their demands.[20]

Today, the juvenile court has a dual role which is contributing to and resulting in its dysfunction as a social institution. Not only is the court expected to carry out its original purpose as a welfare agency for the rehabilitation of wayward youth, it is also expected to protect society from the foul deeds of the juvenile delinquent. It becomes readily apparent that while providing a child with the elements of a good and useful life (education, economic security, and emotional maturity), the court's role may be entirely incompatible with its other function of protecting the public from his or her antisocial behavior.

Burdened with these two obligations, the court can perform neither role to anyone's satisfaction. Regrettably, it is often used as a scapegoat for the problems of delinquency and the juvenile justice system as a whole.

The divergent range of responsibilities given to the juvenile courts has therefore made them somewhat ineffectual. When one realizes that the juvenile court operates foster homes, detention facilities, after-care facilities, treatment facilities, and offers welfare services for young people, the seriousness of the problem becomes clearer.

The court also is expected to handle teenage traffic offenses, child abuse and neglect cases, and, in some instances, provide the legal sanction for the adoption of children. On top of these duties it serves as the disciplinary arm of the schools and community and of parents who cannot control their unruly children.

Status Cases versus Delinquent Cases

Compounding the problems of the courts are the growing numbers of nondelinquent cases which overload court dockets. The juvenile court is generally reluctant to refuse to hear a case for which it has a legal responsibility. For example, juvenile courts are mandated to deal with incorrigible youth. Incorrigible youth fall under the category of dependent children or status offenders. A status offender (see chapter 3) is a child who commits an offense which is an offense only because of age. The offense would not be dealt with in a court of law if committed by an adult. School truancy is a status offense. If schools decide they do not want to handle matters of school truancy, they can shift the responsibility for these incorrigible youth to the juvenile court.

Among those in the juvenile court system and the field of juvenile corrections, it is generally believed that the needs of incorrigible youth or status offenders would be best served by nonlegal social service agencies. The courts would be freed thereby to focus their attention upon the problem of youth who commit delinquent acts, acts which if committed by an adult would be an offense.

In 1974 the juvenile courts in the United States heard and disposed of 1,252,000 delinquency cases.[21] Because no distinction is made in the statistics between real delinquencies and status offenses, there is no way of knowing how many of these cases were actually status offenders. But the President's Commission on Law Enforcement and the Administration of

**TABLE 8-1. DISPOSITION OF JUVENILE CASES AT THREE STAGES
IN THE JUDICIAL PROCESS—1965**

| | PART I | PART II | |
	Most Serious Adult Offenses	All Other Adult Offenses	Juvenile Status Offenses
Court petition after complaint (in percent)	57 N* = (37,420)	33 (52,862)	42 (33,046)
Convicted if brought into court (in percent)	92 N = (21,386)	90 (17,319)	94 (13,857)
Placed or committed if convicted (in percent)	23 N = (19,667)	18 (15,524)	26 (12,989)

*N = number.

Justice has estimated that over one-fourth of all cases heard by juvenile court judges are status offenses.[22]

After a review of juvenile cases in New York City, Paul Lerman determined that:

1. PINS (persons in need of supervision) cases are more likely to be detained than serious delinquents (54% versus 31%).
2. Once detained, PINS are twice as likely to be detained for more than 30 days than are serious delinquents (50% versus 25%).
3. Length of correctional institution stay was two to 28 months for serious delinquents versus four to 48 months for PINS, with the median being nine months for serious delinquents and 13 months for PINS and the mean length of stay being 10.7 months for serious delinquents versus 16.3 months for PINS.
4. PINS are also more likely to receive harsher dispositions and to be sent to correctional institutions than are serious delinquents (26% versus 23%).
5. Nationwide, an estimated 40–50 percent of the residents of correctional institutions for delinquents are PINS cases, who are mixed indiscriminately with serious delinquents in most institutions.[23]

Table 8–1 indicates that in 19 of the 30 largest American cities in 1965, status offenders comprised 42 percent of court cases. Of these there was a 94 percent conviction rate.

An analysis of status offenders in almost every juvenile court across the nation will show that many, if not most, of these children are experiencing trouble in growing up. These problems usually involve school, home, or sex. The harmful effects of unnecessary court referrals upon these youth have been the subject of numerous studies, and it is generally agreed that inappropriate referrals have adverse effects not only on the child but on the juvenile court and the community.[24]

Deed versus Need

Supreme Court rulings in the area of juvenile justice have led to a gradual switch from the court's original concern with the child's needs to a mandate to cope with his deeds. The courts have taken on a definite adversary atmosphere, an atmosphere of the criminal court.[25]

Court rulings such as in *In re Gault* and others have granted constitutional due-process rights to juvenile offenders who have committed criminal acts. Status offenders, however, have committed no criminal offenses. But if these rulings are interpreted literally, the courts could be mandated to provide the same constitutional rights to status offenders. They, too, are in jeopardy of being deprived of their freedom for an indefinite period of time. Status offenders are theoretically entitled to all of the due-process rights granted to adults (with the exception of trial by jury, *McKiever* v. *Pennsylvania*) when they are adjudicated in the juvenile courts. Demands by status offenders that these due process rights be enforced could drastically disrupt and tie up court dockets and create a major crisis for the juvenile courts.[26]

Kobetz and Bosarge state that:

> As long as uncounted numbers of noncriminal cases are allowed to be referred to juvenile courts for disposition, these courts will never have adequate treatment resources to meet the needs of the delinquent child, i.e., the child who has committed a criminal offense. This problem cannot be solved solely by infusing large sums of money into the juvenile court system to enable it to hire additional personnel and improve rehabilitative services. Rather, the answer lies within the grasp of the juvenile courts . . . they must take steps to narrow their own jurisdictions. This means that the juvenile courts must, first of all, determine exactly what their role is to be in administration of justice and, second, to secure and apply procedural changes to allow the juvenile courts to function clearly within their new roles and not within any other roles society may assign them.[27]

Status Offenders

It has been suggested that the issue could be clarified and some of the confusion dispelled if status offenders were removed from the jurisdiction of the juvenile courts. The courts would then be relieved of the responsibilities of service provision to children who, if screened more stringently at intake, would never come before the court in the first place. Judge David Bazelon, chief judge of the U.S. Court of Appeals for the District of Columbia, voicing the opinion of several juvenile court judges who favor eliminating status offenders from the jurisdiction of the juvenile court, writes:

This situation is truly ironic. The argument for retaining beyond control and truancy jurisdiction is that juvenile courts have to act in such cases because "if we don't act, no one else will." I submit that precisely the opposite is the case: *because* you act, no one else does. Schools and public agencies refer their problem cases to you because you have jurisdiction, because you exercise it, and because you hold out promises that you can provide solutions.

There is still vitality in the concept of a separate juvenile court for offenders who are children. The juvenile court can have sensitive intake screening procedures to weed out these technical infractions of law which constitute "crimes" but which ought not to be prosecuted, like the proverbial apple stealing or breaking a neighbor's window by mistake. The juvenile court can have flexible pretrial adjustment tools such as the conciliation conference and the consent decree. The juvenile court can have sensitive investigative machinery for arriving at informed dispositions tailored to the needs of the individual child.

But in the area of borderline predelinquent jurisdiction—beyond control, truancy and the like—where the rationale for intervention seems to be the illusory hope of preventing future crimes, we ought to stop fooling ourselves and the community. You ought to tell the community that you are failures— yes failures—at *preventing* delinquency and crime. As long as the community views you as a prevention agency and refers its social and behavioral problems to you, the root problems will not be attacked.

The battle against juvenile crime can't possibly be won in court, even in the most enlightened court. That is only where we bring the worst casualties and hope that some, with good care, will survive, albeit with scars and crippling disabilities. The name of the game is Prevention, and that's a job for the institutions in the community that can help children. . . .[28]

In further defense of the desirability of removing status offenders from the jurisdiction of the juvenile court, juvenile justice professionals argue that:

1. The broad scope of delinquency statutes and juvenile court jurisdictions has permitted the coercive imposition of middle-class standards of child-rearing.

2. A broad definition has enlarged the limits of discretionary authority so that virtually any child can be deemed a delinquent if officials are persuaded that he needs correction.

3. The presence of juvenile "status" offenses, as part of the delinquency statutes, provides an easier basis for convicting and incarcerating young people because it is difficult to defend against the vagueness of terms like "incorrigible" and "ungovernable."

4. The mixing together of "status" offenders and real delinquents in detention centers and reform schools helps to provide learning experiences for the non-delinquents on how to become real delinquents.

5. The public is generally unaware of the differences between "persons in need of supervision" and youths who rob, steal and assault, and thereby is not sensitized to the special needs of "status" offenders.

6. Statistics on delinquency are misleading because we are usually unable to differentiate how much of the volume reflects greater public and official concern regarding home, school and sex problems, and how much is actual criminal conduct by juveniles.

7. Juvenile ''status'' offenses do not constitute examples of social harm and, therefore, should not even be the subject of criminal-type sanctions.

8. Juvenile institutions that house noncriminal offenders constitute the state's human garbage dump for taking care of all kinds of problem children, especially the poor.

9. Most policemen and judges who make critical decisions about children's troubles are ill-equipped to understand their problems or make sound judgments on their behalf.

10. The current correctional system does not rehabilitate these youths and is therefore a questionable approach.[29]

Professionals in the field are far from the only critics of the present juvenile court system. To the youth being adjudicated, all the court talk of rehabilitation and personalized justice can become meaningless and a cruel joke. For some, contempt for the court system is all they feel. Various features of their court processing may cause juveniles to develop a definite sense of injustice. In *Delinquency and Drift*, David Matza considers how a youth, especially a status offender, might view the court's behavior:

[T]he suspicion that he is being misled regarding the basis of disposition suggests the necessity of exploratory speculation regarding the true bases. Why should persons so important and influential as the judge and his helpers lie to him regarding the true bases of disposition? Why should they insist, as they frequently do, that it is not what he did—which strikes delinquents and others as a sensible reason for legal intervention—but his underlying problems and difficulties that guide court action? Why do they say they are helping him when patently they are limiting his freedom of action and movement by putting him on probation or in prison? What on earth could they possibly be hiding that would lead them to such heights of deception?[30]

Matza contends that the present juvenile court system and process creates an overpowering sense of injustice among youth with first-hand court experience or those who find out indirectly about the courts. Delinquency-generating attitudes became strengthened rather than nullified. Matza states:

The major meanings of fairness are captured, I believe, in the following assertions: it is only fair that some steps be taken to ascertain whether I was really the wrongdoer (cognizance); it is only fair that I be treated according to the same principles as others of my status (consistency); it is only fair that you who pass judgment on me sustain the right to do so (competence); it is only fair that some relationship obtain between the magnitude of what I have done and what you propose to do to me (commensurability); it is only fair that differences between the treatment of my status and others be reasonable and tenable (comparison). Each of these statements poses an elementary component of justice.[31]

It is felt that present-day courts cause juveniles to feel that their access to fairness or justice is being violated. Mixing youth who commit criminal acts with those who are status offenders only adds to their disillusionment. The 10-year-old who is habitually running away from home may not be quite sophisticated enough in his knowledge of court proceeding to understand why he receives the same or harsher punishment as the teenager who steals automobiles.

Taking into consideration the criticisms of professionals in and out of the juvenile justice system, and of the youth themselves, the juvenile court must actively campaign for the diversion and/or removal of status offenders from their jurisdiction and for policies which provide for the utilization of the juvenile court by the community only as a last resort.

The Interdepartmental Council to Coordinate All Federal Juvenile Delinquency Programs has made removal a top, nationwide priority. However, LEAA and HEW, although they have discussed the diversion of status offenders,[32] have carefully avoided a policy supporting separation of status offenders from the juvenile courts. According to Milton Rector, "They fear the wrath of the National Council of Juvenile Court Judges and of child welfare workers who have unfortunately come to regard coercion as an essential tool of social work with children. The 1974 Juvenile Justice and Delinquency Prevention Act is only serving as a grant program to take status offenders out of security confinement but leaves them within the jurisdiction of the court."[33]

Changing State Laws

In an attempt to move in a direction approximating diversion and/or removal of status offenders from the court's jurisdiction, several states have redefined their statutes to clearly distinguish between status offenders and delinquents. New York's Family Court Act is the most notable legislation thus far.[34] The New York Family Court Act separates children into two main categories: juvenile delinquents and status offenders.

These two categories of children are handled and identified in different ways. The act provides for a two-stage proceeding for its intervention in noncriminal (status) juvenile cases. First, there is a fact-finding hearing to determine the juvenile's conduct, and then there is a dispositional hearing to determine whether the court should formally hear the case. In support of this two-stage process for noncriminal cases, Judge Millard L. Midonick of the Surrogate Court of New York County finds:

This dual requirement permits, indeed compels, the court to carefully circumscribe and to gingerly approach the conditions and situations for societal intervention. In this respect, such requirements can be seen as an amelioration of the otherwise broad strictures of ungovernability statutes. Furthermore, for these reasons, in the case of noncriminal ungovernability, these requirements may be constitutionally imposed as prerequisites for juvenile court jurisdiction.[35]

Several states, including California, Colorado, Illinois, Indiana, Kansas, New York, Oklahoma, Texas, Utah, Vermont, and Washington, have banned initial and/or subsequent commitment of status offenders to institutions. Washington's new Juvenile Court Act, for example, provides for the continued removal of status offenders (incorrigibles in particular) from juvenile institutions.[36] It also provides that newly adjudicated incorrigibles may not be sent to an institution and may be committed by the court to a diagnostic and treatment facility for not more than 30 days. This act will force Washington's courts to distinguish between cases that are delinquent and cases that are dependent. Adjudications will, therefore, have to be made carefully.

The removal and/or diversion of status offenders from the juvenile court's jurisdiction must be carefully planned and coordinated within the entire juvenile justice system, the community, and the appropriate governmental agencies, including the legislature. There is a need for traditional youth serving agencies, such as the Scouts, YMCAs, Boys' Clubs, to extend their capabilities to enable them to work toward meeting the needs of these *nondelinquent* youth; such services could include family-child conflict resolution, drug and alcohol abuse counseling, and counseling programs for boy and girl prostitutes. However, the needs of the status offender must be met by someone—if not the court, then social service agencies such as those mentioned above. To abandon this category of youths is not the answer.

Other Problems

Although jurisdiction or nonjurisdiction over status offenders and the failure of the court to define its role and set guidelines for its actions appear to be the major problems to be overcome by the juvenile justice system, the court's problems do not cease here. The juvenile courts have failed also because the states' continued unwillingness to provide the resources— money, people, facilities, and concern—necessary to permit the courts to realize their potential and prevent them from becoming as callous as some of the lower criminal courts.

A recent study by the National Council of Juvenile Court Judges of 1,560 juvenile court judges revealed some disturbing facts.[37] Forty-nine percent of these judges had not received B.A. degrees, and 24 percent were without legal training. Seventy-two percent of the juvenile court judges spent one-fourth or less of their time on juvenile matters. Attention to juvenile matters was viewed as a minor part of their responsibilities in most of the jurisdictions.

Most of the judges in the survey were found to be underpaid. The average salary for a full-time judge was $12,493. Judges not only suffered from low wages, but they were found to be short of adequate help. Approximately one-third of them reported having no probation workers or social workers to assist them. However, while these judges were found to be underpaid and understaffed, compared to police officers and nonjuvenile court judges, they were more social-service oriented and less punitive.[38]

Most state statutes invest the juvenile court judge with the powers to make rules, procedures, and appointments. However, if the judge fails to meet with other court personnel over a period of months or years to review the rules and procedures, the staff's ability to properly conduct the court's business can be greatly hindered. For example, if rules, procedures, and staff needs are not periodically reviewed, they will become outdated and difficult to administer. This could lead to case backlogs, delays, poor morale, and a decreased ability to function.

The operation of the juvenile court involves much more than the judicial treatment of cases. The juvenile court judge should not be expected to manage the entire court operation. The use of a professional court administrator who reports directly to the chief judge would enable judicial staff to devote more of their time to judicial duties. The International Association of Chiefs of Police Delinquency and Prevention/Juvenile Justice Conference participants have recommended that:

> all juvenile courts with more than 25 personnel employ a professional court administrator to manage the planning, administrative, and personnel aspects of the courts' operations and that juvenile court judges be released from primary managerial responsibilities.[39]

Other staff problems within the juvenile court concern the probation officer staff.[40] Many jurisdictions fail to provide merit or civil service coverage to probation staff. In the majority of probation services, staffs are underpaid, inadequately trained, and their caseloads are too high.[41]

Defenders of the juvenile court blame the court's shortcomings on the lack of public support. They assert that the insufficient member of skilled personnel to staff the court's diagnostic and treatment facilities and public disagreement over the court's role in the rehabilitative process are primary causes of court failure. They contend that the juvenile court plan is workable, if only someone would make a serious attempt to try it.

Juvenile courts are troubled by the lack of other resources also. In most court jurisdictions there is a growing need for adequate placement facilities for young people, such as foster homes, group homes, or halfway houses. There is also a lack of needed service provision which could allow the placement of a youngster in his or her own home. Psychiatric services, for example, which are mentioned in most juvenile court *standards* are in fact rarely provided in practice.

To overcome the shortage of placement possibilities and services, many court judges opt for the easy solution and simply commit the child to a juvenile institution. Others, who hesitate to do this, will grasp at the barest of straws to keep the youth in the community. The result is a revolving-door policy. Children are released to the community no better prepared to survive than before they were brought before the bench. Within no time, the same child appears before the court dozens of times. Institutionalization, even to the most sympathetic judge, becomes the inevitable solution. The revolving-door policy extends to youth on parole who find themselves no better equipped to return to the community after being institutionalized than those who are on probation.

In light of the problems discussed in this section, it is no wonder that students of the juvenile court have become extremely critical of the way in which it is run. The lack of adequate placement facilities, undertrained and inadequate personnel, lack of proper training for judges and probation officers (both of whom have broad discretionary powers over the lives of juveniles), and the apparent lack of role definition have led individuals and groups interested in civil liberties, especially the American Civil Liberties Union, to press for reforms. In the past, the outcome has been Supreme Court decisions such as *Kent, Gault,* and others. The nature of future court decisions could depend on how quickly and how far the juvenile justice system moves toward court reform. The IACP conference offers the following as a first step toward solving court problems:

> It is recommended that all juvenile courts which have not undergone major reorganization in recent years seek funds from state criminal justice planning agencies to contract for outside management studies of the court and that the SPA's set aside sufficient funds for these studies to be performed by all juvenile courts which request them.[42]

Juvenile Court Jurisdiction

A good definition of jurisdiction as it applies to the juvenile court is:

> Jurisdiction of a court is that power conferred upon it by law, by which it is authorized to hear, determine, and render final judgement in an action, and to enforce its judgements by legal process.[43]

Before the juvenile court can make its valid, enforceable order, the case must be brought properly before the court and the court must then make a finding. Certain requirements must exist before the case can be brought before the court. The court must have geographical jurisdiction over the accused. The court must also have jurisdiction over the conduct of the juvenile. Almost every juvenile court has jurisdiction over delinquency, dependency (incorrigibility), and abuse cases. Some extend this jurisdiction to adoptions, court-ordered support, paternity actions, divorce, permanent termination of parental rights, custody over mentally ill or retarded children and, less often, family offenses and foster-care placement and review. Therefore, the subject youth upon whom the order is made must by law fall into one of the categories granted by statute to the juvenile court.

The age of the child, both lower (younger) and upper (older), is also a jurisdictional element. Most legislation defining delinquency sets no minimum age limit. Under the majority of state statutes it is hypothetically possible for a child to be defined as a delinquent from the day it is born. However, it is generally thought that the common rule of immunity until age 7 is adhered to. Fox, in *The Law of Juvenile Courts in a Nutshell*, comments:

> It may be significant to note that even in the absence of a minimum age in the statutes, there are no reported cases involving an attempt to charge delinquency against a child under the common law immunity age of seven. Administrative common sense appears to supplement legislative drafting.[44]

Upper age limits vary from 16 to 21 years. The U.S. Children's Bureau recommends age 18, and about two-thirds of the states adhere to this recommendation. However, it is statutorily possible for the juvenile court judge to seek the transfer of a juvenile to a criminal court. This usually occurs when the juvenile is older and has committed certain serious acts, such as murder or rape. Some geographic jurisdictions, in fact, automatically exempt from the juvenile courts juveniles 16 or older "charged by the United States attorney with murder, forcible rape, burglary in the first degree, armed robbery, or assault with intent to commit any such offense."[45] The Supreme Court has passed on such exemptions and has found them to be constitutional.[46]

Although most transfers of jurisdiction, whether sought by the law enforcement official, a probation officer,[47] the prosecutor,[48] the juvenile defendant himself,[49] or the court, involve older youth, the transfer of young defendants is not out of the question.

In most cases, before a transfer can legally take place, one must consider the Supreme Court decision (*Kent* v. *United States*) which has offered some legal safeguards for youth regarding their removal to face an adult criminal court. In the *Kent* decision, the Court nullified the transfer of a juvenile to the District of Columbia Criminal Court because the juvenile court had not held a hearing on the issue.[46] The Court decided that a full investigation which met the essentials of due process and fair treatment should be held in all cases where the transfer of a juvenile to an adult court was being sought. A transfer without such a proper hearing could be deemed illegal and unconstitutional.

Jurisdictional Problems

The juvenile courts are faced with certain problems when they lose jurisdictional rights over a juvenile who has reached the upper age limit. As frequently occurs, the juvenile will pass the upper age limit of the juvenile court's jurisdiction before the charges against him are adjudicated. The juvenile court must then decide from what point in time to measure the juvenile's age for jurisdictional purposes. Some courts measure the youth's age from the date of the offense.[50] Others use the time of the judicial proceedings as the deciding factor,[51] and still others measure from the date the actual trial begins.[52]

When the first alternative is used, there have been some court imposed limitations. For example, in one case the juvenile was under the age of 18 at the time the offense was committed. He was 27 years old before he was finally brought to trial for the offense. A federal court rules that there was no juvenile court jurisdiction even though the offense was in fact committed at an age over which the juvenile court had jurisdiction.[53]

State statutes giving the juvenile court jurisdiction over delinquents within a certain age range apply to dependents as well. The element of need of treatment and rehabilitation becomes a factor here. It is generally conceded that the status offender, who has committed no criminal offense, has different needs from a delinquent counterpart. It is also agreed that these needs, which are not being met by the juvenile court, can best be served elsewhere. In Ohio, a juvenile who attempts to marry without parental consent comes under the jurisdiction of the juvenile court.[54] Georgia makes it illegal for a juvenile to patronize a bar.[55] Adding cases of this nature to the juvenile court docket is questionable, at best. And as previous discussion in this chapter has suggested, the juvenile court's jurisdiction over noncriminal offenders should be seriously questioned, debated, and challenged.

The jurisdiction of juvenile courts varies from state to state. The state legislature or other rule-making body decides what the court's jurisdiction will be. Since there are no federal juvenile courts, juvenile court jurisdiction is a matter for state policy. Juveniles under the age of 18 who violate a federal law not punishable by death or life imprisonment may have their case transferred to the juvenile court of the state in which they reside.

The juvenile court can enforce its orders by legal action and should not therefore make an order which cannot be enforced by such action. According to Hahn, there are three prerequisites which the court must meet before it can make an enforceable, binding order. They are:

1. The subject (person) upon whom the order is made must fall within one of the categories granted by statute to the juvenile court.

2. Service of summons in accord with the particular statutory requirements, and the case law interpreting same, must have been had (subject to emergency orders).

3. After service, a hearing, in accord with the procedures set forth in the *Gault* case must have been had, and the court must have found, not by the civil standard or degree of proof of a mere preponderance of the evidence, nor the equity court standard of clear and convincing evidence, but by the criminal court standard of "beyond a reasonable doubt," that the juvenile has been found to be delinquent or is otherwise within the jurisdiction of the court.[56]

Operations Under the Juvenile Court

The operation of the juvenile court system is not autonomous. It is, instead, dependent upon society at large, the juvenile justice system as a whole, and the dictates of individual communities. Without adequate integration of the court within these parameters, it would be like a horse without a rider—possibly going somewhere, but lacking direction on the best way to get there.

The juvenile justice system is comprised of people who make decisions. It is not institutions, buildings, or agencies. Similarly, the juvenile court, which has been referred to as an institution, should portray itself in a more personal and humanistic way as a group of flesh-and-blood people, both those helping and those being helped.

The Court Intake Function

Most juvenile courts have established a system whereby inappropriate cases are diverted from their attention. Called the intake, screening, and adjustment process, its dominant goal is to divert the juvenile from the court in order to prevent unnecessary court proceedings.

> "Intake" refers to the initial screening stage, at which referrals of delinquency cases first reach the juvenile court. Reflecting the sociological character of the court, it has roots in both the case screening and acceptance procedures and charging agencies and the preliminary examination and charging procedures of the adult criminal courts. Intake exists, in one form or another, in most juvenile courts.[57]

Intake screening actually is initiated outside the court in many cases, by the police. The police make extensive and informal adjustments in the field and at the police station.[58] Gibbons states that Sellin and Wolfgang have reported a number of factors which enter into police screening decisions. They are:

1. The prior record of the youth.
2. The type of offense and the role of the juvenile in it.
3. The attitude of the victim or complainant.
4. The family situation of the offender.
5. The potential community resources which might be utilized for correction.
6. The general appearance and attitude of the offender toward the police.
7. The possible overcrowding at the Youth Study Center.
8. The police officer's anticipation of the juvenile court action should an arrest be made.[59]

Point 8 creates confusion and frustration for both the police and the courts. How often have you heard this statement on one of the police shows on television: "What good does it do for us to arrest them, when the courts just turn around and set them free?" Cooperation is up to the police and the courts on this matter. Police departments must make sure that their staffs are educated as to the legal and technical aspects of juvenile court policy. Juvenile courts must share and update their policies with the police and other agencies which might encounter the delinquent, dependent, or abused child.

If the police determine that court action is appropriate or if a petition has been filed by someone else, it is normally the juvenile court's probation staff which continues the intake screening process.[60] The dispositional screening by the probation staff is the crux of the court's intake and screening process. In its initial stages it will involve short investigations, social studies, and informal hearings which frequently involve both parents and child. After considering and weighing the information gathered at this point of the intake screening process, the probation staff determines a course of action. The case may be dismissed, disposed of in an informal manner such as informal probation, or the probation officer may feel that a formal petition requesting appropriate adjudication should be filed.

The probation staff also determines whether the juvenile should be detained pending court action. While some state statutes extend to juveniles the right to bail, most youths are released to their parents, unless, of course, circumstances of the case actually require detention.

It has already been stated in this chapter that the juvenile courts suffer from a lack of clearly written intake guidelines. Accordingly, in the *Task Force Report*, Burns and Stern have written:

> Many of the current procedures for nonjudicial handling of putative delinquents from prearrest to intake in the court system are inadequate and defective. Few formal guidelines are available to those who are responsible for

exercising discretion in determining which youngsters should be sent deeper into the judicial process. Where those guidelines do exist, their relevance and justice is open to question. Frequently, those who make such decisions, by dint of inadequate experience or training, lack the capacity and the resources to make those decisions wisely. . . . Without a system for the periodic review and correction of criteria and decision-making practices in this area, such practices are infrequently refined and frequently arbitrary.[61]

Coupled with the movement to add further legalized procedures to all stages of the juvenile court proceedings, these criticisms have caused some legislators to seek formal guidelines to govern prejudicial proceedings of which intake and screening are major components. IACP makes the following recommendation:

It is recommended that state legislatures establish legal nondiscriminatory written guidelines to govern prejudicial intake proceedings and that these guidelines set forth in detail those criteria to be followed by the intake officer in making the decision to petition the case or settle it informally.[62]

Attorneys in the Juvenile Court

As the juvenile courts move closer to being adversary in nature, the presence of attorneys in the courtroom will become commonplace. In the *Gault* decision, the Supreme Court held that a juvenile accused of committing a crime had the right to counsel. Legal advocacy can begin at the prejudicial stage of the court process or during the trial itself. While attorneys representing juveniles are now generally accepted as a fact of life, the role of the prosecuting attorney has been less readily accepted. Traditional juvenile court process did not include a prosecutor in the sense of a legally trained person to represent the state in court proceedings. Prior to *Gault*, it was the accepted notion that adversariness (and therefore lawyer-advocates, whether for the child or the state) was best kept out of the juvenile court. Since *Gault*, many such notions have been abandoned.

Thus far, it has not been possible to judge the precise impact of the *Gault* decision upon the role of prosecution in the juvenile court. A recent study, funded by the U.S. Department of Justice, indicates the following propositions to be true:

1. There has been a growing recognition, and appropriately so, that some legally trained person must be available to represent the state in many juvenile court proceedings.
2. In part, this stems from recognition that the assumption of prosecutorial roles by the probation staff or the juvenile court judge creates undesirable role conflicts.
3. Increasing requirements for prosecutors in juvenile courts is reflected in trends in both proposed and recent legislation.

4. There is now a substantial and increasing use of professional prosecutors in juvenile court.[63]

This study examined the system of prosecution in the Boston Juvenile Court as a starting point from which to formulate general principles or objectives for juvenile prosecution. These principles are as follows:

1. The prosecutor is an *advocate* of the State's interest in juvenile court. The "State's interest" is complex and multivalued, and may vary with the type of proceeding and the nature of the particular case. Foremost, it includes: (a) protection of the community from the danger of harmful conduct by the restraint and rehabilitation of juvenile offenders; and (b) concern, shared by all juvenile justice system personnel, as *parens patriae*, with promotion of the best interests of juveniles.

2. To the extent that the State's interest in community protection may conflict with its interest as *parens patriae* in promoting the well-being of a particular child, the prosecutor will be required to balance the interests based upon the nature and facts of the particular case. For example, to the extent that interests have to be balanced in given cases, the balance should be struck in favor of community protection when the juvenile presents a substantial threat to public safety, but of promoting the well-being of a child for most other types of offenses.

3. In his role as *advocate*, the prosecutor has responsibility to ensure adequate preparation and presentation of the State's case, from the stage of police investigation through post-disposition proceedings.[64]

Process and Authority of the Juvenile Court Proceeding

Once a case approaches or reaches the point of an adjudicatory hearing, the judge has the most extensive discretionary power in disposing of the case. It is interesting to note that juvenile court legislation does not specify the type of formal response which the juvenile is to make to the charges brought against him or her. The judge will generally, however, accept the common plea of guilty or not guilty.

The Supreme Court held, in *In re Winship*, that the proof against a juvenile must be beyond a reasonable doubt.[65] In juvenile cases the defense has a great advantage over the prosecution in regard to the standard of proof. The defense need only raise a reasonable doubt. The prosecution must establish each and every element of the crime or ungovernable act, and in so doing, establish the court's jurisdiction beyond a reasonable doubt.

Motions in Juvenile Court Proceedings

The proceedings in most juvenile courts remain informal, with most motions being presented orally. However, it is advisable to put some motions in writing.

That the motion is in writing, and hence ripe for purposes of appeal, is not lost on the judge. Written papers also prevent a judge unfamiliar with the particular question of law from being caught unawares and ignorant of the issues involved. Putting the judge in such a situation is impolitic and can be disastrous to an advocate's case. There is perhaps nothing more difficult than convincing a judge to reverse himself because he was "wrong."[66]

Both the defense and the prosecution should be aware of and be prepared to respond to the various motions which can be made at the pretrial stage of the juvenile court process. There are four such major categories of motions, each with several subcategories. They are:

1. Motions addressed to face the petition.
2. Motions addressed to the preparation of the case.
3. Motions addressed to the conduct of hearings or the trial.
4. Motions seeking the termination of court proceedings.

These motions are listed merely to acquaint the reader with their form. A thorough discussion of each separate motion is beyond the scope and intent of this text.[67]

Plea Bargaining

It is generally conceded that the uncrowded court dockets and the informality of the juvenile court proceedings, coupled with the court's open-ended dispositional power, create little necessity for plea bargaining (pleading guilty to a lesser or a reduced charge) in juvenile court cases. However, in *McKiever* v. *Pennsylvania*, the Supreme Court cited the contention of the juvenile petitioners "that counsel and the prosecution engage in plea bargaining."[68] If a court does not have a prosecutor, plea bargaining can take the place between defense counsel and the probation officer.

The practice of plea bargaining is common practice in adult criminal courts. Done properly and with integrity, plea bargaining can hasten the court process and ease the overcrowded court calendars. Done "under the table," it can allow pressure to be put upon the prosecutor or the defense to the extent that the plea to a lesser or reduced charge is accepted unwillingly and contrary to the best interests of protecting society from crime and criminals. For plea bargaining to work it must not be abused.

The Trial

The entering of the plea, the motions and countermotions, and the plea bargaining are all preludes to the main event (if the case is not diverted first): the actual trial. The juvenile court trial is also referred to as a fact-finding or adjudicatory hearing.

Trial Motions

During the trial, the prosecution and defense present witnesses, seek or deny evidence, and generally argue the points of the case. There are a number of trial motions which can be made by either advocate. They are, commonly: (1) motions to strike evidence or lines of questioning; (2) motions to declare a mistrial; (3) motions to dismiss due to the failure to develop prima facie evidence; and (4) motions to dismiss because of failure to prove the case beyond a reasonable doubt.[69]

Dispositional Stage of Trial

After the opening statements, presentation of evidence, trial motions, and closing statements comes the dispositional stage of the trial. The dispositional power of the juvenile court is far broader and more discretionary than the criminal courts. The criminal courts prescribe sentences and lengths of sentences to meet the particular offense (i.e., five to twenty years for robbery). The juvenile courts do not. The length of juvenile court comitment is indefinite in most states, but cannot exceed the 21st birthday.

In theory, the judges dispotional decision is based on the process "of reading a considered judgment for the best method of handling the child."[70]

Unguided by statutes or appellate decisions, the judges often make decisions which will deeply affect the life and future of both parents and child.

There are restrictions on the broad dispositional powers of the judges, however. Their decisions must be realistically based on the availability of diagnostic, rehabilitative, alternative, and treatment facilities. In fact, the dispositional process is a direct result of the alternatives available to each particular judge in each and every court.

Juvenile court judges are empowered to dismiss the case, suspend judgment pending further study, order protection (i.e., order the parents to desist from behavior linked with causing the child's delinquency), order probation (see chapter 10), or order commitment or placement in an institution.

Whatever the pending disposition, it is wise for the court to be reminded that the more involved an offender becomes with the juvenile justice system, and the more often he or she is moved through it, the greater is the potential for continued delinquent behavior.

While institutionalization is the most controversial and criticized of all juvenile court dispositions, it is also the least often used. Of the 1,052,000 cases which came before the courts in 1970, only 10 percent resulted in institutionalization.

Recently, the criminal and juvenile justice systems have moved away from the traditional court disposition based on judicial discretion. This trend has gained impetus with the juvenile court's coming of age as more of an adversary court. The movement concerns possible mandatory or maximum sentences for juveniles convicted of delinquent acts. A severity index list of crimes is developed and requires a specific, not indefinite sentence based upon the crime committed and the youth's attitude, background, and the potential for rehabilitation. The imposition of mandatory or maximum sentences for juveniles is not yet a widely accepted or even acknowledged alternative to the present open-ended discretional powers of the court. But it may be, in which case the serious student of juvenile justice will wish to keep abreast of its development.

Juvenile court judges often times offer the youth an alternative to institutionalization, such as the payment of a fine or restitution to the victim or public for damages or both.

Organizational Structure of the Juvenile Court

No discussion of the juvenile court would be complete without a look at its basic organizational structures. Figures 8–1 and 8–2 illustrate the two most common organizational structures found in major city courts.

There are arguments for and against each of the above structures. However, all juvenile courts should examine their organizational structures to determine how to effectively meet their needs and the needs of the public. The vertical structure (Figure 8–2) contains the position of professional court administrator, a position for which a need has previously been shown in this chapter. But the size of the court may preclude the appointment of a court administrator and the possibility of dividing the court's functions into the professional service division and the administrative services division. Smaller courts may not be able to either justify or acquire funds for the more sophisticated vertical organizational structure.

Summary

After almost 80 years, the juvenile court must review its current goals and objectives and its functions in light of recent changes in the climate and philosophy of the juvenile justice system. Its roles need to be clearly defined or redefined. It needs autonomy to establish its own priorities. It has been overburdened and underassisted by outside agencies and the public. The court has failed to accomplish its goals of diagnoses, rehabilitation, and treatment because its resources have been too thin. The court's dual role as dispenser of punishment and source of rehabilitation isn't feasible. There is inadequate staff, money, or resources with which to accomplish either, let alone both at once.

The revamping and restructuring of the juvenile court system is a necessity, not a luxury. Contrary to its intended purpose, the court can produce and perpetuate delinquency. In its procedures and its decisions, the court must be sensitive to possible negative and damaging ramifications in what it does. It must acquire realistic, humane, and practical methods of

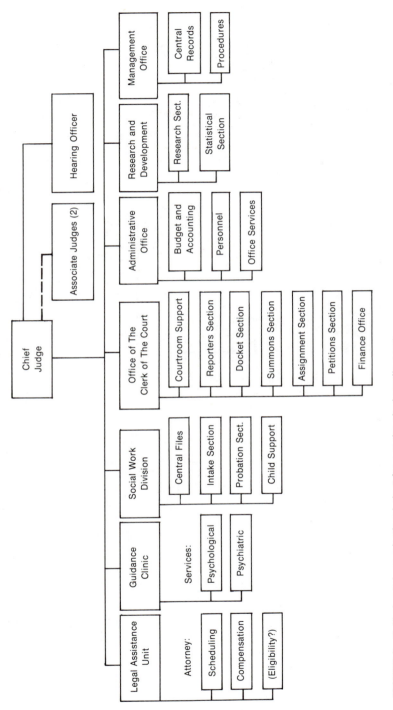

FIGURE 8 – 1. Horizontal organizational chart for a major city juvenile court.

Source: Richard W. Kobetz and Betty B. Bosarge, *Juvenile Justice Administration* (Gaithersburg, Md.: International Association of Chiefs of Police, 1973), p. 210.

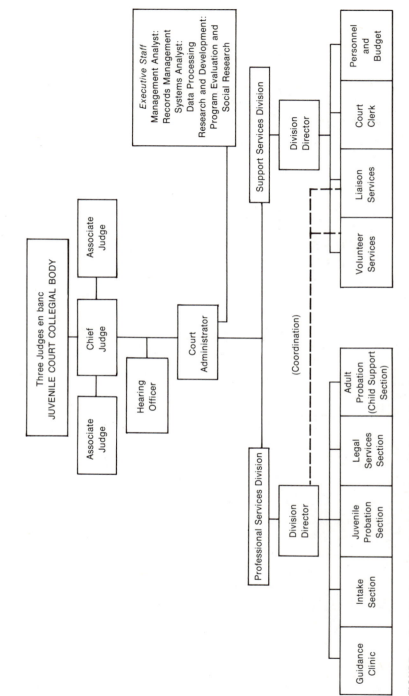

FIGURE 8 – 2. Vertical organizational chart for a major city juvenile court.

Source: Stephen L. Bulfinch and David J. Sarri, "A Study of the Juvenile Court in the District of Columbia, Part II: Administrative Management," in *Court Management Study, Part II* (Washington, D.C.: U.S. Government Printing Office, 1970), p. 206.

processing and treating juveniles if it is to be considered an effective component of the juvenile justice system.

It has been suggested that "volunteer courts" be tried. Volunteer courts provide needed manpower to supervise youths on probation; they do this at no expense by utilizing unpaid volunteers who are appointed Juvenile Court Supervisors. The main objective of a volunteer court program is "to provide each juvenile with individual attention and supervision, change his perhaps begrudging attitude toward law authority and, in the long run, teach him to live a successful life within the limits of society."[71] Each volunteer is urged to emphasize his or her official connection with the court, but at the same time to give the juvenile the individual understanding and help needed to gain respect for the law, himself, and the community. Volunteer courts, such as the one initiated in Missouri's 13th Judicial District, are not courts at all in the physical sense of the word, but rather groups of volunteers providing needed court services to help bridge the gap between the obligation of the juvenile courts and their inability to fulfill that obligation because of limited resources.[72]

REVIEW QUESTIONS

1. Define the following terms:
   a. juvenile court
   b. juvenile court jurisdiction
   c. venue
   d. *parens patriae*
   e. status offender
   f. court administrator
   g. adversary function

2. What are the goals of the juvenile court?

3. What are the major problems facing the juvenile court today? What solutions are available?

4. How does the juvenile court relate to the rest of the juvenile justice system? The juvenile court may become more adversary in nature, i.e. adultlike; would such a change affect the juvenile justice system as a whole? Why or why not?

5. What Supreme Court decision has had the most impact on the juvenile court system? Explain.

6. Based upon your personal experiences, how effective would you say the juvenile courts have been in fulfilling their roles? Explain. How do you think the performance of the court's role can be improved?

7. Keeping the original three goals of the juvenile court in mind, discuss how and why the court has failed to meet these goals. If you feel that the courts have met their goals, please explain.

NOTES

1. Richard W. Kobetz and Betty B. Bosarge, *Juvenile Justice Administration* (Gaithersburg, Md.: International Association of Chiefs of Police, 1973), p. 210.

2. Ibid., pp. 210–13.

3. *Lindsay* v. *Lindsay*; 257 Ill. 328, 100 N.E. 892 (1913) and *In re Turner*, 94 Kan. 115, 145, p. 871 (1915).

4. *State* v. *Overby*, 209 N.W. 552, 554, 54 N.E. 295 (1926).

5. *Bryant* v. *Brown*, 118 So. 184, 188, 151 Miss. 398, 60 A.L.R. 1325 (1928).

6. *In re Santillanes*, 138 P.2d. 503, 508, 47. N.M. 140 (1943).

7. *In re Dargo*, 81 Cal. App. 2d 205, 183 P.2d. 282 (1947).

8. *Kent* v. *U.S.*, 383 U.S. 541, at 555, 556 (1966).

9. *In re Gault*, 387 U.S. 1 at 30 (1967).

10. Ibid., at 31.

11. *District of Columbia* v. *Jackson*, 261 A. 2d 511 (D.C. Ct. of App., 1970).

12. *McKiever* v. *Pennsylvania*, 403 U.S. 528 S. Ct. 1976, 29 L. Ed. 2d 647 (1971).

13. See Milton G. Rector, *Juvenile Justice Issues and Priorities, An Address* (Hackensack, N.J.: National Council on Crime and Delinquency, 1975), pp. 6–7.

14. Jane Addams, *My Friend Julia Lathrop* (New York: Macmillan Co., 1935) p. 137.

15. Children's Bureau, U.S. Department of Health, Education and Welfare, *Juvenile Court Statistics* (Washington, D.C.: U.S. Government Printing Office, 1970 [1971]).

16. Anthony M. Platt, *The Child Savers: The Invention of Delinquency* (Chicago: University of Chicago, 1969), pp. 10–11.

17. Paul W. Tappan, *Juvenile Delinquency* (New York: McGraw-Hill, 1949), p. 173.

18. Ibid., p. 179.

19. Kobetz and Bosarge, *Juvenile Justice Administration*, p. 193.

20. Robert D. Vinter, "The Juvenile Court as an Institution," in the President's Commission on Law Enforcement and the Administration of Justice, *Task Force Report: Juvenile Delinquency and Youth Crime* (Washington, D.C.: U.S. Government Printing Office, 1967), p. 86.

21. Michael J. Hindelang, et. al., *Sourcebook of Criminal Justice Statistics— 1976* (New York: Criminal Justice Research Center, 1977), p. 572.

22. The President's Commission on Law Enforcement and the Administration of Justice, *Task Force Report: Juvenile Delinquency and Youth Crime* (Washington, D.C.: U.S. Government Printing Office, 1967), p. 4.

23. Paul Lerman, "Child Convicts," *Trans-Action,* July–August, 1971, pp. 38–39, 72.

24. Ibid., p. 38 (Adapted by Lerman from data reported by U.S. Children's Bureau).

25. See, for example, "How to Make a Criminal Out of a Child," The National Council on Crime and Delinquency, N.J.; by Charles Mangel and S. Rubin; Children as Victims of Institutionalization; The National Council on Crime and Delinquency, N.J. 1971.

26. Kobetz and Bosage, *Juvenile Justice Administration*, p. 209.

27. Ibid., p. 209.

28. Judge David L. Bazelon, "Beyond Control of the Juvenile Court," *Juvenile Court Journal* 21, no. 2 (Summer, 1970), pp. 6–7.

29. Lerman, "Child Convicts," p. 39.

30. David Matza, *Delinquency and Drift* (New York: Wiley, 1964), pp. 133–34.

31. Ibid., p. 106.

32. Interdepartmental Council to Coordinate All Federal Juvenile Delinquency Programs, *Proposed National Policy Objectives in the Juvenile Delinquency/Youth Development Area* (Washington, D.C.: U.S. Department of Justice Law Enforcement Assistance Administration, 1972), pp. 7–34.

33. Milton G. Rector, President National Council on Crime and Delinquency, Letter to authors, May 17, 1977, p. 2.

34. The first New York Family Court Act in the early 1960s forbade commitment of nondelinquents to institutions. Institutional populations dropped rapidly and career jobs were so much threatened that the next legislative session permitted commitment again, but with the PINS (Persons in Need) label. It took an appellate court decision to finally get nondelinquents out of commitment once again.

35. Millard L. Midonick, *Children, Parents and the Courts: Juvenile Delinquency, Ungovernability and Neglect* (New York: Practicing Law Institute, 1972), p. 18.

36. Engrossed Third Substitute House Bill No. 371. State of Washington, 45th Legislature, April 11, 1977.

37. S. D. McCune and D. L. Skoler, "Juvenile Court Judges in the United States. Part I: A National Profile," *Crime and Delinquency* 11 (April, 1965), pp. 121–31.

38. R. H. Walther and S. D. McCune, "Juvenile Court Judges in the United States. Part II: Working Styles and Characteristics," *Crime and Delinquency* 11 (October, 1965), pp. 384–93.

39. Kobetz and Bosage, *Juvenile Justice Administration,* p. 232.

40. See chapter 10, "Probation."

41. It should be noted that the National Association of Counties, with the support of the National Council on Crime and Delinquency and others, have initiated a national policy position which calls for the removal of the administration of services, probation, detention, etc., from the juvenile court.

42. Kobetz and Bosage, *Juvenile Justice Administration*, p. 227.

43. 14 O Jur (2d); Courts; Section 93.

44. Sanford J. Fox, *The Law of Juvenile Courts in a Nutshell* (St. Paul, Minn.: West, 1971), p. 18.

45. D.C. Code Ann. §16-2301 (3)(A)(1973).

46. *United States* v. *Bland*, 472 F.2d 1329 (D.C. Cir. 1972).

47. See In re John Doe I, 50 Hawaii 620, 446, P.2d. 564 (1968).

48. Example, Cal. Welf. & Instn's Code §707 (West 1973).

49. Example, Fla. Stat. Ann. §39.02 (6) (A)(Cum. Supp. 1973).

50. N.Y. Fam. Ct. Act §714 (McKinney 1973).

51. *Lowry* v. *Commonwealth*, 424 S.W. 2d 841 (Ky. Ct. App. 1968).

52. *Sweet* v. *Porter*, 74 Wash. 2d 869, 454 P.2d 219 (1969).

53. Application of Johnson, 178 F. Supp. 155 (D.C.N.J. 1957).

54. Ohio Rev. Code Ann. §2151 .022(D) (Supp. 1972).

55. Ga. Code Ann. §24A-401 (e)(3) (Supp. 1972).

56. Paul H. Hahn, *The Juvenile Offender and the Law* (Cincinnati: Anderson, 1971), p. 272.

57. M. K. Rosennheim and D. L. Skoler, "The Lawyer's Role at Intake and Detention Stages of Juvenile Court Proceedings," *Crime and Delinquency* 11 (1965), pp. 167–69.

58. See chapter 8, "Delinquents and the Police."

59. Don C. Gibbons, *Delinquency Behavior* (Englewood Cliffs, N.J.: Prentice-Hall, 1976), p. 44.

60. See chapter 10, "Probation."

61. Virginia M. Burns and Leonard W. Stern, "The Prevention of Juvenile Delinquency," in President's Commission on Law Enforcement and Administration of Justice, *Task Force Report: Juvenile Delinquency and Youth Crime* (Washington, D.C.: U.S. Government Printing Office, 1967), p. 396.

62. Kobetz and Bosarge, *Juvenile Justice Administration*, p. 247.

63. U.S. Department of Justice, Law Enforcement Assistance Administration, "Prosecution in the Juvenile Courts: Guidelines for the Future" (Washington, D.C.: U.S. Government Printing Office, December 1973), p. 10.

64. Ibid., pp. 28–29.

65. Winship, 397 U.S. 358, 365–66 (1970). See also chapter 15, "A Juvenile's Legal Rights."

66. Douglas J. Besharov, *Juvenile Justice Advocacy: Practice in a Unique Court* (New York: Practicing Law Institute, 1974), p. 265.

67. The reader interested in learning the particulars of these motions is directed to Besharov's *Juvenile Justice Advocacy* or one of a number of law texts on the subject of juvenile court proceedings.

68. *McKiever* v. *Pennsylvania*, 403 U.S. 528 (1971).

69. Besharov, *Juvenile Justice Advocacy*, p. 362.

70. *Hill* v. *State*, 454 S.W. 2d 429 (Tex. Div. App. 1970).

71. Robert J. Edlen and Betty Adams, *Volunteer Courts, A Child's Helping Hand* (Washington, D.C.: U.S. Government Printing Office, 1973), p. 2.

72. See, for example, Edlen and Adams, *Volunteer Courts*.

9 Probation

In adult court, probation generally refers to the supervision of
offenders in the community as an alternative to incarceration.
For adults, the probation officer's function is largely limited to
diagnosis and supervision. For juveniles, the role of the
probation officer is often much broader. In extreme cases,
such as in the *Gault* case, the probation officer may serve
also as arresting officer, jailer, prosecuting attorney (and also
defense attorney). Often the probation department maintains
treatment facilities and aftercare services which cast the
probation officer as "guard," "psychologist," and "parole
officer." Many problems arise from such a broad definition of
functions, as well as from the questionable assumption that
behavior prediction can be made and appropriate treatment
given.

ROBERT W. WILSON

Today, with the emphasis on community-based treatment, it is recognized
that not all juveniles who are adjudicated as delinquent belong in institutions. Probation is one method of disposition that the juvenile court may
choose, once a young person is determined to be delinquent. In fact,
probation is the most frequently used juvenile court disposition at the present
time. Nationwide, for example, approximately 60 percent of the cases
reaching the dispositional stage in juvenile court result in probation.[1]

In 1970–1971, 54 percent of the juvenile delinquent dispositions for
males and 57 percent of those for females brought before the New York
family court were placed on probation.[2] During this same period, 65 percent
of the male ungovernable and 56 percent of the female ungovernable cases
in that jurisdiction resulted in probation.[3] In 1975, in Washington, 53
percent of all juveniles who were handled formally by juvenile courts were
placed on probation.[4]

Probation as it relates to juvenile offenders is defined as follows:

> Juvenile probation, which permits a child to remain in the community under
> the supervision and guidance of a probation officer, is a legal status created by
> a court of juvenile jurisdiction. It usually involves (1) a judicial finding that
> the behavior of the child has been such as to bring him within the purview of
> the court, (2) the imposition of conditions upon his continued freedom, and (3)
> the provision of means for helping him to meet these conditions and for
> determining the degree to which he needs them. Probation thus implies much
> more than indiscriminately giving the child "another chance." Its central
> thrust is to give him positive assistance in adjustment in the free community.[5]

Historical Background

Modern probation started when those who dispensed the law tried to be both fair and compassionate to the convicted or accused offender by giving him or her an opportunity to avoid punishment under certain conditions. The earliest forms of probation were a sort of suspended sentence. The right to sanctuary, a predecessor of probation or the suspended sentence, permitted a convicted criminal freedom from arrest so long as the person remained in the sanctuary. There are several examples of the right to sanctuary cited in the Bible; in fact, holy places were often set aside for this purpose.[6] This early practice, abandoned in England in the seventh century, was a far cry from probation practices. But it did provide a criminal with a form of reprieve or stay of punishment.

In the Middle Ages, secular punishment could be avoided through a practice called *benefit of clergy*. Persons could use this device to escape the sanguine punishments of English common law, often capital in nature. While benefit of clergy first applied only to members of the clergy, it eventually was extended to any person who could quote Psalm 51 from the Bible and thus beg personally for mercy. Benefit of clergy may be seen as an early form of suspended sentence. As it became available to more and more classes of accused persons, it lost its original intent and clerical meaning and became "a clumsy set of rules which operated in favour of all criminals to mitigate in certain cases the severity of the criminal law."[7] Gradually, the state acquired total jurisdiction from the church and benefit of clergy was eventually abolished. By 1827, it could no longer be claimed by commoners and in 1841 it was no longer available to English peers. Benefit of clergy survived in the American colonies until only shortly after the Revolution.

Another early form of suspended sentence was judicial reprieve. *Judicial reprieve* was the temporary suspension of the imposition or sentence by the court. The granting of such reprieve usually allowed the defendant to go free pending final disposition of the case. Its purpose was to allow the defendant to have time to appeal a case to the Crown or to apply for a pardon. It was also granted when the judge was not satisfied with the evidence presented against the accused. Although judicial reprieve did offer a form of suspended sentence, sometimes indefinite suspension, it did not set forth any conditions by which the accused was to be governed during this reprieve. This form of suspended sentence was not probation, which by earlier definition must carry with it some degree of supervision.

Recognizance (the obligation to appear in court), with or without bail, is deeply embedded in English law. Originally, it was used as a method for assuring that a defendant would appear at trial. It was also used as a form of provisional suspension until the final disposition of a case. Today, it is used for only the first purpose. Recognizance originated as a form of preventive justice. It "consists of obliging those persons, whom there is a probable ground to suspect of future misbehavior, to stipulate with and to give full assurance to the public, that such offense as is apprehended shall not happen. . . . This 'assurance to the public' is given by entering into a recognizance or bond (with or without sureties) creating a debt to the state which becomes enforceable, however, only when the specified conditions are not observed. The recognizance is entered into for a specified period of time."[8]

The United Nations report, *Probation and Related Matters,* states that recognizance and provisional release on bail "in a very real sense [were] the first rudimentary stage in the development of probation."[9]

Early Probation in the United States

The conditional release of youthful offenders to the supervision of their masters or parents was practiced in England as early as 1820 by the Warwick-shire Quarter Sessions, an English criminal court. But a Boston cobbler by the name of John Augustus deserves the title of the "father of probation," for he was the world's first probation officer. Augustus spent a great deal of time observing the proceedings of the Boston police court. He became interested in the common drunks in jail. Because they could not pay their fines, he often paid them himself. In fact, by 1858 he had bailed out over 1,152 men and 794 women and girls. In addition to this, he would offer to help young girls and women who had either no place to go or no one to care for them.

For those he bailed out, Augustus undertook the task of supervising and guiding their behavior during the period prior to the court's final disposition. The courts encouraged Augustus in his endeavors by not sentencing the convicted criminals to the usual stay in the House of Correction. Instead, if they had shown signs of good behavior and reform during the period between their release on bail and their final court date, the judge would impose only a nominal fine and order the defendant to pay court costs.

Augustus' work resulted in the establishment of a visiting probation agent system in Massachusetts, in 1869. This system was devised primarily to assist delinquent children; the method of supervision employed was described as follows:

> If the offense of the convicted one appears exceptional to his general good conduct, and his appearance and surroundings are such as to give promise of future correct behavior, and if it be the first offense, the child is put on probation, with the injunction, "Go and sin no more," and becomes one of the wards of the state by adoption, over whom we exercise such guardianship as we may. If there is hope without strong promise that the offender may do well if released on probation, he is formally and legally committed to the agent of the Board of State Charities, and comes under his control independent of the parents, except as the agent permits; but he is allowed to return to the parents, and remain with them so long as he does well; although he may remain with his parents or friends, he becomes a ward of the State by due process of law, and a subject of visitation.[10]

Because of the humanitarianism of this one man, the nation's first probation law was passed in Massachusetts in 1878. In 1891, a second Massachusetts law required the criminal courts to appoint probation officers and to extend the provisions of the first law generally. By 1900, there were only four other states that recognized and used this new approach for the disposition of criminal cases. They were Missouri, beginning in 1897; Rhode Island, in 1899; New Jersey, in 1900; and Vermont, in 1900. Not until the creation of the first juvenile court in Chicago in 1899 was the idea of probation or suspended sentence with proper supervision considered in regard to juveniles.

By 1927, all but two states had passed laws similar to Illinois's to establish juvenile courts, and all but one of those had established juvenile probation systems. The link between juvenile courts and the provision of probation services for juveniles so prevalent in the system today may be said to have originated at the very beginnings of the juvenile court movement.

> Early probation methods were rather crude, but even the reports of those early officers showed gratifying progress. The personal work has been continuously improved by contributions from social case work, psychology, and psychiatry. . . . However, despite the steady development of probation, it is not a panacea, but rather a method to be used only when a wise and disciplined therapy can be developed.''[11]

The former secretary of the National Probation and Parole Association commented on the probation system as follows:

> A really statewide probation system, and as yet not a single state has a complete one, would mean that every court dealing with offenders would have both men and women trained, experienced, and properly supervised to investigate and report to the judge before sentence, on the history and environment of every single offender. It would mean trying out, under friendly but firm supervision, adapted to the individual's needs, every individual, young and old, whose attitude, past history, and general characteristics appear upon investigation to offer at least a fair chance of improvement and the avoiding of further crime.[12]

Although probation sources have expanded greatly since Mr. Chute made this statement, his remarks still present a valid challenge to practitioners in the juvenile justice system, particularly to the juvenile courts and probation officers, to see that the system does indeed work as intended.

Probation Today

Probation has become a major part of the juvenile justice system as well as a complex social institution which touches the lives of literally hundreds of thousands of young people each year. Underlying the practice of probation is the basic belief that there are juvenile delinquents who pose neither a threat nor a risk to society. Placing such juveniles in institutions would not be in the best interests of the juvenile. Indeed, it could lead to further law violations and more dangerous forms of delinquency. Putting the probationable youth in an institution is also more costly for the state. It costs significantly more to maintain a juvenile in an institution than it does to supervise that same juvenile on probation in the community. A very important task for probation personnel, therefore, is to identify those youths who pose no threat to the community. If the adjudicated delinquent poses no jeopardy to the community and demonstrates law-abiding behavior to the court, it is in the best interests of all concerned to consider placing the youth on probation.

Why Probation?

The primary goal of probation is to provide services designed to help youthful offenders in dealing with their problems and their environment. If the probation is successful, the factors which brought the youth into contact with the law should be resolved, and at the same time, a reintegration process for the youth into the community should be carried out. As mentioned earlier, probation is to be preferred over institutionalization for several reasons:

1. Probation allows the juvenile to function at a fairly normal level in the community, while at the same time affording protection for the community against further law violations.

2. Probation helps the juvenile avoid the negative effects of institutionalization, which often hinder the progress of rehabilitation and the return to law-abiding behavior.

3. The verbal description of the offense in a probation case is often worded in a less severe manner than for other dispositions. For example, instead of a case description of ''grand larceny,'' the words ''bicycle theft'' may be used. This decreases the impact of the labeling process on the juvenile.

4. The youth's rehabilitation program is greatly facilitated by keeping the youth in the community, living at home, and, if feasible, attending school, participating in extracurricular activities, working, and so forth.

5. Probation is much less expensive than incarceration. In fact, 1971 figures indicate that probation costs only one-sixth as much as incarceration.[13] In 1973-1974, for example, it cost the State of Washington $49 per day or $17,885 per year for each institutionalized juvenile. It cost approximately $2,980 a year (or a savings of almost $15,000) to maintain each youth on probation.[14]

Of course, probation is not a suitable or desirable disposition in all cases. In some states there are statutes which define certain offenses as nonprobational. All offenders convicted of these offenses must be incarcerated, regardless of circumstances. In these cases, the court must accept the questionable assumption that dispositional decisions for such offenders can be based on the offense alone and that other conditions such as personality, attitude, and life circumstances are inconsequential factors in the dispositional decision for the offender.

Even if an offense is probational, the community may be so outraged by the crime committed by the youth that pressure is applied on the court to place the youth in an institution. It may also be clear from the youth's past behavior or attitude that there is a predictable risk to the community and that probation would be inappropriate. In most cases, however, probation is feasible if given a chance.

A great deal depends upon the training and attitude of the probation staff and the level of their commitment to making it work. The American Bar Association Project on Standards for Criminal Justice advocates trying to make probation work:

> The automatic response of many in the criminal justice system that imprisonment is the best sentence for crime unless particular reasons exist for "mitigating" the sentence is not a sound starting point in the framing of criminal sanctions . . . quite the opposite ought to be the case . . . that the automatic response in a sentencing situation ought to be probation, unless particular aggravating factors emerge in the case at hand. At least if such aggravating factors cannot be advanced as the basis for a more repressive sentence, probation offers more hope than a sentence to prison that the defendant will not become part of the depressing cycle which makes gates of our prisons resemble a revolving door rather than a barrier to crime.[15]

Juvenile Court Guides

How, then, is the judge to decide between placing a juvenile offender on probation or sending him or her to an institution? The International Association of Chiefs of Police Delinquency Prevention/Juvenile Justice Conference devised criteria to guide the juvenile court judge in such a decision. The factors to be considered are:

1. Does the court have a probation department? If so, is it adequately staffed to insure maximum supervision of and counseling assistance to clients?
2. The nature and circumstances of the offense. How serious is the offense, both to the victim and to the public? What amount of criminal sophistication was evidenced in the planning and commission of the offense?
3. The history and character of the offender. Is he currently on probation for another offense? Was he previously incarcerated? Did he admit his guilt or

involvement? What are his attitudes toward the offense, society, and juvenile justice officials?

4. The offender's family situation. Would placing him back in an unstable family jeopardize chances for rehabilitation? Are the parents willing to assist their child or do they want to ''get him off their hands?''

5. Availability of community resources. The juvenile court judge must establish excellent liaison procedures with community juvenile justice service agencies in order to be able to refer the probationer to these agencies for assistance with his problem. The child's school must be willing to readmit him and assist him in making a satisfactory readjustment.[16]

Formal and Informal Probation

Simply put, formal probation occurs when the child's petition for probation is brought before the court and the court in turn decides that a formal hearing is necessary. A youth must normally be an adjudicated delinquent, dependent, or incorrigible before being placed on formal probation.

If a juvenile is given formal probation, he or she is placed under direct supervision of an assigned probation officer and must abide by the conditions tailored to fit that situation.

A majority of cases never reach the formal court hearing stage. In most states, as many as 50 percent of probational cases are handled on an informal basis.[17] Informal or ''vest pocket'' probation may occur for one of a number of reasons. One of the most common is an overcrowded juvenile court calendar. To place a juvenile on informal probation, a petition must be filed with the court. This petition may be filed by just about anybody, but is usually handled by the police, the probation office, a social service agency, or in some cases by the juvenile court's intake service.

The juvenile court in conference with those involved with the case (i.e., the probation officer, court intake officer, and so forth) reviews the juvenile's case and determines if the offense, behavior, or life circumstances warrant a formal court hearing. If not, the juvenile can be placed on informal probation and is, therefore, technically under the supervision of the probation office.

The President's Conference on Law Enforcement and Administration of Justice, however, points out that informal dispositions are not always in the youth's best interests.

> The rationale for pre-judicial handlings rests on the greater flexibility, efficiency, and humanity it brings to a formal system operating within legislative and other definitive policies. But pre-judicial methods that seek to place the juvenile under substantial control in his pattern of living without anyone's consent are not permissible. The difficult task is to discriminate between the undesirable use of informality, benevolent as well as punitive, and tolerable, desirable modes of guidance.[18]

"Pre-judicial" means that the case does not reach the formal hearing stage, not that the court has not been involved. Most juvenile courts have juvenile probation departments that are defined and legitimized under statute and are part of the court.

Filing a Petition

Generally, a petition is filed when the legal authority of the juvenile court is needed to insure either the welfare of the child or the safety of the community. Anyone who has first-hand knowledge of the case can file a petition with the court. The petition must, however, be reviewed and found to be justifiable by a juvenile probation officer or by a juvenile court intake officer.

While all sections of the petition are essential, the section called "statement of fact" is worthy of special mention. This section of the petition states the allegations which the youth and/or the legal guardian must defend themselves against. If there is no charge in the petition, they will not be required to offer a defense. Although a petition may be amended to include all charges, such an amendment should not be necessary if special attention is paid to completeness and accuracy in the first place.

A completed petition should contain the following sections, if possible:

1. Identification of the child. Name (true and alias), age, birthplace, sex, and residence of the child, so far as known by the petitioner. If not known, the petition shall so state.
2. Identification of the parent or custodian. Names (true and aliases), marital status, residence, relationship to child/children (include whether natural, legal, putative, adoptive or deceased), person with whom the child is residing.
3. Statement of facts. A statement of facts which gives the court jurisdiction over the child and over the subject matter of the proceedings, stated in plain language and with reasonable definiteness and particularity.
4. Request for inquiry. A request that the court inquire into the welfare of the child and make such order as the court shall find to be in the best interests of the child and the community.
5. Previous court orders, if any. Dates of orders and the legal status of the child must be included.[19]

Figure 9–1 is a sample petition used in the Superior Court of Washington for a county juvenile department:

The initial investigation required to enable a person to file a petition is not enough. Once the petition is accepted, the juvenile court intake worker, the probation officer, or any other party who filed the petition must conduct a further investigation. Witnesses (if applicable) must be found and interviewed, evidence must be compiled, and a case must be composed which

IN RE THE WELFARE OF   LEGAL NO.

                                                  PETITION

                          B.D.

_____

        I represent to the Court as follows:

Name of child:
Place of residence:
Name of person child resides
    with and relationship:
Name of father: Residence:
Name of mother: Residence:
Marital status of parents:

        That the child is

        That the child is within or residing within _____
County and is in need of care and planning by the court.
        Wherefore, your petitioner prays that the Court inquire into conditions
and enter such an order as shall be for the child's welfare, pursuant to
Chapter 13.04 of the Revised Code of Washington.

                                          _____
STATE OF WASHINGTON   Petitioner
                          SS
COUNTY OF _____   _____
                                          Petitioner

                                          _____
                                          Agency or Relationship
                                            or Residence

_____ , being first duly sworn on oath,
deposes and says:
        That (s)he is the petitioner herein; that (s)he has read the foregoing
petition, knows the contents thereof,

                                          _____

                                          _____

FIGURE 9—1. A sample petition.

Source: State of Washington, Department of Social and Health Services.

SUBSCRIBED AND SWORN TO before me this ————————————
day of ————————————— , 19————————————— .

SUPERIOR COURT CLERK by Deputy:

————————————————————————

or

————————————————————————

Notary Public in and for the
State of Washington, residing at

————————————————————————

NOTICE TO CHILD AND PARENTS OR CUSTODIAN
READ CAREFULLY

The Court, after appropriate hearings in open court, may:
(1) Commit a delinquent or incorrigible child to the Department of Social and Health Services, Division of Institutions; or
(2) Decline or waive jurisdiction in delinquency cases, to treat a child as an adult by referral to an appropriate adult court or prosecuting authority; or
(3) Place a delinquent, incorrigible or dependent child in the parents' custody subject to a probation plan; or
(4) Place a delinquent, incorrigible or dependent child in the temporary custody of a group home or foster home; or
(5) Make any social plan for the best welfare of a delinquent, incorrigible or dependent child.

Hearing set for:
N & S to:
Officer:

FIGURE 9–1 (continued)

will effectively convince the judge that the court must intercede either to protect the child or safeguard the community.

Functions of Juvenile Probation

The contemporary juvenile probation department serves three major functions: (1) intake and screening, (2) investigation, and (3) supervision.

Intake and Screening

The primary function of intake and screening is to determine whether those juveniles for whom petitions have been made fall under the jurisdiction of the court. Most states have statutes which define what kinds of cases may be handled by the probation department. Thus, each case sent to the department must be thoroughly screened to make sure it is an appropriate referral.

Many referral sources do not have the time, money, or staff to properly explore each case they refer. Often, the probation officer has to confer with the child, the family, and the referral source to find out whether the case should be handled by the probation office directly or by referral to other community resources.

Beside statutory deferment, other circumstances may prevent the involvement of the probation department. For example, most probation offices cannot offer services for the psychotic, the retarded, or the severely handicapped child.

The preliminary investigation at intake should include an interview with the juvenile at which time the juvenile should be advised of his or her legal rights.[20] The probation department should also contact the youth's parents or guardians to inform them of the status of the case and of their right to contact an attorney.

It is possible that the case may be resolved at this early screening stage by what has been previously called an informal disposition. This occurs if it is decided that the juvenile need not go to court but may instead be supervised by the probation department with the consent of the parents or guardian.

A crucial part of the intake and screening process is to decide whether the child should be admitted to, continued in, or removed from detention prior to the final disposition of the case. Removal from the home may constitute a major threat to the child and/or family and may deal a severe psychological blow to the youth. While removal may be necessary and even helpful for some, it may be damaging and inappropriate for others. The problem is rendered even more complex by the fact that in the 1960s and 1970s, many juvenile detention facilities degraded and brutalized their inmates rather than rehabilitating them.[21]

The importance of doing a good job during the intake and screening process must be emphasized. Inappropriate referrals and wrong decisions can do a great deal of harm to the youths involved.

Investigation

In addition to the preliminary investigation mentioned in regard to filing a petition, the probation department must develop a comprehensive social history on each youth who is scheduled for a hearing in juvenile court.

The juvenile court can be a dominant power in the life of a juvenile in trouble. Since the juvenile delinquent may be returned home, placed in an alternative living situation, or removed from society entirely for several years, depending on the action of the court, the social study or diagnostic study is extremely important to the future of the child.

> Such a study involves the awesome task of predicting human behavior. The focal concern is the probable nature of the child's response to the necessary demands of society. Will he or will he not be able to refrain from offending again if permitted to continue to reside in the free community? An even more complicated question is: What will be his adjustment under the various possible conditions of treatment, i.e., if he is returned home without further intervention, or if he is provided differing sorts of community supervision and service, or if he is confined in an institution? Only by illuminating such questions can the social study be of value to the court's dispositional decision.[22]

The probation department staff is charged with a major responsibility. The crucial and difficult task of pretrial investigation requires hard work, dedication, intelligence, and the ability to properly describe human behavior. Effective interview techniques and the ability to coordinate resources and knowledge represented by other disciplines such as law, medicine, and psychiatry must be used as backup to the investigator's own personal skills.

It is not always possible to immediately delineate a child's problems and formulate a precise treatment for those problems after the social diagnosis. The treatment process is often a gradual process in which a continuing relationship between the child and the probation staff is involved. Starting with the problem as defined by the juvenile, and determining what that juvenile wishes to do about it, many other areas of difficulty are uncovered. It is not possible or even desirable for the probation officer to contend with everything that surfaces diagnostically. For example, many fatherless boys are in need of a strong father figure. Casework training may give the probation officer the flexibility to provide such a figure. But time, caseload size, or the danger of the youth's becoming overly dependent upon the probation officer may make this option unrealistic.

Supervision

The overall picture of juvenile probation is muddied by the total lack of standardization. This problem exists in state jurisdictions and in the courts within a single state. This is true in regard to the provision of probation in general and the provision of supervision in particular.

There appear to be no standardized procedures regarding the conditions of probation, the training of probation officers, the organization of the probation staff, or the provision of services. Probation procedures, in fact, seem to be determined by individual courts and by individual cases. This multiplicity of procedures requires that probation supervision be discussed in generalities rather than specifics.

Probation supervision involves three major factors: (1) surveillance, (2) casework service, and (3) counseling or guidance.[23]

1. *Surveillance.* The officer must keep in touch with the juvenile, the parents, the school, and other persons or agencies involved with the case. The degree of this surveillance depends on the amount of time the officer must spend on routine paperwork, the size of the caseload, and the individual philosophy of the court. Surveillance is intended to keep the probation officer informed about the child's progress, attitude, reactions to the treatment plan, the parents' relationship with the child, and other aspects which would indicate the child's progress or lack of progress toward reintegration into the community.

   Surveillance should not be used as a threat to the child. If conducted properly, it can point out the responsibilities and the demands that life and society can make on each member of a community. By acting only as a monitor and reminder of failures, it can be a strong *negative* force.

2. *Casework service.* The probation officer is expected to utilize social casework methods to diagnose, treat, and generally deal with a juvenile. The officer makes home visits, conducts interviews, has discussions with the juvenile and parents, arranges for referrals to services agencies, works with the school, and engages in other tasks which are required in effective casework.

   The officer must determine to what extent the problems confronting the youth may be alleviated by involvement in community services or by his own personal intervention. He must then coordinate such services and present them in an organized program aimed at helping the child and the parents to make effective use of them.

3. *Counseling or guidance.* Guidance in supervision works hand in hand with the other two aspects and makes them both possible to perform.

   The child and family and other persons concerned must be helped to understand and face the existence of the personal or environmental problems productive of the child's delinquency. Frequently, they must be helped to gain some degree of understanding of their roles in the production—and thus in the solution—of such problems. They must be encouraged and stimulated to mobilize their strengths and energies and to invest them in the problem-solving process.[24]

Auxiliary Functions

Depending on the jurisdiction, the probation department provides several other services aside from surveillance, casework service, and counseling. Large probation departments often administer their own treatment or diagnostic services. These programs may include such things as foster care, group homes, drug treatment centers, and forestry camps. They may also be involved in organizing and planning community resources, and some may even operate delinquency prevention programs.

In summary, the supervision of juveniles by the probation department depends on several factors. Some of the more significant are the size and staffing of the department and available financial resources.

> Suppose the judge looks at the youthful misdemeanant, takes time to question him at length, and decides that, with help, the youth has a good chance to lead a useful life rather than be imprisoned at the taxpayers' expense. Then what can he do? He can put the defendant on probation. . . . But the fact is that in at least 90 percent of our lower courts there is no money for a probation or rehabilitation program of any kind. The defendant may be released ''on probation,'' but, unless he commits another offense and is brought back into court, that is the last the judge will hear of him. The estimated 10 percent of lower courts that do have some kind of probation program are usually so short of funds that each probation officer is grossly overloaded with cases.[25]

The amount of success that the probation department experiences in carrying out its supervisory tasks depends in large measure on the ratio of probation officers to juveniles. To emphasize this point, Douglas Besharov, in *Juvenile Justice Advocacy,* offers the following observation regarding juvenile probation supervision:

> The realities of probation supervision do not live up to the hopes of the theory. Few communities are blessed with sufficiently staffed probation services. Many probation departments are so completely overwhelmed that they provide almost no supervision or follow-up. Individuals on probation may be seen as infrequently as once every two months during a perfunctory office interview. This affliction of probation systems is so common that it even has a name: ''token probation.'' Although the available evidence indicates that the size of a probation officer's case load does not affect his success,[26] it is reasonable to assume that the effect of ''token probation'' on a troubled youth is worse than no supervision at all. He sees that the end of court process was a sham and he loses further confidence, or fear in the system.[27]

Conditions of Probation

At the present time the conditions under which probation is granted are not standardized. Some courts dictate these conditions on an individual basis, while other courts follow state statutes. An example of the former is the county courts in Washington, which stipulate the conditions of probation in the court order. The latter is illustrated in a California statute which states:

> The court may impose and require any and all reasonable conditions that it may determine fitting and proper to the end that justice may be done and the reformation and rehabilitation of the ward enhanced.[28]

The conditions of probation that do exist range from vague, general directives like "Stay out of trouble" to specific stipulations, which may include regular school attendance; being home by a certain hour (curfew); getting a job; undergoing specific treatment or counseling; avoiding delinquent peers; refraining from the possession of firearms, dangerous weapons, or an automobile; no drinking or use of drugs; living at home and obeying parents; living in a foster or group home; restoration of damage to victims; doing volunteer public service work or chores; enrolling in special classes for vocational training; and regular reporting to the probation officer.

The purpose of these conditions is to alter the juvenile's environment of past delinquent behaviors in the hope that by removing those factors which were a negative influence, the youth will be less likely to misbehave. Conditions of probation can also apply to the parents or guardians. For example, the court order may stipulate that the parents maintain closer control over the juvenile, undergo family therapy, or participate in other suggested treatment programs.

If the child (or parents) violates the conditions of probation, he or she may be returned to the court for a new disposition based upon the latest misbehavior. Because probation is a means of retaining the youth in the community (and thus a means of eliminating the problems of reintegration after being in an institution), every effort is normally made to refrain from removing the child from the family and community. It is not uncommon for a youth to be returned to probation status time and time again. The courts tend to look for things such as current violations, their impact on the community, the child's past record; his or her attitude toward probation and society, and other factors. These factors were of course considered when the original disposition of probation was granted. The informal probationer who violates the conditions of probation may expect to go before the court for a formal hearing and be adjudicated as either a delinquent or an incorrigible. For the youth on formal probation, the conditions of that probation may be made tighter. Often, the youth has to report more often to his probation officer and the hours under curfew are increased significantly.

If it appears that the youth may have to be brought before the court again, the probation officer can assume disciplinary control over the client. If the officer has a large and unmanageable caseload, disciplinary control has little or no impact. In such a situation, the threat of return to the court becomes an arbitrary action, based on infrequent or totally negative contact with the juvenile.

If one accepts the conventional wisdom that youths should remain in their communities, if at all possible, it is not surprising to see that some courts bend over backwards to avoid sending youths to institutions, even if they repeatedly violate the conditions of their probation. There is a limit, however, to the tolerance of even the most concerned courts. The violation of probation can and often does result in an order remanding the youth to a correctional facility.

There are those who interpret a violation of probation as a failure of the individual officer. This tends to force many officers to make sure that, if a violation does occur, the blame falls on the juvenile and not the officer. To deflect the blame, however, the probation officer must resist committing himself or herself to the youth. Thus, if the probationer does fail, the officer can exonerate himself or herself of any responsibility and say it's all the juvenile's fault. Pressure of this sort certainly does not strengthen the effectiveness of the concept of probational reintegration.

Duration of Probation

As in the case of conditions of probation, the length of time a youth must spend on probation varies from state to state where statutes exist or from court to court within each state. Some statutes limit the maximum amount of time of the probation. For example, in Washington, D.C., probation is limited to one year,[29] in California to six months,[30] in New York to two years,[31] and in Illinois to five years,[32] and in some states, the maximum term of probation may be extended one or more times after required notice and a court hearing.[33]

If a statute is either nonspecific about the limit or does not establish one at all, the maximum extended length is usually considered to be until the juvenile reaches majority, normally age 18.[34]

If the juvenile has proven that he or she can responsibly meet the conditions of probation including no further law violations, the courts can shorten the term of probation and release the youth to the community on a nonsupervised normal citizen status.[35]

Organization and Administration of Probation

Traditionally, the administration of the probation department has been a function of the juvenile court. Probation services, although established slowly throughout the nation, now exist by statute in all fifty states and Puerto Rico.

According to the National Council on Crime and Delinquency, there are three types of organizational structures used by the states in the provision of juvenile probation services:

1. A centralized, statewide system (10 states—Alaska, Connecticut, Maine, New Hampshire, Rhode Island, Tennessee, Utah, Vermont, Virginia, and Wyoming).

2. A centralized county or city system supported by state supervision, consultation, standard-setting, staff development assistance, and partial state-subsidies (28 states—Alabama, Arizona, Arkansas, California, Colorado, Delaware, Florida, Illinois, Indiana, Kansas, Kentucky, Michigan, Missouri, Nebraska, Nevada, New Jersey, New Mexico, New York, North Dakota, Ohio, Oklahoma, Oregon, Pennsylvania, South Carolina, South Dakota, Texas, West Virginia, and Washington).

3. A combined state-local structure, with the largest jurisdictions operating their own probation departments and the state providing services in other areas (11 states—Georgia, Idaho, Iowa, Louisiana, Maryland, Massachusetts, Minnesota, Mississippi, North Carolina, Wisconsin; Montana has a multi-county probation system).[36]

These organizational structures create complex intergovernmental administrative problems, chiefly because most states place the administrative responsibility for juvenile probation services on the shoulders of the juvenile courts.

TABLE 9–1. ADMINISTRATIVE RESPONSIBILITY FOR JUVENILE PROBATION FUNCTION

ADMINISTRATIVE AGENCY	NUMBER OF STATES*
By courts	32
By state correctional agencies	5
By state departments of public welfare	7
By other state agencies	4
By other agencies or combination of agencies	3

*Includes Puerto Rico.

Source: President's Commission on Law Enforcement and the Administration of Justice, Task Force Report: Corrections (Washington, D.C.: U.S. Government Printing Office, 1967).

Juvenile probation has suffered and continues to suffer because there is no uniformity of standardization of administrative procedures. Administration by more than one level of government is a major cause of trouble. If juvenile probation administration continues to be divided among several units of government, then a strong, centralized state-level agency should be responsible for setting goals and standards in probation services for those departments which are unable to set their own.

Where the question of state versus local administration of juvenile probation services is raised, the best solution, from an organizational standpoint, is to have *supervision* from the state and *administration* through the counties. The National Council on Crime and Delinquency recommended the adoption of such a plan because such a pattern:

   a. has greater potential for assuring uniformity of standards and practice, including provision of services to rural areas.

   b. makes more feasible certain kinds of research, statistical and fiscal control, and similar operations.

   c. best enables recruitment of qualified staff and provision of centralized or regional in-service training and staff development programs.

   d. permits staff assignment to regional areas in response to changing conditions.

   e. facilitates relationships to other aspects of the state correctional program.[37]

However, even if everyone agreed that the administration of probation services belongs at the local level, this consensus would not completely solve the problem of intergovernmental relations. County or city probation services are administered either by the court or by an administrative agency which is a separate function of the local government. "Some system professionals feel that the probation function should be part of the local corrections component; conversely, others maintain that the responsibility for probation services should remain with the juvenile court because of the court's legal jurisdiction (the sentence is suspended while the offender is on probation, yet the court maintains legal control and can revoke the suspension, if warranted, and commit the offender to an institution)."[38]

Major police organizations contend that the administration of juvenile probation should be the function of the county or district courts and not at the community level. This is part of the movement toward consolidating such services at more cost-effective levels.

Figure 9–2 shows the recommended organization and administration of juvenile probation services. "This particular organizational structure is recommended for two reasons: (1) the necessity for state supervision of all juvenile probation services in the state to provide for uniformity and standards; and (2) the necessity for local administration by a juvenile court because the court is legally responsible for those children placed on probation. Further, it is felt that this method of providing probation services will strengthen and unify the juvenile justice system, both at the local and state levels."[39]

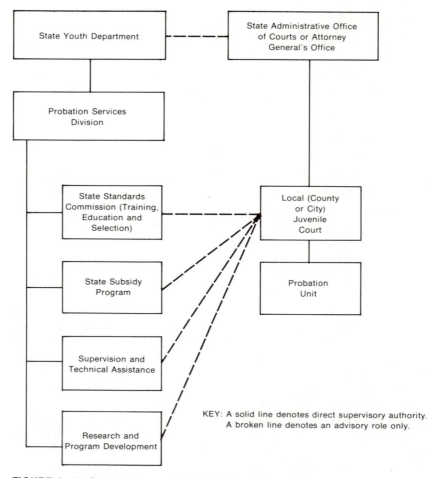

FIGURE 9 – 2. Organization and administration of juvenile
probation services.

Source: International Association of Chiefs of Police.

The Probation Officer

With proper administration, sound organizational structure, and the commitment of state and local governments to providing competent probation services, probation still requires one more ingredient—the dedicated, well-trained, and concerned juvenile or probation officer.

"All juvenile courts have an auxiliary staff to provide the court's social service function. The same staff usually operates the intake and adjustment service, the predispositional investigation and report service, and the probation supervision service. . . ."[40] These staff members are sometimes called juvenile counselors, but more frequently they are known as juvenile probation officers. This name originated because of their traditional role of supervising juveniles on probation.

Generally, state statutes spell out the specific powers and duties of the juvenile probation officer. The following, taken from the Washington State Revised Code, is an example.

> *RCW 13.04.040.* Probation counselors and other persons in charge of detention facilities [regarding their] appointment, powers and duties, compensation. The court shall, in any county or judicial district in the state, appoint or designate one or more persons of good character to serve as probation counselors during the pleasure of the court. In case a probation counselor shall be appointed by any court, the clerk of court, if practicable, shall notify him in advance when a child is to be brought before said court. The probation counselor shall make such investigations as may be required by the court. The probation counselor shall inquire into antecedents, character, family history, environments, and cause of dependency or delinquency of every alleged dependent or delinquent child brought before the juvenile court and shall make his report in writing to the judge thereof. He shall be present in order to represent the interests of the child when the case is heard; he shall furnish the court such information and assistance as it may require; and shall take charge of the child before and after the trial as may be directed by the court.
>
> All probation counselors shall possess all the powers conferred upon sheriffs and police officers to serve process and make arrests for the violation of any state law or county or city ordinance, relative to the care, custody, and control of delinquent and dependent children.
>
> *13.07.040.* Counselors: appointment, term, qualifications. Probation counselors . . . shall be appointed by the court, be subject to its supervision and administration, and shall serve at its pleasure. Each probation counselor so appointed shall in addition to having desirable personal qualification as determined by the presiding judge be of good moral character and hold a bachelor of arts degree from an accredited college or university.[41]

Duties

The duty and responsibility of the juvenile probation officer is to carry out the functions of juvenile probation: (1) intake and screening, (2) investigation, and (3) supervision. How much success the officer has in fulfilling these functions will be determined by several factors, some of which are beyond the officer's control. For example, the number of probation officers a court can hire will be limited by the court's budget, and the number of officers has a direct bearing on the size of each caseload. The training (when there is training) an officer receives is the prerogative of the court under its mandate to provide staff to oversee probation.

Another factor is how the officer interprets his or her role as a probation officer. For example, some officers consider themselves to be social workers, while, in fact, they usually have insufficient or minimal professional training in social work and their prior experience has been more public social service-oriented than treatment-oriented. Even though they perform crucial social service functions, most officers identify themselves with law enforcement officials and also tend to take on an authoritarian role in their work with juveniles.

> [Al]though probation officers talk of their work in terms of "helping" and "supervising" children, social work skills are generally ignored in practice. In place of technical and professional competence, the probation officer identifies common sense and knowledge of local community byways as the fundamental requisites for his work. Hence, the indispensability of practical experience and probation work receives constant stress. In addition, probation officers emphasize getting to know and to be known in the local community . . . these connections are felt to be at the core of probation work, where they both promote exchange of information and favors with community agents such as the settlement houses, schools, and police, and keep the probation officer in close touch with developments in the community.
>
> This particularistic, "common-sense" approach underlies the probation officer's conception of his relationship with delinquents. "Respect," balanced by deserved fairness, must be maintained. . . . Establishing respect requires adapting an authoritarian and disciplinarian stance towards delinquents, not a therapeutic and counseling one.[42]

Although considered low in professional standing within the juvenile justice system, the probation officer generally receives the necessary court backing to enable him or her to do the job effectively. In many respects, the probation officer may be viewed as being second only to the juvenile court judge in the degree of power he or she holds within the juvenile justice system. The probation officer has the power to direct cases to and from the court system, to decide whether a juvenile is to be kept in detention or not, to influence the court's disposition through his or her ability to color the court's picture of the child and the child's family, and to exert a general influence over the outcome of a case.

Qualifications

The juvenile probation officer should possess emotional maturity, integrity, belief in the ability of people to change, interest in helping people, a basic respect for laws, ability to work well with others, desire to grow professionally, and a firm belief in the dignity and worth of young people. These qualities are an essential part of the makeup of a prospective probation officer.

In addition, the Committee on Standards recommends that certain minimal educational requirements be met: (1) a bachelor's degree in arts or social science, (2) one year of graduate study in social work or a related social science, or (3) one year of paid, full-time experience under professional supervision in a recognized social agency. The social agency should be one in which treatment, rather than the routine administration of social services, is stressed. Persons who meet these standards or requirements should receive extensive on-the-job training for diagnosis and treatment of probationers. Unfortunately, it is difficult to find the necessary number of staff who possess these requirements.

> The survey data on the educational qualifications for employment as a probation officer or chief probation officer are not encouraging. They indicate that many appointing authorities have no understanding of the necessary attributes to persons who are to be assigned the task of producing change in human behavior. . . ; [in] 22 percent of the departments included in the survey sample, the educational qualifications for employment of probation officers are below the recommended minimum educational standard. In 74 percent of the departments, that part of the minimum standard calling for at least a bachelor's degree is maintained, but no information is available on the requirement for 1 year of graduate education or 1 year of supervised employment in a social agency.[43]

> It thus appears that most of the country's juvenile courts employ as probation officers and chief probation officers, persons who lack professional training in diagnosis and treatment. This clearly suggests the necessity for extensive use of inservice training and other staff development tools in probation departments.[44]

Training

The President's Commission on Law Enforcement and Administration of Justice recommends that on-the-job training be used to supplement the educational and work-related experience backgrounds of probation officers. This training should begin with an orientation program for new workers to enable them to become familiar with court or agency policies, attitudes, and demands. Inservice training, casework supervision, and the procedures for educational leave should also be included in on-the-job training.

Inservice Training   Inservice training should be designed to meet the needs of the staff at various levels, including supervisory and administrative. Larger agencies should assign a full-time person to conduct inservice training; smaller agencies should be assisted by appropriate state departments in organizing training regionally.

In a recent survey, less than 50 percent of the departments interviewed in the sample had inservice training programs.[45]

Casework Supervision   Casework supervision involves instruction for the probation officer in the proper use and application of diagnosis and treatment. Without specific instruction of this kind, it is difficult for the untrained worker to apply what has been learned in the training program to practical situations involving juveniles, their families, and the community. The President's Commission on Law Enforcement and the Administration of Justice states that "qualified observers who have studied many individual departments find all too often that the supervisor himself is untrained in the professional aspects of probation and does not even regard teaching and consultation as part of his function."[46]

Educational Leave   Probation departments should not only offer but actively encourage educational leave and stipends so that both part- and full-time staff members have the opportunity to broaden their education, meet desired qualifications, and improve their professional abilities and competence.

It is unrealistic to assume that all of the educational and training needs of the probation officer can be met during an inservice training period. In order for this to happen, there must be well-prepared personnel to carry out the necessary supervision and training of those who need it; unfortunately, this is seldom the case. Maximum contributions to the field of probation will not be realized unless staff members are encouraged to advance, learn, and grow. Graduate professional training is an excellent way to accomplish this goal. Advanced professional training can be pursued by taking a Master's in Social Work, which normally requires two full years' work beyond a bachelor's degree, or a graduate degree in sociology, psychology, criminology, or public administration. These degrees require one or two years' study beyond the undergraduate degree.

Method of Appointment

Probation staff should be selected in accordance with civil service laws where there is an organized civil service system. Where these laws don't apply, the staff should be selected on the basis of the merit of the applicants. The selection process should include a thorough review of the applicant's education, experience, and training. A merit examination should be used in making appointments. It should be open to all persons who meet the qualifications.

The evaluation and/or examination should test basic skills and knowledge required for good performance. It should not be concerned with matters that are meant to be learned on the job. Once appointed, the new probation officer should be given a reasonable period of time in which to become acquainted with his or her new duties and responsibilities.

Salaries

Salaries for newly appointed probation officers are as nonstandardized as the functions and terms of probation itself. Probation standards call for salaries commensurate with employment in similar positions of trust and responsibility. However, starting salaries for the chief probation officer run from less than $3,000 to more than $18,000, with a median of $8,000–$9,000; salaries for staff supervisor range from $3,000 to $11,000, with a median of $7,000–$8,000; and salaries for probation officer range from under $3,000 to about $11,000, with a median of between $5,000 and $6,000.

Because of low salary rates, most of the nation's probation departments cannot compete with other government agencies in recruiting the caliber of staff member which they need and want. It is little wonder that the majority of probation departments identify lack of staff as their biggest problem in effectively administering and conducting juvenile probation services.

Caseload Size

As mentioned earlier, a decisive factor in the quality of probation services is the size of the officer's caseload. All facets of the probation officer's work, from preliminary investigation to supervision, are affected by the caseload. An overcrowded caseload will usually result in a cursory investigation in which many pertinent and potentially crucial facts may be totally overlooked.

Supervision, other than formal reporting and infrequent checks at school, work, and home, is literally impossible with a large caseload. Large caseloads not only limit supervision to a cursory police-type function, but they also tend to move probation services further away from professional social casework standards for diagnosis and treatment to a more authoritarian role.

According to Kenney and Pursuit:

> The generally recognized minimal standard, developed from practice experience, calls for a caseload of not more than fifty units of work a month. One case under probation supervision is counted as one unit; a new investigation and diagnostic study counts as five units since, if properly done, it may be expected to require about five times as much time and effort as will a case under supervision in one month.[47]

> Minimal though it is, this 50-unit standard is seldom met in practice. The median load in agencies surveyed falls between 71 and 80 cases under supervision. Of all the children being served, .2 percent were in caseloads where the number of supervision cases was less than 20. On the other hand, 10.6 percent were in loads where the number of supervision cases was over 100. The highest average supervision caseload reported was 281.

In most probation departments at least half of the officer's time is spent on social studies (investigations in new cases). Therefore, a number of work units in the departments included in the survey is at least twice the number of cases under probation supervision reported above.[48]

Probation Subsidy

No discussion of juvenile probation would be complete without a look at what has come to be known as the probation subsidy program. It has been pointed out that the lack of staff and the overload of case assignments can greatly lessen the impact that probation might otherwise have on diverting juveniles from the formalized system. The probation subsidy program was started to alleviate this situation; it is used in several states today.

Simply stated, probation subsidy provides funding and guidance necessary to enable participating courts to develop and implement community-based treatment programs as alternatives to institutionalization. Normally, funding is provided by the state to the local courts. It is based on the number of youths which each court is able to divert from the state system.

The aim of the subsidy program, therefore, is to reduce the necessity for commitment of juveniles to state correctional facilities by strengthening and improving the supervision of juveniles placed on probation by the juvenile courts. The program encourages the courts to develop a wide range of special programs that may include counseling and placement services; contracts for psychiatric, psychological, and medical services; special day-care centers; vocational and educational programs; family and group counseling; tutoring services; extensive use of volunteers; use of case aides, work and recreational programs, educational counseling, and a myriad of other services integral to effective probation supervision programs.

Washington's juvenile probation subsidy, modeled after the one started in California in 1968, is an example of a probation subsidy program and shows how it might work. As the program evolved under the guidance of Washington's state and county juvenile court directors, five specific objectives were defined. They are to: (1) reduce commitment rates to state juvenile rehabilitation facilities by 25 percent or more in participating counties . . . [90 percent of Washington's 39 counties participate in the program.] . . . ; (2) reduce overall costs to the state for rehabilitating selected delinquent youth; (3) provide higher quality probation services to selected youthful offenders through (a) reducing probation officer caseloads and (b) making funds available for purchase of additional services as needed; (4) provide increased protection to the community through more consistent, uniform supervision of probationers; and (5) reduce the extent to which youth become involved in repeated offenses.[49]

The functions of probation (that is, intake, investigation, and supervision) are also functions of probation subsidy workers. Essentially, except for funding base and allocations, regular probation and probation subsidy officers operate in a similar manner. Staff assignments and caseload sizes may vary, however, for probation subsidy officers. For example, several county courts in Washington have regular probation officers who handle the nonsubsidy probation caseloads and probation subsidy officers who handle nothing but subsidy cases.

Since probation subsidy is meant to go beyond regular probation in diverting children from the correctional program, subsidy officers generally have caseloads comprised of youth who are on informal probation or who have not yet reached the formal hearing stage. This type of caseload, which generally requires less routine paperwork, allows the subsidy workers to spend more of their workday providing or coordinating direct services for youths on their caseloads.

The probation subsidy program, where it has been tried, has had a far greater success rate than ever anticipated. It has reduced the social and individual cost of juvenile delinquency by reducing treatment costs, reducing the pattern of institutional commitments, and meeting the treatment needs of delinquent youth within the community.[50]

Volunteers in Probation

The use of volunteers to supplement the efforts of paid correctional and juvenile justice system personnel is an increasingly common practice. It is enthusiastically endorsed by most probation department administrators.

Probation itself, the reader will recall, actually began as a volunteer service in the nineteenth century. In recent years, rising probation caseloads, lack of staff, and increased costs have brought about a renewed dependence on the assistance of community volunteers in probation. With the emphasis today on community-based programs for both adult and juvenile offenders, community volunteers are especially useful, and in the courts, the number of volunteers has increased significantly in the past fifteen years.

Voluntary work in probation is a documented subject, and several works have been written that explain all facets of volunteer programs in probation.

In a volunteer program, the probationer remains under the supervision of the Probation Department after having been placed on probation. However, the youth's primary contact is with a volunteer, usually on an individual basis within the community setting.

Case assignments are made on a common sense basis. Volunteers and children should be matched for the most rewarding relationship. The matching should be based on the needs of the probationer and the skills and interests of the volunteer. Both the youth and the volunteer must feel comfortable with each other or nothing will be accomplished. Many of the larger probation departments have a volunteer coordinator who oversees and supervises the pairing of youth and volunteer and the supervisory responsibilities during the probation period.

There are risks involved in matching probationers and volunteers. One of the risks concerns matching that ends in failure. This is a major problem because the professional staff member must pick up the pieces and attempt to keep the youth interested in the program and out of trouble. The youth may already be badly alienated from the system and may cause the regular probation officer more concern and problems than if the child had been assigned to his or her caseload in the first place. Under these circumstances, regular professional probation officers become resentful or extremely skeptical of volunteers who may undermine the system through their inexperience, lack of professional training, or inability to perform probationary tasks.

The evaluation of the Lincoln Program indicates that it was successful in what it attempted to do. Here is a summary of the results of that program.

A 1972 study of the program's effectiveness produced highly favorable results of comparisons between high-risk probationers who were assigned to volunteers and probationers who proceeded through regular probation programming. Statistically significant differences were found between the two groups in the number of new offenses committed during the probationary year, as well as in the seriousness of those offenses. Even more striking differences occur in the year prior to probation as compared to the probationary year for the two groups. Reductions were found in all offense categories for volunteer program participants, with an overall percentage reduction of 62 percent. In contrast, the group in regular probation had an overall reduction in offenses of 11 percent, which included increases in theft-related, antisocial, and minor traffic offenses. In general, volunteer counseling relationships are "successful" in about three of four cases.

Statistical Profile of Probationers

The average probationer caseload is about 200, half of whom are in the high-risk category. The average age of the probationer population is about 19 years, and about 90 percent are male (although there is an increasing trend in the number of female offenders). Data from the 1972 study suggest that offenses committed by high-risk probationers break down approximately as follows:

Theft-related	10%
Anti-social behavior	16%
Alcohol/Drug	22%
Major traffic	35%
Minor traffic	17%

Psychological testing indicates that the personality characteristics of the high-risk population are remarkably similar to inmate populations in California and delinquency-prone youth in other jurisdictions.

Statistical Profile of Volunteers

During the past eight years, 336 citizens from the Lincoln community have served as volunteer counselors for 472 high-risk offenders. Approximately 80 volunteers are currently associated with the program. Volunteers have ranged in age from 18 to 69 years, with the average being about 27 years. About 60 percent were men, and about 60 percent of the volunteers were married. Thirty-nine percent had previous counseling experience, formal training, or work experience with other community service agencies, sometimes in a volunteer role. Twenty-one percent expressed an interest in a counseling career. The average educational level was a little over 14 years. Over 90 percent of the volunteers expressed a religious affiliation.

Volunteer probation counselors come from all walks of life and socioeconomic levels in the community. Blue collar workers, professors, housewives, plumbers, attorneys, college students, and retirees have served as volunteer counselors. About 70 percent of the volunteers who are assigned to counsel a probationer agree to be reassigned. Because of the care taken in recruiting and screening applicants, the number of volunteers who must be dismissed is minimal. The major loss in volunteers is caused by persons moving from the community.[51]

Summary

In *Juvenile Justice Advocacy,* Douglas Besharov issues a warning in regard to the success of probation—careless overuse.

> Probation supervision tends to be a dumping ground for all those difficult juveniles whom the judge is afraid to send back into the community without some protection from future misgiving or criticism. He does not wish to place them and yet he "must do something" with them. Mentally retarded children, who are in need of very specialized types of services, also are often placed on probation because there is no other place for them. The effect is the dilution and misapplication of limited resources. For many juveniles, then, the circumstances of probation invite failure.[52]

The trend in corrections is more and more toward community-based programs, programs which are being asked to offer diagnosis, diversion, and treatment. As this trend continues, greater use will be made of probation as an alternative to institutionalization. With this increased use comes the threat of overuse of the program as an effective means of dealing with youth in trouble.

The National Commission on Criminal Justice Standards and Goals has recommended the nationwide use of probation as the preferred disposition, preferably without the subsequent adjudication of guilt within the particular case. It has also been recommended that volunteers serve in all capacities in the probation process.

There are persuasive arguments in favor of probation over institutionalization. They are: (1) a reduced stigma for the youth involved; (2) the advantage of remaining in the community; (3) the availability of a wealth of resources offered in the community which are generally absent in the institution; (4) the number of youth served and diverted from the formal system; and, most important, (5) the reduced costs of probation compared to institutionalization.

REVIEW QUESTIONS

1. Outline the historical beginnings of the modern probation system.

2. Define the term *probation*. Explain what is meant by formal and informal probation.

3. What are the functions of probation today? How are they best administered?

4. What is a petition and how is it filed? Why is it filed?

5. What qualities are important in an applicant for the job of probation officer? Are these qualities or qualifications being met?

6. Explain probation subsidy. How does this program and the use of volunteers in probation fit into the goals of probation? Cite any experience or knowledge you have regarding subsidy or volunteer programs.

7. Do you think probation works? Why or why not?

NOTES

1. National Center for Juvenile Justice, U.S. Department of Health, Education, and Welfare, *Juvenile Court Statistics* (Washington, D.C.: U.S. Government Printing Office, 1970).

2. *The Judicial Conference, 17th Annual Report* (Albany: State of New York, 1972), p. 363.

3. Ibid., p. 370

4. Washington Association of Directors of Juvenile Court Services, *Washington State Juvenile Court Statistics* (Olympia, Wash.: Department of Social and Health Services, 1975).

5. President's Commission on Law Enforcement and Administration of Justice, *Task Force Report: Corrections* (Washington, D.C.: U.S. Government Printing Office, 1967), p. 130.

6. Joshua 20: 2–6 and Numbers 35: 6.

7. W. S. Holdsworth, *A History of English Law,* vol. 3, p. 294, quoted in *Probation and Related Matters* (New York: United Nations, Department of Social Affairs, 1951), footnote, p. 17.

8. Robert M. Carter and Leslie T. Wilkins, eds. *Probation, Parole, and Community Corrections* (New York: Wiley, 1976), p. 83.

9. Department of Social Affairs, *Probation and Related Measures* (New York: United Nations, 1951), p. 22.

10. Board of State Charities of Massachusetts, *Sixth Annual Report* (Boston: State of Massachusetts, 1869), p. 269.

11. H. E. Barnes and N. K. Teeters, *New Horizons in Criminology* (Englewood Cliffs, N.J.: Prentice-Hall, 1959), pp. 554–555.

12. Charles L. Chute, "Probation versus Jail," *Jail Association Journal,* January–February, 1940, p. 5.

13. Advisory Commission on Intergovernmental Relations, *For a More Perfect Union: Correctional Reform* (Washington, D.C.: U.S. Governmental Printing Office, 1971), p. 3.

14. "Budget Report," Department of Social and Health Services, Juvenile Rehabilitation Program, Olympia, Washington: RCW 13.06, 72.05, 1974, p. 268.

15. American Bar Association Project on Standards for Criminal Justice, *Standards Relating to Probation* (New York: Institute of Judicial Administration, 1970), pp. 1–2.

16. R. W. Kobetz and B. B. Bosarge, *Juvenile Justice Administration* (Gaithersburg, Md.: International Association of Chiefs of Police, 1973), p. 325.

17. National Center for Juvenile Justice, U.S. Department of Health, Education, and Welfare, *Juvenile Court Statistics* (Washington, D.C.: U.S. Government Printing Office, 1972), p. 12. The intake divisions of probation departments in the U.S. disposed of some 58 percent of referrals in an informal manner.

18. President's Commission on Law Enforcement and Administration of Justice, *Task Force Report: Juvenile Delinquency and Youth Crime* (Washington, D.C.: U.S. Government Printing Office, 1967), p. 16.

19. These sections of a petition are taken from a bulletin entitled "Structure and Procedures of Juvenile Probation Departments and Juvenile Courts", from the Department of Social and Health Services, State of Washington, pp. 15–16. Note that while these factors are particular to Washington state, they may apply in general to other courts and states throughout the country and may serve as a guide for them.

20. See chapter 15, "A Juvenile's Legal Rights."

21. President's Commission on Law Enforcement and Administration of Justice, *Task Force Report: Corrections,* pp. 130–41.

22. Ibid., p. 132.

23. Ibid., p. 132.

24. Ibid., p. 132.

25. Joe Alex Morris, *First Offender, A Volunteer Program for Youth in Trouble With the Law* (Pleasantville, N.Y.: Readers Digest, 1970), pp. 7–8.

26. M. Adams, "Some Findings from Correctional Caseload Research," 31 Fed. Prob. 48 (December 1971).

27. Douglas J. Besharov, *Juvenile Justice Advocacy, Practice in a Unique Court* (New York: Practicing Law Institute, 1974), p. 383.

28. Cal. Welf. and Inst'ns. Code §730 (West 1972).

29. D.C. Code Ann. §16-2322 (a)(3) (1973).

30. Cal. Welf. and Inst'ns. Code §725 (a) (West 1972).

31. N.Y. Fam. Ct. Act §757(b) (McKinney 1973).

32. Ill. Ann. Stat. ch. 37, §705-3(1) (Smith-Hurd 1972).

33. Ga. Code Ann. §§24A-2701, 24A-2302(b) (Supp. 1972); D.C. Code Ann. §16-2322(c) (1973).

34. Ariz. Rev. Stat. Ann. §§8-241(2)(b), 8-246(B) (Supp. 1972); Md. Ann. Code art. 26, §70-19 (1973).

35. D.C. Code Ann. §16-2322(a)(3) (1973).

36. Kobetz and Bosarge, *Juvenile Justice Administration,* pp. 330–31.

37. Ibid., pp. 333–34.

38. Ibid., p. 335.

39. Ibid., p. 337.

40. Besharov, *Juvenile Justice Advocacy,* p. 159.

41. Title 13, Juvenile Courts and Juvenile Delinquents, RCW 13.040 and 13.07.040. pp. 2, 10.

42. Quoted in Besharov, *Juvenile Justice Advocacy,* pp. 160–61.

43. President's Commission on Law Enforcement and the Administration of Justice, *Task Force Report: Corrections,* p. 137.

44. Ibid., p. 137.

45. Ibid., p. 137.

46. Ibid., p. 138.

47. John P. Kenney and Dan G. Pursuit, *Police Work with Juveniles and the Administration of Juvenile Justice* (Springfield, Ill.: Thomas, 1975), p. 345.

48. Ibid., p. 345.

49. Community Services Division, *Juvenile Probation Subsidy Program: An Evaluation* (Olympia, Wash.: Department of Social and Health Services, 1975), p. 3.

50. For a further discussion of probation subsidy, see Paul Lerman, *Community Treatment and Social Controls* (Chicago: The University of Chicago Press, 1975).

51. Richard Ku, *The Volunteer Probation Counselor Program, Lincoln, Nebraska: An Exemplary Project* (Washington, D.C.: National Institute of Law Enforcement and Criminal Justice, 1973), pp. 5–6.

52. Besharov, *Juvenile Justice Advocacy,* p. 384.

10 Group Homes, Foster Home Care, and Adoption

> Adoption of children is an ever-changing tradition. In ancient Rome, the purpose of adoption was to provide elder men with sons to carry on the family name. By the mid-1920s in the United States, the goal was to find children for childless couples. Today the emphasis is on what is best for the adopted child.
>
> *JOAN McNAMARA*

The present trend in corrections is to make the community responsive to and responsible for the well-being of all its citizens, including juveniles who are delinquent or dependent. Several states have enacted legislation to prevent dependent or incorrigible juveniles from being sent to institutions. Washington was among the first states to pass such legislation.

> To the Department of Social and Health Services: Provided, that only a child found to be delinquent may be placed in a facility . . . except that a dependent child whose dependency arises from incorrigibility . . . may be committed to a diagnostic facility for not more than thirty days if the court finds that (a) the conduct of the child evidences a substantial likelihood of degenerating into serious delinquent or criminal behavior if not corrected and (b) other, less restrictive alternatives have failed, and (c) custodial treatment in a diagnostic and treatment facility is available and is reasonably expected to correct such degeneration: Provided, that such housing and treatment shall be entirely separate from that of delinquents.[1]

Cutting back on sending delinquents to institutions and eliminating altogether their possible use for dependent or incorrigible youth, however, may not be as obtainable or realistic a goal as many in the field of corrections would like it to be.

What should the juvenile justice system do with the troubled youths with whom it comes in contact, youths who often have nowhere to go except an institution? Avenues other than institutionalization must be explored. All elements of the juvenile justice system—the police, the probation officer, the judge, the parole officer, the institutional staff, and other professionals—agree that youths should be kept out of institutions. But of course these children cannot simply be let loose in the community. There have to be other choices, alternatives that are both acceptable and promising, or an institution may be the only choice left.

Some administrators operate on the "conventional wisdom" that the child's own home, no matter how bad, is better than no home at all. However, too often a bad or abusive home environment has caused the child to exhibit the very behavior that has resulted in involvement with juvenile justice in the first place. To return the child to such a home is analogous to patching the bulletholes in a target and then returning it to the shooting range. Some parents are not physically, mentally, emotionally, or financially capable of providing their children with proper care and supervision. In such cases, the problem can often be resolved with professional treatment or casework intervention. However, it may still be necessary to remove children from the home during rehabilitation, and a temporary placement may be the proper environment in which to carry this out.

If the home is simply not suitable for the return of the child, permanent alternatives must be sought. This chapter will examine three of the most commonly used alternatives to institutionalized or home living, either temporarily or permanently. These alternatives are *group homes, foster care,* and *adoption.*

The President's Commission on Law Enforcement and the Administration of Justice, in its *Task Force Report on Juvenile Delinquency and Youth Crime,* indicates a clear need for these alternative placements in community-based programs:

> The greatest need in juvenile correctional programs is to develop a graded series of alternatives to the traditional disposition of probation or incarceration in youth institutions. A central part of that process will be to build stronger links between correctional programs and the local communities.[2]

This need becomes even more apparent if one considers that approximately 70 percent of the $320 million spent on all juvenile correction programs throughout the country each year goes to institutional programs even though 48 percent of all those institutionalized for juvenile crimes became repeaters.[3] Institutions are obviously not the answer.

Group Homes

Group homes are a relatively recent development in America. There are those who contend that today's group homes, both private and public, are simply an extension of the halfway-house concept. At their onset, in the early 1960s, group homes may indeed have been halfway houses. At the time, they were perceived as a way to ease the rehabilitated youth's reentry into the community. In fact, they could be viewed as a kind of halfway-*out* house. The group home was primarily responsible for providing additional direction and support to the child, support needed to make the final adjustment to community living.

At first, group homes placed emphasis on making a youth self-sufficient, self-responsible, and self-reliant. To insure the likelihood of success, institutions were often discouraged from referring to group homes boys or girls who had serious behavioral problems. This practice tended to rule out such offenders as the repeat automobile thief, the sexually deviant offender, or those who might commit extreme acts of violence to themselves or others.

In short, early group homes looked after the "low-risk" youth who could be eased into the community from the institution with the minimum amount of treatment or trouble. It was a rare occurrence for the group homes to accept a youth who had not gone through the institutional "softening up" process.

Today, those responsible for group home operations shy away from the term *halfway house*. It is felt that this label connotes nonpermanence, both to those who find themselves as residents and those on the outside. In fact, for many residents, the state group home has become a more permanent home than they have ever known. In this situation, the name "halfway" becomes disturbing to those who may be experiencing their first feeling of belonging.

Group homes exist throughout the country in one form or another. Most states sign contracts with private group homes and do not run the homes directly. A few states, including Washington, run homes owned, staffed, and operated by the state.

In the 1970s group homes have broken out of the image of "transition warehouses" of the 1960s. Many are now providing extensive treatment. These new group homes are willing to work with youths from institutions, institutional rejects, and those assigned directly from a centralized diagnostic center. Their main purpose is the same—to ease the youth's reentry to society—but they also provide group care, counseling, and/or treatment for whatever period seems to be appropriate.

Purpose of the Group Home

The group home is generally a small residence for 6 to 15 youths. It is meant to be a place where adequate peer relationships can be formed, but where affectional ties to and demands from adults are kept at a minimum. Group homes impose needed external controls, but youths are not required to accept "substitute parents," as is the case in the foster home setting. Acceptance of a dependent role can be particularly difficult to the youth, who in his or her normal course of maturing, is in the process of achieving emotional independence from parental figures. Because in most cases those considered for group home placement are children between ages 13 and 18, group homes can promote the socialization process through small group interaction, interaction which does not involve a father or mother figure.

The group home, which was first introduced in 1916, offers interaction in small groups in which confidence and conflicts with a limited number of people provide the requisite emotional support and growing experiences. "Large institutions, except for the most socially disoriented persons, may be a thing of the past. Every creative child- and youth-serving residential program is moving to some adaptation of group homes located in the community."[4] In fact, over 150 agency-operated group homes have been established in the last decade.[5]

> The group home concept is the result of the findings of interrelated studies conducted in various settings in which socialization takes place (i.e., the family, the community-treatment centers, and institutions) and of theoretical insight into what makes a person develop into a mature member of society (i.e., the normal development process).[6]

In the Washington Group Home Study, seven characteristics common to group homes are listed.

1. They are residential.
2. They provide group care.
3. They contain between 6 and 10 residents.
4. They are community-based.
5. They provide social services.
6. They have a full-time staff.
7. They serve youths who are capable of living in the community but who need, for a variety of reasons, an alternative to their natural homes.

The study also contains a good definition of a group home.

> A group home is a small, community-based residential facility for a group of youths for whom a community-living situation is desirable, but who need an alternative to their natural homes. A full-time staff supervises the youth's activities and is responsible for coordinating the provision of social services, whether these services come from staff members themselves or from the community.[7]

Group homes are not a family enterprise. Professional and custodial staff are employed to run group homes (state or private) on a salaried basis. Unlike foster homes or adoptions, a "normal" or "normative" family atmosphere doesn't generally exist in a group home. Members of a group home often receive community services in a fragmented or piecemeal way from a number of unrelated agencies. With this kind of setup, the youth is not overburdened with outside involvement, involvement which is not only unrelated but sometimes not well coordinated.

School Facilities and Education

School facilities in the larger, more institutionalized group homes may be on the grounds of the home. The teaching staff is drawn from the group home staff. However, children in group homes often attend public schools in the community in which the home is located. Successfully integrating youths from group homes into the public schools depends in part on the cooperation and coordination efforts of group home staff, children, the public schools, and the community. Through their efforts, children with problems can be smoothly assimilated into schools designed to serve the average child.

In Washington, the problem of integrating group home children in the public school systems is conducted in a unique manner. Five full-time certified teachers, one part-time certified, and one full-time noncertified teacher have been employed to carry out the Title I program at the state's six group homes. The duties of these Title I teachers are to:

1. Evaluate each child's needs on entering the group home to determine individual program scope.
2. Serve as liaison between school and group home in providing continuous communication feedback on individual children in a coordinating effort.
3. Develop and institute special classes in reading, math, and English to meet the needs of children in residence at the group homes.
4. Provide a tutoring class for each child with a need.
5. Maintain information on each child to be used in evaluating the total Title I program.
6. To direct youth in need of a GED to the appropriate facility to obtain the necessary material resources in order to aid this effort.[8]

The Title I teachers conduct classes at the local school or, in those situations that warrant, at each individual group home. Classrooms are set aside for Title I teachers to use as they require them. Group home youths are given credit for work completed at school or carried out at the group home level. The credit is granted by the local school officials in coordination with the Title I teachers.

The major objective of Washington's Title I Group Home Project is to develop a means whereby every child can receive a fundamental and meaningful education whatever their point of entry into the program, tested ability, behavioral difficulty, or motivation. The project has four specific goals.

1. To provide special, individualized programs in reading, math, and English for all children found to be below grade level in these areas. Due to the complexity of this problem, the level of deficiencies these children experience, and following review of prior years' program results in this area, a realistic goal of bringing each child up to the equivalent of two grade levels in each area of weakness seems in order.

2. To provide tutoring and counseling services of all children in group home services determined as needing this assistance. This will reduce by 100 percent those children who are now having academic-related behavior and motivation problems as determined by the needs assessment.

3. To provide appropriate program scheduling for all youth referred irrespective of their date of placement into the group home or their previous school enrollment. This will reduce by 96 the number of children now being affected by this problem.

4. To provide special GED preparatory instruction to a minimum of 15 youths during the period of the project.[9]

A recent survey of children referred to Group Home Services during fiscal year 1976 indicates why the Title I project might become an important part of meeting the needs of group home youth. Of a sample of 200 youths assessed for educational needs, 48 percent showed marked deficiencies in educational training. To accommodate these children, individualized course work is necessary in which the child can learn at his or her own pace. This remedial-type learning experience then enables the student to progress to a regular academic schedule in time.

Thirty-one percent (61) of the sample was found to be below average intelligence and in need of remedial studies. Of these 61 youths, 10 were one grade below their expected level; 15 were two grades below the norm; 24 were three grades; and 19 were four grades below. Twenty-one tested at an intelligence level which required special help in all subjects. Forty-six youths were found to be below grade level in math, 42 in reading, and 56 in English.

Eighty-seven (44 percent) of the children reviewed continued to demonstrate a lack of motivation which resulted in behavioral problems which could not be coped with in the traditional public school setting. Reasons for this widespread lack of motivation are many and varied.[10]

Youths who enter state group homes often come from an *institutional* educational program, where positive reinforcement methods are likely to be used. Positive reinforcement provides rewards, such as privileges and good grades, for exhibiting desired behavior. When youths from this environment are subsequently placed into a public school in the community near the group home, they suffer from a form of educational shock. The more stringent demands of the public school system cause these youths to become discouraged and their motivation wanes. Past experience has shown that some of these youths create disciplinary problems in the classroom, problems which result in their being removed from school. Sometimes, dismissal is what they wanted in the first place.

Teachers in the Title I Group Home Project act as tutors, guidance counselors, and overall educational coordinators for residents. In these capacities they ease the educational shock syndrome and help the youth solve motivational shortcomings and ease tensions leading to disruptive behavior in the classroom. Relieved of this responsibility, the public school classroom teacher has more time to teach, time which might otherwise be wasted in overcoming behavioral problems.

Group Home Admissions

In recent years, group homes have grown significantly. Between July, 1969, and January, 1973, the number of group homes in Washington (exclusive of state group homes) increased from 9 to 68.[11]

In most cases, a youth must be under court order or jurisdiction upon entering either a state or private group home. Until 1976, youths in Washington's group homes were there on a parole status. When a group home youth did something wrong, his or her parole had to be revoked in order to send him or her back to an institution or incur other disciplinary action. To avoid red tape and waste of the staff's time, the Bureau of Juvenile Rehabilitation changed the status of state group home youth from parole to continued "institutional" status. Instead of revoking a youth's parole, it is now possible to simply transfer the child from the group home to an institution.

Licensing

Most states have the authority to license group homes as a specific category of child-care services. In order for a home to be licensed, it must meet certain criteria:

> A group home must be a single-family-type dwelling or apartment neither adjacent to nor part of an institutional campus, nor one of a group of child-care units in one building, caring for a group of not more than 10 children.[12]

Licensing requirements also provide a description of the group home's function to serve children and young expectant mothers. They are those:

1. Who need foster care but who cannot ordinarily adjust to the close personal relationships normally required by a foster family home.
2. Who leave an institutional setting for a transitional period of care prior to returning to their own home or prior to achieving independence [for example]—job, armed services, college.

3. Who need emergency placement pending more permanent planning or during temporary disruption of a current placement.
4. Who are emotionally disturbed or physically or mentally handicapped, or whose behavior is so bizarre as to be unacceptable to most foster parents; provided that the supervising agency, through its own program or by the marshalling of appropriate community resources, can provide the necessary specialized services that may be required by the group which the facility serves.[13]

Many states stipulate that group home operators must become licensed by the state. Licensing of operators insures that professional standards are applied to group homes in order to prevent abuse and the existence of group homes of poor quality. There are some precedents which offer guidance to those concerned with the licensing of group home operators. Each state, for example, has a Nursing Home Administrator's License Board. This board interviews prospective operators, gives them a written test regarding their abilities as nursing home operators, and generally evaluates their capabilities, training, and experience. "The problem with developing a written test for group home operators, however, is that there is no agreement among those in the field on a common body of knowledge which all group home operators require. This may reflect the fact that there has been no sufficient definition of the group home's role and responsibilities."[14]

Program Services

The adequate provision of program services to juveniles is perhaps the single most important issue facing group homes today. These program services, which include educational counseling, tutoring, job placement, individual counseling, and life skills counseling, are essential to the group home's goal of successfully reintegrating juveniles into the community. Those in the group home field should have a common understanding of what services group homes should offer and how those services fit into existing community resources.

The provision of services needed to adequately treat juveniles instead of "warehousing" them has emerged as a genuine concern of group home professionals in recent years. Problems with the provision of needed services to group home youths may arise if such factors as (1) whether the youths with varying needs and problems can be successfully accommodated within the same group home setting, or (2) whether youths in different age groups are compatible and able to be treated together are not taken into consideration.

Program evaluation is essential to the provision of program services and any treatment which may result. Proper evaluation can answer such questions as (1) what is the best way of assuring that a group home is actually providing quality services as efficiently and as effectively as possible, and

(2) which client assignments, staffing patterns, and interfacing with outside service agencies are in the best interests of the juveniles being served. The proper evaluation of group home services will move group homes a major step forward in their realization of their full potential as a child care resource.

To evaluate its group home program, the California State Youth Authority conducted a three-year study of the differential use of group homes for teenage delinquent boys. The study, referred to as the Group Home Project, identified six types of homes in terms of preadmission tests of the boys' level of maturity. The boys were then placed in homes that varied in controls and restrictiveness. "Behavioral ratings by the parents and parole agents at 2, 4, 6, and 8 months revealed important decisions . . . the parents noting positive changes at the end of 4 months and significant changes for the worse at 8; the parole agents perceiving consistent changes for the better in the 4-, 6-, and 8-month ratings. This raises, but by no means begins to settle, the point of diminishing return in group home placements."[15]

Group Home Referrals

What a group home program evolves into may be a far cry from what that program was actually intended to be. One reason for this is that inappropriate referrals are frequently made, referrals which often redefine the role and purpose of the group home and thus endanger its survival. In the Washington Group Homes Study, several factors that cause inappropriate group home referrals were identified:

1. Juvenile justice referral options are often mistakenly viewed chronologically, with the group home seen as the resource to be used after a foster home failure but before commitment to an institution, rather than as the most appropriate resource for a particular youth at a particular time.

2. Referring agencies often do not have adequate knowledge of available group home programs and the services which they provide.

3. Because many referring agency personnel are extremely reluctant to send youths to the State's juvenile institutions, they frequently use existing group homes inappropriately.

4. Since some caseworkers are primarily interested in placing youths as quickly as possible, they may refer them to the most readily available group homes rather than those best suited to meet the youth's needs.

5. Many group home operators knowingly accept inappropriate referrals because they cannot afford to have empty beds.[16]

These findings suggest some definite problems in regard to the referral functions of both the juvenile justice system and the group home programs. If the group home concept is to remain a viable child-care service, solutions must be found to these problems.

Staffing of Group Homes

The program of rehabilitation at a group home is determined by the kinds of residents in that home and their particular needs. It is the staff's function to see to it that the program meets those needs and that there are sufficient personnel resources to support it. In general, there is no single staffing pattern which will fit the needs of all group homes.

Group home staff and supplementary volunteers should be suited for the job, and they should be fully aware of and trained for the demands of the particular home's program. Although not a prerequisite for group home houseparents, a college degree is an asset because of the semiprofessional aspects of the job.

Personal characteristics and attitudes such as sincerity, maturity, concern, patience, and an empathy with youth are extremely important attributes for group home houseparents. However, group homes find it difficult to recruit good houseparents because of the low levels of salaries. Few people with the desired character traits of good group home houseparents can afford to take the job.

In addition to the personal characteristics mentioned above, the operators of group homes should have administrative skills and the ability to act as liaison between the home and the community. A college degree is also useful for the group home operator. Group home operators may find that they are required to provide an in-service training period for new staff.

If the group home claims to provide a therapeutic service for its youth, then at least one person on the staff should have the credentials to act as a counselor.

Future Prospects for Group Homes

Among many beneficial findings and suggestions of the 1973 Washington Group Homes Study are the following recommendations for future action in the group home field.

1. As a prerequisite for licensing, each group home should provide a comprehensive description, in writing, of its proposed service delivery plan.

2. Copies of all new or updated description packages should be made available to all potential child-placing agencies and/or individuals. Such descriptions can often prove useful knowledge for the determination of an appropriate placement, and as such can save the referral agency and the child time and trouble.

3. In order to involve the community and to limit responsibilities for group home operations to a few individuals, each group home should be required to appoint a board of directors.

4. In order to facilitate the functions listed in 3 above, no member of the board of directors should be in a position to benefit financially from the group home's operation.

5. Each group home should be evaluated based upon the development of a sound methodology.

6. The evaluation of the group home should take place at least every six months.

7. State-sponsored training should be provided for all group home staff personnel.

8. Diversification in programs offered by group homes is beneficial to both the juveniles being served and to the community.

9. As a means of evaluating success rates and of tracking the post-placement progress of former group home residents, these former residents should be subjects of appropriate follow-up studies.

10. Coordination of the development of all group home programs, including future programs, should be strongly considered. Such a centralized group home planning function is essential to the provision of quality services which appropriately meet the needs of juveniles placed in a group home setting.[17]

Because of their general nature, these recommendations could be readily adopted by the group home operators of other states.

As far as the role of the group home in the juvenile justice system of any particular state is concerned, the state must define that role. Of special importance is the relationship between institutions and group homes. When the purpose of the group home is clearly defined and programs are funded and begun, only then can the group home programs realize their full potential as community-based juvenile corrections alternatives.

Foster Home/Family Care

The concept of *parens patriae* is that society shall have the ultimate parental responsibility for all children in the community. Thus, when a youth cannot remain at home, society must provide a substitute home. One such alternative is foster care. "Foster care is a generic term applied to any kind of full-time substitute care of children outside their own home by persons other than their parents."[18] Although this generic term could be used to describe institutional care, group home care, or adoptions, here it will mean specifically foster family care.

A foster home, unlike the group home, offers services to the youth who still has fairly strong dependency needs, rather than to the young person who is struggling to be free of adult control.

A foster home is a family paid by the state or local government to board a neglected, abused, or delinquent child. If the court feels the child does not need the controls of a correctional institution, but is not yet ready for the move to independence offered in a group home, the child will most likely be placed in a foster home.

In 1933, 47.2 percent of the dependent, neglected, and emotionally disturbed children needing substitute care were placed in foster family homes, while the remaining 52.8 percent were institutionalized.[19] The trend in the past 30 years has been away from institutional care to foster care.

Background of Foster Care Homes

The feudal practice of indenture, in which parents contracted to place their child with a master craftsman to learn a trade, is the forerunner of foster home care. In return for teaching the child a trade, the craftsman had his or her services for a given length of time.

While the feudal system vanished, the practice of indenturing youth remained in the form of private and public placements of dependent or destitute children. Delinquent children were also indentured. From 1853 to 1879, the Children's Aid Society of New York placed 48,000 children in homes in southern and western states. These placements were unpaid—that is, the family agreed to feed, house, clothe, and educate the child at its own expense. In 1866, Massachusetts started placing children who were charged with delinquent acts with families who were paid board.[20] The Massachusetts plan was the first systematic attempt at providing foster home care for delinquent youths.

With the rise of the juvenile court movement in 1899 and the consequent effort to remove the stigma of delinquency, the use of foster home care emerged as a preferred alternative to correctional placements.

In Boston and Buffalo, in the 1930s, foster homes were used to provide care for youths who needed secure custody. Foster parents were guaranteed a flat sum with an additional per capita rate for each child in residence.

The use of foster care homes has shown a steady growth in the second half of the twentieth century. But in the 1960s, concern was voiced about the effectiveness of foster care programs. During that period professionals were becoming aware that the supply of foster homes was limited, that the needs of children coming into care were changing, and that the sheer number of youths in need of service was growing at alarming rates.

However, in spite of this, foster care continues today to be the most frequently used alternative home placement for children of all ages. For example, the state of Washington, in fiscal 1975, had 4,155 foster family homes licensed for use by the Department of Social and Health Services. For 60 private child-placing agencies there were approximately 1,500 licensed foster family homes.[21]

The Need for Foster Care

Specific reasons why foster care may be needed can be grouped into two main categories: (1) *parent*-related problems and (2) *child*-related problems. The most frequent parent-related problems are:

- parental inadequacy
- parental rejection
- mental illness
- child abuse
- child neglect

- abandonment
- addiction to drugs
- alcoholism
- imprisonment
- inability to cope

The most frequently observed child-centered problems are:

- parent-child conflict
- delinquent behavior
- incorrigibility
- emotional disturbance

- physical handicap
- mental handicap
- child-sibling conflict
- sociopathic behavior

Given the fact that one or more of these problems does exist, the following questions then arise: What type of child can be expected to benefit from an experience in a foster care home? What type of child would not be suitable for foster care placement?

While these questions are difficult to answer, experience and common sense do offer some basic clues for the right course of action. Eldefonso and Hastinger suggest the following:

> First, a minor who clearly needs a close relationship with an adult parental model and is capable of responding to affection and individual attention is probably a good candidate for foster-home placement. In addition, as noted above, minors whose offenses are not serious ones and who do not have a long record of prior violations are much better foster-home risks than those whose backgrounds reflect a pattern of continual delinquent behavior—particularly in such areas as arson or sexual perversion, which suggest deep emotional problems.
>
> . . .
>
> Another reason for placing a minor in an institution rather than a foster home might be a need for specialized education or training that the community does not provide.[22]

Separation of a child from its parents can become necessary for a wide range of reasons. A study of 425 families with children in foster care was conducted by Shirley Jenkins and Mignon Sauber to learn about such families prior to placement. On the basis of the results, the families were classified into five groups, according to family problem:

1. The most frequent factor was found to be the physical condition of the mother, i.e., physical illness (21 percent) or confinement for current pregnancy (8 percent).
2. Mental illness of the mother (11 percent).
3. Emotional problems of the children (17 percent).
4. Severe neglect or abuse (10 percent).
5. Family problems (33 percent); this category included deserted children, arrested parents, and conflicts within the home.[23]

This study found that 40 to 50 percent of these placements could have been averted by providing adequate income, medical care, housing, or child supervision. However, a residual group appeared to be placement-prone because of severe psychological problems.

If there were a profile of the ''average'' child in foster care, it would indicate that most children entering foster home care come from broken homes with either one or both parents absent. The children are usually from lower-class, chronically deprived families that are living a crisis-oriented existence. The principal source of referrals for the children coming into foster care is their parents, followed by social service agencies, the courts, and the police. Five-year-olds make up the largest age group of those referred. And of whites and nonwhites, white children are most prevalent in foster home care.[24] The average length of stay for children in foster family care is less than one year. However, 25 percent of all children placed in foster family care can expect to remain for three years or more.[25]

Selecting the Foster Home

Once the decision to separate the child (or children) from the parents is made and all the pertinent placement information is gathered, the process of choosing a home to meet the child's specific needs should begin.

The criteria for an appropriate home are realistically determined by the range of homes available to the child-placing agency, whether private or public. In the past the majority of foster homes were located in low-income urban or rural areas. The need to supplement income with the money received for taking in a foster child has often been criticized in cases where it seems the sole reason why a family will take a foster child in the first place. In these cases, the benefit to the child being placed should be questioned. In recent years, social agencies have been focusing their home-finding efforts in higher income suburban areas.

The findings of this study suggest that social agencies would be well advised to undertake foster-home recruitment in higher income suburban areas. They also suggest that churchgoing women in such areas might be motivated to sponsor children from institutions or children in critical life situations, and in doing so might become interested in further work with social agencies on behalf of children.

Assuming that delinquents from various ethnic backgrounds have a better chance of adjusting in a familiar environment, efforts have also been made of late to place minority children in ghetto areas. According to Mother Michaels, in foster home care, and particularly the ghetto home, psychosocial dynamics are crucial to a successful placement.[26] "Even though complex economic and social problems plague the ghetto community as a whole, the tightly knit family units encourage strong interpersonal relationships that can build the values on which good social adjustment depends."[27]

A good foster home, regardless of location, will generally possess the following characteristics:

1. The foster father has a high degree of participation in the minor's care.
2. The foster parents accept the natural parents as significant persons in the minor's life.
3. The foster family is well accepted in the neighborhood and the community.
4. The foster parents' own children seem secure and well adjusted.
5. Relationships within the family are characterized by mutual respect.
6. The foster parents help the minor understand that he can be loved.
7. The foster parents give affection without expecting immediate returns.
8. The foster family has a clear set of "ground rules" for behavior but a teen-ager's need for privacy and group activities is recognized.[28]

Foster Family Care: A Changing Image

Recently, foster family care has come under criticism from experts in the field. Child-care professionals are now somewhat more reluctant to favor foster family care as an alternative placement service than they once were. Foster family care has been so widely used that it has become looked upon as a panacea for the ills of delinquent, dependent, or abused youngsters.

Available research indicates that more adequate services to children in their own homes, more adequate assistance grants, and greater availability of some specific services, notably protective services, homemaker services, and day care, would tend to reduce the number of children needing foster care.[29]

Assuming the above to be true, one could make the further assumption that children being placed in foster family care come from families where parents will not or cannot respond to the array of services being offered. Many youths, therefore, are coming from homes which are beyond rehabilitation. Consequently, the "temporary" nature of foster care has been greatly changed. More and more youths are apt to spend all their minority years in foster families. The longer a child remains in foster care, the more likely he or she is to remain there. One solution to this problem is to insure that maximum efforts at providing needed services are made early in the case history, services such as day care, homemaker services, protective services, and appropriate financial and medical care services.

Foster Family Care Studies

Considerable interest has been shown in the outcome of adoption but the outcome of foster family care is infrequently studied. Relevant findings by those who have conducted studies follow.

Elizabeth G. Meier found that the vast majority of former foster children were "indistinguishable from their neighbors as self-supporting individuals, living in attractive homes, taking care of their children adequately . . . sharing in the activities of the neighborhood, and finding pleasure in their association with others."[30] However, her studies also indicated that former foster children had a diminished sense of well-being. Girls were found to be concerned with "what" they were, and boys, because of a lack of parental relationships (especially male), were left with a void in their feelings as to "who" they were.

Paula Van Der Waals did a follow-up study of 200 children in extended foster family care. She found that many of these children felt unsuccessful, dissatisfied, distressed, and emotionally maladjusted. About 25 percent of the former foster children interviewed had regular contact with their mothers and apparently were more self-confident than those who had little or no contact. She states "This feeling of being loved by their own mothers evidently helped in their relationship with the foster parents, for these respondents also tended to speak kindly of their foster parents."[31]

Eugene A. Weinstein also suggests that a continuing contact with natural or adoptive parents has a positive effect. His study indicates that foster children who had little or no contact with their natural parents (even though they appeared to identify positively with their foster parents) had a sense of well-being far less than that of foster children whose natural parents visited them on a regular basis. Children who identified with their natural parents, and not their foster parents, were shown to have the highest sense of well-being of any group in his study.[32]

These studies indicate that the child's feeling of personal worth is essential to his or her full development and to a well-adjusted life. An individual achieves a positive identity and thus a feeling of self-worth through the mastery of a succession of developmental stages: (1) the dependent age (birth to 1 year); (2) the self-assertive age (1 year to 3–4 years); (3) the play-work age (3–4 to 6–7); (4) the age of accomplishment (6–7 to 12–13); (5) the becoming-an-adult age (12–13 to 21); and finally (6) the adult age (21 and over). Studies indicate that foster children often are unable to complete one or more of these developmental stages or they take longer than other children in moving from one stage to another.

Focusing on the Problem

Traditional emphasis in foster care has been on the children. Focus must now be centered on the failures of our social and economic systems which lead to the dysfunctioning of the family, which in turn can lead to the need for foster care.

The Jenkins-Norman study, which was a component of a child research project carried out at the Columbia University School of Social Work, clearly pinpointed where changes should take place.

> Knowledge about the kinds of family situations which lead children to enter foster care has implications for both practice and policy. It would, of course, be an oversimplification to consider all the families of children in placement as constituting a homogeneous group. But with the exception of some families of emotionally disturbed children, there are many characteristics common to this parent population. These common areas include pervasive poverty, high incidence of minority group membership, frequent receipt of public assistance, one-parent families, and physical and mental illness.
>
> It is apparent that the social service system as presently structured does not have the capability to provide basic preventive services to strengthen family life. A majority of the families in the study were known to social agencies before the placement crisis. Yet these agency resources did not prevent the movement of these children into foster care. The child welfare system is forced to operate like firemen arriving after the house has burned . . . fulfillment of its service task is hampered by the extent of damage done prior to agency intervention. Disadvantaged circumstances, extreme pathology, and inadequate parenting are common precursors of placement, thus handicapping the most sincere professional efforts to give such children a chance before they reach adulthood.[33]

The characteristics that are common to the parent population in this study are also those often linked with the causes of crime and delinquency. Obviously, programs which would be effective in curbing the movement of children into foster care could prove useful in preventing delinquency. Basic preventive services to strengthen family life would, therefore, serve the juvenile justice system as a whole, inclusive of the families of children who must enter foster care.

Jenkins and Norman point out, however, that there are no complete solutions to the child-rearing dilemma. "In any society there will always be some children in need of substitute parenting. But enlightened social policies designed to improve living conditions of the urban poor could effect significant reductions in the number of children entering care."[34]

Until such time as social and economic services are made available to those who now rely on foster care, foster home placement as a private alternative to government-operated correctional institutions will be valuable to the juvenile justice system. To cite one reason, the return rate of delinquent youths placed in foster homes and later assigned to juvenile correctional institutions has been found to be significantly lower than the return rate for minors placed on aftercare supervision after release from correctional institutions.[35]

Adoption

The third and final alternative to institutionalization is adoption. "Adoption is the social and legal process of becoming a parent. After adoption, parents and children have essentially the same reciprocal rights and responsibilities as if they were biologically related."[36] The problems which face natural parents and children are much the same, therefore, as those facing adoptive parents and adopted children. This is true in all aspects of family life, including those which could bring the children and parents in contact with the juvenile justice system. Children from group homes or foster homes may end up being adopted, and adopted children may end up being placed in a group or foster home.

Historical Background

The practice of adopting children, which can be traced to the beginning of recorded history, was instituted by the ancient Assyrians, Egyptians, Babylonians, Greeks, and Romans in order to acquire heirs to their thrones. The adoption of Moses by Pharaoh's daughter and of Esther by Mordecai are both recorded in the Bible. The ancient Chinese considered ancestor worship so significant that they established the custom of allowing a childless male to claim the firstborn son of his younger brother. Over four thousand years ago, the Babylonians in the Code of Hammurabi, emphasized the importance of perpetuation of the family in the following section of their code:

> If a man take a child in his name, adopt him as a son, this grownup son may not be demanded back.[37]

Primitive tribes were known to have used the practice of adoption to settle quarrels with one another. One tribe would adopt a child, usually a male, belonging to a member holding status in another tribe.

Modern adoption law has its beginnings in the Roman Empire, where adoption became very popular for both social and religious reasons. The Roman father had total authority over his children and descendants, including the power of life and death. This dominance had a crucial effect on the development of adoption; it meant that the adoptive father had complete control over his adopted children. All previous biological family ties, such as legal, religious, and economic, were severed. Once an adoption was formalized there was no possibility of its being reversed.

The adoption of children was practiced in European countries during the Middle Ages: However, it was unknown to the common law of England, a law from which much of American law is derived. The emphasis on blood lineage was the major reason why English common law lacked regulations regarding the adoptive process. Feudal tradition was such that only a biological child born during wedlock could inherit his parents' rights and property. A child born out of wedlock or one who was adopted was not a legal heir.

That is not to say that the English were not concerned with the plight of homeless, parentless children. They were, but until the Adoption of Children Act of 1926, they chose means other than adoption to meet those needs. Apprenticeship or indentured servitude were two methods in common use, and when the English founded colonies overseas, these practices went with them. In the seventeenth century, a vast number of destitute English children became apprenticed as child laborers in Virginia, Massachusetts Bay, and other colonies. "The apprenticing of poor children to the Virginia Company began as early as 1620. . . . A record of 1627 reads: 'There are many ships going to Virginia and with them 1400 to 1500 children which they have gathered up in diverse places.' "[38]

During the eighteenth and nineteenth centuries in America, the apprenticeship system was still the preferred method of taking care of homeless children. No governmental or legal sanction existed for adoption. Blood relatives began taking complete responsibility for their families' orphaned or dependent children. And soon it became a common practice for them to specify in their wills the relative with whom the orphaned child should live. Mark Twain's *Tom Sawyer* illustrates this practice. Tom was raised by an aunt after his own parents died.

Apprenticing of children began to die out during the rapid industrialization of America in the mid-nineteenth century. Machines replaced apprentice tradesmen and craftsmen. Child welfare agencies were formed, agencies which attempted to place needy children in institutions or in foster and adoptive homes.

The placement of homeless children in private homes was often criticized by opponents of adoption. Responses to such criticism, however, were often overzealous and lent a decidedly paternalistic air to the subject. Unfortunately, the paternalistic attitude continues today. This attitude is well illustrated by the following quote from the founder of the New York Children's Aid Society:

> It is feared that these children would corrupt the morals of the families to which they are sent. . . . We must remind such persons [the critics of adoption] of the wonderful capacity for improvement in children's natures

under new circumstances; and we assert boldly, that a poor child taken in thus by the hand of Christian charity, and placed in a new world of love and of religion, is *more likely to be tempted to good,* than to tempt others to evil.[39]

Early adoption laws were considered to be private laws, that is, laws made available only to those select individuals to whom knowledge of a specific child to be adopted was made available. Members of the general public as a rule were uninformed of the adoption laws or of how they themselves could adopt a child. It was thought that only a member of the elite society could be entrusted with the duty of converting a poor, ignorant little child into a God-fearing member of decent society. The very notion that others less fortunate than themselves could be good, loving parents to adopted children probably never even entered the minds of the lawmakers of the day or those for whom the laws were made.

Adoption Today: Why and Who

In our society, a childless family has generally been thought to be an incomplete family. Consequently, the inability to conceive or bear children has been one of the primary reasons why people adopt. A new sense of social responsibility, and a growing concern and awareness about overpopulation is leading many who are already natural parents to adopt children in need of parents. They are inclined to feel it is better to adopt a child who is already here than to have a new child and add to the population of the world.

Adoption is open today for children of any age, not only infants. Furthermore, more attention is being paid to children who traditionally were difficult to place, such as older children, siblings, mentally, emotionally, or physically handicapped children, and children of a minority or mixed racial background.

Approximately 2 percent of the child population under age 18 is adopted in this country and 50 percent of these children have been adopted by relatives.

In 1970 there were some 176,000 adoption petitions granted by the courts in the United States. About 49 percent of these adoptions were by relatives. Of the some 89,200 nonrelative adoptions, 78 percent were arranged by social agencies and the remainder by the concerned parties independently. About 88 percent of the children adopted by nonrelatives are born out of wedlock.[40]

In the United States, adoption statutes vary from state to state. Generally, however, any unmarried adult, single parent, or married couple, where both are adults, may file for the adoption of a child. If either of the prospective parents is a minor, the parties may jointly adopt the other spouse's child.

In many states, anyone who is a resident of that state is allowed to adopt.[41] Other states require that the adopting parents be a specific number of years older than the person to be adopted.[42]

Rights and Responsibilities in Adoption

Every child has the right to have his or her own parents, and no child should be unnecessarily deprived of this right. In the summer of 1976, a young man from California filed suit against the state for failing to provide him with a permanent adoptive home as an infant, as had been his natural mother's wish. Instead, he was shuffled from one foster home to another until he turned 18. Bureaucratic red tape was blamed for this not atypical situation.

A child has a right to grow up in a reasonably wholesome family setting that should offer affection, security, and the desire to see that the child develops in the best manner possible by providing all the necessities of childhood, including adequate medical care. As for responsibility, the child is obligated to obey the adoptive parents and to perform any other responsibilities that would be expected of a child by his or her natural parents.

Natural parents of children who may be adoptable have rights, too.

> In our culture and under our law, the natural parents or, if they are not married to each other, the mother, have the right to custody and control of children born to them. They also have the responsibility for their support, care, and upbringing. This right of the parents must be exercised for the child's benefit, and if not, must yield to the child's interest and welfare. A parent may not be deprived of his rights nor divest himself of his responsibility for the care of a child except through process of law with full protection of the child.[43]

Natural parents also have the right to have counseling in arriving at a decision to give up their child for adoption, and they must have a full understanding of their rights and of the consequences of their decision, especially of the irreversibility of such a decision once the adoption is made final in court.

Problems in Adoption

In an adoption placement, several factors can slow or completely hinder its success; for example:

1. Adoptions arranged primarily for the convenience of the natural parents, to meet the need of the adoptive parents, or for the profit of the intermediary parties. In all such arrangements the welfare of the child is a secondary objective, if it is an objective at all.

2. Delay in placement. . . . Loss of time in making permanent, adequate placement for an infant endangers his opportunity for healthy development and deprives his adoptive parents of their share of an interesting and significant period of his life.

3. Multiple home placements. . . . When a child is subjected to multiple placements, whether by plan or default, his emotional development is jeopardized.

4. Placement in a home that ultimately proves incapable of providing the wholesome atmosphere considered to be the child's right. A poor emotional environment is destructive to the child's development. Competent casework with the child's prospective parents prior to placement reduces the incidence of the abuse represented by gross misplacement.

5. Failure to resolve problems of the natural parents. . . . The lack of able counsel at the proper time contributes to the persistence of unresolved conflicts in the parents that may affect their lives for a long time. Such trauma most often occurs when the decision to relinquish a child is made without a careful exploration of alternatives. Difficulties can be minimized by competent counseling.

6. Unnecessary social or economic poverty, including a lack of medical care for the unmarried mother and her child. Well-developed social services for unmarried mothers exist in many metropolitan areas and offer help that prevents impoverishment and degradation through misfortune.

7. Failure to provide and interpret significant medical information to prospective adoptive parents may put both child and parents at a disadvantage. Skilled interpretation of the implications of pertinent medical information for the future life and development of the child is of utmost importance.[44]

If it is decided that the adoption of a child is a desirable and acceptable alternative to institutionalization, whether to prevent placement in an institution or as an after-institutional placement, the above-mentioned problems must be resolved in order for that placement to work.

Since a large number of children in our juvenile delinquent or dependent populations come from broken homes, homes with both parents missing, abusive or neglecting homes, and no homes at all, the goal of matching a child with a family that can provide a permanent home, love, and proper care can be beneficial in many ways. Fulfilling this goal could lead to a significant reduction in the number of children who are out on the streets, committing delinquent acts or wandering aimlessly through life with no hope for a secure future and who have a good chance of coming in contact with the juvenile justice system.

Follow-up studies of adopted children tend to indicate that 70–80 percent of adoptions are successful."[45] A stable and secure home environment has consistently been shown to be a major factor in forming a child's ego, personality, and social competence. It has also been shown that such an environment is best provided by the parent-child relationships and role exchanges within the traditional family setting. Unfortunately, many children in the United States are denied the love and security of a family of their own, and in spite of the well-intended efforts of social service agencies, some of them are forced to spend their entire childhood in foster homes or institutions. Adoption is the most desirable solution to the problem of the child without a parent or parents.

Summary

This chapter has discussed three of the more common alternatives to institutionalization of children. Under ideal conditions any of these alternatives may be the right one for a child, depending upon his or her needs and the circumstances of the individual case. Group home living has been traditionally utilized as a placement for children who have already been in contact with the juvenile justice system and for whom an alternative to home living is generally mandated.

Ideally, foster care should be of as short a duration as possible. It is a temporary solution to the problems of a dysfunctioning home, whether the dysfunction is parent- or child-related. Foster care is often used as an interim placement. Good foster homes may enable some youths to remain outside the institutional experience altogether. For others, it may speed their release by offering them someplace to go.

For the child who should be removed from the influence of adults in parental authority roles, the group home is often a better solution than foster care.

Foster care, the reader will recall, is mainly intended for the child who needs the guidance and care of his or her parents but who cannot get that care from the present home situation.

Because it can provide a permanent, loving, caring home which offers the child a substitute family, adoption is actually more of a preventive measure than it is an alternative to institutionalization. By providing such a home to children who may otherwise have none—children who could end up drifting from one foster home to another—adoption helps prevent these children from being exposed to environmental conditions, lif-styles, and experiences which often lead to crime or incorrigibility.

The adopted child can develop a permanent sense of belonging and security about where he or she will be from day to day. The foster child, however, is not quite as fortunate. For example, it is not uncommon to remove a child who has problems from a foster home once these problems appear to be settled and signs of progress are evident. The child then finds himself back in his own home where the problems often reoccur all over again. If this experience is repeated often enough, the child will soon learn that to succeed in a foster placement is a *disadvantage*. Such frustrating experiences for an already troubled young mind can only jeopardize the chances of the child's having a healthy outlook about himself and society.

Whether the choice is to place the child in a group home, foster home, or adoptive home, the procedures in each of these placements must keep in mind and must be based on pursuing the best interests of the child.

REVIEW QUESTIONS

1. Define the following terms:
   a. group home
   b. foster home
   c. adoption
   d. alternative placement

2. Discuss the following:
   a. What types of children are best served by each of the alternatives discussed in this chapter? Why?
   b. What characteristics differentiate each of these placements from one another?

3. What is the historical background of each of the following:
   a. group homes
   b. foster care
   c. adoption

4. What factors cause inappropriate referrals to group homes?

5. What characteristics are generally found in a *good* foster home?

6. What are some of the problems which may be encountered in the adoption of a child?

7. How does each of the three alternatives discussed in this chapter fit into the present-day juvenile justice system?

NOTES

1. State of Washington, Senate Bill No. 3116, Chapter 71, Laws of 1975–76 2nd Extraordinary Session, 44th Legislative Session, p. 2, lines 4–19.

2. Stanton Wheeler, Leonard Cottrell, and Ann Romasco, "Juvenile Delinquency, Its Prevention and Control," in "Task Force Report: Juvenile Delinquency and Youth Crime," Appendix P 2 to *Report on Juvenile Justice and Consultants Papers*, President's Commission on Law Enforcement and the Administration of Justice.

3. Seattle, Model City Program. Group Homes work plan, 1971–1972, Law and Justice Division (1971), p. 2.

4. Edward Eldefonso and Alan R. Coffey, *Process and Impact of the Juvenile Justice System* (Encino, Ca.: Glencoe Press, 1976), p. 172.

5. M. Gula, "Agency-Operated Group Homes," Department of Health, Education, and Welfare, Children's Bureau (Washington, D.C.: U.S. Government Printing Office, 1964), p. 2.

6. Eldefonso and Coffey, *Process and Impact of the Juvenile Justice System*, p. 172.

7. Northwest Regional Council, *State of Washington Group Home Study*, "Comprehensive Analysis of Major Program Components: Specific Finding and Recommendations," vol. 1, Zaring Corporation, October, 1973, pp. 19–20.

8. Program Component—ESEA Title I, Fiscal Year 1976, Department of Social and Health Services, Bureau of Juvenile Rehabilitation, p. 3.

9. Ibid., p. 2.

10. Ibid. p. 1. (Note: All percentages related to the 200 youths reviewed are derived from the same source as in footnote 7.)

11. Northwest Regional Council, *State of Washington Group Home Study*, p. 3.

12. Washington Administrative Code 388-64-055.

13. Ibid.

14. Northwest Regional Council, *State of Washington Group Home Study*, p. 57.

15. Howard Polsky, "Child Welfare: Residential Treatment Homes," *Encyclopedia of Social Welfare*, vol. 1 (New York: National Association of Social Workers, 1971), p. 140.

16. Northwest Regional Council, *State of Washington Group Home Study*, pp. 21–22.

17. Ibid., p. 73.

18. Alfred Kadushin, "Child Welfare: Adoption and Foster Care," in *Encyclopedia of Social Work*, vol. 1 (New York: National Association of Social Workers, 1971), p. 104.

19. Ibid.

20. Herbert D. Williams, "Foster Homes for Juvenile Delinquents," *Federal Probation* 13 (September 1949): 46–51.

21. *Child Foster Care Program Review* (Olympia: State of Washington Department of Social and Health Services, Community Services Division, 1976), p. II–3.

22. Edward Eldefonso and Walter Hartinger, *Control, Treatment, and Rehabilitation of Juvenile Offenders* (Encino, Calif.: Glencoe Press, 1976), p. 183.

23. Shirley Jonkins and Mignon Sauber, "Paths to Child Placement" (New York: Community Council of New York, 1966), pp. 62–80.

24. Kadushin, "Child Welfare: Adoption and Foster Care," p. 105.

25. Ibid.

26. Mother M. Ann Michaels, "Community-Centered Foster Family Care," *Children* 13 (January–February 1966): 8–9.

27. Eldefonso and Hartinger, *Control, Treatment, and Rehabilitation of Juvenile Offenders*, p. 184.

28. Leslie W. Hunter, "Foster Homes for Teenagers," *Children* 11 (November–December 1964): 234.

29. Kadushin, "Child Welfare: Adoption and Foster Care," p. 105.

30. Elizabeth Meier, "Current Circumstances of Former Foster Children," *Child Welfare* 44, no. 4 (1965): 196–206.

31. Paula Van Der Waals, "Former Foster Children Reflect on Their Childhood," *Children* 13, no. 1. (1960): 29.

32. Eugene A. Weinstein, "The Self-Image of the Foster Child," (New York: Russell Sage Foundation, 1960), pp. 17–18, 68–70.

33. Shirley Jenkins and Elaine Norman, "Filial Deprivation and Foster Care," (New York: Columbia University Press, 1972), p. v.

34. Ibid., p. 258.

35. Arthur W. Witherspoon, "Foster Home Placements for Delinquents," *Federal Probation* 30 (December 1966): 48–52.

36. Kadushin, "Child Welfare: Adoption and Foster Care," p. 107.

37. Albert Kocourck and John C. Wigmore, *Source of Ancient and Primitive Law, Evolution of Law, Select Readings on the Origin and Development of Legal Institutions* (Boston: Little, Brown, 1951), p. 425.

38. Arthur W. Calhoun, *A Social History of the American Family*, vol. 1 (New York: Barnes and Noble, 1960), pp. 306–307.

39. Charles L. Brace, *The Best Method of Disposing of Pauper and Vagrant Children* (1859), pp. 13–14.

40. "Adoption of Children," Committee on Adoption and Dependent Care, American Academy of Pediatrics, Evanston, Illinois, 1973, p. 2.

41. Delaware, Indiana, and Minnesota use the word "resident," whereas Maine, Colorado, and Alaska use the term "inhabitant."

42. Arizona, California, Georgia, Montana, New Jersey, New Mexico, North Dakota, Oklahoma, South Dakota, Utah, and West Virginia.

43. "Child Welfare League of America Standards for Adoption Service," Child Welfare League of America, New York, 1968, p. 17.

44. Committee on Adoption and Dependent Care, "Adoption of Children," pp. 11–12.

45. *Encyclopedia of Social Work*, p. 109.

11 Institutions

Institutions holding children include not only training schools but prisons and reformatories. Also, they are put into adult institutions not only by courts but by administrators. It is fairly common for training schools to transfer to a prison or reformatory, sometimes with court approval, sometimes not, children they consider to be unruly, or who have grown older than the main body of the children, who are about 15.

SOL RUBIN

No matter what it is called—juvenile institution, training school, correctional facility, detention center, shelter, youth camp, ranch, halfway house, jail, reformatory, or prison—each of these places is an institution in which a delinquent and dependent youth can be held.

In 1973 there were 794 publicly operated juvenile detention and correctional facilities in the United States. Of this number, 367 were operated under state auspices and 427 by local governments. There were 319 detention facilities, 19 shelters, 17 reception and diagnostic centers, 187 training schools, 103 ranches, forestry camps, and farms, 59 halfway houses, and 90 group homes. California alone accounted for 104 of these facilities, while Vermont had only one.[1]

The total number of facilities grew from 722 in 1971 to 794 in 1973, an increase of almost 10 percent. State-operated facilities increased by more than 15 percent, from 318 to 367, and local facilities by about 6 percent, from 404 to 427.[2]

The number of juveniles being held in these facilities in 1973 was 45,694. Of this number, 30,403 were in state-operated facilities and 15,291 in local facilities. By far the greatest number of youth (26,427) were being held in training schools. Detention centers held 10,782; the remaining 8,485 were distributed among the shelters, reception and diagnostic centers, ranches, forestry camps, and farms, halfway houses, and group homes.[3]

Of the 45,694 juveniles held in detention and correctional facilities in 1973, 33,385 were adjudicated delinquents, 4,551 had been declared in need of supervision, and 6,397 were held pending disposition by court. The remaining 1,361 juveniles were either awaiting transfer to another jurisdiction or were classified as voluntary commitments or dependent and neglected children.[4]

Commenting on the rising number of commitments to juvenile correctional institutions, Sol Rubin states: "This trend is wrong; it is bad for children, and it is needless. A community that undertakes to build larger institutions for children is doing a disservice to children and to the community."[5] Milton G. Rector, President of the National Council on Crime and Delinquency, in pointing out the extravagant cost of imprisonment, has commented: "Adoption of a policy of nonimprisonment of the nondangerous would signal a shift from a reactive to a proactive response to crime and would result in the reallocation of vast sums presently earmarked for institutional construction. It requires legislative action."[6]

The per-capita operating expenditure by public juvenile detention and correctional facilities was $9,582 in 1973.[7] Estimates for fiscal year 1978 indicate that it will cost Washington approximately $22,800 to maintain a youth in one of its four major juvenile institutions for one year and $13,550 to maintain a youth in one of its forestry camps for one year.[8]

A juvenile institution is intended to provide specialized programs for children who must be under some form of restraint in order to be treated. Accordingly, it normally houses the more hardened, unstable, or nontreatable youths who do not even meet the liberal standards for juvenile probation. The institution program attempts to prepare the youth for return to the community. Whether this reintegration with society will work depends on several interrelated factors, one of which is the quality of aftercare services, which are necessary to strengthen and reinforce changes begun in the institution that can only be tested and proved during the course of normal community living.

Professionals in corrections and juvenile justice are split on the use of institutional confinement for juveniles. A "get tough" attitude toward dealing with crime and criminals, both adult and juvenile, seems to be current in America. Connected with this "get tough" attitude is a trend toward fixed sentences and the abolition of parole both for juveniles and adults. The Scandinavian countries have abolished parole and 27 states have abolished or are considering abolishing parole for adults. The American Bar Association Commission on Juvenile Justice Standards is calling for fixed terms of institutionalization for juveniles. Such a plan stresses the gravity of an offense and the juvenile's prior record rather than individual *needs*. Protecting society first and the rights of the individual offender second is the emphasis of the "process model."

In recent years, many demands have been made for the phasing out of major juvenile institutions. Such institutions have been criticized for being overregimented, isolated, and totally ineffective in rehabilitating youth. In their place, many advocate the creation of less secure, more treatment-oriented, community-based alternatives to incarceration. With increased use of community-based facilities there has still been no major decline in the use of juvenile institutions.

> Spending months or years in confinement away from family, friends, and familiar circumstances is an odious prospect for a person of any age. For a young person the prospect is especially frightening. Compared to the juvenile court's other dispositional options, institutional placement of a juvenile in a residential facility is the court's ultimate dispositional power. It is the court's most severe and only really feared disposition.[9]

In the *Gault* decision, the Supreme Court emphasized the reality of institutionalization for a juvenile:

> Ultimately, however, we confront the reality. . . . A boy is charged with misconduct. The boy is committed to an institution where he may be restrained of liberty for years. It is of no constitutional consequence . . . and of limited practical meaning . . . that the institution to which he is committed is called an Industrial School. The fact of the matter is that, however euphemistic the title, a "receiving home" or an "industrial school" for juveniles is an institution of confinement in which the child is incarcerated for a greater or lesser time. His world becomes "a building with whitewashed walls, regimented routine and institutional hours. . . ." Instead of mother and father and sisters and brothers and friends and classmates, his world is peopled by guards, custodians, state employees, and delinquents confined with him for anything from waywardness to rape and homicide.[10]

Adult prisoners on death row or serving life sentences in New Jersey prisons have initiated a program designed to inform juvenile offenders what they can expect if they end up being sent to an adult prison. While it is too new to predict its effect, this program allows juveniles to tour the adult prisons and to talk to the "lifers" face to face. They are told about impending dangers such as homosexual rape, theft, extortion of one's family for money to prevent physical abuse, total loss of freedom, and so forth.[11] Programs of this nature give a sober, realistic warning to "shape up" before it's too late. Through shock, such programs may divert some youths from the path of crime.

Is there a realistic and practical need for the juvenile institution? Dr. Jerry Miller, the former youth commissioner for the State of Massachusetts, thinks not. Miller was responsible for the closing of juvenile institutions in Massachusetts. Miller's critics are legion, with few juvenile correctional administrators outside Massachusetts following his lead. In fact, most do not believe that institutions *are* inherently destructive or that they should be eliminated. One California Youth Authority administrator who respects Jerry Miller stated that what he did in Massachusetts was tragic, and that he would hate to see other states initiate it.[12] To date, Miller's one-man crusade in Massachusetts has failed to gain a large enough following to pose a significant threat to the existence of juvenile institutions nationwide.

Historical Survey

America's early juvenile institutions were patterned after nineteenth-century European models. In 1817, the London Philanthropic Society was founded and included in its purpose and practice the reformation of juvenile offenders. This organization opened the first English house of refuge for children, which became the prototype of similar houses of refuge in the United States.

Houses of Refuge

Houses of refuge were the first organized attempt to control and treat juvenile delinquency. These institutions marked a major shift away from family-oriented discipline and toward treatment administered by society in specialized facilities. As houses of refuge spread throughout Europe and America, they retained a reformatory atmosphere, associated with education and with mechanical labor, as in the trades. Rauhe Haus, founded in Hamburg, Germany, in 1833 by Dr. John Henry Wichern, served as a model for the institution combining reform and refuge.[13]

New York, Boston, and Philadelphia were the centers of urban population in the early 1800s. The woeful plight of wayward youths confined with adults in jails in these cities prompted groups to study the ways in which juveniles were being handled in Europe. The philosophy upon which early American juvenile institutions were founded was, therefore, an indigenous one. It can be traced to several European leaders and educators such as Johann Heinrich Pestalozzi (1746–1827), who established a school for orphans at Neuhoff, Switzerland, in 1775.[14] Unfortunately, Pestalozzi's legacy to American school children—the reduction of physical abuse and punishment in common schools—made little impression on those who ran the houses of refuge or the reform schools.

The New York Society for the Reformation of Juvenile Delinquents, founded in 1823, organized the first of the institutional movements. Originating from a movement among the Society of Friends, the New York Society opened the first reformatory in the United States, the New York House of Refuge, in 1825. The New York House and those opened in Boston and Philadelphia generally accepted destitute and orphaned children as well as youths convicted of crimes in state and/or local courts. Life was hard for the children who grew up in these special houses. Their parents were looked down upon as too poor or too degenerate to provide them with the basic necessities of life. The refuge house managers considered immigrant youth, white female delinquents, and blacks of both sexes (generally, blacks were totally excluded from the refuges) inferior to white, American-born males.

The New York House of Refuge experienced a rapid growth rate and similar growth occurred in other houses of refuge. Before long, they became overcrowded and filled with a mixture of hard-core juvenile delinquents and orphans. New York's answer was Randall's Island institution in the East River. Randall's Island allowed the Society for the Reformation of Juvenile Delinquents to apply a more systematic reformatory regime, one which they felt was the answer for dealing with delinquent and wayward youth.

The first public juvenile institution was a municipal reformatory for boys established in New Orleans in 1845. Prior to that, the operation and maintenance of the institutions was a joint effort responsibility of state and private agencies. The first state reform school for boys was opened in 1845 in Westboro, Massachusetts. Known as the Lyman School for Boys, it was closed only recently, in 1972.

The prevailing philosophy and educational practice of the times had a great deal of influence on the operation of juvenile institutions. During this time, it was believed that behavior was entirely a matter of self-control, so related influences were given little consideration. The early methods used in institutions were concerned with strict discipline, the inculcation of regular work and school habits, and the extensive use of punishment.

New York established a state agricultural and industrial school in 1849, and Maine, a training center in 1853. By 1870, Connecticut, Indiana, Maryland, Nevada, New Hampshire, New Jersery, Ohio, and Vermont could boast separate institutions or training schools for delinquents. By 1900, 36 states had followed suit, and today they are located in every state.

The original functions of the houses of refuge, reformatories, and juvenile institutions were threefold: (1) to get the poor, the wayward, and delinquent youth off the streets; (2) to separate youths from adult criminals; and (3) to save juveniles from crime through a regimented life-style, education, and training. Although juvenile institutions attempted to protect the children from the bad influence of adult institutions, the courts were still permitted to commit juvenile offenders to adult prisons if they desired.

Although the efforts to rescue juveniles in the early 1800s were crude and haphazard, they did offer a beginning. The religious environment and training of the early houses of refuge was largely Protestant, in keeping with the religious affiliation of early settlers in the eastern United States. To counter this Protestant influence, several private sectarian institutions were established. The Roman Catholic order of the House of Good Shepherd established institutions for girls and the Christian Brotherhood assumed responsibility for parochial schools and for institutional care of delinquent Catholic boys. Protestant denominations also established institutions for delinquent youth of both sexes. After the major Jewish migrations near the end of the nineteenth century, American Jews began to build orphanages and training schools as well.

Reform Schools

During the period 1859–1890, the movement to set up houses of refuge was replaced by the reform school and preventive agency movement. The Boston

House of Reformation was one of the more notable reform schools. Juvenile asylums were established, and the practice of "placing children out" became popular.[15] By 1890 nearly every state outside of the South had some type of reform school for delinquent youths that was also responsible for the care of numerous destitute children. One of the major problems facing the reform schools then still exists today: the problem of agreeing to a legal definition of juvenile delinquency. Because of this, youths who had committed crimes, youths who had neither committed nor been convicted of a crime, and youths who were convicted of a crime for which the law had no penalty were all held together in the same school. Also housed there were children who had been abused or abandoned by their parents, or youths who had been committed by their parents for being unruly or unmanageable.

Although the reform schools devoted more time to schooling (usually half a day or more), many of them were otherwise indistinguishable from the early refuges. Most were large congregate institutions with regimented workshop routines. Many reformers sought to change the routines of these reform schools by introducing a more varied and aesthetic institutional life for the children, with guidance aimed at bettering the total child and not simply at making him conform to the rigors of strict discipline, work, and training.

Cottage Reform School

The cottage reform school plan, founded by Wichern at Rauhe Haus, offered an opportunity to break away from the congregate placement of children in the institutions. Wichern's cottage plan was described thus:

> Each house is to be a family, under the sole direction and control of the matron, who is the mother of the family. . . . The government and discipline are strictly parental. It is the design to give a home interest, a home feeling and attachment, to the whole family.[16]

Cottage reform schools spread widely throughout the United States. New Jersey (1864) and Indiana (1866) opened cottage schools, and some older institutions converted from the congregate to the cottage plan. The cottage system for housing institutionalized juveniles continues to be the most popular form in use today.

State Reformatories

The 1870s saw the beginning of yet another type of institution: state reformatories for young men 16 to 30 years old who were first offenders. This development aided in resolving the category of children referred to as juvenile delinquents. American penal reformers, influenced by European innovations, established the New York State Reformatory at Elmira in 1877, the Massachusetts Reformatory for Men in 1884, and a reformatory for women and girls convicted of misdemeanors, chiefly those involving sex offenses, in New York in 1893. With the growth of the reformatory movement, some juvenile delinquent institutions were relieved of their older and often more troublesome inmates, a relief that was welcomed.[17]

Deficiencies of the Reform Movement

Early juvenile institutions had many failings. In the eastern states, they were located in the large metropolitan cities and these locations afforded the juveniles little change from the conditions which had so much to do with their being delinquent. With a vast amount of open land, western states overcame this shortcoming by locating their schools in the countryside and organizing their institutional programs around agricultural work. By the 1890s, most western reform schools had introduced vocational education, along with military drill and organization, into their routines. But they were otherwise very similar to the older eastern institutions and were bound toward a common destiny.

In the South, no provision was made for juvenile lawbreakers until long after the Civil War. The Populist political movement ushered in badly needed reforms. Prior to that time children were put in jail, in convict camps, and in the country road gangs or in prison farms along with adults.

During the last half of the nineteenth century, A. O. Wright of the Wisconsin Board of State Charities summarized the feeling of child-saving philanthropies of the time:

> If I were to classify the order of places, best or worst, in which people may be placed, especially children or young people, I say first of all, a good home; second best, a small institution rightly managed under proper persons, meaning by a small institution, one or two hundred inmates or less; thirdly, a large institution; fourth, a bad home.[18]

Punishment in reform schools was often brutal, and reformatory institutions became known, in the words of one superintendent, as "not the first aid to the injured . . . the forlorn hope. . . .' At the Illinois Reformatory a boy was hung by chains on the wall for nearly three days. He was alternately beaten and given the "water cure" until he died with his back broken in three places.[19]

Noncriminal youth who did not attend school regularly or who were unruly in school were spared the unhappy fate of reform school when parental or truant schools were started in 1900 just for these children. Thus youths who didn't belong among the populations of juvenile institutions were kept out of them.

Strongly influenced by popular scientific notions about juvenile delinquency and its probable causes, reform school managers and institutional superintendents emphasized everything from physical conditioning, strict military discipline, and the learning of a trade to the attainment of "decent" moral standards. Little progress has been made beyond the attempts of early correctional administrators. Today, basically the same problems are being faced. They are overcrowding, lack of public support and proper legislation, and a continuous debate on the link between cause and treatment of delinquency. The systems and practices started in the early houses of refuge, reform schools, reformatories, and juvenile institutions have remained with us. Throughout the country, many of our institutions are relics of the nineteenth century. In many cases, their programs have changed little since the founding date was put on their corner-stones.

Institutions Today

Directors of early juvenile institutions were chiefly concerned with the protection of society. Youths confined within institutional walls were judged enemies of society, and their custody was looked upon as a disciplinary measure. How far have things advanced since then? Has there been measurable progress in the search for an answer to the problem of juvenile delinquency? For the past several decades juvenile institutions have been subscribing, at least superficially, to a philosophy of social responsibility for the rehabilitation of deviant youth. As a consequence, today's institutions call for greater emphasis on education, vocational and personality training, and the inculcation of socially accepted living habits. Although recent Supreme Court decisions, such as *In re Gault*, have moved away from the *parens patriae* concept, it is still a widely held belief that society is responsible for juvenile delinquency.[20] The collective social conscience of America has reacted with an incredible variety of programs meant to alleviate the problem.

Society has a way of placing its concerns in an order of priority, concerns that are social and technological. One often hears the inquiry, "If we can put a man on the moon, why can't something be done about crime?" Social problems which lead to, cause, or are associated with crime and delinquency might be solved if top priority were given to solving these problems using the finest minds in the world and an unlimited budget. Such efforts aren't likely in the near future, however, so debate, half-measures, and temporary solutions will have to do for the foreseeable future.

In the meantime, juvenile crime increases, public schools cease to function,[21] and organized and armed youth gangs reemerge as a menace in the community. A return to the extensive use of imprisonment, which stigmatizes youthful criminals as the enemies of society, may well be the future for juvenile corrections. While not all youths belong in juvenile correctional institutions (e.g., status offenders, mentally or emotionally disturbed youth, or first-time offenders), economic pressures may force a line to be drawn. The proponents of community-based programs and treatment for troubled youth may argue against it, but a return to old-fashioned discipline, large congregate institutions, and the reform school-style institutions, while not the most desirable response, may be unavoidable.

However, if the increased use of institutions and the "get tough" policy is to be effective, the public will be faced with staggering costs for new and bigger institutions with more staff and an increasing drain on limited resources.

Detention

The National Council on Crime and Delinquency (NCCD) provides a clear, simple definition for detention care: "The temporary care of children in physically restricted facilities pending court disposition or transfer to another jurisdiction or agency."[22] To provide the child with a constructive experience, NCCD notes further that detention should meet four basic objectives:

1. Secure custody with good physical care in a manner that will offset the damaging effects of confinement.
2. A constructive and satisfying program of activities to provide the child with an opportunity to develop and recognize strengths and to help him find socially acceptable ways of gaining satisfaction.
3. Individual and group guidance to help the child use his detention experience positively.
4. Observation and study to provide screening for undetected mental or emotional illness as well as a diagnosis upon which to develop an appropriate treatment plan.[23]

Authorities generally agree that only certain youths should be involuntarily detained. They include those who would probably disappear prior to their hearing, those with a high probability of committing a dangerous offense while awaiting court disposition, and those who must be held for another jurisdiction. Federal guidelines emphasize that no youth should be unnecessarily detained, and those who can safely remain in their homes should be allowed to do so. These guidelines also specify that juveniles needing diagnostic evaluations should be able to receive them without being subjected to the detention experience.[24] In all, open facilities should be used for all youth not explicitly requiring a secure custodial setting.

Guidelines and recommendations, no matter how well intended or thought out, are useless unless they are put into practice. They are, however, useful as a yardstick against which to measure the real-life findings encountered by students of the juvenile justice system.

Of all facilities being used in the United States to incarcerate youth, the detention facility is the most common. Detention facilities can include jails, centers located above the juvenile court, converted mental wards, or anything in which youth can be imprisoned, pending a hearing or transfer. Five out of every six children held in all juvenile facilities are in detention. In 1971, 531,686 juveniles were admitted to all types of juvenile facilities; 494,286 of this total were admitted to detention.

The typical detainee is a male, with a median age of 14.7 years, who lives in a metropolitan area. A LEAA census of 11,748 youths indicates that nearly two-thirds were being detained pending a court hearing. Twenty-nine percent were adjudicated delinquents; four percent were dependent or neglected; and another four percent were awaiting transfer to another jurisdiction.[25]

One of the more tragic aspects of juvenile detention is that most single jurisdictions do not have enough youthful offenders to justify the construction of separate juvenile detention facilities. Therefore, an estimated 50,000 to 100,000 juveniles are being detained in local jails or police lockups for adults each year.[26] Nineteen states have statutory provisions for the detention of juveniles in jail, as long as they are segregated from adult offenders. Some states have statutes or policies prohibiting the detention of juveniles in jails, but practical solutions to juvenile detention problems require the frequent violation of such statutes.

Facilities designated for the exclusive purpose of detaining youth are usually not the best examples of how an ideal juvenile correctional facility should be designed or operated. Most of these structures were originally built to serve another purpose and have been converted to their present use. A 1969 survey found that the average capacity of juvenile detention facilities was 61; however, most were overcrowded before reaching that number.[27]

The emphasis on custody, which pervades the adult institutions, also shapes the general environment of juvenile detention facilities. Most of these facilities are located in urban areas and virtually sealed off from the community by their physical structure and other security measures. The youths are placed in dreary single cells or barrack-type housing with fixed furniture.

The chance of leaving a detention facility to return to a nondelinquent life-style is remote when one considers the lack of services and programs for youth in detention. They are denied most of the good in the adult programs, and are subjected to the worst aspects of institutional living.

Placing a Youth in Detention

There are several critical factors which have been linked with the courts' decision to place a youth in a detention facility:

1. Location of the detention unit;
2. The time of the youth's apprehension;
3. The location of that apprehension;
4. Availability of intake personnel to screen referrals;
5. The credibility of the referring source; and
6. The degree to which the court sees its detention policies as an area of community interest.[28]

For example, it has been observed that:

1. The further the detention unit is from the referring police units, the lower the rate of placement;
2. If a juvenile is apprehended after court office hours, he is more likely to be held in detention;
3. Youth are more likely to be detained if apprehended on the street or in public buildings where parents or concerned adults are less likely to be available to intervene;
4. When intake personnel are available for thorough screening and for detention hearings, juveniles are less frequently held in detention;
5. The higher the credibility of the referring source with court personnel, the greater the likelihood that a juvenile will be detained;
6. Time of year . . . especially as related to the school calendar, public attitudes, and interorganizational relations of the court with other community agencies also affect how detention polices are implemented.[29]

Length of Stay

In approximately 86 percent of the cases, the average length of stay in a juvenile detention facility is less than one month. The larger the facility, the more likely a youth is to remain longer than one month, despite concerns of overcrowding or lack of resources. Table 11–1 shows the average length of stay for a population observed and reported on by Rosemary Sarri in her book *Under Lock and Key*.

As noted in the opening paragraph of this section, the primary purpose of detention is *temporary* care. Lengths of stay of one month or more exceed the "temporary" nature of the stay and are difficult to explain in terms of the philosophy of detention. They may reflect inadequacies in the rest of the juvenile justice system, such as court backlogs, lack of sufficient probation staff and/or court intake personnel, overcrowded training schools and institutions, or a lack of adequate alternate placements within the community. NCCD recommends a detention program geared to last ten days to two weeks. "Children who stay much beyond that time usually deteriorate in morale, lose whatever gains they may have made, and frequently make it

TABLE 11-1. AVERAGE LENGTH OF STAY (in percentages)

AVERAGE NUMBER OF MONTHS	SIZE OF UNITS			ALL UNITS
	25 or Less	26 to 75	76 or More	
Less than 1	93	75	84	86
1 to 3	5	21	16	12
3 to 6	1	1	—	1
6 to 12	1	3	—	1
Total	100	100	100	100
(N of Units)	(134)	(71)	(37)	(242)

Note: Figures rounded to nearest percentage.
Source: Rosemary C. Sarri, *Under Lock and Key: Juveniles in Jails and Detention* (Ann Arbor: University of Michigan, 1974), p. 44.

impossible for children detained for the usual period to derive full value from detention programs."[30]

Youths detained because of abuse by parents—or because their parents claim they are unmanageable (status offenders)—are frequently placed in the same facility or cell with delinquent youth who have committed violent or assaultive crimes. While various guidelines have been written recommending that status offenders be separated from delinquents, they are seldom implemented. The results can be disastrous, not only in detention facilities but in institutions as well. In *Hard Cores Don't Come From Apples,* the authors explain:

> There's a great system for training criminals operating on a grand scale throughout the United States. It involves taking juvenile offenders, booking them, and then jamming them into the meat grinder of overcrowded inadequate juvenile courts and massively overburdened penal institutions, which are themselves crammed to overflowing with dangerous hard core criminals and sexual perverts. This system which is maintained and endorsed by lawmakers, law enforcement agents, educators, juvenile officials, and the voters, turns out hardened law breakers. It's an expensive system, but it works! Trained medical personnel assigned to juvenile halls across the country have said, in essence, that juvenile halls sustain the type of atmosphere that supports continued further anger and hatred toward a system that today has become intolerant and illiberal with the American juvenile. If society doesn't believe, nor even wonder, that violence, sex attacks, inadequate medical facilities, and indiscriminate mixing of juvenile offenders—some first-time offenders—with hardened criminals can produce more criminals, merely examine the latest crime statistics. Look at the ages of the thieves, drug users, rip-off artists, kill-for-kicks practitioners, and violent sex perverts. They are young—and getting younger![31]

The National Advisory Commission made specific recommendations with regard to juvenile detention facilities:

1. The detention facility should be located in a residential area in the community and near court and community resources.

2. Population of detention centers should not exceed 30 residents. When population requirements significantly exceed this number, development of separate components under the network system should be pursued.

3. Living area capacities within the center should not exceed 10 or 12 youngsters each. Only individual occupancy should be provided, with single rooms and programming regarded as essential. Individual rooms should be pleasant, adequately furnished, and homelike rather than punitive and hostile in atmosphere.

4. Security should not be viewed as an indispensable quality of the physical environment but should be based on a combination of staffing patterns, technological devices, and physical design.

5. Existing residential facilities within the community should be used in preference to new construction.

6. Facility programming should be based on investigation of community resources, with the contemplation of full use of these resources, prior to determination of the facility's in-house program requirements.

7. New construction and renovation of existing facilities should be based on consideration of the functional interrelationships between program activities and program participants.

8. Detention facilities should be coeducational and should have access to a full range of supportive programs, including education, library, recreation, arts and crafts, music, drama, writing, and entertainment. Outdoor recreational areas are essential.

9. Citizen advisory boards should be established to pursue development of in-house and community-based programs and alternatives to detention.

10. Planning should comply with pertinent state and federal regulations and the Environmental Policy Act of 1969.[32]

Institutions: Functions and Theories

While the stated purposes of the juvenile detention facility and the juvenile institution (or state training school) are ideologically different, what they produce is quite similar. Adult prisons and juvenile institutions have been repeatedly criticized for their inherently degrading and dehumanizing effects on inmate populations. However, the continued use and survival of institutions indicates that they are performing functions and purposes acceptable to society, which continues to tolerate them.

In an article entitled "Tear Down the Walls? Some Functions of Prisons," the authors, Charles Reasons and Russell Kaplan, suggest that the actual survival of prisons and institutions depends on their "fulfilling four important manifest functions in varying degrees: (1) reformation, (2) incapacitation, (3) retribution, and (4) deterrence."[33] However, Reasons and Kaplan also suggest that there are eleven latent functions of institutions more significant than the four manifest functions, and which also serve various interests and needs: "(1) maintenance of a crime school, (2) politicization, (3) self-enhancement, (4) provision of jobs, (5) satisfaction of authoritarian needs, (6) slave labor, (7) reduction of unemployment rates, (8) scientific research, (9) do-gooderism, (10) safety valve for racial tensions, and (11) birth control. These latent functions, largely unintended and generally unrecognized, suggest that abolition of the prison may not be as assured as some reformers suppose."[34]

In light of the fact that institutions are considered the most expensive and least successful method of handling juvenile offenders, one must question whether these functions of institutions (or ones similar to them) are preserving them despite the costly operations and lack of success attributed to juvenile institutions. Alternatives to institutionalization, such as the provision of supervision and treatment in the community, are under close scrutiny to prove themselves. It no longer suffices simply to state that these services exist. With less tolerance for crime and criminals, adult and juvenile, these community services will have to prove effective almost immediately in order to be continued. All juvenile programs are under such scrutiny today; however, programs that break with tradition and contemporary innovations are usually most suspect and subject to early curtailment.

It appears, then, that the manifest and latent functions of institutions *do* outweigh their high cost and their lack of success with offender populations. To make this answer more palatable, there are those who contend that junior prisons in America are not all that bad. However, this contention assumes that their purpose is *custody* as opposed to *treatment*. Unfortunately, the emphasis on custody as the prevailing model creates the same problems of civil rights at the juvenile level as it does at the adult level. The dangers that juvenile institutions hold for the civil rights of the offender were forcefully brought to public attention in the *Gault* decision.

The *two basic theories* favoring the institutionalization of youths may be increasingly challenged in the near future. The first theory (that incarceration is an effective device for changing people and at the same time deterring others) is debatable, irrespective of the *Gault* decision. Unfortunately, national statistics on recidivism after incarceration are generally not available to substantively refute this theory. A review of juveniles incarcerated in federal institutions revealed that slightly over 40 percent recidivated after their release and were reimprisoned. Better statistics on the rate of recidivism of juvenile institutional populations after release would certainly provide us with useful information on the supposed deterrent effect of institutions.

The second theory favoring institutionalization is that the youthful offender should be removed from the community and the influences which caused his or her delinquent behavior in the first place. This theory, however, also lacks support. As noted in chapter 7, the research on the effectiveness of treatment within correctional institutions indicates that juvenile correctional systems have had varying degrees of success at best. The success of the treatment programs and the validity of treatment statistics is under constant challenge. Robert Martinson suggests from his review of much of the correctional research that:

> These data, involving over 200 studies and hundreds of thousands of individuals as they do, are the best available and give us very little reason to hope that we have, in fact, found a sure way of reducing recidivism through rehabilitation. This is not to say that these instances have been isolated, producing no clear pattern to indicate the efficacy of any particular methods of treatment.[35]

Daniel Glaser states that:

> A review of a half century's research in corrections reveals much that is useful, yet a study of its influence suggests that the primary contribution of past research to correction progress is not in its answers to the questions that were investigated, but in its guidance to more fruitful questions.[36]

Glaser also indicates that "we know that no single policy or service rehabilitates all offenders, and we have saved millions by vetoing proposals from practitioners who still recommend these costly expenditures for everyone."[37] In a study of the effect of institutionalization on self-image, Robert Culbertson found that:

> It is impossible to ignore the fact that by using a cross sectional design, the self-concept scores for delinquents not previously incarcerated did decrease significantly . . . involvement in the juvenile justice system commences a negative labelling process and the result is a depreciated self-concept for those children so labeled.[38]

The incarceration of youth, in fact, can reach a point of diminishing returns. Studies have indicated that communities spend enormous sums of money keeping juveniles locked up longer than is necessary, so long, in fact, that the chances of realizing rehabilitation are greatly decreased. The findings of a California report emphasize the absence of a positive correlation between time served in institutions and subsequent criminal or delinquent behavior.[39]

The juvenile justice system suffers from two basic mistaken notions regarding the functions of institutionalization: first, punishment is of little importance, and, second, punishment and rehabilitation can occur in the same setting. In an article "When to Punish, When to Rehabilitate," Ellsworth Fersch suggests a two-step process—first punishment, then rehabilitation. He contends that this would restore faith in the criminal justice system and respect for the individual and society. "We need to separate these critical functions and provide short, swift, and humane punishment, followed by voluntary rehabilitation."[40] Fersch may be right, although the effects of punishment on a frightened youthful offender may well neutralize his or her receptivity to rehabilitative programs. Even voluntary participation by the youth may be consent merely to gain release from the institution or rehabilitative setting. If a system such as Fersch's is adopted, those responsible should take care to maintain the fine difference between being viewed as prison "screws" or "rehabilitative agents."

In review, there are four *manifest* and eleven *latent* functions which are attributable to juvenile institutions, and two *basic* theories which favor their existence. We feel that the continued existence of juvenile institutions may be the result of their successful fulfillment of the latent functions, while fulfillment of the functions of reformation, incapacitation, retribution, and deterrence are of secondary consequence. But it is apparent that today's juvenile institutions have fallen far short of providing conclusive proof that the two basic theories in their favor are, in fact, valid.

Institutional Treatment and Rehabilitation

The National Advisory Commission on Criminal Justice Standards and Goals offers the following guidelines and standards in order to assist the juvenile institutions in their reexamination of educational and vocational training programs:

1. Each institution should have a comprehensive continuous educational program for inmates.
2. Each institution should have prevocational and vocational training programs to enhance the offender's marketable skills.
3. Features applicable both to educational and vocational training programs should include the following:
   a. Emphasis should be placed on programmed instruction, which allows maximum flexibility in scheduling, enables students to proceed at their own pace, gives immediate feedback, and permits individualized instruction.
   b. A variety of instructional materials—including audio tapes, teaching, machines, books, computers, and television—should be used to stimulate individual motivation and interest.
   c. Selected offenders should participate in instructional roles.
   d. Community resources should be fully utilized.
   e. Correspondence courses should be incorporated into educational and vocational training programs to make available to inmates specialized instruction that cannot be obtained in the institution or the community.

  f. Credit should be awarded for educational and vocational programs
     equivalent to or the same as that associated with these programs in the
     free world.[41]

Unfortunately, in spite of these standards and guidelines, actual experience has shown that most youths committed to juvenile institutions
are simply "doing time." Their release is more often based on such
nontreatment-related factors as overcrowding, administrative decisions, and
incredibly, *nontreatability*. Instead of being a constructive and maturing
experience, incarceration in a juvenile institution is often harmful for the
juvenile. Nonconstructive time spent away from family and community
leads to a lessening of the sense of belonging and responsibility.

> Delinquency institutions today—with few exceptions—manifest practices
> based on the concepts of retaliation . . . strict obedience enforced through
> military-type discipline, protection through custodial care, education through
> provision of mostly vocational and often outdated training, sometimes individ-
> ual or group therapy unrelated to the rest of the milieu, and especially an
> overall separation from the community.[42]

The institutionalization of juveniles is currently being viewed by both the
public and the juvenile justice professional as a last resort, an alternative to
be used when nothing else is available. In fact, there has been a recent
decrease in the rates of institutionalization of juveniles at a time when
juvenile court delinquency cases—the primary source of commitments to
institutions—appear to be increasing. The decrease in institutional care,
therefore, may reflect the recent emphasis on finding alternatives for the
treatment of youthful offenders, using incarceration only where it is absolutely necessary to the child's welfare and/or protection of the community.[43]

Services in Institutions

Institutionalized juveniles, for whatever reason they are in institutions, must
be provided access to services required for individual growth and development. These services include meaningful, quality education and adequate
vocational training programs.

Irving Kaufman suggests that to accomplish this end, all sentences should
be fixed terms. Any subsequent change should be imposed by the court upon
show of good cause. "Indeterminate sentences have been rejected by the
commission as a game of chance based on arbitrary decisions. Frequently in
the past the most violent juveniles were released from institutions because
they were, ironically, difficult to control. Power to determine the actual
length of stay of a juvenile is thus removed from the hands of correctional
authorities. To encourage good behavior, correctional administrators are
allowed to reduce a youth's sentence by no more than 5 percent. The

maximum term of incarceration should not exceed two years for any offense.''[44]

Currently, even when the treatment staffs does plan a potentially meaningful program, they can seldom be assured of how long they have with their "client." As long as release is possible at any time, training programs are practically worthless. To believe, therefore, that youths are released from juvenile institutions only when they are successfully rehabilitated or "cured" is to believe a fantasy.

The use of fixed-length sentences would allow the juvenile to complete useful training programs. One must keep in mind, however, that the length of time a youth spends in an institution and the degree to which he is rehabilitated are not always related. To assume, for example, that the longer a youth spends incarcerated the more he will be rehabilitated, and vice versa, is not always true. To justify the use of fixed-length sentences, therefore, on the basis of allowing enough time for the completion of adequate training programs and then not to provide these programs would be in violation of the principle of "right to treatment." Under a system of fixed-length sentences, it would be necessary for the institutional staff to tailor treatment programs to fit the varying periods of time youths could spend in the institution. It would defeat the purpose of the treatment plan, for example, if a youth sentenced to from two to four months were placed in a treatment program which required at least 10 months to complete.

Morales v. Turman

Many people have assumed that a juvenile has the right to treatment once he or she comes under the auspices of the juvenile justice system, or at least that treatment does exist. However, the *right* of a juvenile to rehabilitation and/or treatment (whether or not treatment actually exists) in a correctional institution has until very recently gone uncontested. Most court cases concerning rights to treatment generally have involved adults, but in 1974, the U.S. District Court for the Eastern District of Texas in *Morales* v. *Turman* determined that constitutional rights of incarcerated minors had been violated and ordered the parties involved to submit a comprehensive plan for righting these violations.[45] This case has raised a wide range of issues regarding the nature and adequacy of procedures and programs adopted by the Texas Youth Council (TYC). The TYC has the responsibility under Texas law for minors adjudicated delinquent and involuntarily committed to its custody. In this case, the court withheld issuing a permanent order of relief in favor of the plaintiffs in order to give TYC a chance to make amends and to present a treatment plan favorable to all parties involved. This was done because the granting of requested relief could quite possibly entail extensive changes in virtually every phase of the TYC operations.

The court's ruling presupposes a constitutionally-based right to rehabilitative treatment in juvenile correctional facilities, and involves a sustained attack on a wide range of practices, policies, procedures, and resultant conditions authorized by the TYC. The plaintiffs in this case have questioned whether TYC had violated the youth's rights regarding: (1) First Amendment freedoms of speech, expression, religious choice, and the right to petition for redress of grievances; (2) the freedom from unreasonable search and seizure under the Fourth Amendment; (3) the protection from cruel and unusual punishment as guaranteed by the Eighth Amendment; (4) privacy, as assured by the First, Fourth, Fifth and Ninth Amendments; (5) freedom from involuntary servitude under the Thirteenth Amendment; (6) equal protection of the laws vis-à-vis adults fined or imprisoned for the same offenses under the Fourteenth Amendment; (7) *rehabilitative treatment* administered in a manner least restrictive of their liberty, assuming judicial determination that such a right exists under the due process clause of the Fourteenth Amendment; and (8) freedom from discipline while institutionalized, arbitrary transfer between institutions or groupings, and parole revocations, without due process of law.

The breadth of relief requested would require the court to order the defendants to assure: (1) that safe and sanitary conditions would be restored to and be maintained at TYC schools and facilities; (2) that architectural and design changes would be made to facilitate rehabilitation; (3) that incarcerated youths would be accorded essential preventive and therapeutic medical, dental, and mental health services, including complete physical and mental examinations upon admission to TYC and periodically thereafter; (4) that classification and confinement schemes would be organized to prevent grouping multiple offenders with youths having less serious records; (5) that an individualized treatment plan would be developed as each individual youth enters TYC custody with the participation of psychiatrists, psychologists, counsellors, and other professionals, and that the individual treatment plans thereafter would be implemented accordingly; (6) that adequate educational, vocational, and work programs would be established; (7) that TYC staff would be recruited, selected, trained, and employed to insure that staff members in sufficient numbers and with adequate education and experience would be available; (8) that confinement in isolation cells would be eliminated, and that practices and procedures governing disciplinary confinement of any kind would be ameliorated; (9) that visiting regulations and facilities would be established which would ensure decency, comfort, privacy, reasonable and frequent visiting periods, and which would place no restrictions on the identity of visitors; (10) that adequate, unmonitored telephone access would be provided: (11) that corporal punishment would be prohibited; (12) that extensive procedural protection could be invoked by an inmate before any disciplinary measures could be taken against him or her; and (13) that inmates would be permitted to speak, write, and receive letters in languages other than English.

The crucial test of this case may well surround a further request by the plaintiffs that the defendants be restrained from engaging in any of the unlawful acts, practices, or omissions itemized at length in connection with their right to treatment, and that if the defendant failed to submit and implement a satisfactory plan, further incarceration and detention of the plaintiff class in deficient TYC facilities should be enjoined.[46]

The District Court granted virtually all the relief that was requested by the plaintiffs. A few examples of the requirements that the decision imposes on the TYC follow: (1) the District Court found that the Gatesville State School for Boys, the school with the largest capacity in the state, and Mountain View State School for Boys, the maximum security facility for the entire TYC system, were "places where the delivery of effective rehabilitative treatment is impossible" due to the "history of brutality and repression" at those institutions.[47] The court ordered that these schools should be abandoned as soon as possible,[48] and it did something which may be viewed as facilitating treatment in its own system which should serve as an example throughout the country. The court disparaged the TYC policy of using large institutions located in small rural towns far from urban population centers because of the difficulties created thereby for involving the youth's family and community in the treatment plans and for attracting qualified professional staff.[49] The court further held the TYC "must cease to institutionalize any juveniles except those who are found by a responsible, professional assessment to be unsuited for any less restrictive, alternative form of rehabilitative treatment,"[50] and that they must "create or discover a system of community-based treatment alternatives adequate to serve the needs of those juveniles for whom the institution is not appropriate." In addition, "those few juveniles for whom close confinement is appropriate must be surrounded by a staff trained to meet their special needs, in a virtually one-to-one ratio."[51]

What the plaintiffs in this case accomplished was nothing less than an exhaustive attack on a set of policies and programs which, when taken as a whole, represent no less than a state's entire juvenile correctional system. The assurances requested by the plaintiffs should serve as examples to be followed by similar court action throughout the United States. *Morales* v. *Turman* and its implications for correctional attitudes, settings, and treatment rights is crucial to the future of the juvenile justice system. Although this case specifically applied to Texas, the conditions described therein are similar to those in a large number of other states in this country. It is hoped that these systems which have been or are moving in the direction of providing requests and assurances similar to those contained in the *Morales* case will continue to do so, and that states which find their programs sadly behind the times and lacking in humane treatment practices will soon follow suit. If not, court action similar to that brought against the TYC may leave them no choice.

The whole concept of treatment or lack of treatment within our juvenile institutions raises the basic question, "Is it our intention to punish youth who violate the law or to rehabilitate them?" Put another way, this question is, "Are we for justice, or are we for laws?" According to Rossi and Dumm,

In the juvenile area, the system for training criminals throughout the United States is complete. Hardly a course is overlooked in the education of youth when they enter this exceptional and unequalled academy of learning. Quickly and proficiently they develop into criminals. Yet, juveniles are not brought into this world as potential, hard-core criminals. A criminal, like a surgeon, requires training and enlightenment, growth and extension. The manner and means of training and development a juvenile receives will determine whether or not he or she will become a criminal. Crime is not a talent! It is a means of survival and self-preservation and a way of life for many young individuals. It's not an artistic, creative endeavor such as music, painting, or architecture.[52]

If law is to be upheld, then a juvenile who violates the law should be accorded every right currently granted to adult offenders, including the right not to be detained or incarcerated for status offenses or incorrigible acts. If justice is to be served, we should see to it that only those youths for whom no alternative exists other than incarceration are committed to juvenile institutions, and at the same time accord them all rights granted adults. Furthermore, incarcerated youth should be guaranteed humane rehabilitative treatment and nonincarcerated youth should be placed in community-based treatment programs which promote their remaining in society as useful citizens.

The use of laws to deprive a person of justice is too common. Justice is supposed to be blind, yet youths and adults receive separate treatment when it comes to constitutional guarantees and access to treatment and rehabilitation.

Today, there are millions of American juveniles who are nothing but a lingering mass of bewildered humanity. They are continually faced with highblown pacifying rhetoric, spewing from the mouths of nearly every faction in adult society, from the highest levels of government to the lowest gorges of domesticity. The American juvenile is engulfed with layer upon layer of compounded political, incompassionate, discriminating deceit. That's not much of a party, but it's one hell of a cake! If our system is a responsible system, if society is a dignified society, then the juvenile justice system must surely be restructured to a more humanistic level of care and *treatment*.[53]

Escape and Unauthorized Leaves

Among the many serious problems confronting juvenile correctional administrators and staff is escape or unauthorized leave from juvenile institutions. Unauthorized leaves both disrupt and destroy a juvenile's participation in residential treatment programs designed to make possible a successful reentry into the community. In the past few years, professional staffs at institutions have become increasingly aware of this problem. In Washington, for example, over a five-year period ending June 30, 1975, there was

FISCAL YEAR	AVERAGE DAILY POPULATION	UNAUTHORIZED LEAVES
1971	996	838
1972	848	718
1973	812	831
1974	756	906
1975	752	689

approximately one escape from juvenile rehabilitation institutions each year for each youth in the average daily population of these institutions.[54]

Authorized leaves from juvenile rehabilitation institutions are an essential, significant component of the overall treatment planning for individual youth. However, failure to return to the institution after the leave period has expired is counterproductive to treatment. Although authorized leaves are a vital part of the rehabilitative process, the risk of extended approved leaves without authorization should be minimized.

At present, little information is available to assist institutional program staffs in developing a program modification or new programs to reduce the frequency of escapes or unauthorized leaves. Detailed information about the characteristics of juveniles who are likely to escape or take an unauthorized leave; or about the personnel, situational, and institutional circumstances that lead to unauthorized leaves; or about what juveniles actually do when on unauthorized leaves is generally lacking in the field of juvenile corrections. Obviously, there is a need for substantive research in this area.

Increasing rates of unauthorized leaves apply nationwide. It is the authors' belief that the frequency and length of unauthorized leaves can be controlled. Reduction in the frequency of unauthorized leaves should reduce the rate of criminal behavior committed by juveniles in the community and should make the juvenile more available for treatment. A long-range reduction in delinquency is also probable.

An interstate agreement for juveniles (called the Interstate Compact on Juveniles) was formulated in the early 1950s to cope with the many problems involved in supervising and controlling juveniles and juvenile delinquents. A major purpose of this agreement was to provide for the return of escapees to the state from which they had escaped. Forty-seven states are signatories to the Interstate Compact on Juveniles; the prospects for all states joining in the near future are favorable.

Under the compact, when the runaway child is apprehended in another state, the arresting agency usually contacts the institution or agency from whose jurisdiction the child ran. If problems are encountered, the Interstate Office may assist whenever possible.

The constitutionality of the compact has been challenged on the grounds that it has not received the consent of Congress and that it violates the protection privileges and immunities and due process clauses of the Fourteenth Amendment.[55] Ruling in a case which challenged the compact (*Chin v. Wyman et al.*), a New York court said that in respect to the possible violation of due process, a hearing should be held in the state to which the youth had fled, on the question of whether he or she should be returned to the home state. Such a hearing, the court said, was necessary in order to satisfy due process requirements.[56]

Before leaving the subject of escape and unauthorized leave, the reader should consider two things:

1. The granting of full constitutional protection to juveniles carries potential hazards unrealized by many. For example, adult convicts attempting to escape from an institution can be legally shot. How acceptable would it be to allow a 13-year-old joyrider to be subjected to the same sort of life-endangering threat?

2. Of the thousands of young people who escape or take unauthorized leave from juvenile institutions each year, many are never caught and are not heard from again. Could it be that perhaps they have found their own successful means for rehabilitation outside the world of our institutional treatment programs? (At least one juvenile institution recognizes this possibility and calls it self-placement.)[57]

Institutional Punishment

Horror stories of brutal punishment, sexual and homosexual abuse and assault, and convict child labor were once commonly reported in newspapers, magazines, and other media. For the most part, the juvenile justice system has overcome these abuses; however, children still may suffer many dehumanizing acts when they are locked away in jails, institutions, and "kid prisons."

Often funds and resources which could be used for education, health care, and positive treatment of youth are used up on negative programs. Many institutions continue to emphasize punishment or the threat of punishment as their primary means of controlling their youthful populations.

> They duplicate—with untried, unconvicted children—the typical shortcomings of the whole American correctional system.
>
> Only a minority of all children detained are dangerous to society. Many more have difficulties dealing with authority. Whatever a child's problems, the use of force reinforces those problems. Children's courts and institutions were not meant to punish, but to help. This is especially true of institutions for children who are only suspected of or charged with misconduct. But what was intended is seldom achieved.
>
> When children in detention attempt to release pent-up energy, bred of inactivity and idleness—when they talk back to staff, speak when the rules command silence, smoke, fight, or violate institutional regulations—they may be beaten, placed in solitary confinement, stripped, or otherwise abused and humiliated.[58]

Bizarre corporal punishments are common in juvenile institutions and detention facilities. A Harvard student, for example, who posed as a

16-year-old inmate of the John J. Connally Youth Center in Roslindale, Massachusetts, reported that one commonly used punishment was to hold a boy's head under water, and for minor infractions of the rules youths were beaten by the fists of teenagers forced to participate under threat of a beating themselves.

The use of solitary confinement or isolation is as widespread in juvenile detention facilities and institutions as is corporal punishment and the administration of calming or tranquilizing drugs. Its use continues despite condemnation by theoreticians and practitioners.

In Washington's juvenile institutions, isolation is used only as a vehicle of treatment policy, rather than a means of juvenile punishment. For juveniles confined to one of Washington state's youth camps, there are 26 grounds for isolation. They are:

1. Fighting with any person (except in self-defense).
2. Threatening another with bodily harm or with any offense against his person.
3. Loaning of property for profit.
4. Intentionally mutilating, altering, defacing, or destroying property either of the State or of other persons.
5. Refusing to, or being inexcusably absent from, work or other regularly scheduled assignment.
6. Refusing to obey a lawful order of any staff member.
7. Abusive language directed to any other person.
8. Lying or knowingly providing a false statement to a staff member or to the hearing panel.
9. Interfering with a staff member in the performance of his duties.
10. Being present in an unauthorized area with knowledge of the lack of authority to be there.
11. Intentional failure to follow published safety, health, or sanitary regulations.
12. Using any equipment or machinery which is not specifically authorized.
13. Gambling.
14. Assaulting any person.
15. Extortion.
16. Giving or offering any official staff member anything of value for a service or favor.
17. Unauthorized leave (run away).
18. Stealing property or knowingly possessing stolen property.
19. Refusing to submit to a body search, blood test, or urinalysis when lawfully ordered to do so by institutional staff and when medically acceptable conditions are proffered.
20. Possession or introduction into the institution of a gun, firearm, weapon, sharpened instrument, knife, or unauthorized tool.

21. Possession or introduction of an explosive or any ammunition.

22. Possession, transfer, or use of any narcotics, controlled substance, or intoxicant other than those prescribed for the juvenile by the medical staff.

23. Rioting or inciting others to riot.

24. Soliciting, conspiring, attempting, or aiding others to commit the above infractions.

25. Being otherwise dangerous to the welfare and security of one's self, the institution, or others.

26. Personally and voluntarily requesting placement in isolation where such isolation is determined by the institution staff to be in the child's best interest.[59]

The youth camp's policies show a degree of humane treatment even in the extreme practice of isolation. Examples of these practices are:

A. *Isolation Hearing:* Any juvenile confined to isolation shall be given a hearing, unless the hearing is waived by the juvenile, or unless isolation was at the juvenile's request. If a hearing is not granted within 24 hours the juvenile must be released from isolation. The purpose of the hearing shall be to determine both the truth of the allegations and the reasonability for isolation. The juvenile's rights at such hearing shall be:

B. *Conditions of Isolation:*
1. Except as provided in subsection (3), no juvenile shall at any time be placed in any isolation facility without provisions for the following:
   a. A room equipped with lighting sufficient for the occupant to read by during reasonable hours.
   b. Sufficient clothing to meet seasonal needs.
   c. Bedding, including blankets, sheets, mattresses, pillows, and pillow cases.
   d. A daily change of clothes.
   e. Minimum writing materials; Paper, a pen or pencil, and envelopes.
   f. Prescription eye glasses, if needed.
   g. Approximately equivalent access to all books, periodicals, and other reading materials located in the facility.
   h. At least hourly access to personal hygiene facilities and supplies, such as sink and toilet, and daily access to a shower or bath.
   i. Access to medical facilities reasonably equivalent to those enjoyed by the institution inmates who are not in isolation.
   j. Three full meals per day, in reasonable quality and quantity.
   k. Daily opportunity for at least one-half hour of large muscle physical exercise.
   l. Communication by the isolated juvenile via the mails or telephone, subject only to those limitations which apply generally to all inmates of that juvenile facility.

    m. Education through the use of comparable books and materials as those used for juvenile inmates in the general population, but such education in the isolation chambers shall be conducted only on an indirect basis. Indirect here means any communication between the juvenile and the education instructor other than face-to-face communication.

2. There will be at least one staff member on duty at all times within calling distance of the isolation units. This staff member must be equipped to properly and within three minutes respond to emergencies involving the juvenile in isolation.

3. Where specific evidence before the hearing panel, or before the Superintendent or his representative, indicates that the health or safety of the detained juvenile or that of others would probably be endangered by providing any of the rights guaranteed in subsection (1) hereof, that a likelihood of escape would be created, or that malicious destruction of property occur, then the right(s) may not be provided so long as the danger exists.

C. *Reporting and Recording:* Each incident of isolation will be reported to the Lodge Supervisor at the earliest convenience. On those occasions when the situation is of a more serious or emergency nature the supervisor will be notified immediately. The Officer of the Day will be contacted and he will arrange for the hearing as necessary. All other staff on duty in the living unit will be notified of the isolation, the reason for it, and what approach to take with the juvenile.[60]

Organizational Traditions and Punishment

Within juvenile correctional institutions, organizational traditions exist which compound the problems caused by mixing treatment and punishment. In treatment philosophy as in punishment philosophy, the primary source of the delinquent or incorrigible behavior is sought *within* the offender. As a consequence, the treatment philosophy has never really challenged the social functions of institutional punishment, nor has it indicated the extent to which caste-like correctional organizations may seriously hamper efforts at rehabilitative treatment. There is a tendency for youths to view whatever is done to them as punishment rather than treatment.

    "Part of the reason for this perception lies in the fact that treatment personnel, even if highly trained (and they are in short supply in most juvenile training schools), have a symbiotic relationship with clients which is subtle and paradoxical. The status of the professional, his helping role, his very place in the whole scheme of things depends heavily upon the client remaining in a subordinate relationship to him. The paradox is, therefore, that although the professional role ostensibly exists to help the client, it is, in fact, one which relies upon a superordinate-subordinate relationship. As a result, it is difficult for the client to change unless his relationship to those above him changes also. Organizational arrangements are not available by which to encourage him to stop conceiving of himself as delinquent, inmate, or patient, and to conceive of himself, instead, as non-delinquent, employee, or student."[61]

Although some institutions are taking steps to move inmates step by step into new roles, there are still too few organizational structures within correctional institutions which allow the youth to be anything but an inmate and a delinquent. There are, therefore, two types of punishment practiced within our juvenile institutions: (1) actual physical punishment such as beatings, isolation, restraints, and so forth; and (2) a form of psychological feeling which causes the youth to view everything happening to him or her, while at the hands of an adult power structure, as punishment—even if that action is intended to be treatment oriented and in the youth's best interest.

The Future of Juvenile Institutions

The questions about institutions are numerous. Who should be institutionalized? For what purpose? For how long? By whose decision? According to what criteria? Should youth receive a fixed or indeterminate sentence? Is parole the only acceptable mechanism for early release? How does one adequately measure the outcome of the correctional process on society? What impact does the institutional experience have upon the youth who is processed through it? How does the labeling of a youth by the police, courts and institutions affect his or her abstention from delinquent behavior?

In recent years, delinquency has increased, and this has stimulated the development of numerous kinds of programs for the juvenile institutional field. Four of the most significant of these new programs are briefly described as follows:

A. *Community-Based Treatment Services.* As the name implies, these services include various methods of handling juveniles in a community setting as alternatives to commitment or for reducing the number of commitments. They are of special interest because of their relative economy compared with institutional commitment and because of the advantages of treatment in a setting as normal or "close to home" as possible.

The principal vehicles include intensified and selected probation and parole caseloads offering special counseling and community help plus "in and out" and trial furloughs; group homes and agency-operated residential treatment programs; "day care" in specialized institutional programs that return youngsters home at night and on weekends; regional detention centers with diagnostic service intended to reduce "dumping" into institutions; special "closed" local facilities with intensive counseling; and family involvement.

B. *Group Treatment.* Group treatment techniques offer essentially the advantage of economy over one-to-one counseling relationships, plus treatment advantages gained from insights on behavior through viewpoints pressed from several sources. In the institutional setting they have included families of the trainees. Their common goal is acceptance of responsibility rather than satisfaction with shallow conformity.

C. *Diversification*. Development in this direction is represented by the growth of small camp programs, halfway houses, group-treatment centers, reception and screening centers, vocational training centers, and special short-term programs.

D. *Decriminalization and Deinstitutionalization* Detention of juveniles would be drastically reduced if PINS and dependency-neglect cases were removed altogether from juvenile court jurisdiction. Decriminalization of conduct which is prohibited "for children only," would remove thousands of children from court-controlled institutions. This shift would work only if alternatives were available to respond to neglected and troubled children. One such mechanism is the system of "Youth Service Bureaus" advocated by the President's Crime Commission in 1967.[62]

In the future, juvenile justice administrators must guarantee that alternatives to institutionalization are as readily available to the children of the poor as to the middle- and upper-class children. One may argue that poor children commit more wrongs, but the unequal handling of criminal cases may be due to the fact that upper- and middle-class families are more often allowed to deal with the problem *outside* of the system. Ironically, poor children are often placed in juvenile institutions for their own protection and good, regardless of the seriousness of their offense(s), while children from prosperous backgrounds are usually released—also for their own good— even though they may have committed more serious offenses.

Summary

Juvenile institutions are as good and as bad as those in the adult system. Most people dislike seeing youths detained in jails and lockups, but this practice still persists in jurisdictions where there are no alternatives. From numerous research projects conducted over the years, it is clear that detention and incarceration in juvenile institutions harm many youths. Despite the failures of the adult corrections system, society seems to prefer using a similar type of system for the youths who come in contact with the juvenile justice system. To counter this attitude, standards of treatment and guidelines for handling the problems of delinquents must be carefully applied to these youths in trouble. Otherwise, the impact upon society can be more negative than positive. The impact of *Morales* is just being felt. This and other cases in which the Supreme Court ruled in the post-*Gault* era will shape and mold the future of the institutionalization of delinquent juveniles.

Just as important as the institutions are the alternatives to institutionalization offered by juvenile corrections administrators. The rights and recourses available to adults in the adult corrections system will probably soon be accessible to juveniles as well. While the two systems are not yet equal, the movement toward equalization seems irreversible. It is the job of the juvenile justice professional to ensure that these similarities are more on the positive side than the negative.

To conclude this chapter, here is a list of recommendations, in response to the problems of juveniles, made in a recent national commission report on corrections:

> Each State should enact legislation by 1975 limiting the delinquency jurisdiction of the courts to those juveniles who commit acts that if committed by an adult would be crimes.
>
> The legislation should also include provisions governing the detention of juveniles accused of delinquent conduct, as follows:
>
> 1. A prohibition against detention of juveniles in jails, lockups, or other facilities used for housing adults accused or convicted of crime.
> 2. Criteria for detention prior to adjudication of delinquency matters which should include the following:
>   a. Detention should be considered as a last resort where no other reasonable alternative is available.
>   b. Detention should be used only where the juvenile has no parent, guardian, custodian, or other person able to provide supervision and care for him and able to assure his presence at subsequent judicial hearings.
> 3. Prior to first judicial hearing, juveniles should not be detained longer than overnight.
> 4. Law enforcement officers should be prohibited from making the decision as to whether a juvenile should be detained. Detention decisions should be made by intake personnel and the court.
>
> The legislation should authorize a wide variety of diversion programs as an alternative to formal adjudication. Such legislation should protect the interests of the juvenile by assuring that:
>
> 1. Diversion programs are limited to reasonable time periods.
> 2. The juvenile or his representative has the right to demand formal adjudication at any time as an alternative to participation in the diversion program.
> 3. Incriminating statements made during participation in diversion programs are not used against the juvenile if a formal adjudication follows.
>
> Legislation, consistent with the following modifications, should be enacted for the disposition of juveniles:
>
> 1. The court should be able to permit the child to remain with his parents, guardian, or other custodian, subject to such conditions and limitations as the court may prescribe.
> 2. Detention, if imposed, should not be in a facility used for housing adults accused or convicted of crime.

3. Detention, if imposed, should be in a facility used only for housing juveniles who have committed acts that would be criminal if committed by an adult.

4. The maximum terms, which should not include extended terms, established for criminal offenses should be applicable to juveniles or youth offenders who engage in activity prohibited by the criminal code even though the juvenile or youth offender is processed through separate procedures not resulting in criminal conviction.[63]

Although this legislation (recommended for passage by 1975) has yet to be realized on any large scale, those in the system should not be discouraged from moving in the direction outlined.

REVIEW QUESTIONS

1. Define *detention* and *institutionalization*. What is the basic difference between them?

2. What is the purpose of juvenile institutions? Is that purpose realistic, given the structure of today's society? Why or why not?

3. What is meant by "right to treatment"? Discuss the major aspects of *Morales* v. *Turman* and how that case may have impact on the national juvenile justice system as a whole.

4. Define and discuss the following terms:
   a. unauthorized leave
   b. isolation
   c. institutional alternatives.

5. Discuss the future of juvenile corrections in terms of detention and institutions.

6. Discuss the issue of punishment versus treatment as the most realistic goal of the juvenile institutions of the past, today, and the future.

NOTES

1. National Criminal Justice Information Statistics Service, *Children in Custody: Advance Report on the Juvenile Detention and Correctional Facility Census of 1972–73* (Washington, D.C.: U.S. Government Printing Office, 1975), p. 1.

2. Ibid.

3. Ibid.

4. Ibid.

5. Sol Rubin, "Children as Victims of Institutionalization" (Hackensack, N.J.: NCCD, August 1974), p. 11.

6. Milton G. Rector, "The Extravagance of Imprisonment," *Crime and Delinquency,* October 1975, p. 323.

7. "Children in Custody," p. 1.

8. Bureau of Juvenile Rehabilitation, "Estimated Cost Figures: Juvenile Institutions and Youth Camps" (Olympia, Wash.: Department of Social and Health Services, 1977).

9. Douglas J. Besharov, *Juvenile Justice Advocacy: Practice in a Unique Court* (New York: Practicing Law Institute, 1974), p. 384.

10. *In re Gault,* 387 U.S. 1, 27 (1967).

11. Columbia Broadcasting System, "60 Minutes," March 1977.

12. This remark is attributed to Allen Breed of the California Youth Authority as reported in "Juvenile Corrections in Massachusetts—The View from Other States," *Corrections Magazine,* November/December 1975, p. 7.

13. Robert W. Mennel, *Thorns and Thistles: Juvenile Delinquents in the United States, 1825–1940* (Hanover, N.H.: University Press of New England, 1973), pp. 52–54.

14. Ibid., pp. 25–26.

15. See chapter 1, pp. 20–25, of this text for a discussion of reform schools and the practice of "placing children out."

16. Horace Mann, "Account of the Hamburgh Redemption Institute," (n.p., 1843), pp. 3–7.

17. Mennel, *Thorns and Thistles.*

18. National Conference of Charities and Corrections Proceedings (1881), p. 305.

19. H. W. Charles, "The Problem of the Reform School," *Proceedings of the Conference for Child Research and Welfare* 1 (1910): 86. Clarissa Olds Keller, *American Bastilles* (Washington, D.C.: Carnaham Press, 1910), pp. 8–9.

20. See chapter 9.

21. According to federal Justice Department statistics, 60,000 teachers and 300,000 students were openly assaulted in public schools in 1976, and enough damage was done in the schools to provide funds for the hiring of 50,000 teachers for one year.

22. National Council on Crime and Delinquency, *Standards and Guidelines for the Detention of Children and Youth* (Paramus, N.J.: NCCD, 1961), p. 3.

23. Ibid., p. 6.

24. Robert J. Gemignani, "Youth Services Systems: Diverting Youth from the Juvenile Justice System," *HEW Delinquency Prevention Reporter,* July–August 1972, pp. 3–7.

25. U.S. Bureau of the Census, *Inmate Survey* (Washington, D.C.: Law Enforcement Assistance Administration, U.S. Department of Justice, 1974), p. 1.

26. National Advisory Commission on Criminal Justice Standards and Goals, *Corrections* (Washington, D.C.: U.S. Government Printing Office, 1973), p. 258.

27. Nicholas A. Reuterman, *A National Survey of Juvenile Detention Facilities* (Edwardsville, Ill.: Southern Illinois University, 1970), p. 39.

28. Rosemary C. Sarri, *Under Lock and Key: Juveniles in Jail and Detention* (Ann Arbor: University of Michigan, 1974), p. 21.

29. Ibid., pp. 21–22.

30. NCCD, *Standards* (1961), pp. 3–7.

31. John Rossi and Rickley Dumm, *Hard Cores Don't Come from Apples* (Pasadena, Calif.: Ward Ritchie Press, 1976), p. 41.

32. National Advisory Commission, *Corrections,* p. 269.

33. Charles E. Reasons and Russell L. Kaplan, "Tear Down the Walls? Some Functions of Prisons," *Crime and Delinquency* 21 (1975): 360–72.

34. Ibid.

35. Robert Martinson, "What Works? Questions and Answers About Prison Reform," *The Public Interest,* Spring 1974, p. 49.

36. Daniel Glaser, "Achieving Better Questions: A Half Century's Progress in Correctional Research," *Federal Probation,* September 1975, pp. 3–9.

37. Ibid.

38. Robert G. Culbertson, "The Effect of Institutionalization of the Delinquent Inmate's Self-Concept," *Journal of Criminal Law and Criminology,* March 1975, p. 93.

39. California State Assembly, "Deterrent Effects of Criminal Sanctions" (Sacramento, 1968), pp. 31–32.

40. Ellsworth Fersch, "When to Punish, When to Rehabilitate," *American Bar Association Journal* 61 (1975): 1235–37.

41. National Advisory Commission on Criminal Justice Standards and Goals, *Report on Corrections* (Washington, D.C.: U.S. Government Printing Office, 1973), pp. 368–70.

42. A Konopka, "Our Outcast Youth," *Social Work,* October 1970, pp. 76, 80.

43. U.S. Department of Health, Education, and Welfare, *Statistics on Public Institutions for Delinquent Children* (Washington, D.C.: U.S. Government Printing Office, 1970), p. 2.

44. Irving R. Kaufman, "Of Juvenile Justice and Injustice," *American Bar Association Journal* 62 (1976): 730–34.

45. *Morales* v. *Turman,* ED Tex., 1974 383 F Supp. 53.

46. *Morales* v. *Turman,* No. 74-3436, U.S. Court of Appeals, Fifth Circuit (July 21, 1976).

47. *Morales* v. *Turman,* 383 F Supp. at 121, 58, 59, 72, 76.

48. Ibid., at 125.

49. Ibid., at 123–24.

50. Ibid., at 125.

51. Ibid., at 125.

52. Rossi and Dumm, *Hard Cores Don't Come from Apples,* pp. 51–52.

53. Ibid., pp. 102–103.

54. Department of Social and Health Services, Bureau of Juvenile Rehabilitation Statistics; Olympia, Washington (1976).

55. *Chin* v. *Wyman et al.* (Supreme Court Westchester County, December 31, 1963) 246 N.Y.S. 2d. 306.

56. For further discussion on the subject of escapees and/or runaways, the reader is referred to: *Smallwood* v. *Hindle,* District Court of Iowa, Black Hawk County (October 11, 1964) and the Runaway Youth Act, Title III of the Juvenile Justice and Delinquency Prevention Act of 1974 (P.L. 93-415).

57. The Institution referenced is Training Institute of Columbus, Ohio.

58. *Naselle Youth Camp Policy—Isolation* (Olympia, Wash.: Department of Social and Health Service, February 14, 1975), pp. 2–3.

59. Ibid., pp. 4–5.

60. Gary B. Adams et al., eds., *Juvenile Justice Management* (Chicago: Thomas, 1973), p. 460.

61. President's Commission on Law Enforcement and Administration of Justice, *Task Force Report: Corrections* (Washington, D.C., U.S. Government Printing Office, 1967), p. 149.

62. Ronald Goldfarb, *Jails: The Ultimate Ghetto* (Garden City, N.Y.: Anchor Press, Doubleday, 1976), p. 315.

63. National Advisory Commission on Criminal Justice Standards and Goals, *Detention and Disposition of Juveniles* (Washington, D.C.: LEAA, 1975), p. 573.

12 Parole

The success of any institutional treatment program depends
to a large extent upon supervision done after a youngster is
released on "juvenile aftercare." The Commission found,
however, that aftercare is perhaps the most neglected aspect
of the juvenile justice system. Juvenile aftercare, where it
exists, entails cursory contact by underpaid, overworked
counselors with excessive caseloads who often do not meet
minimum qualifications to be counselors.

ROBERT W. WINSLOW

Before discussing juvenile aftercare, it is useful to define *parole*. This will
help eliminate some of the misconceptions regarding it. The terms *probation*
and *parole* are often confused. In many instances, the word *parole* is used
imprecisely when referring to various methods of release from an institution
which may or may not be included in its actual meaning.

Juvenile parole is defined as the conditional release of a juvenile from a
correctional institution at a time when he or she can best benefit from release
and continued life in the community under the supervision of a counselor or
parole officer. Parole is a method whereby society can be protected and the
juvenile can be provided with continuing treatment and supervision.

There is no direct tie between juvenile court probation and juvenile parole
as part of one correctional process. *Probation* is administered, in most cases
by the courts on a county level; *parole*, on the other hand, is generally
administered on a state-wide basis by the agency which is responsible for
providing institutional services. Juvenile probation is a preinstitutional procedure; parole is part of the correctional process and is used only after the
juvenile has spent some time in a juvenile correctional institution.

The term *aftercare* has also been used in reference to juvenile parole,
although it is not widely accepted or used within the field of juvenile
corrections, *aftercare* will be used here interchangeably with *juvenile parole*
to encourage its usage. Those who are concerned about providing social
services to youth prefer this term to its adult counterpart—parole. Generally
speaking, the practice of juvenile aftercare has gained more acceptance than
the term itself.

The word *parole* derives from the French language, in which it means to promise. The term was probably first used in a correctional context by Samuel Howe, a Boston penal reformer of the mid-1800s.

Unlike the probationer, the parolee (one who is on parole) has already completed part of the period of his or her commitment. Release is conditional, and may be revoked if the terms of the parole are violated prior to the end of the youth's parole period.

Parole, unlike probation, is administrative and quasi-judicial. It is an attempt to bridge the gap between the institution and the community and to ease the transition period from the institution to the community. Parole is meant to help the youth remain in the community and to decrease the likelihood of becoming involved again in delinquent behavior. The parolee is usually more of a problem to the parole officer or counselor than the probationer is to probation staff. The paroled juvenile has been locked away and may be bitter, resentful, remorseful, and hostile, and may exhibit more acting out or antisocial behavior than a probation counterpart. Behavior is not predictable, however, for sometimes the parolee will be more cooperative, docile, and content than a probationer. The parolee can have parole revoked and can be returned for another taste of institutional life, which is something that many juveniles on probation can only conjecture about and have not experienced. Whatever the individual youth's reaction to parole, hostile or cooperative, juvenile corrections is responsible for providing aftercare services as long as institutionalization of juveniles continues and as long as the mechanism of parole is an alternative "way out."

Brief History

Parole, unlike probation, is basically more English and European in its roots than American. In England in the early nineteenth century, transportation, indenture, and other practices of placing children and adults in involuntary labor in both private and public settings became common practice. These programs, motivated by economic pressures rather than humanitarian concerns, offered a conditional release from prison. As in parole, the transported or indentured individual was not altogether free, but rather was forced to work for a certain period of time (often as long as seven years) to regain his or her freedom.

In early American history, offenders were sentenced to prison for a fixed length of time, and they were not released until that time had been served. Breaking with this tradition, New York, in 1817, was the first state to pass a so-called good time law. Good time laws allowed for a reduction in a prisoner's sentence based upon his or her cooperative good conduct and behavior in accordance with institutional rules. Subsequent good time laws passed by other states had rules which were firm and straightforward, but which varied from one state to another. New York's, for example, enabled the correctional administrator to "reduce by one-fourth the sentence of any prisoner sentenced to imprisonment for not less than five years, upon certificate of the principal keeper and other satisfactory evidence, that such prisoner behaved well, and acquired in the whole, the net sum of 15 dollars or more per annum."[1] By 1916, all states and the District of Columbia had passed some form of good time law.

While good time laws were a step in the right direction, they were really not much better than the methods used to gain pardons for prisoners serving excessively long sentences. Early laws sometimes dictated such oppressively long sentences for a prisoner that the *jury* often petitioned the governor to grant a pardon. Not unlike current practices, pardons were often used to empty out prisons to make room for newly sentenced offenders. Obviously, overcrowding of penal institutions is an age-old problem.

By 1832, a new concept in corrections—the indeterminate sentence—was being developed and experimented with. The idea of the indeterminate sentence is attributed to the combined efforts of England's Alexander Maconochie and Ireland's Sir Walter Crofton. At the 1870 meeting of the National Prison Association, the effectiveness of Crofton's "Irish System" was discussed. Crofton presented a paper on indeterminate sentencing at that meeting. The system devised by Crofton consisted of a series of stages, each bringing the prisoner closer to freedom. In the first stage, the new prisoner was placed in solitary confinement and assigned to dull, monotonous work. The second stage involved assignment to public works and a progression through various grades, periods of time in which conduct was to improve. In the last stage, the prisoner was assigned to an intermediate prison where there was no supervision and the prisoner moved in and out of the free community. If his conduct continued to be good and if he was able to find a job, he was returned to the community on a conditional pardon or "ticket of leave." This pardon could be revoked at any time within the span of his original fixed sentence if conduct was not up to standards established by those who supervised the conditional early release. Crofton's plan was the first effort to establish a system of conditional liberty in the community.

In 1867, the Michigan legislature passed an indeterminate sentence act under continued pressure from the superintendent of the Detroit House of Corrections, Zebulon Brockway. Brockway pressed for the use of parole and the indeterminate sentence mainly because of the large number of prostitutes who were being shuttled in and out of his institution.

Indeterminate sentencing and parole as advocated by Crofton and Brockway were introduced in 1876 at the Elmira Reformatory in New York. In the form of parole worked out at Elmira, the prisoner was kept under the supervision and control of the prison authorities for an additional six months following release. By 1891, eight states had authorized the indeterminate sentence but only for first-time offenders. New York excluded first-time women offenders altogether.

For adult prisoners, true indeterminate sentencing has won acceptance more slowly than parole. However, a genuine indeterminate sentence (one having no minimum or maximum length) has been used in the juvenile justice system for some time. One might question, however, if the juveniles aren't released because of their willingness to conform to the model used to determine their ability to return to a free society (as is the case in a *genuine* indeterminate sentence). Another question is whether they aren't released periodically merely because of overcrowded conditions, lack of sufficient funds and resources, or for other shortcomings of the system.

The American Law Institute's Model Youth Correction Authority Act of 1939 introduced the practice of granting the court the right to commit delinquent or dependent youths to the local Youth Authority for diagnosis and placement. This act is significant because it focused much attention on the Youth Authority model in the 1940s and 1950s. The model promoted the concept of parole release and aftercare supervision for committed youth. Today, every state has statutory provisions for both juvenile and adult parole.

Parole for juveniles can be traced back to the early houses of refuge established for children in the latter half of the nineteenth century. "Juvenile parole developed for several years as part of the general child welfare field, but recently, while still retaining a close involvement with child welfare programs, has assumed a more distinct status."[2] The concepts of foster care and group homes have also led to the emergence of parole as a specific practice. However, juvenile parole still remains one of the least developed of all aspects of the juvenile justice system.

Juvenile Parole Today

After release from correctional institutions, most juveniles eventually go back to the neighborhoods from which they came. Unless the youth dies in the institution or is transferred to an adult correctional facility, he or she will be released and will be the charge of the juvenile justice system for some period of time. The excessively long sentences of the nineteenth century usually meant that few offenders, adult or juvenile, left prison unembittered or unbroken. Today, almost every offender has a chance for parole before completing a prison term. The adult offender is usually released on parole long before the expiration of the maximum sentence. In the case of juveniles, they are usually paroled long before institutional treatment programs have reached them, or long after they have become hardened by and immune to the whole system.

In 1967, a survey for the President's Commission on Law Enforcement and Administration of Justice included data from state-operated special aftercare programs in 40 states. The states reported a total of about 48,000 youth under aftercare supervision. Based on a projection of that figure, approximately 59,000 youths were under aftercare supervision in the whole United States. The number of juveniles in individual states' programs ranged from 110 to 13,000.[3]

Statistics for Washington indicate that of the 838 youths released from correctional institutions during fiscal year 1974, 622 or 74 percent of them were released on parole status; during fiscal year 1975, 608 (or 63 percent) of the 951 youths released were released on parole status.[4]

Although nationwide statistics exclude data on numbers of juveniles paroled from correctional institutions, it is estimated that virtually all of them are released under some type of aftercare supervision—about 60,000 per year nationwide.[5]

Today, a nationwide study of aftercare would be futile because of the unreliability of statistics gathered from the states. The gaps in vital information are so great that validity of the survey would have to be viewed with extreme caution. Efforts are being made to correct this situation, but they will require extensive organizational programming for statewide or nationwide data collection to become a reality.[6]

Currently, there are a number of legal issues involved in the commitment and subsequent release of delinquent youth on parole status. The most important are: (1) stipulated periods of time that a youth must spend incarcerated before being paroled, and (2) the necessity of obtaining approval from a committing judge before release is granted. The National Survey found that only three states stipulate by law a minimum period of confinement before a youngster can be paroled. One state has an 18-month minimum, another 12 months, and a third has varying minimums. In several other states, minimum terms are established by administrative action and consequently the facts of the individual case are often ignored. Unnecessary confinement in correctional facilities results and psychological injury can accompany such practices.[7] "While the usefulness of the minimum sentence is debated extensively in the adult field, no authorative body advocates their use for juveniles."[8]

More widespread than the practice of minimum confinement periods is the practice of requiring the committing judge to become officially involved before a juvenile can be paroled. Nine states have such a procedure. The problem with this practice is that the judge, often already too busy with court matters, must be aware of the child's problems and behavior in the institution, as well as current provisions and conditions in the child's local community. Providing both kinds of information to the judge has been difficult at best, and therefore the judge is required to act on incomplete or outdated knowledge. Another problem is that control by the court may impede institutional programs for the child by treatment staff who have the duty of preparing the youth for release. Judicial control over the release of committed juveniles has been done away with by the vast majority of states and should be done away with by others.[9]

Parole's Purposes and Functions

Experts in the field of juvenile aftercare agree that the aims of parole are based on two separate but not mutually exclusive objectives: (1) the protection of the community and (2) the proper adjustment of the offender. With a growing emphasis on the integration and coordination of institutional and parole services, it becomes increasingly evident that the most important objective of the total correctional process is the *protection of society*. It seems to us that the question should not be the protection of society *versus* the rehabilitation of the delinquent, but rather the protection of society *through* the offender's rehabilitation.

The immediate purpose or objective of parole is to assist the parolee in understanding and coping with the problems faced upon release, to get used to the status of being a parolee. The long-range goal of parole is to assist in the development of the juvenile's ability to take independent action and to make correct choices regarding behavioral standards which will be acceptable to society. This latter goal is essential, for it is of permanent benefit to both the parolee and the community.

The basic functions of juvenile aftercare are three: (1) classifying the offender to determine readiness for release and the risk factor upon release, among other things; (2) the rehabilitation and reintegration of the juvenile into the community; and, (3) the reduction in the likelihood of the juvenile's committing further delinquent acts, that is, reduction in recidivism.

Classification

Classification is a systemized attempt to match the youth with potentially successful treatment modalities and placement facilities, and to make a reasonable judgment about whether the youth is ready for release to the community. (An in-depth discussion of classification and classification schemes is found in chapter 4.) A California Corrections-Field Services Report, in its discussion of classification as related to parole, states:

> Considerable time and effort is expended in reception centers and other institutions to classify all wards by one or more systems that have relevancy to treatment techniques. However, much of this effort seems lost when youths are paroled. For example, two-fifths of all line agents indicated that they use no classification system whatever with their clients. An additional 30 percent replied that they used one, but found it of no significant help in treating their clientele. . . . One agent classified all his cases according to astrology, supposedly facetiously, and felt that it was as meaningful as anything else. Task Force staff found little evidence to dispute this.[10]
>
> There were a few noteworthy exceptions to the situation described above. These were found in special programs with significantly reduced caseloads, such as the Community Treatment Project and the Guided Group Interaction Program.[11] A particularly progressive direction pursued in some units was the

"matching" of workers and clients according to the worker's ability to deal with a particular type of youth. However, the normal differentiation seemed to be merely the one mentioned in the Parole Agent Manual, viz. "regular supervision cases", which were to be seen once a month, and "special service cases", to be seen twice a month.[12]

The above report also recommends that the California Youth Authority (as well as other states' equivalents) should strengthen its ongoing development and use of classification systems, with a particular emphasis on integrating such efforts between institutions and parole.[13]

Rehabilitation and Reintegration

The second of the three basic purposes of juvenile aftercare is rehabilitation and reintegration. Rehabilitation and reintegration are related in part to the success or failure of the classification scheme used, and may be viewed as having a positive or negative influence upon the rates of recidivism by virtue of their success or failure.

The California Parole Task Force Report states:

IN THEORY

The California Youth Authority has long been in the forefront nationally in planning and developing correctional strategies. In keeping with this tradition, the Department has recently drawn up and endorsed one of the most progressive policy statements on program planning in existence. While this document is brief and, in many respects not implemented, it clearly sets forth a series of premises for correctional planning which "represent the conceptual framework and guide used for comprehensive program planning by the Department of the Youth Authority."[14]

1. Divert from the system
2. Minimize penetration into the criminal justice system
3. Maximize capacity for differential care, treatment, and custody
4. Normalize correctional experience
5. Maximize the involvement of the volunteer and the offender as an agent of change
6. Minimize time in correctional system
7. Maximize research and evaluation for feedback and organizational change

The Parole Task Force concurs totally with all these principles and suggests the addition of another, perhaps implied in number 5: Maximize the use of community resources.

IN PRACTICE

The Youth Authority has a number of carefully planned, experimental treatment programs in operation, primarily in large urban centers. These programs (notably the Community Treatment Project, Guided Group Interaction, Part Way Homes and Community Parole Centers) have been described and evaluated in regular CYA reports.[15] Unfortunately, however, the youths participating in these programs comprise only 10 percent of the total parolee population (approximately 13,500 wards).[16] The great majority of rehabilitation/reintegration efforts take place in excessively large caseloads and are left up to the ingenuity and skills of the individual agent. (The new Increased Parole Effectiveness Program attempts to ameliorate this situation by reducing caseload size and requiring a differential case approach, involving careful and ongoing case planning between agents and supervisors.)

Also noteworthy is increased Departmental effort to integrate institution and parole services. By placing both components of the system in one Division of Rehabilitation Services, and by pilot programs which assign cases to parole agents while wards are still confined, some progress is being made toward coordinating the services of both.[17]

Reduction in Delinquent Behavior

The third basic purpose of a successful juvenile aftercare program is the reduction of future repetitive delinquent behavior by the youth once he or she is released to the community. In its report, *Corrections,* the National Advisory Commission on Criminal Justice Standards and Goals specifies:

> Few things about parole evoke consensus, but there is some agreement that one objective and measure of success is reduction of recidivism. Even this consensus quickly becomes less firm when two specific functions are examined: (1) provision of supervision and control to reduce the likelihood of criminal acts while the offender is serving his sentence in the community (the 'surveillance' function), and (2) provision of assistance and services to the parolee, so that noncriminal behavior becomes possible (the 'helping' function).[18]
>
> To the extent that these concerns can be integrated, conflicts are minimized, but in the day-to-day activity of parole administration they frequently clash. Decisions constantly must be made between the relative risk of a law violation at the present time and the probable long-term gain if a parolee is allowed freedom and opportunity to develop a legally approved life style. Resources are needed to clarify the choices and risks involved. Key requirements for this kind of assistance are development of clear definitions of recidivism and creation of information systems that make data available about the probabilities of various types of parole outcome associated with alternative decisions.[19]

Overall, the usefulness and effectiveness of parole in achieving its goals and purposes depend on whether it performs two social tasks. The first is sound case disposition. This encompasses the selection of those juveniles among the institutionalized offender groups who would benefit from return to the community at a certain point in time instead of remaining in the institution. Since most juveniles are eventually paroled, the primary concern becomes more one of *when* to release, as opposed to *who*. The second social task is social treatment, which includes providing the offender with access to adequate community resources to aid in reintegration.

Both of these social tasks place immense responsibility on the correctional system within juvenile justice. Case disposition involves "people processing," to select the right course of action to meet the needs of each individual youth, and social treatment necessitates intervention (sometimes welcomed, often not) into the social situation in which the individual functions in an attempt to change attitudes and behaviors. The final outcome is often nothing less than the actual shaping of the present and future lives of human beings. Thomas Callanan states:

> Parole, for all intents and purposes, replicates probation supervision. It is designed to assist offenders who are released to the community prior to the expiration of their sentences. However, parole boards have been reluctant to release inmates whose institutional careers have not reflected the docile and submissive behavior that is expected. Too often, parole reviews are stereotyped, fast, and superficial examinations of inmate eligibility. Denial of parole is often used to reinforce conformity to institutional norms; and as such, becomes another form of punishment.
>
> No system of community supervision is workable unless there is adequate support from the community and an adequate and dedicated staff of professionals. Too often community-based correctional budgets are miniscule, and ancillary services such as psychological testing, job training, remedial education, and other necessary assistance are not available. Supervision caseloads are often too high to allow the fullest supportive assistance, which makes the job frustrating and causes high turnover and low morale.[20]

The Parole Decision Process: Who Decides and How

Parole services in the juvenile justice system should be administered by the same state agency that is responsible for the institutional and related services to delinquent and dependent children. This agency is called the juvenile paroling authority.

However, as Table 12–1 shows, the organizational arrangements through which juvenile parole services are actually administered vary widely among the states and Puerto Rico. Unlike other programs for youths, such as public education, which is nearly always administered by a state educational agency, juvenile parole has no clear-cut organizational pattern. It may be administered by a Youth Authority, a child welfare agency, an adult correctional agency, a lay board, or the correctional institution staff.[21]

Differing patterns of local jurisdiction have emerged for various reasons. Some state officials have chosen to give jurisdiction to local agencies, on the assumption that youth would receive better care from them than from the centralized, state-operated programs. In other states, the jurisdiction for

TABLE 12–1. ORGANIZATIONAL ARRANGEMENT FOR ADMINISTRATION OF AFTERCARE[22]

TYPE OF STRUCTURE	NUMBER OF STATES*
State Department of Public Welfare	13
State Youth Correction Agency	12
State Department of Correction	10
Institution Board	6
State Training School Board	4
State Department of Health	1
Other	5
	51

*Including Puerto Rico

parole fell to local agencies by default; there were simply no state agencies which could provide the needed supervision at a local level.

To ameliorate such nonstandardized organizational arrangements for the administration of aftercare services, it is recommended that the law under which the youth is committed to a juvenile correctional institution should provide that the agency granted legal custody also be given the right to determine when the youth shall leave the institution.[23]

For purposes of this text, the administering agency of juvenile parole will be referred to as the ''Juvenile Paroling Authority.''

When to Release

Unlike the adult parole boards, the juvenile paroling authority does not determine the length of time (at the post-sentencing stage) of an offender's prison term.

Some juvenile paroling authorities do, however, require that the juvenile remain incarcerated for a certain period of time before release on parole. The time period varies among states and jurisdictions. In most instances, however, the youth's length of commitment is determined by what is called the ''progress toward rehabilitation.'' Progress is sometimes measured by a token system which awards a specific number of points for various positive actions. In most states, the criteria for measuring successful rehabilitation (and therefore, time of release) is whether or not the juvenile conforms or causes problems. Unfortunately, there exists no valid measure of a genuine rehabilitation or change of attitude. The youth's behavior may be tempered by knowledge of the release date or may be motivated solely to please the ''man.'' By appearing to have been reformed, the youth receives the quickest release possible.

Institutions with the most adequate treatment services are the best prepared to judge the youth's readiness for parole. In these institutions, staff members should have the opportunity to come to know the juvenile as an individual, for they can then judge more accurately the progress, risk, and potential for successful reintegration into the community. In institutions where the *process* model has replaced the *treatment* model, the decision as to when a particular youth is ready for parole can be based upon little more than the behavior shown by that youth while institutionalized. In this case, factors to consider are the number of times isolation had to be used, the number of fights, or other behavioral problems caused by the youth. If the process model is to become the model used within juvenile correctional institutions, guidelines based on criteria other than good behavior are needed in determining preparedness for release.

For purposes of parole, there is general agreement that the youths should be released as soon as operative criteria determine they are ready. The use of the fixed sentence, with a minimum and a maximum, could well interfere with this conceptual approach.

Gains made by the youth in the institution (if any) must be strengthened when they are returned to the community, by the basic functions of the parole process. Good release planning is a key to the success of the youth's "return life" in the community. Institutional staff, working in conjunction with parole staff, should prepare the juvenile for any negative reactions or other stumbling blocks to reintegration that may be encountered in the community. This pre-release planning should include the utilization of community resources during incarceration, if possible, and pre-release classes and/or meetings with parole agents to anticipate and discuss post-release problems, thus helping to bridge the gap between the institution and the community.[24]

The question of when to release a juvenile on parole depends on the youth's future behavior and how far one can predict that behavior. There are several policy considerations which should be evaluated prior to granting parole:

1. Whether the juvenile has profited by his or her stay in the institution.
2. Whether reform has taken place so that it is unlikely that another offense will be committed.
3. Behavior in the institution.
4. Whether suitable employment, training or treatment is available on release.
5. Whether the juvenile has a home or other place, such as a group home, to which to go.
6. The youth's perception of his ability to handle reintegration into the community.
7. Seriousness of past offenses and the circumstances in which they were commited.

8. Appearance and attitude prior to release.

9. Behavior on probation and/or former parole, if applicable.

10. The institutional staff worker's perception for the youth's successful return to the community.

In making parole selection decisions, the paroling authority generally runs the risk of making one of two types of error. The first is granting release to a juvenile who will commit new offenses or parole violations. The second is not granting release to a youth who would have completed parole without violation. Since over 95 percent of all those committed to institutions are eventually released,[25] the chances are that, sooner or later, both these errors occur often. A thorough evaluation of the policy considerations previously mentioned, coupled with a good knowledge of the youth, the system, and the setting to which the juvenile will be returned will certainly aid the paroling authority in their decision when to release.

Parole Services

Parole services consist of all of the various components of the juvenile justice system required to facilitate the goals and basic purposes of parole. These include: institutional efforts at classification, the efforts of the parole staff and Juvenile Paroling Authority to assist the youth in re-entry to the community, and efforts of the community on the juvenile's behalf.

Juvenile parole services begin with preparole investigations and contacts used to establish the groundwork for parole supervision and to obtain the necessary background information on the child and family. Parole services continue until the discharge of the parole case. The average length of time the juvenile will spend on parole status varies from state to state. Some states keep their juveniles in active aftercare supervision programs for an average of one year or less; others give aftercare supervision for an average of one year or more. Girls generally are maintained on parole longer than boys; the reason may lie in society's attitude that the young female offender requires protection through supervision for a longer period than does the young male.[26]

The service of supervising a paroled youth is a form of social work; hence it is helpful if the parole officer has had some social work training. Unfortunately, as is the case with probation and institutional staff, many of them do not. Parole officers experience many of the same problems as their probation counterparts: too many children to supervise, too large a territory to cover, and too much time spent in travel.

It is unrealistic to assume that the parole officer can be all things to all youths. Community involvement in the youth's rehabilitation is paramount to the success of any aftercare services program. Even though the parole agent can identify the juvenile's *problems,* developing *solutions* to these problems ultimately lies within the community. The community must be willing to re-accept the child and through its acceptance, facilitate the primary goal of individual rehabilitation. Juvenile aftercare services should therefore act as an agent of community change.

The Professional Standards Division of the International Association of Chiefs of Police suggests two steps which can be taken by the aftercare program administrator to secure community involvement. They are:

> First, he must utilize public relations/community relations techniques to educate individual citizens about their responsibilities in the rehabilitation of juvenile offenders. The residents of the community must be convinced that the youngster deserves a second chance; further, the community must be convinced that it is, in part, responsible for any further criminality by the youngster if he cannot obtain an education, a job, adequate housing, or financial assistance.
>
> Second, those citizens most directly responsible for providing the physical means for a youngster to achieve social responsibility must be encouraged to participate in rehabilitation programs. This means that employers must be willing to provide jobs for youths with records; that bonding agencies provide security if the particular job requires it; that banks and stores extend credit to the youngster for justifiable purposes; and that realtors be willing to rent or sell him desirable housing.[27]

The Community Resources Management Team (CRMT) approach to parole and probation includes seven assumptions concerning probation and parole services:

1. Probation and parole services are in need of improved delivery system models.

2. Most offenders are not pathologically ill; therefore, the medical (casework) model is inappropriate.

3. Most probation and parole officers are not equipped by education and experience to provide professional casework counseling even if it is needed.

4. Existing probation parole manpower is not likely to be expanded. Consequently, these people must come to view their roles in different and perhaps radically new terms if they are to deal with the increasing numbers of offenders under supervision.

5. Services needed by the offender to "make it" in society are available in the community social service network rather than in the criminal justice system.

6. Probation and parole staff must assume advocacy roles in negotiating appropriate community-based services for offenders. They must assume a community organization and resource development role for needed services that do not exist.

7. A team approach represents a powerful and viable alternative to the autonomous and isolated individual officer and "case" relationship.[28]

TABLE 12-2. AFTERCARE CASELOADS IN STATES HAVING SPECIAL AFTERCARE STAFF

SIZE OF CASELOAD*	NUMBER OF STATES	NUMBER OF CHILDREN UNDER SUPERVISION	CATEGORY'S PER-CENTAGE OF TOTAL NUMBER UNDER SUPERVISION
Under 30 cases	3	536	1.12
30–40 cases	10	8,612	17.98
41–50 cases	5	4,339	9.06
51–60 cases	5	2,244	4.68
61–70 cases	6	23,382	48.81
71–90 cases	9	4,875	10.18
Over 91 cases	2	3,914	8.17
	40	47,902	100.00

*Number of children under aftercare supervision. Does not include children in institutions.

Source: President's Commission on Law Enforcement and Administration of Justice, *Corrections* (Washington, D.C.: National Council on Crime and Delinquency, 1967), p. 101.

Caseload Size

The report of the President's Commission on Corrections called for a maximum caseload of 50 juveniles (see Table 12–2 for existing caseloads) for the aftercare counselor (active supervision cases). One prerelease investigation was held to be equal to three cases under active supervision.

Aftercare programs should be set up for proper counseling and direction for all categories of offenders. It is preferable for the juvenile to maintain *personal* contact with the parole officer to insure adequate supervision. Caseload sizes should not be so large that routine contact between the parolee and the parole agent is conducted only through telephone calls.

Although it is claimed that a reduction of the size of a parole officer's caseload would result in greater success for parolees, there is no evidence to prove it. Proposals to reduce caseload size still gain wide acceptance on the basis of promised improvement in success rates, even though research suggests that reducing the caseload size alone is not the answer.

> "The institutionalization of the fifty-unit concept is now firmly entrenched. Budgets for operating agencies, testimony before legislative bodies, standards of practice, and projections for future operational needs all center about this number. There is no evidence of any empirical justification for fifty; nor for that matter, any other number."[29]

Parole Staff

Without adequate staff, aftercare programs are likely to remain the stepchild of the juvenile justice system. The President's Commission on Law Enforcement and the Administration of Justice stated that the juvenile justice system spends ten times more money and resources to incarcerate a juvenile than it does for probation or aftercare. Low salaries, large caseloads, and lax professional standards are not conducive to attracting highly trained and qualified professionals to enter into a career of juvenile aftercare.

Ideally, parole staff should possess a master's degree in social work or a related field because of the nature and complexity of their tasks. This standard has proven virtually impossible to attain, however. To compensate for the lack of formal professional training in the diagnosis and treatment of behavioral problems, extensive inservice training and other methods of staff development are highly recommended.

Adherence to this recommendation would help solve many problems currently facing juvenile aftercare staff. Furthermore, the staff could get down to the business of supervising and helping youth in need. This would be a clear improvement over simply trying to survive in a system which often seems not to give a damn.

Role of the Parole Agent

Eldefonso and Coffey have defined the role of the parole agent as a diverse one requiring a thorough grounding in both casework and investigative techniques. They state:

Special skills must be utilized in three broad areas of supervision.

1. Control, including case observation, surveillance, and, when necessary, arrest.
2. Case assistance and the development and use of community resources, including counseling, group work, job finding, and special placement efforts.
3. Decision-making, especially in areas that affect the legal status of the parolee.

Therefore, the agent must (a) closely observe the parolee's behavior, (b) assist in improving his social and emotional adjustment through the use of individual and group counseling, (c) arrange outpatient psychotherapy in some cases, (d) provide or initiate specialized assistance where necessary in such areas as vocational and marital adjustment, (e) make proper referrals for educational, legal, medical, religious, and recreational assistance, (f) maintain specialized controls such as antinarcotic testing and surveillance, (g) investigate alleged or known criminal activity, (h) make arrests and place parolees in confinement when necessary, and (i) both report and make recommendations to the paroling authority whenever the parolee violates certain conditions of his parole.

In performing these various roles, the agent must communicate and establish relations with many different private and public groups within the community, such as employers and family members, local law enforcement agencies, probation departments and the courts, various private and public welfare agencies, and a number of other community groups whose activities may have some direct or indirect bearing on the parolee's adjustment.

The parole agent pursues his principal objective of protecting the community by employing all of the above techniques to prevent a reoccurrence of criminal activity on the part of the parolee. Preventive measures such as educational opportunities, job placement, and appropriate counseling services are stressed. In addition, every attempt is made to detect adjustment problems that may contribute to a resumption of deviant behavior as quickly as possible and to institute immediate remedial action.

Where conditions are such that the continuance of an individual on parole constitutes a major risk to the community, the agent must arrest the parolee and report this matter to the paroling authority with an appropriate recommendation. It is also a function of the agent to recommend early termination of parole when a subject has made a good adjustment in the community and further controls and assistance are no longer deemed necessary.[30]

Effective parole supervision requires the efforts of many individuals and community agencies, not just the immediate parole agent. Providing parole services is not a one-man effort. To redirect and reeducate an individual with criminal and/or antisocial behavior is an involved, complex matter requiring the careful coordination and cooperation of a variety of activities and services.

Conditions of Parole

Although the conditions under which a juvenile is released in the community on parole are not quite as stringent as those for adults, they are complex. Among the specifications generally included in the conditional release of the juvenile are: (1) not committing further offenses; (2) staying off drugs and away from alcohol; (3) not hanging around with the old gang or other persons who are known offenders or who could have a potentially damaging effect on the youth on parole; (4) reporting on a regular basis to the parole officer or other designated person; (5) staying in a specified geographical area; and (6) getting a job or obtaining training which will lead to gainful employment.

Several states have an actual parole contract which the youth is required to read, understand, and sign prior to release. Washington is one of these states. The juvenile parole contract or order of parole conditions of Washington is seen in Figure 12–1 on page 294.

As indicated within the "Order of Parole Conditions" conditions may be changed and renegotiated after consultation with the juvenile parole counselor. This provision, practiced by other states as well, is an attempt to make the terms of a juvenile parole as flexible as possible, adjusting realistically to changing needs, desires, and opportunities.

DEPARTMENT OF SOCIAL AND HEALTH SERVICES
BUREAU OF JUVENILE REHABILITATION
OFFICE OF JUVENILE PAROLE

IN THE MATTER OF THE   )
)
PAROLE OF _____   )   **ORDER OF**
)
BJR # _____   )   **PAROLE CONDITIONS**
)
DATE OF BIRTH _____   )

Parole is a provisional release from an institution. The provisions are that certain conditions and/or restraints are placed on your movements and activities in the community to which you are paroled. In order for you to remain on parole and ultimately be eligible for discharge from the Bureau of Juvenile Rehabilitation, you are hereby instructed as to what these conditions are. If you have any questions, or are in doubt about what these conditions mean, you should ask for clarification immediately.

   1. You are under the direct supervision of your assigned Juvenile Parole Counselor. You are ex-
      pected to report to your Juvenile Parole Counselor as instructed for whatever reason and as
      often as requested.

   2. You must secure (written) permission from Juvenile Parole Services before changing residence
      or traveling outside the (county) (State) in which you now reside.

   3. You are expected to obey all federal and State laws as well as local ordinances defining crime,
      and you are not to behave in a manner that is defined as incorrigible under the provisions of
      RCW 13.04.010(7).

   4. Other special conditions are as follows: (use attached sheet if necessary)

Parolee's Statement

      I have read, or have had read to me, the above conditions, and I understand them. Furthermore,
I understand that these conditions may be changed and re-negotiated with my Juvenile Parole Counselor.
Before I sign a new condition of parole order, I also understand I have a right to have, or I may waive
my right to have, a parole conditions conference. I further understand that any violation of any of the
above conditions may result in my detention and/or the revocation of my parole.

_____   _____
Signature of Parolee   Juvenile Parole Counselor

_____   _____   _____
Parents, Guardian, Witness   Date   Place

The conditions of parole as outlined in this document are granted by the authority of the Review Board
of the Bureau of Juvenile Rehabilitation under RCW 13.04.095.

FIGURE 12–1. Order of parole conditions.

Source: State of Washington, Department of Social and Health Services, Bureau of Juvenile
Rehabilitation.

Violation of the conditions of parole can result in revocation by the parole
authority. However, the only valid reason for parole revocation is clear
evidence that the youth just cannot make it in the community. The following
guidelines are generally relevant to the revocation decision:

   1. Conditions of aftercare should be realistic and should be aimed to
      strengthen the minor's law-abiding tendencies. Aftercare conditions should
      vary from case to case, depending on each individual's needs and problems.

2. Minors placed on aftercare should be made to understand the limits of their new status. Merely signing conditions of parole or aftercare does not necessarily mean that the minor understands these conditions.

3. All adjudicated new offenses should be brought to the attention of the parole or aftercare authority. Arrest for a specific delinquent act is not grounds for revocation, though adjudication and proof that the minor was involved may be. However, it does not follow that revocation automatically results from adjudication of a delinquent act.

4. The revocation of aftercare merely through inability to keep appointments, failure to obey curfew ordinances, and so forth, probably serves little or no purpose. However, a generally unfavorable attitude and deliberate non-compliance with the conditions of aftercare may necessitate reinstitution-alization.

5. To assist the authority, whether a superintendent, a board, or a court, in deciding a matter of revocation, a formal report should be submitted by the parole agent. The report should contain details of the alleged violations and factors that seem to underlie the violation, the minor's attitude toward the violation, a summary of his conduct and attitude during supervision, and the agent's specific recommendation.

6. The minor and/or his counsel should be provided with a copy of the report and an opportunity to respond to it, so that the minor's rights can be safeguarded.[31]

Once the decision to grant parole is made, the specifications attached to that conditional release often become the measure of a youth's freedom and responsibility. Since failure to observe a condition of parole may result in revocation, its legal significance is clear. The value of such conditions is that both the youth and the community are made to understand that parole, while a mechanism for release from the institution, is not absolute freedom. The right to decide parole conditions within individual jurisdictions, the way in which these conditions are actually imposed, and the discretionary right of an individual parole officer to enforce these conditions are crucial continuing legal safeguards in both adult and juvenile corrections.

The basic legal issues associated with parole conditions may be summarized as follows:

1. Conditions often affect such basic constitutional freedoms as religion, privacy, and freedom of expression.

2. Too often they are automatically and indiscriminately applied, without any thought given to the necessities of the individual case.

3. In many instances, conditions lack precision and create needless uncertainty for the supervised individual and excessive revocation leverage for those in authority.

4. Some conditions are extremely difficult, if not impossible, to comply with.[32]

Revocation of Parole

Ordinarily, it is the function of the juvenile paroling authority (if one exists) to revoke a juvenile's parole. In most jurisdictions, the paroling authority must issue a warrant, or order, if it intends to detain a juvenile suspected of violating parole. A few states permit detention for parole violation without such a warrant. The discretionary powers of the paroling authority are very broad regarding its decision to revoke the juvenile's parole.

When the parolee is placed in detention pending a decision as to guilt or innocence in regard to the alleged parole violation, a statement of the allegations is often presented to the youth for acknowledgement or denial. In Figure 12–2, a "Statement of Allegations," the form used in Washington, is shown.

Until recently, the paroling authorities could do almost anything they chose in regard to the revocation of the parolee's status. Adult parole boards often used the threat of revocation to insure that their "charges" did exactly as they were told. In its discussion of parole revocation and revocation hearings, the National Advisory Commission on Criminal Justice Standards and Goals has stated:

> Until the late 1960s, procedures in many jurisdictions for the return of parole violators to prison were so informal that the term "hearing" would be a misnomer. In many instances revocation involved no more than the parole board's pro forma approval of the request of the parole officer or his field staff supervisor. In many jurisdictions the revocation decision represented almost unfettered discretion of parole authorities. In addition to minimal procedural formality, the grounds for revocation also were nonspecific, involving such assessments as "generally poor attitude" or allegations of "failure to cooperate," rather than specific breaches of conditions or commission of new offenses.
>
> This was particularly true in revocation of the aftercare of juveniles, where the decision to revoke was viewed primarily as a casework determination. Ostensibly, it did not involve a breach of conditions but was simply an action for the youth's welfare.
>
> This general stance of casual and quick return of both adults and juveniles rested primarily on the "privilege" or "grace" doctrine of the parole grant. To many parole officials, revocation did not warrant much concern with due process, procedural regularity, or matters of proof, hearing, and review.
>
> In 1964 a study of parole board revocations showed that there was no hearing at all in at least seven States. In those States providing a hearing, the alleged violator frequently was returned to prison directly from the field on allegation of the field agent or on a warrant issued by the board. An actual hearing or review of this return by the parole board did not take place until weeks, sometimes months, after the parolee had been returned to the institution.[33]
>
> In a small minority of cases, board members canceled the warrant or field complaint and permitted the prisoner again to resume parole. However, since

DEPARTMENT OF SOCIAL AND HEALTH SERVICES
OFFICE OF JUVENILE REHABILITATION
JUVENILE PAROLE SERVICES
STATEMENT OF ALLEGATIONS

It is hereby alleged that _____ has violated the conditions of his/her parole as stated herein:

BEFORE YOU ARE QUESTIONED YOU ARE ORALLY AND IN WRITING ADVISED OF YOUR RIGHTS, AS FOLLOWS:

1. You need not say anything.

2. Anything you do or say may hereafter be used for or against you in court proceedings. If you are under the age of 18, anything you do or say may hereafter be used for or against you in Juvenile Court; or, if you are transferred to an adult status, then anything you say may be used for or against you in criminal proceedings in an adult court.

3. You may, immediately or at any time, obtain the services of an attorney for advice, and you may have an attorney with you at any or all times during periods of questioning.

4. If you cannot afford an attorney, you may request the court to appoint one for you before you answer any questions.

5. You may stop answering questions at any time, even though you have commenced answering questions. You may do this without asking for an attorney.

I understand the above-listed allegations and I acknowledge and understand the above rights.

_____   _____
Signature of Youth   Juvenile Parole Counselor

_____   _____
Date Delivered   Place Delivered

OPTIONAL

I admit to the violations of my Parole Agreement as specified below:

_____   _____
Signature of Youth   Juvenile Parole Counselor

_____
Date

FIGURE 12 – 2. Statement of Allegations.

Source: State of Washington, Department of Social and Health Services, Bureau of Juvenile Rehabilitation.

the parolee had been moved to the institution, employment and family relationships already were disturbed. In effect a canceled revocation order meant that the parolee once again had to be transported to his local community and begin the readjustment process all over again. Counsel rarely was permitted to represent the alleged violator at such hearings. Any witnesses to the alleged violation almost always were seen outside the hearing at the parole board offices, rarely subject to confrontation or cross-examination by the parolee. While at the time of the survey some States allowed parolees to have "assistance" of lawyers, no jurisdiction assigned counsel to indigent parolees.[34]

Irregularities and failure to provide legal representation at revocation hearings have received careful scrutiny by Appellate Courts and, most recently, by the U.S. Supreme Court.

This new vigor is consistent with a general distinction in administrative law between granting a privilege (as in parole) and taking it away once it has been given (as in revocation). Courts generally have held that initial granting or denial of a privilege can be done much more casually and with fewer procedural safeguards than taking away a privilege once granted.

Development of court-imposed requirements for procedural due process in parole revocation has been somewhat erratic. One of the important leading cases in the Federal jurisdiction was *Hyser* v. *Reed*, decided in the D.C. Circuit in 1963 (318 2d 225, 235). The decision in this case generally supported the common position that revocation was strictly a discretionary withdrawal of a privilege not requiring adversarial hearings at which inmates are represented by counsel and so forth. . . .

Subsequent to the *Hyser* decision, however, courts in some Federal and State jurisdictions reversed the first part of the decision; namely, the lack of any right, constitutional or otherwise, for due process to be applied at revocation proceedings. Most courts that departed from *Hyser* in this regard did so on the basis of the Supreme Court decision in a case involving "deferred sentencing" or probation revocation. In *Mempa* v. *Rhay*, 389 U.S. 128(1967), the Supreme Court held in 1967 that a State probationer had a right to a hearing and to counsel upon allegation of violations of probation. A number of courts interpreted the principle of *Mempa* to apply to parole as well.

The extension of *Mempa* procedural requirements to parole revocation was fairly common in both State jurisdictions and in various Federal circuits. In almost all cases, conformity with *Mempa* requirements meant a reversal of former legal positions and a major change in administrative practices. . . .

The rationale most often used as a basis for the requirement of procedural due process at parole revocation was expressed in another Federal Circuit Court case, *Murray* v. *Page*, 429 F. 2d 1359 (10th Cir. 1970):

Therefore, while a prisoner does not have a constitutional right to parole, once paroled he cannot be deprived of his freedom by means inconsistent with due process. The minimal right of the parolee to be informed of the charges and the nature of the evidence against him and to appear to be heard at the revocation hearing is inviolate. Statutory deprivation of this right is manifestly inconsistent with due process and is unconstitutional; nor can such right be lost by the subjective determination of the executive that the case for revocation is "clear."

By and large parole officials have resisted attempts by courts, or others, to introduce procedural due process requirements into parole revocation and at other stages of parole. Resistance has rested not simply on encroachment of authority but also on the possible negative effects of stringent procedural requirements on parole generally and on administrative costs. Some parole officials argue that elaborate revocation hearings would create demands on the parole board's time grossly incommensurate with personnel and budget. Other opponents of procedural elaborateness have argued its negative effects on the purpose and use of revocation.[35]

In late June, 1972, the U.S. Supreme Court decided the most important case thus far regarding parole revocation and revocation hearings. The case of *Morrissey* v. *Brewer* contained facts which were fairly typical of the standard practices regarding parole revocation as it existed in approximately 20 states where no hearings were held to determine the appropriateness of revoking the offender's parole.[36]

The petitioners in *Morrissey* were two parolees originally sentenced to prison in Iowa for forgery. Approximately six months after being released on parole, their parole was revoked for alleged violations. The two men appealed an appellate court's decision on the ground that the revocation of their paroles without a hearing had deprived them of due process of law guaranteed by the Fourteenth Amendment.

The appellate court, in affirming the district court's denial of relief, reasoned that parole is only "a correctional device authorizing service of sentence outside a penitentiary"[37] and concluded that a parolee is still "in custody"[38] and not entitled to a full adversary hearing, as would be mandated in a criminal proceeding. The Supreme Court reversed the Court of Appeals decision and held that:

> the liberty of parole, although indeterminate, includes many of the core values of unqualified liberty and its termination inflicts a "grievous loss" on the parolee and often on others. It is hardly useful any longer to try to deal with this problem in terms of whether the parolee's liberty is a "right" or a "privilege." By whatever name, the liberty is valuable and must be seen as within the protection of the Fourteenth Amendment. Its termination calls for some orderly process, however informal.[39]

The "orderly process" has since been guaranteed by the Supreme Court when it laid down guidelines establishing minimum standards of due process regarding parole revocation. In referring to these guidelines, the Court stated:

> They include (a) written notice of this claimed violations of parole; (b) disclosure to the parolee of evidence against him; (c) opportunity to be heard in person and to present witnesses and documentary evidence; (d) the right to confront and cross-examine adverse witnesses (unless the hearing officer specifically finds good cause for not allowing confrontation); (e) neutral and detached hearing body such as a traditional parole board, members of which need not be judicial officers or lawyers; and (f) a written statement by the fact finders as to the evidence relied on and reasons for revoking parole.[40]

Although these requirements refer to the actual revocation hearing, the Court required substantially the same requirements at a preliminary hearing conducted at a time prior to the revocation hearing and shortly after arrest or detention. The Court said that this preliminary hearing should be "conducted at or reasonably near the place of the alleged parole violation or arrest and as promptly as convenient after the arrest while information is fresh and sources are available . . . to determine whether there is probable cause or reasonable ground to believe that the arrested parolee has committed acts that would constitute a violation of parole conditions."[41]

There is no doubt that the Supreme Court's ruling in reviewing *Morrissey* v. *Brewer* has enhanced the rights of a parolee, but it has also left several questions unanswered.

> The extent to which evidence obtained by a parole officer in an unauthorized search can be used at a revocation hearing was not considered. Nor did it reach or decide the question whether the parolee is entitled to the assistance of retained counsel or to appointed counsel if the parolee is indigent.
>
> While the Court did address certain features of the parole revocation process prior to a formal revocation hearing, it did not specify requirements for the process by which offenders are taken and held in custody. Present law and practice in many jurisdictions empower individual parole officers to cause the arrest of parolees for an alleged violation and to hold them in custody for extensive periods.[42]

Revocation Rates

The rate of parole revocation is often used to measure the effectiveness of various parole programs. Prus and Stratton suggest that:

> if one is to use revocation rates as a measure or program success, one should be highly conscious of the processes by which decisions to revoke parolees are made. While known infractions draw attention to the parolee and make his status as a parolee problematic, violations are subject to multiple interpretations and the seriousness of a given offense can be readily defined away. The decision to revoke a parole reflects the agent's personal orientations and his perception of self-accountability to the goals and personnel of the system in which he works. Revocation is not a structured response to parole violations; it is a socially influenced definition.[43]

It cannot be stressed too strongly that parole revocation rates are meaningful only when the reasons and procedures by which parole may be revoked are clearly understood.

Discharge from Parole

In most jurisdictions, the juvenile on parole status may be recommended for discharge by the parole officer at any time after the juvenile's release from the correctional institution. Release from parole is, however, conditional, and is based on criteria similar to those used in determining release from the institution. Keeping in mind that the major goal of parole is the protection of society *through* the rehabilitation of the offender, it is paramount that there be a reasonable assurance that the parolee can continue to adjust satisfactorily in the community once the parole supervision is removed. In many states, the discharge of the juvenile from parole jurisdiction is reserved for the juvenile paroling authority or its agent. The juvenile's parole counselor is responsible for recommending discharge and for submitting this recommendation in writing to the paroling authority prior to the actual discharge of the parolee.

The decision to discharge a juvenile from parole can have as many potential pitfalls as the decision to place him or her on parole in the first place. For some youngsters on parole, survival in the community is possible because they can depend on their parole counselor. At least the officer is supposed to have some interest in their existence. Once this crutch is removed the parolee may regress in both behavior and attitude and may well end up back on the road to crime. Most jurisdictions are reluctant to discharge a juvenile from parole for at least one year after release from the institution. Hopefully, this is enough time for the competent and observant agent to recognize and work on the youth's long-range needs and to help achieve independence from the juvenile justice system.

It was stated above that juvenile aftercare is the poor stepchild of the juvenile justice system. Similarly, post-aftercare services are the abandoned child. Once discharged from parole, most juveniles are left to their own devices until they either become 18 (and are considered adults) or commit crimes and are returned to the courts for yet another trip on the juvenile justice merry-go-round. This is too often a ride they must take because somewhere someone failed to prevent the circumstances leading to their original delinquent acts.

Research on post-parole success rates is generally scant, even though there is a definite need for it. In the absence of solid data, juvenile justice officials continue to play youth and society against one another.

Parole as the Juvenile Sees It

The following material contained in Sophia M. Robison's *Juvenile Delinquency—Its Nature and Control,* is based on the unpublished doctoral thesis of a young man who spent 6 months at Ralston, his fictitious name for an actual institution for juveniles in New York. We present some of this material to offer the reader a look at parole from the inside.

PAROLE

One of the explanations of the many runaways was unfavorable review by the committee which decided the date of the boy's release. When a boy knew that he had met the committee's standards and was returning home in a few weeks, he relaxed his hostile attitude toward the administration. When, however, the committee's decision was unfavorable, the animosity smoldering just below the surface flared up. It is reported that some of the worst riots in Ralston were engineered by ringleaders in revenge for unfavorable reviews of their progress. The virulence of these sentiments in their mildest form was expressed by an angry boy's wish to castrate all the male officers and rape all the female ones.

As the day of his release neared a boy counted the minutes until he was on the school bus starting back to the city. Often he jeered at and mocked those who remained behind. Sometimes he said he wished the place would burn down. As he neared his home he talked about the pleasures that he anticipated. He competed with the other boys in boasting how many pints of liquor he would kill, how long he would "lush it," how many women he would possess and how his future criminal exploits would exceed anything he might have done in the past. He was no longer afraid of being caught.

By the Observer

Unfortunately most of these boys return to the surroundings which fostered their precommitment activities. By virtue of their time at Ralston, their status and prestige among their friends and acquaintances is not diminished but enhanced. The Ralston experience, according to the observer, has chiefly been an introduction to the occupational risk of the professional criminal. . . .

Cures at Ralston could be claimed only for the very small minority able to assimilate the "ethos" of the greater society through a particularly meaningful relationship with an individual officer. The majority of the boys experienced no change in their values or philosophical orientation. They learned only to accommodate by withdrawal through fantasy, which protected their personal will against boredom or invasion by the institution.

By the Boys

The boys with whom the observer talked were unanimous in expressing strong feelings of hate. They said they had not learned anything good. One boy who broke parole and was returned to Ralston expressed the sentiments of many others in saying: "This damn place is no good. Look at these hands, all chapped. That's the only thing you get out of the place. It's no good. All it teaches is things that the boys shouldn't know about. They don't know about punking but when they come up here, they learn. It doesn't teach you nothing." He continued by commenting on the language which the little boys picked up so quickly.

One boy said that when he got out he was going to rob and steal. Maybe this was just talk, but he certainly wasn't talking about being honest.[44]

Summary

In this chapter it was shown that the concepts of juvenile *parole* and juvenile *aftercare* are used interchangeably. *Probation*, which takes place before the institutionalization of a juvenile as a diversionary procedure, is separate from parole. Juvenile parole (aftercare) is used to bridge the gap back to the community after incarceration. The juvenile under the guidance of the juvenile parole officer is more likely to be a problem than the juvenile reporting to the juvenile probation officer. Parole for juveniles has a dual purpose: that of protection for the community and proper adjustment of the parolee.

Many attempts have been made to classify youths in correctional institutions as potentially "good" risks on parole. While the concept of classification is discussed at length in Chapter 4, the classification referred to in this chapter is aimed more at prediction models of behavior. Classification, if properly applied, contributes significantly in the assignment of parolees to the appropriate type of parole officer. More effort must be expended in this direction if juvenile parole is to be maximally effective.

The juvenile parole decision-making process is fragmented and varied throughout the states. Fragmentation is a major problem and one that needs to be squarely addressed in determining the kind of organizational structure for a juvenile paroling authority. Organizational muddle, combined with excessive rhetoric and little action, have tended to push juvenile parole into the same model as the adult systems. Whether this movement will prove useful or harmful remains to be seen.

REVIEW QUESTIONS

1. Describe the difference between probation and parole.

2. How does the historical background of parole differ from that of probation?

3. List and discuss the major goals and three basic purposes of aftercare. How are these being realized?

4. Discuss the importance of the decision of the United States Supreme Court in *Morrissey* v. *Brewer*.

5. What factors should be considered for the successful release from an institution to parole status and for the discharge of a youth from parole? Are these considerations similar? Why or why not?

6. Explain how parole fits into the juvenile justice system and how it relates to the rest of the system.

7. Who decides when to parole and on what basis?

8. In your opinion is juvenile parole working? Why or why not?

NOTES

1. H. E. Barnes and N. K. Teeters, *New Horizons in Criminology*, 3rd ed. (Englewood Cliffs, N.J.: Prentice-Hall, 1959), p. 568.

2. The President's Commission on Law Enforcement and Administration of Justice, *Task Force Report: Corrections* (Washington, D.C.: U.S. Government Printing Office, 1967), p. 60.

3. Ibid., p. 151.

4. Juvenile Parole Services, *Juvenile Rehabilitation April–January 1975 Quarterly Report* (Olympia, Washington: Department of Social and Health Services, 1975, table 15.

5. National Advisory Commission on Criminal Justice Standards and Goals, *Corrections* (Washington, D.C.: U.S. Government Printing Office, 1973), p. 389.

6. R. M. Carter and L. T. Wilkins, eds., *Probation, Parole, and Community Corrections* (New York: Wiley, 1976), pp. 305–306.

7. The President's Commission on Law Enforcement and Administration of Justice, *Task Force Report: Corrections*, p. 63.

8. Ibid.

9. Ibid.

10. *California Correctional System Study, Final Report* (Sacramento: Human Relations Agency, Board of Corrections, July 1971), p. 23.

11. Department of Youth Authority, *A Guide to Treatment Program* (Sacramento: State of California, April 1970).

12. Department of Youth Authority, *Parole Manual* (Sacramento: State of California, August 1, 1966), Section 501.

13. *California Correction System Study, Final Report*, p. 24.

14. Don C. Gibbons, *Changing the Lawbreaker* (Englewood Cliffs, N.J.: Prentice-Hall, 1965); R. M. Carter and L. T. Wilkins, "Some Factors in Sentencing Policy," *Journal of Criminal Law, Criminology, and Police Science* 58, no. 4 (1967): 503–504; Department of Youth Authority, *The Status of Current Research in the California Youth Authority* (Sacramento: 1970) p. 5.

15. The President's Commission on Law Enforcement and Administration of Justice, *Task Force Report: Corrections*, p. 29.

16. Ibid., p. 189; Department of Youth Authority, *Standards for the Performance of Probation Duties* (Sacramento: 1970), p. 11.

17. *California Correction System Study, Final Report*, pp. 24–25.

18. See American Correctional Association, *Manual of Correctional Standards* (Washington, D.C.: ACA, 1966), p. 114.

19. National Advisory Commission on Criminal Justice Standards and Goals, *Corrections*, p. 393.

20. H. B. Acton et al., *Punishment, For and Against* (New York: Hart, 1971) pp. 96–98.
Note: Reference within this material is made to: John M. Stanton "Murders on Parole," *Crime and Delinquency* 15 (January 1969): 149–55.

21. William E. Anos and Raymond L. Manella, *Readings in the Administration of Institutions for Delinquent Youth* (Springfield, Ill.: Thomas, 1965), p. 188 ff.

22. The President's Commission on Law Enforcement and Administration of Justice, *Task Force Report: Corrections*, p. 151.

23. Ibid., pp. 151–52.

24. Edward Eldefonso and Walter Hartinger, *Control, Treatment and Rehabilitation of Juvenile Offenders* (Encino, California: Glencoe Press, 1976), pp. 207–209.

25. Edward Eldefonso and Alan R. Coffey, *Process and Impact of the Juvenile Justice System* (Encino, California: Glencoe Press, 1976), p. 168.

26. The President's Commission on Law Enforcement and Administration of Justice, *Task Force Report: Corrections,* pp. 152–53.

27. Richard W. Kobetz and Betty B. Bosarge, *Juvenile Justice Administration* (Gaithersburg, Maryland: International Association of Chiefs of Police, 1973), p. 582.

28. Frank Dell 'Apa et al., "Advocacy, Brokerage, Community: The ABC's of Probation and Parole," *Federal Probation* (December, 1976), p. 38.

29. Carter and Wilkins, eds., *Probation, Parole, and Community Corrections,* p. 212.

30. Eldefonso and Coffey, *Process and Impact of the Juvenile Justice System,* pp. 169–70.

31. Eldefonso and Hartinger, *Control, Treatment and Rehabilitation of Juvenile Offenders,* p. 209.

32. Carter and Wilkins, eds., *Probation, Parole and Community Corrections,* p. 667.

33. See Ronald Sklar, "Law and Practice in Probation and Parole Revocation Hearings," *Journal of Criminal Law and Criminology* 55 (1964), p. 75.

34. National Advisory Commission on Criminal Justice Standards and Goals, *Corrections,* pp. 404–405.

35. Ibid., pp. 405–406.

36. *Morrissey* v. *Brewer* (1972, 408 U.S., 471).

37. Ibid., pp. 471–89.

38. Ibid., pp. 471–89.

39. Ibid., p. 489.

40. Ibid., p. 489.

41. Ibid., p. 485.

42. National Advisory Commission on Criminal Justice Standards and Goals, *Corrections,* p. 407.

43. Robert Prus and John Stratton, "Parole Revocation Decision Making: Private Typings and Official Designations," *Federal Probation* (March, 1976), p. 48.

44. Sophia M. Robison, *Juvenile Delinquency: Its Nature and Control* (New York: Holt, 1964), pp. 392–94.

13 Juvenile Justice Administration

According to the labeling and stigmatization process, at least
part of the responsibility for the development of an identity
and subsequent career as a "juvenile delinquent" appears to
rest with the handling of the juvenile offender by the police
and the courts. Ambiguity in the laws governing juvenile
conduct places a great deal of emphasis upon the exercise of
discretionary powers.

HAROLD J. VETTER

The juvenile justice administrator's major problem is lack of control resulting from the extreme fragmentation of the juvenile justice "system."
Viewing the administration of juvenile justice as a series of articulated and
coordinated efforts amounts to a convenient fiction; the reality is far from
this rosy picture. The nature of the juvenile justice system poses many
serious obstacles in the way of effecting intelligent administration. All three
elements of the criminal justice system—the police, the courts, and
corrections—have developed special ways for dealing with children and
young people in trouble. Because of the need to protect information
regarding juveniles and because of conflicting purposes and missions within
these three subsystems, the fragmentation problem is even more exacerbated
in the juvenile system than in the adult system.

Police departments have responded to the problems of juvenile crime in a
number of different ways, usually through specialized units for juvenile
control. The juvenile courts, sharing their duties with other tribunals, have
also developed special philosophies and procedures to deal with their wards,
but the recent movement away from the legal philosophy of *parens patriae*
to one which stresses due process and constitutional safeguards for juveniles
has placed the courts in need of change. Juvenile and adult institutions
developed independently and have in large part remained autonomous in the
United States until the past two decades. Recently, several states have
recognized the practical, economic value of combining the services and
institutions of the adult and the juvenile systems of corrections. Further, the
use of probation as an alternative to incarceration has always been more

accepted in the juvenile system than in the adult system. As a result, juvenile corrections has moved in the direction of community-based programs at a faster rate than the adult corrections.

Although the juvenile justice system has a number of shortcomings, it is operated in general by persons who are better educated and who possess a higher level of skills than their adult counterparts. Also, the juvenile justice system is *usually* better financed, is provided better facilities, and is afforded better services. Despite these advantages over the adult system, the juvenile crime rate continues to increase faster than the juvenile population, recidivism rates continue to rise, and an increasing number of juvenile criminals are becoming adult criminals. With the hopes of the treatment model fading, a new area of promise seems to be in better organization and administration of existing programs and a gradual revision of most juvenile justice systems along the lines of the "process" or "social justice" model. This chapter will examine some of the problems in various parts of the juvenile justice "system"—or the components that are viewed as comprising this *non-system*—and offer some tentative solutions for the administrator.

The Police: First Point of Contact

The restrictive procedures by which the law protects juveniles tend to create many administrative problems for the police, who are charged with a mandate to enforce all the laws. A youth's age, for instance, is a major factor in determining criminal responsibility. Below the age of seven years, children are normally considered free of criminal responsibility. Between the age of 7 and 16 or 18 (depending upon the jurisdiction), the offender is considered a juvenile delinquent rather than a criminal. The problem is further clouded by the fact that about half of all juveniles who come in contact with the police are "status offenders" whose conduct would violate no criminal statute if they were adults (e.g., runaways, dependent children).

The police officer (in this case, the administrator of juvenile justice) who comes into contact with a juvenile offender has a number of alternatives available. He can ignore the delinquent behavior altogether and go on his way. The contact could be very casual, with light conversation and inquiry to identify participants in the offense. The police may then escalate from questioning to search, an order for dispersal, or other more "official" action. Even after deciding to intervene, the officer can still decide to take the offenders home, warn them or their parents, or take some other "street corner justice" action. Only when informal alternatives seem to be inadequate to the task at hand will most police officers take formal and official action to start the juvenile through the justice system. The decision as to how far to go regarding these alternatives is often determined by departmental policy, whether explicit or implicit. The effect of policy varies greatly between departments, and rigid enforcement of policy within a department is difficult in the environment of freedom of action and discretion enjoyed by the police.

Juvenile crime should concern *all* personnel in a modern police department. While it is important to have the specialized skills required for many juvenile problems available, separate sections should be set up only if a demonstrated need for them has been established. Separate juvenile units are needed to handle special investigation techniques for the processing of juveniles, disposition requirements, and coordination with family and community. Since juvenile offenders react to the criminal justice process differently from adult offenders, special interrogation skills and handling techniques are needed to help expedite cases. The delinquency specialist is attuned to the community and to the needs of the juvenile in a way that the "regular" patrolman usually is not.

The juvenile specialist is *supplementary* to the operations of the patrol division in most agencies, so the patrol field unit is responsible for all preliminary investigation procedures. The initial report of a crime seldom identifies the perpetrator as a "juvenile" or "adult," and juvenile investigators do not generally become involved until after the initial contacts have been made and an initial investigation has been completed.

A number of names have been used in the past for juvenile units in police organizations. "Crime Prevention Bureau," "Juvenile Bureau," "Youth Aid Bureau," and the more recent "Juvenile Control Bureau" are but a few. Kenney points out some of the functions of a Juvenile Bureau, the term we shall use throughout this chapter although it is not the most common one:

Logically, the functions of a juvenile unit seem to be as follows:

1. Discovery of delinquents, potential delinquents and conditions including delinquency.
2. Investigation of delinquency and causes of delinquency.
3. Disposition or referral of cases.
4. Protection of children and youth.
5. Community organization.

Although these functions are general in nature, they provide the basis for the operation of the juvenile unit. When viewed in terms of the overall departmental objectives for juvenile control as discussed in the previous chapters, they provide the basis for the juvenile control unit's operation.[1]

The smaller department has less of a problem with organization and administration. In agencies with from one to fifteen persons, every officer must be prepared to assume *all* the police functions; specialization for juvenile cases would be an impractical and expensive use of limited resources. One person in the department, often the chief, may be assigned as the juvenile case coordinator. Because the juvenile problem often impacts on the community in a different manner from adult crime, the small department chief tends to follow it closely.

In departments larger than fifteen officers, the assignment of a juvenile bureau, even if it is composed of only one officer, seems to be the rule. This bureau will often be assigned a number of duties such as bicycle patrol, school safety patrol, "Officer Friendly" programs, and others aimed at the juvenile population sector. It has often been the practice to assign a capable police*woman* to the juvenile bureau, even the one-person bureau. Until the recent opening of police roles to women, juvenile duty was likely to be considered one of a number of female-oriented roles within the agency.

An exhaustive list of the kinds of details that might be set up within a juvenile bureau would be too space consuming. Some of the more important are as follows.[2]

1. Investigation Section
2. Patrol and Inspection Section
3. Coordination, Disposition, and Referral Section
4. Felony Detail or Adult Investigation Detail
5. Boys' Detail
6. Girls' Detail
7. Juvenile Missing Persons' Detail
8. Dance Hall Detail
9. Bicycle Detail
10. Records Unit
11. Truancy Detail
12. Big Brother Unit
13. Big Sister Detail
14. Detention Detail
15. Special Events Detail

The organization of police agencies is changing. Kenney and Pursuit relate the changes in police organization to juvenile justice as follows:

> The impact of the human relations approach to organization based upon a recognition of the importance of the socio-psychological behavior of man on organization has modified the traditional approaches. Stringent adherence to the so-called principles of organization emphasizing hierarchy, command, and superior-subordinate relationships no longer reflects the real world of organization. Organization, in fact, is the relationships which exist between members of the organization. The human relations approach has treated the relationships as a reflection of informal organization, that which exists alongside of the formal organization as reflected in the traditional approaches, but influencing operations because it does reflect relationships.
> . . .

Trend toward a team approach to policing is increasing. Some departments are integrating the juvenile and detective operations for investigation purposes with teams consisting of juvenile officers and detectives working together. The juvenile officer continues in his specialized role as necessary in the investigation process and has responsibility for dispositions. Another change in larger departments is to integrate operations at the precinct or station level. Specialist juvenile officers and detectives are assigned under the direction of the station or precinct commander rather than reporting directly to headquarters. A much more flexible type operation results. Likewise, there is increasing tendency in many departments to follow the Vollmer approach to organization, placing greater responsibility on the uniformed field officer with detectives and juvenile officers fulfilling a support role.

A team policing organizational model calls for constituting what has traditionally been command level officers as a top management team principally responsible for planning and policy clarification and for providing general direction for operations. Primary responsibility for operations is delegated to operations teams consisting of the traditional middle management, supervisory and first line operating personnel. Each operations team is collectively held responsible for all program implementation.

The top management team will consist of the chief of police and high level specialists in each of the functional program areas. The program areas include investigation, patrol, traffic, juvenile control and services, and a specialist for operations. It is the responsibility of the team with assistance from supporting personnel to identify departmental needs and to develop comprehensive plans and policy guidelines for implementation. The concern of each specialist is with his program area of competence. Decisions are made on a collective basis with a view of integration of all programs for feasible implementation. The operations specialist works with the operations team in the implementation of programs. The juvenile control specialist in this arrangement would be primarily a planner rather than a command officer.

The operations teams would be responsible for taking the program plans developed by the top management team for implementation. Each team would consist of lead personnel whose responsibilities would be primarily that of planning the operations to meet the program requirements established by the top management team. Operational personnel would consist of the necessary number of specialists and generalists to perform all of the work necessary to meet all program requirements. Thus, there would be the generalist field personnel and specialists including juvenile officers and detectives working side by side.

In a medium-sized department there may be two operations teams. Each team would be responsible for all police work occurring between designated hours, the division to be determined by workload. The team leader would deploy and assign personnel as necessary to accomplish the work. The traditional three shifts would no longer prevail. Perhaps a policy would be that personnel shall work eighty hours within a two-week period. This would make it possible for personnel to work longer than eight-hour periods in one day and provide greater flexibility for assignment.

Where would the juvenile officers fit into such a scheme? They would be specialist members of each team fulfilling essentially the same functions as previously outlined. However, all members of the team would share responsibility for performance of the juvenile control program as they would all other programs. Likewise the juvenile officers would share responsibility for implementation of all other programs.[3]

As police organizations adjust to meet the changes in the juvenile control mission, the problems of the police administrator are magnified. The administrator, working in an environment that is changing from protective to punitive, must try to upgrade juvenile bureau personnel while cracking down on juvenile crime. He or she must justify some of the progressive changes in the police sector while social attitudes toward juvenile crime are hardening. Continuing to protect the *rights* of juveniles and protecting the juveniles *themselves* from the harsh realities of the enforcement sector of the adult system remains another continuing headache for the police administrator.

The Juvenile Court: The Heart of the System

The juvenile probation system is usually under the direct control of the juvenile court. The hypothetical "overall juvenile administrator" (in reality, no such person exists), may have difficulty understanding how these two concepts fit together.

The juvenile probation system can be seen as both a pre-adjudicatory and post-adjudicatory alternative for the juvenile delinquent. Direct referrals to the probation system are usually made by police citation, with specific instructions for the juvenile to report at a particular time to a specific place. After an initial interview, the probation officer decides whether or not to refer the case to nonjudicial or judicial action. The probation officer has a number of discretionary choices for action should he decide to settle the matter through nonjudicial means:

1. *Dismissal*—this action is justified when the preinterview investigation, and the facts disclosed in discussing the case with the juvenile and his parents, indicates to the probation officer that the case is unfounded, or the evidence is untrustworthy or insufficient and does not warrant or sustain the charges.
2. *Referred to Resident Jurisdiction*—this referral is appropriate when the juvenile resides elsewhere and the problem does not justify action where the act of misconduct occurred.
3. *Referral to Other Local Agencies*—this is proper action when the investigation and discussion indicates another local agency is better equipped to handle the juvenile and his problem (usual referrals are to the welfare or mental health agencies).
4. *Counseling and Dismissal*—this action goes beyond outright dismissal, but not beyond a simple counseling session in which all concerned discuss the problem and plan possible solutions.
5. *Informal (consent) Supervision*—this is the most serious nonjudicial alternative. It involves the provision of probation supervision to the juvenile

with the consent of the parents (parent or guardian), and is only justified when it is apparent that the juvenile requires professional assistance in solving his problem. When initiated, the case is then processed through the probation agency to determine the supervision and counseling services that will be necessary, and the juvenile becomes part of the informal supervision caseload of the probation agency.[4]

The probation officer must also determine just *which* factors to consider in his role as administrator.

In making a decision as to alternatives for a judicial processing of a juvenile, probation officers often attempt to isolate and identify the most important single factor. Was it the current offense, the prior record of delinquency, or the attitude of the juvenile and his parents? (At this initial probation interview the intensive social-history case study needed to file a petition for juvenile judicial appearance has not been made.) The decision may be a combination of all three factors. Injustice can occur when the offense alone (except at felony levels) justifies referral to juvenile court. The previous history data of an offender at this stage of the screening process is generally no more than brief references, and usually fails to indicate if the current offense is part of a general pattern of delinquency—really the only justifiable grounds for considering past misdeeds when making this decision.[5]

After all screening or diversionary actions have been taken or all nonjudicial alternatives exhausted, the juvenile that is still a problem will finally be referred to the juvenile court for disposition. The following material, based on the *National Advisory Commission on Criminal Justice Standards and Goals,* focuses on the juvenile court and some of the problems faced by the administrators of this system.[6]

Juvenile offenders pose special problems and raise special hopes. Although their past actions indicate that these juveniles are a danger to the community, their age creates a reluctance to use adult procedures in dealing with them. Society's response to this reluctance to use adult methods in dealing with juvenile offenders has been the use of the juvenile court.

The structure of juvenile court systems varies widely. In some jurisdictions, the juvenile court is a separate court—or a distinct division of a trial court with a broader jurisdiction—that hears nothing but juvenile cases. Since judges of these courts do not divide their efforts between juvenile and other cases, they have an opportunity to develop expertise in juvenile matters. In other jurisdictions, courts hearing juvenile matters also have other judicial duties; probate courts, for instance, are sometimes given jurisdiction over juvenile matters. Judges on these courts focus less of their attention and efforts on juvenile matters, and therefore have fewer opportunities to develop the specialized skills that most juvenile matters require.

Despite such structural variations, however, juvenile courts have at least five unique characteristics in common. In part, these create the special problems that juvenile courts pose in the court system's fight against crime.

Philosophy

Although today's juvenile court personnel have shed the naive expectations of early reformers, the juvenile courts, more than other courts with criminal jurisdiction, are still imbued with a rehabilitative orientation. Less emphasis is placed on punishing particular offenders to deter others, or on frightening particular offenders into abstaining from future offenses. More emphasis is placed on using scientific methods to change offenders' motivation so that they have alternative methods of satisfaction and no longer desire to commit criminal acts.

Jurisdiction

The limits and breadth of the jurisdiction of juvenile courts also set them apart. This jurisdiction generally is limited to individuals under a specific age, which varies from 16 to 21. However, authority over these juveniles is much broader than the corresponding authority of courts of general criminal jurisdiction over adult members of the community. Juvenile courts ordinarily may assume control over a juvenile—take jurisdiction over him—if he has performed an act that, if performed by an adult, would constitute a crime. But the juvenile court may also assume control of a juvenile, even though his actions would not authorize a court of general criminal jurisdiction to exercise any control if he were an adult, as in case of truancy and running away. A person of the required age who has committed any of these acts generally is described as delinquent or in need of supervision.

Juvenile court authority may even extend to individuals who have not committed any overt act that demonstrates that they pose a danger to society. Mere circumstances demonstrating that a juvenile is not being properly provided for by persons with responsibility for him is often sufficient to justify the juvenile court's assuming jurisdiction over the juvenile. If this failure on the part of the parents or other responsible persons is deliberate, the juvenile traditionally has been designated neglected; if not, the child may be labeled dependent.

The terminology used to describe juveniles within the jurisdiction of the juvenile court varies from state to state. To an increasing extent, the traditional labels of delinquency, neglect, and dependency are being combined or replaced. New York, for example, includes within juvenile court jurisdiction a broad category of juveniles labeled Persons in Need of Supervision, or PINS.

Whatever the appellation applied, however, most juvenile courts have jurisdiction over a broad category of persons who come within certain age limits. This broad jurisdiction reflects the underlying philosophy of the juvenile court. Since the objective of juvenile proceedings is regarded as treatment rather than punishment, the power of the court has been defined in terms of the need for treatment rather than in terms of demonstrated dangerousness for which punishment is justifiable.

Procedure

Juvenile courts have traditionally had more flexible procedures than their counterparts in the adult criminal justice system. Many of the procedural devices used to guard against conviction of an innocent defendant in the adult process have not been utilized in juvenile court. Since a juvenile court's proceeding results in treatment rather than punishment, the stringent procedural safeguards against unjustified punishment have been considered unnecessary. Moreover, treating has been viewed as requiring more flexibility than the procedures of the adult system permit. The philosophical objective of the juvenile courts, then, has justified the use of more flexible procedures than are allowable in the adult system.

Differences in procedure, as well as the desire to set the juvenile system apart from the adult system, have resulted in the development of specialized terminology with different shades of legal meaning for the juvenile court system. The document upon which proceedings are brought, for instance, does not *charge* delinquency, neglect, or dependency; it *alleges* it. The document is not an *indictment* or *information*, but a *petition*. The court, in determining whether the juvenile who is the subject of a petition is in fact delinquent, neglected, or dependent does not *convict;* it *adjudicates*. The process of deciding what to do with a delinquent, neglected, or dependent juvenile is not *sentencing*; it is *disposition*.

Intake or Screening

Juvenile courts have had a relatively organized process for determining which individuals are to be brought before the court on a petition alleging delinquency, dependency, or neglect. This initial screening function is usually performed by an intake unit, consisting of caseworkers functioning as a court-attached agency. The court, then, has control and supervision over the intake unit. In many systems, the intake unit performs functions other than screening, such as conducting diversion programs involving informal supervision over juveniles who are not the subject of formal court petitions.

Dispositional Alternatives

The juvenile court has available a broader range of dispositional alternatives than the adult court. This also is based on their difference in philosophy: Since the object of the proceeding is treatment, access to a broad range of potential treatment programs is essential.

The juvenile courts have come under attack in recent years for failing to adopt all of the procedural safeguards afforded a defendant in an adult criminal prosecution. In part, this criticism has been based on the conclusion that despite the supposed difference in philosophy between the adult courts and the juvenile courts, for all practical purposes being adjudicated a delinquent is no different from being convicted of a crime. The critics also believe that differences between the juvenile system and the adult system are no justification for relaxing safeguards against unjustified state exertion of power over individuals. Under this view, protections against unjustified treatment are as important as protections against unjustified punishment.

Such criticism was translated into judicial edict in *In re Gault*, 387 U.S. 1 (1967). After commenting that "the constitutional and theoretical basis for this peculiar system is—to say the least—debatable," the U.S. Supreme Court concluded that the proceeding at which it is determined whether a juvenile is a delinquent "must measure up to the essentials of due process and fair hearing." In delineating this due process and fair hearing, the Court held in *Gault* that the subject of such a proceeding had to be accorded adequate notice of the specific charges against him, the assistance of counsel, the right to confront and cross-examine witnesses used against him, and the privilege against self-incrimination. In *In re Winship*, 397 U.S. 358 (1970), the Court held that due process required that in a delinquency proceeding the State prove "beyond a reasonable doubt" every fact necessary to establish the juvenile's delinquency.

It is clear, however, that the U.S. Constitution does not require that all aspects of adult criminal procedure be applied in juvenile court. In *McKeiver v. Pennsylvania*, 403 U.S. 528 (1971), the Court held that due process did not require that an alleged delinquent be extended the right to trial by jury. The Court's language indicated that it retained hope for the preservation of the juvenile court system as a separate and distinguishable process:

> The juvenile concept held high promise. We are reluctant to say that despite disappointments of grave dimensions, it still does not hold promise, and we are particularly reluctant to say . . . that the system cannot accomplish its rehabilitative goals. So much depends on the availability of resources, on the interest and commitment of the public, on willingness to learn, and on understanding as to cause and effect and cure.

Reform, in other words, should not render the court processing of juveniles indistinguishable from the processing of adult criminal defendants. Rather, it should improve the effectiveness of the court process as part of a rehabilitative juvenile justice system and strike a reasonable balance between the need to maintain flexibility and the need to prevent unjustified findings or labels of delinquency, neglect, or dependency.

There are two crucial areas in which reform is essential. The first is the place of the juvenile court in the criminal justice system, including its breadth of jurisdiction over juveniles, its location within the judicial system of jurisdiction to hear such cases, and its relationship to other agencies. The second area for reform is procedures, including procedures used during the formal hearing as well as methods by which the decision is made to detain a juvenile prior to the formal hearing itself.

The appropriate administrative approach to the processing of delinquency cases is the formal court procedure, which should vary little from that the procedure in adult criminal prosecutions. Processing of juvenile cases should differ from that of adult cases primarily in a greater willingness to use informal nonpunitive measures. If, however, formal court action is sought and the juvenile contests the facts upon which court jurisdiction is sought, the procedure for resolving the dispute should not differ substantially from that used in adult cases. Such an approach can preserve the value of the juvenile justice process as a means of dealing with young offenders without unduly sacrificing the right of alleged offenders to a full and fair determination of whether official action is justified.

The juvenile judge is in a real position of conflict in today's justice environment. He or she is pressed from one sector for more humane sentencing practices, more diversion, and differential decision-making despite limited information. From another sector there is pressure to "get tough"—to inflict more punishment, impose longer institutional confinement, and exhibit less interest in the juvenile's rights. Not surprisingly, the juvenile justice process as a means of dealing with young offenders without problems of overcrowding and repeat offenders. Organization of the courts along the lines suggested by the National Advisory Commission would surely be a worthwhile beginning in solving some of these problems.

Juvenile Corrections

Juvenile corrections seems to be at a crossroads. Partly because of the emphasis on juvenile rights and partly because of the failure of past models, juvenile correctional administrators are looking for new answers to old questions. We are indebted to the Bureau of Juvenile Rehabilitation, Department of Social and Health Services, State of Washington for providing us with much of the following material.[7]

Conflicts Between Models

The current issue is: Do we continue to pursue the treatment model or do we adopt the justice model? In order to perceive this issue more clearly, one needs historical perspective. The first juvenile probation law was established in Massachusetts in 1869. The first juvenile court act was applied in Cook County, Illinois, in 1899 at the urging of medical and social science experts. All but two states had similar acts setting up noncriminal courts by 1928. For about 35 years literature on the courts, institutions, and parole emphasized the treatment aspects of juvenile programs, and social service schools and staff development programs focused on the treatment rehabilitation model. Since the Supreme Court's first juvenile case, *Kent* v. *United States,* in 1967, there has been much more attention given to the issues of due process, juvenile civil rights, separation of dependent from delinquent youth, and distinguishing between delinquent youth with the new category of "status offender" and those who have committed adult-type violations. Court decisions since 1967 have affected the following areas: First Amendment freedoms, access to courts, protection from harm, medical aid, discipline, classification and transfers, rehabilitation and treatment, physical condition, parole, and civil liberties.

The criminal justice system or model based on the constitution, criminal procedures, and special legislative enactments, operate in conformity with the law. The justice system is composed of police agencies, court systems, and correctional systems which cover the political jurisdictions of cities, counties, states and the federal government and include both private and public agencies. The adult justice system is concerned today with plea bargaining, bail, pre-trial release, diversion programs, the adversary approach in court, designated sentences for crimes, prisoner rights, and much greater focus on custody and punishment. The courts, until 1967, had taken a position of nonintervention regarding the juvenile corrections system. Today there is considerable intervention in the internal administration of programs and considerable concern for youths' constitutional rights.

As noted previously, it is misleading to assume that there is a juvenile justice *system*. The word *system* implies organization, connection, and togetherness, but police, county prosecutors, the courts, and correctional agencies have different objectives and goals which often are in conflict. Because of such conflicts there are ongoing programs which not only cancel each other out, but may even threaten each other's existence. One example of this is the clash between treatment and custody which occurs in almost every juvenile institution. Another is society's pressure for punishment as well as individualized treatment. Still another example is the clamor for more community-based programs in the face of protests on the part of the community itself. Correctional policies must be developed and applied which attend to the interests of the offender and the community, even though these interests are frequently in conflict.[8]

The *treatment model* typically includes study and *diagnosis*, which allows social workers to determine positive factors before prescribing social treatment. *Individualization* of treatment is needed to meet the needs of each person at a given point in time. *Focus and objectives* treatment aims for a step-by-step process of personality change rather than anything dramatic or sudden; objectives are set which are the basis for the treatment plan. The offender and the worker must establish an effective, professional *relationship* in which the worker exercises a conscious, controlled use of himself. A fifth aspect of the treatment model is *participation:* the social worker and the individual must be involved together in working out the individual's problems and encouraging his or her motivation to change. The sixth aspect is the *use of resources* available to help the individual being served. *Continu-*

ous evaluation is needed to improve effectiveness, with flexibility enough to change with what is happening to the individual being served.[9] This list of elements of the treatment model can certainly be broadened, but these aspects are typical. The treatment model presupposes adequate staffing and adequate resources, including a general community acceptance of what is being done.

It can be safely assumed that those who developed the various juvenile court laws, established probation, and brought about juvenile court acts would be disappointed in what has actually been accomplished. Research in juvenile treatment programs seems to indicate that we are succeeding with only about 50 percent of our youth, though the whole matter of the reliability of such statistics and the meaning of success is currently being challenged. What cannot be disputed is that the general public feels that our programs are not accomplishing what they should: programs are very expensive; the crime rates continue to rise; youth go through our system and come back as recidivists, and there is no decline of juvenile crime.

Although we talk about community diversion programs, we are aware that the courts do not have the resources to give adequate individualized treatment. We also are aware of the limited capacity of the court to affect necessary changes in conditions external to the child. In the past the jurisdiction of the court was based on a desire to help children in "loco parentis" (in place of their parents), but this concept is being challenged. Individualized treatment requires exhaustive analysis and evaluation of the youth and all the internal and external influences which may bring about change in the pattern of behavior—including the diagnostic services of medicine, psychology, psychiatry, social work, and education. Many of our courts still do not have these services.

The current purpose of juvenile rehabilitation is well expressed in the objectives of a Washington institution listed in their *Manual for Parents.*

> The purpose of the program is to bring about a change in the attitudes of the behavior of the delinquent youth in order to affect the reduction in delinquent behavior and prepare him for more adequate functioning in society. Emphasis is placed on the realistic responsibilities that each member in society faces in relation to himself, his family, and the community.
>
> It is essential in working with delinquents to view their delinquent activities as symptoms of problems which are not effectively treated by severe punishment or by placing them in a situation where they can have little or no opportunity to develop mentally, physically or emotionally. Youth need to develop feelings of self-worth, dignity, competence, and responsibility through their own achievements and a variety of activities through their associations with both institutional staff and interested community people. Staff recognize that each youth is a unique human being and that each youth arrives at the institution with his own personal, familial, and societal problem. Since it is imperative that the institution provides programs that recognize the individual

complexities, it does provide a combination of treatment, rehabilitation and custodial programs.[10]

Corrections—Problems

Any evaluation of correctional programs, either in the institution or in community services, indicates varying degrees of success. Deficiencies in current programs are frequently found in the following areas: stigma, labeling, the inability to demonstrate success, the difficulty of correct diagnosis, and the exorbitant costs of care and treatment. The cost per day of maintaining a child in the Washington State Diagnostic Center is about $49, and the average annual cost for a child in one of Washington's large institutions is about $17,923. Another deficiency is inadequate community resources and money. State programs frequently wind up with youth because they are the only resource available for the particular kind of problem the youth has. Some youth need coercion or an authoritarian setting before they will recognize that they have a problem or do anything about them; some must be incarcerated for the protection of the community or themselves. Many community programs cannot handle youth needing control.

Some additional obstacles to juvenile corrections reform are the fragmentation of corrections, the variety of governmental authorities involved, and, most of all, a lack of overall correctional planning that assigns each segment of the system specific involvement and accountability. Corrections may be overused for some crimes; the political protester and conscientious objector, for example, are not effectively treated in our correctional programs. Overemphasis on custody is another obstacle. An additional obstacle, as has been implied, is the ambivalence of the community: they want treatment but they also want punishment; they want good programs but they do not want to pay the price for these programs; they want offenders incarcerated but they do not want jailbirds back in the community after they have been released. Lack of sufficient information upon which to base good planning is one more serious deficiency.

The focus on diversion, particularly for status offenders, causes some legal problems. For example, if a child referred to a social agency fails, should he be processed through the courts for the same offense? If so, a case could be made for double jeopardy.[11] Status offender cases—for example, drunkenness, truancy, incorrigibility—might well be treated in a separate system, but most jurisdictions cannot afford one juvenile correctional system, so there is little probability of setting up a separate status offender system. Another problem is the amount of discretion that already exists in our system. Juvenile court judges, the police, the correctional programs, and the district attorney have a wide discretion in the decisions they make. Depending on how one views the system, this discretion could be a major problem because of a lack of consistent standards.

The juvenile justice model, which focuses on juvenile rights, is currently being given nationwide attention. The question of whether to follow the treatment model or justice model implies that we have a choice, when in fact treatment and justice are intertwined, and we are already committed to both.

The juvenile corrections administrator has no choice about whom the court commits to his care but has had the choice of determining how long they are kept. Financial pressures outside the control of the juvenile rehabilitation administrator are forcing the shortening of the length of stay, which means youth are going back to communities before juvenile corrections staff feel they are ready. Consequently, recidivism rates go up. The justice model focuses on sentencing and custody which would effect basic treatment and philosophy. Length of stay could not be controlled and an attempt to reconcile the merits of both systems and live with the liabilities could be made.

The ability of the juvenile corrections administrator to alter or change the direction of juvenile justice is very difficult to determine. The administrator has little choice but to continue in the current direction because of the requirements of Supreme Court decisions and subsequent administrative directives. He or she is not in control of most of the elements which effect change in his own system.

The model most used in the past centers around a benevolent judge acting as a guardian of the youth's rights in the name of the state *(parens patriae)*. But this approach to the juvenile as a *delinquent* rather than a *criminal* has resulted in overly casual juvenile justice procedures in which the offender's rights are ignored instead of protected.

The basic organizational structure of the juvenile court was designed to keep the judge in control at all stages of the procedure, from adjudication to release back to the community. When the concept of corrections and rehabilitation emerged in the adult criminal justice system, the gap between the goals of the two systems narrowed. The provision of due process and many other rights within the adult system highlighted their absence in most juvenile courts. The U.S. Supreme Court's decision *In re Gault* decreasing emphasis on *parens patriae* and affirming due process in the juvenile system, has made it obvious that new organizational structures are necessary.

The President's Commission on Law Enforcement and the Administration of Justice proposed a juvenile justice system that includes all the incarceration alternatives and rehabilitation opportunities available to adults. This system (Figure 13–1) is administered by a Youth Services Bureau, which ensures that juvenile offenders have access to these alternatives before the case goes to court. This correctionally-oriented organization tempers the court's authority, furnishing help for each youth's needs without necessarily removing him from the community or labeling him as a delinquent. The youth services approach is one direction for the future, but the organizational concepts to implement this approach will have to be worked out in each

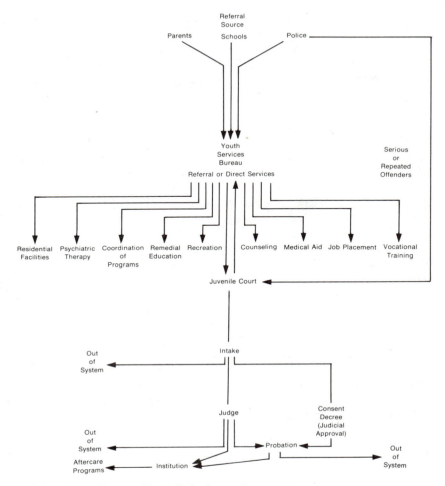

FIGURE 13–1. Proposed juvenile justice system.

Source: The President's Commission on Law Enforcement and Administration of Justice, *The Challenge of Crime in a Free Society* (Washington, D.C.: U.S. Government Printing Office, 1967), p. 89.

jurisdiction. And, as noted in chapter 16, the youth services concept has received less than enthusiastic support in the 10 years since it was devised.

The juvenile justice administrator comes in several different forms: policemen with great discretion, probation officers who must respond to several constituencies, judges faced with many problems in protecting both public and juveniles. The juvenile correctional administrator has the most clearly defined role, but even it suffers from fragmentation of jurisdictional control among cities, counties, and states. Only a few states have seen fit to consolidate juvenile and adult corrections under a single authority. The lingering fear of the ''terrible'' adult institutions still inhibits the vast majority from taking that difficult but seemingly logical step. The management muddle of our juvenile justice "non-system" can only be cleared up when American society decides whether it wants to *punish, protect,* or *treat* its miscreant youth. That prospect seems dim, so we struggle on, trying to make programs work in an environment of administrative uncertainty whose byproduct is uncertain administrators.

Summary

The administration of the juvenile justice system is in some ways more difficult than its adult counterparts; and in other ways, it is much easier. The problem of whether the police, the courts, and the corrections agencies should develop complete and separate apparatus for juveniles or absorb them into the existing criminal justice agencies is one of long standing. The separate subsystems have had varying degrees of success in seeking autonomy for juveniles. The most successful of these has been the juvenile courts, which have had almost absolute power over the juvenile offender under the doctrine of *parens patriae.*

Currently, the trend in administration seems to be heading toward a more selective jurisdiction over the offenders, not merely their status as juveniles. As attitudes change toward making juvenile offenders more and more accountable for their actions, the adult and juvenile systems will become less distinguishable. As a result, the administration of juvenile justice will become more and more formalized and the traditional *parens patriae* approach will give way to a legalistic process instead. Administration officials, who want and need rules as guidelines, will favor this process, but its impact upon the children is yet to be determined.

REVIEW QUESTIONS

1. Why has the concept of *parens patriae* become difficult to maintain in the present juvenile justice environment?

2. What alternatives are *usually* used by the police in juvenile incidents?

3. Where do juvenile probation officers get their referrals? Where do *most* come from?

4. Women have been used in juvenile bureaus in the past. Is this a reasonable use of these females within the organizational structure of the police force? Why or why not?

5. What is the difference between the "treatment" and "justice" models of juvenile justice, as outlined in the text?

NOTES

1. J. Kenney and D. Pursuit, *Police Work with Juveniles and the Administration of Juvenile Justice,* 4th ed. (Springfield, Ill.: Thomas, 1976), p. 119.

2. Ibid., pp. 104–107.

3. Ibid., pp. 109–113.

4. P. Weston and K. Wells, *Criminal Justice: Introduction and Guidelines* (Pacific Palisades, Calif.: Goodyear, 1976), pp. 269–70.

5. Ibid., p. 270.

6. National Advisory Commission on Criminal Justice Standards and Goals, *Courts* (Washington, D.C.: U.S. Government Printing Office, 1973), pp. 289–92.

7. Bureau of Juvenile Rehabilitation, "Do We Pursue the Treatment Model or Do We Adopt the Justice Model?" Unpublished report (Olympia, Wash.: Department of Social and Health Services, 1976).

8. Vincent O'Leary, "Correctional Assumptions on Their Program Implications," (November 1967) p. 13.

9. Gordon Hamilton, "Theory and Practice of Social Casework;" Chapters, I, II, III, VIII, and IX (1956).

10. *Parents Brochure* (Chehalis, Wash.: Greenhill School for Boys, 1974).

11. The U.S. Supreme Court ruled on May 27, 1975, in *Breed* v. *Jones,* that trial of a juvenile in criminal court for the same offense for which he had been tried in juvenile court places him in double jeopardy and is therefore unconstitutional.

PART IV

Changes in the System

14 A Juvenile's Legal Rights

> The extension of positivism into criminal law has created an untenable position wherein the legal rights of juveniles, alcoholics, addicts, and the mentally ill are ignored in the name of treatment while at the same time the defendant is not afforded treatment which can make any claim to effectiveness or impact on future behavior.
>
> *C. RAY JEFFERY*

What is said to *be* true and what *is* true often have little to do with one another. For at least a century, much has been said of the legal rights of children, but little has been done to implement them. It is futile, therefore, to simply list the natural or legal rights of a minor. Even the noblest of judicial rulings has done little more than change a *badly* inequitable situation into a *poorly* inequitable one. "The gradual extension of official control to protect children from physical abuse and exploitation has led not to greater freedom and respect for the child but to a 'partial exchange of masters'."[1]

Although children are now protected from unreasonable demands by parents or guardians, and a court's treatment of them may be officially correct, they are still expected to conform closely to social norms and legal sanctions even though their rights and individualities are largely ignored.

Even in the juvenile court of today, where a so-called revolution in the rights of juveniles is supposed to be occurring, a "rather deep disrespect among judges for the integrity of adolescents" continues unabated.[2] Furthermore, among attorneys, juvenile clients are treated as subordinates and "nonpersons."[3]

Justice for the child is touted as an official goal for a modern society. However, in practice children are often dealt with in ways that would be totally unacceptable for adults. Their constitutional rights are often violated and there is little regard for their integrity, human dignity, and privacy.

Television, which attempts to reflect the realities of our society, has many popular series involving the police. But seldom does one see a *juvenile* being informed of his or her constitutional rights (*Miranda* decision) prior to being taken into custody by the police. In reality, children are not guaranteed the privilege of being informed of their rights.

Police must have probable cause for stopping, detaining, or even questioning an adult suspect. If the police handle an arrest incorrectly, it is quite possible that the adult offender cannot be held—guilty or not—because of a technicality. However, it is not uncommon practice for police to stop, detain, and question a juvenile with little or no cause. Seldom is a juvenile offender released from custody because of a legal technicality resulting from improper arrest procedures by the police.

It is an irony of the 1970s that the rights of blacks, Jews, homosexuals, women, unborn children, and adult criminals are being championed while the rights of our children in trouble are overlooked.

There are, nevertheless, significant efforts being made to change the legal and social position of minors. The moving forces behind these efforts include the courts, lawyers and legal associations, private persons and agencies, legislatures, universities, educational groups, and juveniles themselves.

In this chapter, juvenile rights will be explored. Emphasis will be placed on what has been done, and on what seems to remain to be done to reach equity. If juveniles are expected to abide by the law, does it not logically follow that they, too, should have equal protection under the law?

Brief History

The earliest precedent related to the development of a modern-day juvenile code is the case of the *Duke of Beaufort* v. *Berty* (England, 1721?). The basic principle of that case was that children should be treated differently from adults, primarily for the purpose of prevention rather than punishment. The principle of this case did not receive immediate acceptance, but it is considered to be fundamental to juvenile law.

The principle of individualized justice for youth came with the decision *Rex* v. *Delaval* (England, 1763). The concept of *parens patriae,* which allows the state through the courts to assume parental responsibility for any child under its purview, evolved from *Ellesley* v. *Ellesley* (England, 1828).

Early American practices did not reflect a strong feeling for children, as evidenced by their treatment in the New England colonies. In fact, children who committed crimes in colonial times were often punished more severely than adults.

By the nineteenth century, however, several champions surfaced to lead the crusade for children's rights. More and more Americans were becoming aware that children may not be as responsible for their criminal acts as adults. By 1858, in California, a youth industrial school was established as an institution for children under the age of 18 who were leading "idle or immoral" lives. And, in 1887, California held that it was unlawful to confine children under the age of 16 years in jails.

The nation's first juvenile court was established in Cook County, Chicago, in 1899. *Mill* v. *Brown* (Utah, 1907) states the importance of the laws establishing early juvenile courts: "The juvenile court law is of such vast importance to the state and society that, it seems to us, it should be administered by those who are learned in the law and versed in the roles of procedure, effective and individual rights respected. Care must be exercised in both the selection of a judge and in the administration of the law."

In 1923, the National Probation Association's Annual Conference proposed a Standard Juvenile Court Act. The last state to adopt this act was Wyoming, in 1945. Between 1925 and 1945, various states defined their own juvenile codes.

The "new" court system, which was over one hundred years in coming, defined all procedures of the juvenile courts as civil rather than criminal. (*Civil* suits relate to and affect only individual wrongs, whereas *criminal* prosecutions involve public wrongs.)

It is evident, therefore, that the greatest effort in the juvenile justice system has been aimed at creating a separate court system for youths and delinquents. This separate system, and the perpetuation of the doctrine of *parens patriae*, have resulted in a system which has largely ignored juveniles' legal rights. Those rights accorded adults, such as a speedy trial, trial by jury, right to bail, right to confront one's accusers, and protection from self-incrimination were seen as unnecessary for juveniles.

However, as the rights of adults (i.e., *Miranda* v. *Arizona*) were being pursued, some court decisions did have bearing on juvenile rights. The decision in *Gideon* v. *Wainwright* [372 U.S. 335 (1963)] set the stage for legislation regarding due process. Although concerned with the right to legal counsel in adult, noncapital felony cases, several states have required that indigent children who request counsel be so provided and at public expense.[4]

In the landmark opinions in *Kent* v. *United States* [383 U.S. 541 (1966)] and *In re Gault* [387 U.S. 1 (1967)], the Supreme Court at long last evaluated juvenile court proceedings and the constitutionally guaranteed rights of children. In *Kent* v. *United States,* the Court noted that the child involved in certain juvenile court proceedings was both deprived of constitutional rights and at the same time not given the rehabilitation promised under earlier juvenile court philosophy and statutes. It pointed out in a rather dramatic matter that "there may be grounds for concern that the child receives the worst of both worlds."[5] In the *Kent* case, the Court did not have occasion to pass directly on the right to counsel and the notice of this right because the juvenile involved had been provided with counsel within 24 hours of his arrest.

The next year, however, the Supreme Court did have occasion to render a decision on these rights in *In re Gault*. On May 15, 1967, the Supreme Court rendered its first decision in the area of juvenile delinquency procedure. Gerald Gault allegedly made a telephone call to a woman living in his neighborhood, during which he used some obscene words and phrases. The use of a telephone for such purpose violates an Arizona statute, and hence

Gerald, aged 16, was subject to adjudication as a juvenile delinquent. The adjudication was in fact made after a proceeding in which he was not offered the basic procedural protections to which he would have been entitlted had he been charged in a criminal court.

In this decision, Justice Abraham Fortas ruled that a child alleged to be a juvenile delinquent had at least the following rights:

1. Right to notice of the charges in time to prepare for trial.
2. Right to counsel.
3. Right to confrontation and cross-examination of his or her accusers.
4. Privilege against self-incrimination, at least in court.

With the *Gault* decision, the presumption that the juvenile courts were beyond the scope or purview of due-process protection was ended. The primary lesson learned here was that juvenile courts would have to become courts of law and follow standard procedures concerning the constitutional rights of those on whom they passed judgment.

In re Gault did, however, fail to answer one vital question. It is whether a juvenile must be advised of his or her rights at some point in the prejudicial stage. Where serious offenses are involved and the juvenile might be transferred to an adult criminal court, some police forces are giving such warnings. Some states like California apply *Miranda*[6] restrictions to juvenile interrogations generally.

In another case related to the *Gault* decision, *In re Winship* [397 U.S. 35851 Ohio op. (2d) .323, 25, L.Ed. (2d) 368, 90 Sct. 1068 (1970)], the Supreme Court held that to justify a court finding of delinquency against a juvenile, the proof must be beyond a reasonable doubt that the juvenile committed the alleged delinquent act. Prior to this case the requirement seemed to be that the judge should be influenced only by a preponderance of evidence against the accused delinquent.

Finally, the Supreme Court, in 1971, agreed to hear arguments whether juveniles had a constitutional right to a jury trial. In *McKeiver* v. *Pennsylvania* [403 U.S. 528 (1971)], implying that the due process standard of "fundamental fairness" applied, the Court rejected the concept of trial by jury for juveniles. The Court contended that the "juvenile proceeding has not yet been held to be a 'criminal prosecution' within the meaning and reach of the Sixth Amendment. . . ."[7] The Supreme Court stated that it was as yet unwilling to "remake the juvenile proceeding into a full adversary process" and put "an effective end to what has been the idealistic prospect of an intimate, informal protective proceeding."[8] The Court concluded by encouraging the states to "seek in new and different ways the elusive answers to the young."[9]

The Supreme Court has not been the only source of change in the area of juvenile rights. Federal acts and legislation have also played an important role. For example, until the Uniform Juvenile Court Act of 1968, a child could still be taken into custody by police or others in a situation where the Fourth Amendment would have exempted an adult. The Uniform Juvenile Court Act therefore set some limits on nondiscriminatory home removals of children. It provides for the removal of a child from his or her home only if there are reasonable grounds to believe that the child is suffering from illness or injury or is in immediate danger from his environment and that removal from that environment, therefore, is necessary.

In 1974, the U.S. Congress passed the Juvenile Justice and Delinquency Prevention Act (Public Law 93-415). This act requires

> a comprehensive assessment regarding the effectiveness of the existing juvenile justice system. This legislation also provides the impetus for developing and implementing innovative alternatives to prevent juvenile delinquency and to divert status offenders from the criminal justice system. The intent of the Act is to clearly identify those youth who are victimized or otherwise troubled but have not committed criminal offenses and to divert such youth from institutionalization. Simultaneously this will promote the utilization of resources within the juvenile justice system to more effectively deal with youthful criminal offenders.[10]

It appears, then, that the courts and the legislative bodies (state and federal) are still reluctant to allow children to be treated as legal equals to adults. As a doctrine, *parens patriae* is as deeply and firmly entrenched as is the tendency to treat children who violate laws by having them, in the old days, "whipped and put to bed without supper."

Juveniles do not have full protection under the law, and their constitutional rights are being violated. However, once equitable protection is recognized, then delinquents will have to be considered (in most cases), to be criminally responsible for their misbehavior.

Equal protection under the law can work both ways. Present juvenile court procedures, while denying some rights to juveniles, do, nevertheless, extend to them certain privileges and immunities not afforded to adults. A new legal system for juveniles will of necessity imply trade offs of these immunities in return for the granting of full constitutional rights.

Procedural Rights

As a result of the Supreme Court cases mentioned earlier in this chapter, the juvenile court is now a *court of law*. Procedural guarantees are therefore mandatory, as stated in the due-process provisions of the Fourteenth Amendment of the Constitution, which protect the rights of accused juveniles.

Procedural rights are rights dealing with statutory laws. Procedural rights are accorded to juveniles during the fact-finding process of a juvenile case.

Such rights range from the right to a trial by jury (not yet a reality) to the right to legal counsel. The Supreme Court decisions regarding juveniles have thus far dealt with only the procedural rights of children.

Procedural rights accorded juveniles in court are still lagging behind those of adults. The *McKeiver* decision, which declared that the concept of due process in juvenile court proceedings does not include the right to a jury trial, is the most significant of these.

Thus far, the procedural rights guaranteed to juveniles in court proceedings are: (1) the right to adequate notice of charges against him or her; (2) the right to counsel and to have counsel provided if the child is indigent; (3) the right to confrontation and cross-examination of witnesses; (4) the right to refuse to do anything that would be self-incriminatory; (5) the right to a judicial hearing, with counsel, prior to transfer of a juvenile to an adult court; and (6) the right to be considered innocent until proven guilty beyond a reasonable doubt.

Notice of Charges

The Gault case has established that a juvenile has a constitutional right to a timely notice of charges against him or her. This is required in order to give the juvenile's defense counsel adequate time to prepare for the trial.[11]

To provide *this* timely notice, most states use a summons. A *summons* is the legal instrument to give notice to the accused of the proceedings against him or her. Many states issue a copy of the court petition with the summons. The petition provides the accused with a more complete explanation of the charges.

The summons orders the accused juvenile or the juvenile's parents to appear in court at a specified date and time. The question of who should be served the summons is debatable; in some states it is served directly upon the juvenile, in others upon the parents, and in still others, upon both juvenile and parents.

The *Gault* decision held that the due process requirements of notice in juvenile court proceedings were to be the same as in other criminal or civil proceedings. This left the door open for the serving of the summons to be handled in one of two ways. Some states, following criminal procedures, have the summons served by the sheriff, the juvenile probation officer, or by another person so designated by the court. In such cases, the summons is served in person. Other states, following civil procedures, use substitute means of serving the summons. Some use the mails and others place a notice in the newspaper, if the child's address or whereabouts is unknown.

The juvenile courts also have flexibility in deciding what constitutes "timely notice" in order for defense counsel to prepare the case. Some juvenile court acts specify one day, some as much as one week; if mail service is used, a longer period of time is allowed.

> Because the civil rules of procedure are applied, the question arises whether improprieties in the manner of services and even the total lack of service

should be deemed waived if the accused voluntarily appears in court. Although the authorities are in disagreement, most jurisdictions seem to adopt the view that once the accused enters the courts the defects are waived and the court gains jurisdiction over him.[12]

Right to Counsel

In the *Gault* decision, it was held that the accused juvenile has the right to counsel. The counsel may be of the person's own choosing or appointed by the court for financial or other reasons.

By the time of the *Gault* decision several states had already taken steps to provide legal counsel to juveniles. Since *Gault,* the regular participation of defense counsel in juvenile court has become a commonplace occurrence. However, if the juvenile uses either private counsel or an assigned counsel, there is a likelihood that such defense counsels will be unfamiliar with the proceedings of a juvenile court, for many will have had only civil court experience. The public defender's office is more likely to provide counsels who know their way around the juvenile court and who will be less likely to be intimidated by the police, probation officer, or the judge.

Notice of the juveniles right to counsel must be clearly understood by both the child and the family, and should be given both in writing and orally. This notice contains two important elements: (1) the child and parents, or either of them, may be represented by counsel, and (2) if they cannot afford and therefore cannot employ counsel, the child and parents are, in the absence of a competent waiver, entitled to be represented by counsel at public expense.

Procedures direct that notice of the right to counsel shall be given to the child and parents at the first intake interview, or when the child is admitted to a detention center or shelter care facility. It may often be necessary to give separate notice to the parents, who may not always be available at the point of initial contact.

Generally, there are four possible responses to the notification of the right to counsel; the juvenile court must be prepared to deal with each.

First, the child and parents may request counsel immediately. In this case any intake interviewing must cease, and the officer in charge must seek the assistance of counsel for the juvenile. In large jurisdictions it may be feasible to arrange with a legal services agency to provide representation on call, or with a bar association to provide for volunteer attorneys at initial intake. In other jurisdictions the officer must notify the judge or the court clerk, as soon as possible, of the request for counsel.

In many cases, counsel will often advise family to proceed with intake and with attempts at informal adjustment. Counsel's major role may be to simply explain the juvenile justice system to the family and to reassure them that full participation in the intake process may be in their best interest. Under standard operating procedures for most juvenile court jurisdictions, statements made during the intake stage are inadmissible at the adjudicatory hearing. If this provision applies and is made clear to the family, it is likely that the need to provide counsel for representational support during the intake process will seldom occur.[13]

The second possibility is that a request for counsel for any proceedings before the court will be made. In this case, the officer in charge should notify the clerk of the court. If a petition is then filed, the judge can immediately assign counsel and avoid any unnecessary delays in affecting the assignment of counsel.

The waiver of the right to counsel is another possibility, but it must be made by both the child and the parents because both have the right to be represented. Of course, the child's ability to exercise good judgment in arriving at such a decision is often questionable. In cases where there is doubt regarding the validity of the waiver, the intake officer should obtain an attorney to consult with the family on the question of representation. If counsel is waived before an adjudicatory hearing, a new inquiry into that waiver must be made by the judge when the hearing begins. If counsel is appointed at this time, any statements made without counsel present or facts uncovered as a result of such statements should not be admitted into evidence, for any prior waiver of the right to counsel in a case of this nature may be considered to be invalid.

And finally, the court may receive no response whatsoever to the notification of right to counsel. In cases of indigent parents whose educational backgrounds are severely limited, this is often what happens. It may be extremely difficult to impress upon them the importance of obtaining counsel. Counsel *must* be appointed for the duration of the court proceedings in such cases. The mere failure to request counsel may not be taken as a waiver of counsel; waiver is an affirmative act and not one to be presumed.[14]

Counsel should be provided to children in all possible cases. No simple action holds more potential for achieving procedural justice for the juvenile in court than does legal representation. The presence of an independent legal representative of the child, or of his or her parents, is the basis of a whole structure of guarantees that a minimum system of procedural justice requires. The right to confront one's accusers, to cross-examine witnesses, to participate meaningfully in the dispositional process, and to make an appeal have substantial meaning for the majority of juveniles brought before the courts only if they are provided with attorneys with the ability to invoke these rights effectively.[15]

Rights of Confrontation and Cross-Examination

The juvenile's right to confront and to cross-examine hostile witnesses was upheld in *In re Gault*. Most states apply this ruling to only the first phase of the criminal court proceedings, that is, that part dealing with the determination of one's guilt or innocence. However, many statutes and cases allow the juvenile the right of confrontation and cross-examination at dispositional hearings where the second phase of criminal court proceedings designed to determine appropriate sentencing is carried out. For example, in *Strode* v. *Brorby*,[16] a commitment order which would have sent a boy to an industrial school rather than place him on probation was reversed. The court ruled that the juvenile had been refused the opportunity to present witnesses in his favor who would have testified that he deserved probation rather than institutionalization.

Right of Privilege Against Self-incrimination

The Fifth Amendment right to remain silent (that is, the privilege against self-incrimination) is the last entitlement concurred upon juveniles by the *Gault* decision. The court concluded that the constitutional privilege against self-incrimination is as applicable in juvenile cases as it is in adult cases.

If the juvenile court judge in the *Gault* case had reached a decision as to Gerald Gault's guilt based upon Gerald's own admissions, it would have been based on admissions obtained without regard to his privilege against self-incrimination.

In ruling on the *Gault* decision, Justice Abraham Fortas obviously felt that juvenile court judges should not be influenced by confessions, admissions, and like acts which may have been obtained under dubious circumstances and without regard to the provisions of the Fifth Amendment.

Right to a Judicial Hearing

In 1966, *Kent* v. *United States*[17] was argued in the U.S. Supreme Court; this case raised the issue of whether juveniles receive less legal protection than adults.

Morris Kent, who was 16 years old at the time, was arrested for house-breaking and rape. The District of Columbia's juvenile judge, on the basis of Kent's past record (he had been on probation since age 14), waived juvenile jurisdiction and transferred Morris to the District Court for trial proceedings as an adult. Kent's counsel requested a hearing on this waiver of jurisdiction, but was denied. Kent's counsel also requested access to all of his previous arrest records; this request was also denied. The waiver stated that "after a full investigation, I hereby waive. . . ," and Kent was consequently tried as an adult and received a sentence of 30–90 years. Had he been tried as a juvenile, the maximum disposition would have been only five years.

The Supreme Court ruled that the lower court decision was unconstitutional. It found that: (1) in waiver of jurisdiction, a hearing must be granted; (2) assistance of counsel at such hearings must be granted; (3) the plaintiff's counsel must have access to social service records; and (4) a statement of the facts of the full investigation and a statement of the judge's reasons for waiver must accompany the waiver. In making this ruling, the Court emphasized that juvenile court procedures were still civil in nature and consequently juveniles are not entitled to all the protections given adult criminals, but waiver hearings must provide all protections implied in the Fourteenth Amendment's due-process clause.

Proof Beyond a Reasonable Doubt

In 1970, in the *Winship* case, the Supreme Court held that juveniles were entitled to have accusations and/or charges against them proven beyond a reasonable doubt.

Twelve-year-old Samuel Winship was adjudicated delinquent as the result of a theft of $112 from a woman's purse. Consequently, he was committed to a training school for one and one-half years subject to annual extensions of commitment until his eighteenth birthday. The case was appealed to the New York Court of Appeals and was upheld by that court. The U.S. Supreme Court, however, later reversed that decision. The Supreme Court contended that the loss of liberty is no less significant for a juvenile than for an adult. Therefore, no juvenile may be deprived of his or her individual liberty on evidence less precise than that required to deprive an adult of his or her individual liberty.

With this ruling the Court mandated that the *criminal* law burden—rather than the traditionally less stringent civil law burden of the mere preponderance of all evidence—is applicable in juvenile cases. The Court emphasized that "civil labels and good intentions do not themselves obviate the need for criminal due process safeguards in juvenile courts."[18]

The Supreme Court did, however, limit its holding in the *Winship* case to cases involving alleged delinquent behavior and not ungovernability. State courts taking the ruling one step further have assumed that proof beyond a reasonable doubt is a requirement in ungovernability or incorrigibility cases as well.[19]

As in adult cases, the defense now has an advantage over the prosecution in regard to the burdens of proof. The prosecution must prove every allegation with facts, while defense merely has to raise a reasonable doubt.[20]

Trial by Jury

As stated earlier, in 1971, the Supreme Court held, in *McKeiver* v. *Pennsylvania*, that due process of law does not require a jury in juvenile court trials. However, the Supreme Court was careful to note that there "is nothing to prevent a juvenile court judge in a particular case where he feels the need, or when the need is demonstrated, from using an advisory jury."[21]

The use of an advisory jury in a juvenile case has already been approved by the courts; in the case to which we refer it was determined that the use of such an advisory jury was in the best interests of reaching a fair and impartial decision in the case.[22] Jury trials for juveniles in most cases, however, are the exception rather than the rule unless a motion specifically requesting the statutory provision of a trial by jury is made in the court jurisdiction in which the case is to be heard.[23]

Addressing the subject of when a trial by jury is and is not in the best interests of a defendant, Besharov says: "Trial by jury is the keystone of the Anglo-American system of justice. Most experienced criminal defense attorneys say they never waive trial by jury unless the trial judge is exceptionally fair and open-minded, or unless the facts are particularly gruesome and inflammatory, or unless a successful defense will rely upon a careful application of legal technicalities."[24]

Unless one or more of the above-cited reasons would apply to a juvenile's case, it is likely that denial of a trial by jury is not in the best interests of the juvenile's defense.

Until the door to jury trials for juveniles accused of crimes is opened wide, young people will not receive fair treatment through procedural rights in the courts and will remain the second-class citizens that so many persons in the juvenile justice system feel they are.

In addition to procedural rights in court, juveniles do have certain other procedural rights within the various stages of the juvenile justice system. Those rights will now be examined.

Procedural Rights at Other Stages of the Juvenile Justice System

The Supreme Court has not yet considered the question of whether the constitutional rights of individuals who come into contact with police (i.e., for questioning, temporary detainment, arrest, or other perceived intrusions upon their freedom) apply to juveniles. However, many courts, police departments, and legislatures have made the assumption that they do. It has been reported that there is a trend in the amendment of juvenile court acts to extend arrest laws to juveniles and the Uniform Juvenile Court Act does include a section regarding search and seizure.[25, 26]

Arrest

Before further examining procedural rights, let us briefly look at the general principles of arrest. These principles are derived from the Fourth Amendment of the Constitution. Under the Fourth Amendment the police must have an arrest warrant or have probable cause to believe an offense is being committed in order to make a legal arrest.

In felony cases, probable cause as a reason for arrest is based on several factors. Hearsay, a tip from a neighbor, and suspicious circumstances are among these factors. The arresting officer does not need probable cause if he or she is acting under the orders of superiors or as the result of communcation with another officer. Sometimes, the court may have trouble determining whether probable cause existed at the time of the arrest. In such cases, the court usually considers the officer's record, experience, and expertise.

One must consider, however, that there are literally thousands of children taken into custody each year who are not arrested. The Department of Health, Education, and Welfare Children's Bureau reported in 1969 that "In the past, statutes have provided that taking into custody shall not be deemed an arrest; however, for all practical purposes, this has been a legal fiction since the child is being held in involuntary custody."[27]

Many states, though they do not consider the taking of a child into custody by police to be an arrest, do require that this act be legal under the state's and the national constitution.[28] Since the *Gault* decision, many courts have required that the police have probable cause before taking a child into custody as a suspect of a criminal act. "In the near future, courts will have to decide whether the taking of a juvenile into custody for noncriminal misbehavior, ungovernability, is subject to these or other standards. Certainly, there are some constitutional limitations on how the police handle problem children."[29]

While laws applicable to the arrest of adults may be applicable to the arrest (or taking into custody) of juveniles, provisions relating to detention, custody, and interrogation which are found in juvenile acts may differ decidedly from those accorded adults.

Interrogation

The issue of whether warnings (*Miranda* decision) must be given at the stage of interrogation of a juvenile suspect has yet to be decided by the Supreme Court. As noted earlier, the *Gault* decision gives the accused juvenile the right to refuse to give self-incriminating evidence; however, this privilege has generally been applied to court proceedings only. In fact the Supreme Court in the *Gault* decision declined to discuss the questioning of juveniles by the police.

In 1948, in *Haley* v. *Ohio*,[30] the Supreme Court held that a confession obtained from a 15-year-old youth after five hours of continuous questioning by police was involuntary. In its ruling, the Court stressed that juveniles "cannot be judged by the more exacting standards of maturity; that which would leave a man cold and unimpressed can overcome and overwhelm a lad in his early teens."[31]

In a similar case *Gallegos* v. *Colorado*,[32] the Court negated the confession made by a juvenile which was obtained after five days of questioning during which the police refused to allow the juvenile's mother to see him. "Various lower courts also have pointed out the need for extra precautions to safeguard juveniles' rights and to insure the reliability of their confessions."[33]

The police have developed and used many methods, now considered either illegal or unethical, for extracting confessions from accused suspects. Among them are such tactics as the "Mutt and Jeff routine." This tactic employs the use of a two-man team, one of which is a hard-nosed belligerent personality and the other an easy-going nice guy. To frighten the suspect, the nice guy tells him that he can only hold off the belligerent officer for so long and he begs the suspect to talk now and avoid what may happen at the hands of his partner. Another tactic is the false line-up in which one or more witnesses under police orders wrongly identify the suspect.

If a juvenile remains silent throughout questioning, the police often make that silence appear to be an admission of guilt and urge the suspect to cooperate and talk. Along similar lines, if two or more juveniles are arrested together, police try to get one of them to tell everything by intimating that the others have already talked. Thus if one of the suspects being questioned is actually guilty, he faces the better-him-than-me dilemma.

Is a frightened teenager who finds himself being questioned in a police station able to withstand such police practices? In its decision in *Miranda* v. *Arizona,* which reviewed these and other methods used by police to obtain confessions, the Supreme Court concluded that "the very fact of custodial interrogation exacts a heavy toll on individual liberty and trades on the weakness of individuals."[34] If the Court felt this way about confessions abstracted from adults, it would appear logical that they would be even more sensitive to those obtained from juveniles.

If, according to *Miranda,* an individual does not knowingly waive his or her constitutional privilege against self-incrimination, then the police cannot submit that person to custodial interrogation. If a confession is obtained during interrogation, then it is up to the prosecution to prove that there was a proper waiver; if not, the confession cannot be submitted as evidence.

The question arises whether a juvenile is capable of understanding his or her right against self-incrimination when being interrogated by police, and whether a waiver of this right by a youth is valid. In answer to this question, the police should consider (as should the court when evaluating confessions obtained by police) whether the child is sufficiently mature and intelligent to understand the meaning of waiving the right against self-incrimination. In judging maturity, the police should consider the child's age, intelligence, education, experience, mental capacity, complexity of the charges, knowledge of legal matters, arrest background, and other circumstances such as the time of day or night, and whether the child's parents or counsel are present. The court may challenge any confession if after considering the above circumstances it finds a discrepancy in the facts being presented or questions in any way the nature of the confession.

In summary, regarding the precourt interrogation of juveniles by police, the following seems to be true. Several courts have already taken the position that a confession or statement of guilt by a juvenile during prejudicial investigation (interrogation by police or probation officers) is not admissible in court unless the juvenile was previously notified of the right to remain silent and right to counsel, and knowingly waived those rights. This implies, therefore, that there are efforts to bind the police to the requirements of the *Miranda* decision when dealing with juvenile suspects.

In *The Police Role and Juvenile Delinquency,* Richard Kobetz offers the following policy guide for police in respect to juveniles.

> When gathering evidence of an offense, there must be no differences in procedural operations within a police agency if a juvenile is involved instead of an adult suspect. Through a competent investigation, the degree of proof required is no less for a juvenile than for an adult. Every care must be exercised to assure the rights of the child; he is guaranteed the same rights as an adult.[35]

By following this policy, police forces will be in tune with the current practices regarding a juvenile's legal rights, and will thereby be offering the juvenile fair treatment in their hands.

Detention and Bail

Since the decision to detain a juvenile prior to court proceedings affects the way the court will later see that child, it is important that this decision is right. Placing a juvenile in a detention facility simply because he or she has noplace else to go, for example, appears to be a questionable practice, especially in light of the potential harm it may cause the juvenile. Also, statutory law and appellate courts in some states require that a juvenile be given a formal detention hearing with the right to confront and to cross-examine the witnesses.[36]

Most courts throughout the country will normally require precourt detention of a juvenile either because they fear he or she will not appear for the court appearance or because the juvenile presents a potential threat to self or others. The latter reason for precourt detention has not been challenged in court so far. However, if a juvenile is detained for the first reason—fear of failure to show up—then the issue of the right to bail arises. Currently, less than 20 states allow the use of bail in juvenile cases.

> Some make bail a statutory right, while others provide for bail as the sole means of release. Most states traditionally have not provided bail procedures in juvenile cases. A few states even prohibit the use of bail. Through the years courts have been divided over whether there is a federal or state constitutional right to bail.[37]

Although the question of bail as a constitutional right for juveniles was brought before the Supreme Court in 1968, the Court failed to rule on this issue, and it has yet to be resolved.[38]

There are many factors which need to be seriously considered when discussing the subject of bail for juveniles. For example, where does a 14-year-old teenager get the money for bail, especially when his or her parents cannot pay it? Would the right to bail simply widen the gap concerning justice between the rich and the poor? Bail is a constitutional guarantee in most adult cases, and the disparity between rich and poor exists there. Possibly, the use of or access to bail by poor adults would shed some light on what types of problems a poor juvenile would encounter.

In adult cases, the adult who posted bail usually suffers if he or she skips bail, especially if the bail money was his or her own or a friend's or a relative's. Would a juvenile feel any responsibility to the person who put up money to ensure his temporary freedom? Would bail bondsmen be willing to provide bail money for an indigent juvenile, especially one who receives no financial support from his or her parents?

These and other questions will have to be considered in devising a system of bail for juveniles accused of criminal acts, especially if the courts rule in favor of this provision as a constitutional right to juveniles. A ruling to this effect appears imminent in light of the current trend in the area of juvenile rights. Will the juvenile justice system be prepared to implement the provisions of such a ruling? It will have to be if the juvenile is to move closer to full protection under the Constitution.

Incarceration

The last of the procedural rights of juveniles at other stages of the juvenile justice system involves the rights of incarcerated juveniles. Concern for incarcerated or institutionalized juveniles comes from a similar concern in adult cases. The primary issues are prisoner rights and the right to treatment.

In its examination of the causes of the Attica prison riot, the McKay Commission cited a long record of disregard of legitimate grievances arising from inadequate medical care, bad food, and the absence of recreational facilities; obstacles to any form of communication with the outside world; rules that were "poorly communicated, often petty, senseless, or repressive and . . . selectively enforced," and a "relationship between most correctional officers and inmates that was characterized by fear, hostility, mistrust, nurtured by racism."[39]

If proper grievance practices existed at the time, the riot at Attica might never have happened. The need for just grievance procedures is as real in juvenile institutions as it is in those for adults, for although there has been no juvenile equivalent to Attica, there are injustices within juvenile institutions which quite often surface only after rioting, destruction of property, or attempted escapes.

The Justice Model

An exhaustive effort is currently underway to find a replacement for the much derided rehabilitative model of corrections which has dominated penology for most of this century. In its place, a successor model is discernible which has as its core a sense of fairness in grievance procedures for inmates, among other things. This model is commonly referred to as the justice model.

> Justice is the first virtue of social institutions, as truth is of systems of thought. A theory however elegant and economical must be rejected or revised if it is untrue; likewise laws and institutions no matter how efficient and well arranged must be reformed or abolished if they are unjust. Each person possesses an inviolability founded on justice that even the welfare of society as a whole cannot override.[40]

The justice model is beginning to emerge as an approach to corrections, but there have been few applications of it to date. Those that have been attempted include a grievance procedure involving independent arbitration introduced by the California Youth Authority (CYA) in 1973. This CYA program is seen as a means of promoting justice and demonstrating a democratic process within an authoritarian setting;

> "Kids who turn delinquent have a very keen sense of fairness, maybe because they've learned to recognize the lack of justice in how they've been handled before they got to us." Young offenders ask themselves, he said, why they should act in a law-abiding manner when they are constantly treated in a way that doesn't seem fair.[41]

This statement was made by the director of CYA in explaining his motivation for introducing a form of the justice model into California Youth Institutions.

In a correctional policy statement published in 1974, the Group for the Advancement of Corrections, a body made up of current and former correctional administrators, commented on grievance procedures for prisoners as follows:

> Grievance procedures must be made available to *all* offenders. At a minimum, these procedures must provide for guaranteed responses to all grievances within specified time limits and review by some person or body outside the correctional agency and acceptable to both offenders and employees.[42]

The National Council on Crime and Delinquency has drawn up a Model Act for the Protection of the Rights of Prisoners, which states:

> The director of the State Department of Corrections (or the equivalent official) shall establish a grievance procedure to which all prisoners confined within the system shall have access. Prisoners shall be entitled to report any grievance, whether or not it charges a violation of this Act, and to mail such communication to the head of the department. The grievance procedure established shall provide for an investigation of all alleged grievances by a person or agency outside of the department, and for a written report of findings to be submitted to the department and the prisoner.[43]

This act also recommends the prohibition of inhumane treatment and suggests standards for the use of solitary confinement, disciplinary procedures, judicial relief, and visiting.[44] However, it does not specifically mention juvenile inmates. Logically, the juvenile inmate should be accorded the same rights and protections within a correctional facility as the adult; after all, juvenile training schools and institutions are prisons and offer juveniles punitive confinement. But until this fact is admitted, court action to protect the juvenile inmate is likely to be limited to the prohibition of inhumane conditions in institutions, and will continue to ignore such things as the right to uncensored mail, legal libraries within institutional walls, and sophisticated grievance procedures.

The juvenile inmate will fare much better in terms of the second area of rights for incarcerated youth, the right to treatment. This is true because rehabilitation has been the primary reason given to justify the incarceration of children. And rehabilitation is accomplished by means of treatment.

Many courts have held that an institutionalized child *must* receive appropriate treatment or else be released. Some states, therefore, require periodic progress reports on the juvenile,[45] and cases have been brought before the courts to require juvenile correction systems to improve institutional services and to release children when these services are inadequate,[46] or in violation of the juvenile's right to an "acceptable home substitute" as their place of detention.[47]

In *Creek* v. *Stone,* the Court of Appeals for the District of Columbia interpreted the local juvenile court act to mean that a juvenile has a statutory right to treatment.

> The purpose stated in the 16 D.C. Code §2316(3)—to give the juvenile the care "as nearly as possible" equivalent to that which should have been given by his parents—establishes not only an important policy objective, but an appropriate case, a legal right to a custody that is not in conflict with the *parens patriae* premise of the law.[48]

Whether a juvenile has a legal right to treatment and whether the concept of the right to treatment and the treatment itself are accepted and applied within the confines of the juvenile justice system may in reality be worlds apart.

> Unless viable dispositional alternatives become a reality, most courts will continue to close their eyes to the inadequacy of treatment resources in fear of sending dangerous juveniles into the community. It is difficult to conceive of the time when the widespread awareness of the juvenile court's inadequate resources will translate into a judicial turning away from troubled youth. The need to maintain the illusion of helping will be too strong unless forceful public action is the attitude of the general public.[49]

Many of the major court rulings (especially in adult cases) regarding the right to treatment came about because the plaintiff was confined involuntarily in a mental institution or treatment facility. Because the inmates of training schools and juvenile institutions are confined against their will, the right to treatment issue was inevitable. And rehabilitation and the treatment used to achieve it are inherent in the doctrine of *parens patriae*, a doctrine which is being stubbornly retained by many persons within the juvenile justice system.

In 1974, the U.S. District Court for the Eastern District of Texas in *Morales* v. *Turman* determined that the constitutional rights of incarcerated minors had been violated by the Texas Youth Council (TYC) by its failure to provide proper care and treatment for its institutionalized juveniles.[50] This is the first major case which has raised serious questions regarding a juvenile's right to treatment when he or she is incarcerated against his or her will. An in-depth discussion of this is provided in chapter 12, ''Institutions.''

There are two rights not widely discussed or generally examined in a text on juvenile delinquency: (1) the right to refuse treatment and (2) the right of punishment.

The right to refuse treatment normally is claimed in cases involving mental patients, but it can be used by an inmate of a correctional facility. The acceptance or rejection of treatment seems at first to be the individual's prerogative. However, if a patient or inmate is allowed to refuse treatment, he or she would more than likely remain a burden on society.

One could hypothesize that the increasingly high rate of recidivism among juveniles released from institutions may be a result of their refusal to accept treatment; this is, however, doubtful. One would have to prove that treatment had been offered in the first place before one could conjecture that it had been refused.

The right to refuse treatment is closely related to, but not the same as, the right to choose punishment rather than treatment. Both of these proposed rights are alternative and theoretical companions to the right to treatment. The courts have both supported and refuted the right to refuse treatment, but they have yet to decide a case involving the issue of ''right to punishment.''[51]

The right to choose punishment may seem absurd at first, but it is plausible when looked at in the following manner. Just as the right to treatment is based on statutory law, the right to punishment under the law is supportable under the same concept. This concept is applicable to the offender who is criminally responsible for his or her crime. The delinquent could object to conventional treatment by citing the First Amendment right to privacy and then demand a statutory right to punishment based on a state criminal code designating a specific length of imprisonment as punishment for the crime for which he was convicted or committed.

The theoretical approach to a right to punishment is clarified further by the following argument. Treatment often takes place in confinement. Confinement itself has been defined as punishment.[52] Therefore, treatment, when it takes place in confinement, can be punishment. If the inmate has the right to accept or refuse treatment and possibly even choose what kind of treatment, then it would seem that the inmate may, therefore, have the right to choose punishment (confinement) as his or her treatment. This may seem somewhat oblique, but such an interpretation is theoretically correct and could be put into practice. Courts have not decided such a case, but individuals sentenced in criminal or juvenile court who are classified as psychopaths and receive indeterminate sentences may be expected to raise this issue in the near future.[53]

Procedural Rights Outside the Justice System

Do juveniles, both delinquent and nondelinquent, have rights other than those specifically associated with the juvenile justice system? If so, what are they? To a limited extent, juveniles do have the same rights as other citizens. The term *limited extent* is used because these rights are not always acknowledged or honored. One of the major reasons for this lack of acknowledgment is that a juvenile's age of majority (adulthood) is adult-defined and until this age is attained, a juvenile is considered a child or second-class citizen. They include such things as their rights under laws governing employment and employment practices, driving, contracts and legal agreements, voting, drinking, drugs, marriage, sex, abortion, operating a business, rights in educational institutions, rights of children with regard to parents and home, and their right to the means to maintain an adequate standard of living.

The two most important institutions which hold almost totalitarian control over the life of the juvenile are the school and the family. We will look at the rights of the child vis-à-vis these institutions. In *Children's Rights, The Legal Rights of Minors in Conflict with Law or Social Custom*, Klapmuts explains:

> The child has little legal recourse against school or family and conflict with either can land him in juvenile court, under present definitions of court

jurisdiction. Together the parents and the school have the power and the means to deny the child the degree of liberty and independence (commensurate with his capabilities and level of maturity) that is necessary for his growth and development. As long as parents can turn their children over to the courts or institutions as "incorrigible," and as long as schools can suspend, expel, or otherwise discipline students arbitrarily and without challenge, the rights of children are in serious danger.

Because both parents and schools are responsible for controlling and disciplining minors to some extent, finding a proper balance is not a simple matter. Between the extreme positions of those who argue for complete self-government by children and those who advocate a return to old-fashioned authoritarian discipline, another view is gaining acceptance in the literature and in the courts: that due process and fair procedure, which permits the child to make himself heard, is required in decisions that importantly affect a child's life and future development.

Courts and legislatures have been understandably reluctant to intervene in the child's relationship with parents and the home except in cases of neglect or physical abuse. The right of parents to deal with their children as they see fit has only recently been questioned. This new emphasis on a child's right to protection from exploitation, even by those who act as his guardians, is summed up in a draft charter of children's rights published by the Advisory Centre for Education in England. One of several provisions which distinguish this charter from earlier efforts states that "children have the right to protection from any excessive claims made on them by their parents or others in authority over them . . . no one shall have the power to infringe a child's rights."[54]

In addition to recommendations that the child be entitled to separate counsel when his interests conflict with those of his parents, recent efforts to protect the child from his protectors have included (1) claims that counsel for the child must defend the child's stated interests rather than his own or others' opinions about what is best for him;[55] (2) measures to insure the child's right to be heard in custody litigation, to have independent counsel, and, if he is old enough, to choose where and how he will live; and (3) some statutory changes to define the juvenile as "emancipated" for limited purposes, such as to obtain medical treatment without parental consent or knowledge. The legal status of emancipation, whether applied to all juveniles for a specific purpose or broadly conferred on individuals who qualify as emancipated minors,[56] is one means of achieving some balance of rights and responsibilities and protection from the inappropriate exercise of parental authority.

The rights of the child as student are somewhat better defined. While the law is still undeveloped and court decisions have not been consistent, a significant body of court rulings favoring student rights is forming as litigation by students against schools increases. An overview of the pertinent decisions in the context of recent developments in juvenile court is provided in a handbook for school personnel, published by the National Juvenile Law Center.[57] Decisions have dealt with constitutional rights of students in substantive questions such as dress codes and hair length, picketing and demonstrations, censorship of school newspapers, and marriage and pregnancy, but the emphasis has been on due process requirements that restrict the schools in disciplining students who violate school rules and regulations. Recognizing the severe consequences of denial of an education through expulsion from school, courts have established the general rule that a child may not be expelled or given lengthy suspension for misconduct unless he has been notified of the charges against him and given a hearing.[58] Although the full protections of a court hearing as outlined in *Gault* are not usually required, some schools have set up procedures that approximate court review.[59]

The right to an adequate standard of living is reflected by the number of children receiving public assistance in the form of Aid for Dependent Children (ADC). "In 1974 there were approximately 10.2 million children under 18 in low-income families; 3.29 million of them were under age six."[60] There were about 3.0 million families on ADC in 1973.[61] Aside from ADC, the Social Security system and the Veterans Administration provide assistance to qualified families, regardless of income level. There is also Child Development Head Start, Child Development–Child Welfare Research and Demonstration Grants, Public Assistance–Social Services, Work Incentive Programs, and Community Service Training Grants.

While some people may decry "welfare cheaters" and claim most persons on welfare are not willing to work, it is generally accepted that children, at least, should receive public assistance. ADC expenditures may be seen as a "necessary evil."

Another right of juveniles is the right to employment and protection against employer abuses.[62] The labor market experiences of juveniles has been discussed in national juvenile justice administration policy sessions for many years. Initially, there was concern because of the high rate of unemployment, but later the emphasis shifted to poor job preparation and insufficient occupational training for youths who enter the labor market with less than a college degree.

Substantive Rights of Minors

Substantive rights are the basic rights of a human being, such as life, liberty, and the pursuit of happiness, which are not dependent on manmade laws. While there has been some resolution in the area of procedural rights for juveniles, the issue of their substantive rights has remained virtually unexamined.

Substantive rights are especially important when discussing children who present no real threat either to themselves or to society. These children are often controlled by laws, regulations, and rules which would make an adult's life-style unbearable.

Substantive rights used to be expressed in terms of protection and welfare. The new substantive rights are a decidedly different breed; they include the right to refuse an unwanted service, the right to make or participate in choices that affect one's life, and the right to be free from unnecessary restrictions in individual development. "Underlying all efforts to define these new rights is the question of whether children, as well as adults, have a fundamental interest in privacy that might be expressed as the 'right to be left alone'."[63] According to Klapmuts,

> When Justice Brandeis described the "right to be left alone" by the government as the right "most valued by civilized men,"[64] he was concerned with the right of *adult* citizens to at least some freedom from public intrusion. Since then, the right to privacy has received some attention, but its scope, even for adults, remains untested. This right, based on a combination of the Fourth and Fifth Amendments and related to the First and Third, has been invoked in a number of cases to invalidate laws governing the private behavior of adults. While the right of the child to be left alone has not been tested in court, the concept has been used to measure the extent of undue interference in the lives of children whose behavior does not conflict with a compelling interest of the state.
>
> . . .
>
> Should the courts come out strongly in favor of the child's right to be left alone, this right would undoubtedly be invoked to test the constitutionality of a wide range of laws and official actions that currently limit the freedom of minors. The right to privacy and free choice in decisions to behave in a manner which, though socially disapproved, is not demonstrably harmful is already implicit in recommendations to decriminalize victimless behavior (including that of juveniles) and in court decisions holding that the behavior and appearance of students can be restricted only upon proof by the school that the learning process is thereby disrupted. It might be used to test the extent and nature of the state's interest in compulsory education (already dealt with by courts in the case of the Amish), or to determine the legality of a host of involuntary measures now officially imposed on "predelinquent" or otherwise troublesome juveniles. The right to be left alone most obviously underlies the dissatisfaction that many have expressed with the broad and vague jurisdiction of the juvenile court and justice system.[65]

Summary

We have discussed the procedural rights of juveniles within the court system and their substantive rights in this chapter. What will be the eventual impact of the recent "revolution" in juvenile rights on the juvenile justice system has yet to be determined. However, as juveniles gain equal rights and protections under the law, they are losing the sometimes useful and heretofore "protective" cover of *parens patriae*.

For example, Attica proved that violent riots can result in the deaths of inmates. If juveniles are eventually treated as equals with adults, will they then be also exposed to the potential dangers which might befall adults? If an adult attempts an escape from prison he or she may be shot and even killed in the process. Thousands upon thousands of youth "run" or escape from training schools and juvenile institutions each year. What would be the public reaction if several of them were wounded or killed in their attempts?

Adult correctional facilities, staffed with armed guards, are places where security and control are guiding considerations. Should we turn our relatively insecure youth camps into likenesses of these facilities?

Currently juveniles are protected from being identified in newspapers and from being fingerprinted until age 16. Should we change these practices and ensure exacting equality between juveniles and adults?

One thing is relatively clear: the juvenile offender of today is potentially the adult offender of tomorrow. How we treat and react to these juveniles now may have great bearing on whether or not we will have to deal with them later, as adults when they are at least guaranteed their full constitutional rights.

REVIEW QUESTIONS

1. Define the following terms:
   a. Procedural rights
   b. Substantive rights
   c. Due process

2. Discuss the major court cases upon which the procedural rights of juveniles within the court are based.

3. What ramifications would the right to trial by jury have on the juvenile justice system? Explain.

4. What are the advantages and disadvantages of juveniles receiving the same protection and constitutional rights as adults?

5. What is meant by the "right to punishment"? How could this right be applied within the juvenile justice system?

NOTES

1. Nora Klapmuts, *Children's Rights* (Hackensack, N.J.: 1974), National Council on Crime and Delinquency, p. 27. (See R. H. Bremner, ed., *Children and Youth in America—A Documentary History,* vol. 2, 1866–1932, parts 1–6 (Cambridge, Mass.: Harvard University Press, 1971), p. 487.

2. Martin T. Silver, "The New York City Family Court: A Law Guardian's Overview," *Crime and Delinquency* 18 (1972): 93–98.

3. Anthony M. Platt, *The Child Savers* (Chicago: University of Chicago, 1969), p. 168.

4. See *Gallegos* v. *Colorado,* 370 U.S. 49, 3 LED (2d) 325, 82 SCT 1209, 87 ALR (2d) 614 (1962) for further discussion on right to counsel and the waiver of such a right.

5. M. L. Midonick, *Children, Parents, and the Courts: Juvenile Delinquency, Ungovernability and Neglect* (New York: Practicing Law Institute, 1972), p. 1.

6. *Miranda* v. *Arizona,* 384 U.S. 436, 448 (1966).

7. Ibid 403 U.S. 541 (1971).

8. Ibid at 545.

9. Ibid at 547.

10. Juvenile Justice and Delinquency Act of 1974: P.L. 93-415: Signed into law September 7, 1974.

11. *In re Gault,* 387 U.S. 1,33 (1967).

12. Douglas J. Besharov, *Juvenile Justice Advocacy: Practice in a Unique Court* (New York: Practicing Law Institute, 1974), p. 227. [(See, *Doe* v. *State,* 487 p. 2d 47 (Alaska, 1971); Cal. Welfare and Institutions Code §660 (b) (West 1973). But see *Casanova* v. *State,* supra n. 7 (holding that a juvenile lacks the capacity to waive service of notice)].

13. Council of Judges of NCCD, *Provision of Counsel in Juvenile Courts* (New York: National Council on Crime and Delinquency, 1970), p. 21.

14. Ibid., p. 20.

15. Frederick L. Faust and Paul J. Brantingham, *Juvenile Justice Philosophy* (St. Paul, Minn.: West, 1974), p. 247.

16. 478 p. 2d 608 (Wyoming, 1970).

17. 383 U.S. 541 (1966).

18. *Winship,* 397 U.S. 358, 365–66 (1970). (See also *Debacher* v. *Bainard* 396 U.S. 28, 6Crl 3001).

19. See for example *In re Richard S.,* 27 N.Y. 2d 802, 264 N.E. 2d. 353, 315 N.Y.S. 2d 861 (1970).

20. The doubt expressed must be one which a reasonable man or woman would express when presented with all of the evidence.

21. *McKiever* v. *Pennsylvania* 403 U.S. 548 (1971).

22. *Ex parte* State *ex rel.* Simpson, 288 Alabama, 535, 263, So. 2d. 137 (1972).

23. For example, see *M.* v. *Superior Court,* 4 Cal. App. 3d 370, 482 P.2d 664, 93 Ca. Rptr. 752 (1971).

24. Besharov, *Juvenile Justice Advocacy,* p. 287.

25. E. Z. Fester, and T. F. Courtless, "The Beginning of Juvenile Justice: Police Practices and the Juvenile Offender," *Vanderbilt Law Review* 22 (1969): 567–608.

26. Commissioners on Uniform State Laws, Uniform Juvenile Court Act, Section 27 B, 1968.

27. Children's Bureau, U.S. Department of Health, Education, and Welfare, "Legislative Guide for Drafting Family and Juvenile Court Acts" (Washington, D.C.: U.S. Government Printing Office), p. 20.

28. Ohio is one example of such a state. [See Ohio Rev. Code title 21 §2151.31 (supp. 1972); Uniform Juvenile Court Act §13(b) (1968).]

29. Besharov, *Juvenile Justice Advocacy,* pp. 104–105.

30. 332 U.S. 596 (1948).

31. Ibid. at 599.

32. 370 U.S. 49 (1962).

33. Besharov, *Juvenile Justice Advocacy*, p. 97. [See *Charling* v. *U.S.*, 295 f. 2d 161 (D.C. Cir. 1961); *In re Gregory W.*, 19 N.Y. 2d. 55, 224 N.E. 2d. 102, 277 N.Y.S. 2d 675 (1966)].

34. *Miranda* v. *Arizona* 384 U.S. 436, 448 (1966).

35. Richard Kobetz, *The Police Role and Juvenile Delinquency* (Baltimore: International Association of Chiefs of Police, 1971), p. 132.

36. See, for example, California Welfare and Institutions Code §702.5 (West 1973).

37. Besharov, *Juvenile Justice Advocacy*, p. 231.

38. *In re Washington*, 391 U.S. 341 (1968).

39. J. Michael Keating et al., *Grievance Mechanisms in Correctional Institutions* (Washington, D.C.: U.S. Government Printing Office, September, 1975), p. 1.

40. Ibid., p. 5.

41. Quoted in "Prison Grievance Procedures: A National Survey of Programs Underway", *Corrections Magazine*, January–February, 1975, p. 41.

42. The Academy of Contemporary Problems, The Group For The Advancement of Corrections, "Toward A New Corrections Policy: Two Declarations of Principles," 1974; p. 10.

43. National Council on Crime and Delinquency, "A Model Act for the Protection of Rights of Prisoners" (Paramus, N.J.: NCCD, 1972), p. 17.

44. Ibid.

45. For example, see Michigan Comp. Laws 712-A (supp. 1973).

46. Jeffrey E. Glen and Weber, J. Robert, *The Juvenile Court: A Status Report* (Washington, D.C.; National Institute of Mental Health: 1971). See also: Supreme Bench of Baltimore City, Memorandum Opinion: Juvenile Detention Center, Baltimore City Jail, Baltimore, August, 1971, pp. 9–12.

47. Juvenile Court of the District of Columbia, In the Matter of: Joseph Franklin Savoy and Tony Hazel, p. 16.

48. *Creek* v. *Stone*, 379 f. 2d. 106,111 (D.C. Cir. 1967).

49. Besharov, *Juvenile Justice Advocacy*, p. 435.

50. *Morales* v. *Turman*, No. 74-3436, U.S. Court of Appeals, Fifth Circuit (July 21, 1976) and *Morales* v. *Turman*, ED Tex. 1974 383 F Supp. 53.

51. B. G. Toomey, C. E. Simonsen, and H. E. Allen, "The Right to Treatment: A Socio-Legal Examination," Program for the Study of Crime and Delinquency, The Ohio State University, 1974, p. 39. (Unpublished monograph.)

52. *Cross* v. *Harris*, 418 F. 2d 1095.

53. Toomey, Simonsen, and Allen, "The Right to Treatment," pp. 39–40.

54. Advisory Centre for Education, "A Draft Charter of Children's Rights," Cambridge, England, 1971.

55. Stephen Wizner, "The Defense Counsel: Neither Father, Judge, Probation Officer, or Social Worker," *Trial* 7 (1971), pp. 30–31.

56. An "emancipated minor" is generally above a certain age (usually 16 to 18), living apart from family, and adequately supporting himself or herself.

57. National Juvenile Law Center, *The Legal Rights of Secondary School Children Charged with an Act of Delinquency or Violation of School Rules* (St. Louis: St. Louis University, 1971).

58. Ibid., pp. 18–19.

59. Klapmuts, *Children's Rights*, pp. 14–16.

60. Department of Justice, Office of Juvenile Justice and Delinquency Prevention, "First Comprehensive Plan for Federal Juvenile Delinquency Programs" (Washington, D.C.: G.P.O., 1976), p. 48.

61. Ibid.

62. See Frances Fox Piven and Richard A. Cloward, *Regulating the Poor* (New York: Pantheon, 1971).

63. Ibid., p. 77.

64. Klapmuts, *Children's Rights*, p. 19.

65. *Olmstead* v. *United States*, 277 U.S. 438, 478 (1928).

15 Preventing Delinquency

Two major myths concerning delinquency prevention permeate the American scene—first, that "nothing can be done about it," and second, that "somewhere there is a neat and simple cure for the problem." The average citizen frequently finds himself floundering between these two extremes.

WILLIAM C. KVARACEUS

The problem of preventing delinquent behavior and youth crime becomes increasingly important as the number of juvenile offenses continues to climb. Because of the paucity of effective programs aimed at the prevention of juvenile delinquency, the Law Enforcement Assistance Administration (LEAA) allocated $10 million for priority discretionary programs in this area in November, 1976. The authors have extracted relevant materials from the background paper contained in that program announcement bulletin, from the volume of the National Advisory Commission on Criminal Justice Standards and Goals, *Community Crime Prevention,* and from the President's Commission on Law Enforcement and the Administration of Justice, *Task Force Report: Juvenile Delinquency and Youth Crime.* These are the most authoritative current sources for this critical area of study in the juvenile justice system.

Background to the Prevention Problem

Preventing is unmistakably preferable to punishing delinquency. By the time a youth has become involved with the juvenile justice system, too much damage has already been done. It is clear, though, that prevention is a long-range and complex goal and that ways must yet be found to deal with the causes of delinquency among contemporary youth and to disrupt the sequence of events that results in wrongdoing. The design of prevention strategies can only be guided by our admittedly limited knowledge of the origins of delinquent behavior.

Over the past fifty years, numerous approaches to delinquency and delinquency prevention have been proposed, written about, and tested. However, the prevention aspect of juvenile delinquency is the least sophisticated aspect of delinquency intervention. Very little that has been done to prevent lawbreaking activities has seemed to work. There is a shortage of hard data to describe its dynamics. But whatever approaches are taken to resolve the problem will have to consider a few core characteristics.

The first of these characteristics is a dramatic increase in juvenile crime during recent years. This does not refer to changes in status offenses, but to increases in arrests for offenses which would be crimes if committed by adults. From 1960 through 1974, official statistics show an increase of 138 percent in youth arrests for all crimes, and an increase of 254 percent in youth arrests for the four violent index crimes—murder, rape, robbery, and aggravated assault. Even allowing for a substantial margin of error because of changes in reporting procedures and growth in the size of the youth population, the increase in arrests implies a rapid and major increase in real offense rates.

A second characteristic is that disproportionate numbers of youth from low-income, low-status families in the inner city fill the court records and juvenile correctional facilities of this country. What these figures mean continues to be a subject of debate. Studies which distinguish between "official" delinquency and delinquent behavior have argued that official records more often reflect differential rates of apprehension, disposition by the police, and adjudication by the courts than real differences in delinquency rates. Other observers argue that real delinquency rates remain especially severe among youth from poor, crowded, urban environments. Whether the statistics reflect real differences in offense rates or real differences in arrest rates, they do delineate an especially severe problem in the inner city.

Delinquency Prevention Overview

The many approaches to delinquency prevention that have been proposed may, for purposes of an overview, be classified according to several foci: the individual offender; the offender's social and physical environment; and the delinquency-defining process. These categories overlap, and the differences among them are, in part, a matter of emphasis. They are helpful in calling attention to the variety of approaches to delinquency prevention that have been considered, however, and a summary review of activities representative of each of these three approaches is given below.

The *individual approach* dominated the field from the 1920s until the 1950s, and is still a component of many prevention programs. This position focuses on the pathology of the individual as a contributing factor; it includes the identification of emotional, motivational, and attitudinal factors that could explain delinquency. In general, advocates of prevention from the individual perspective see psychotherapy, social casework, individual counseling, or behavior therapy as the means by which clients will be able to resolve their personality conflicts and assume a positive orientation toward society.

One of the first programmatic expressions of the individual approach was the series of Child Guidance Centers established by Healey in the 1920s. The goals of these centers were to study psychiatric problems of predelinquent and delinquent children and to develop means of treating them. Similar counseling programs became predominant during the 1940s and 1950s, but social scientists recognized that not all delinquent behavior resulted from repressed desires, unconscious conflicts, or any other ready psychiatric explanations. Typologies were developed to distinguish among delinquent types. One of the most prominent of these has been the Interpersonal Maturity Level Classification of Sullivan, Grant, and Grant, modified by Warren, which was designed to facilitate a match between the treatment strategy and the individual's level of functioning.

The individual approach to delinquency is still the basis of the vast majority of existing delinquency prevention programs. Innovations in the approach also continue as problems within the individual are seen to interact with programs based on other approaches.

The *environmental* approach views situational conditions as the dominant factor in stimulating and perpetuating delinquent activity. This approach assumes that cultural and social systems produce reactions in individuals which cause them either to conform to or deviate from legitimate standards. It further assumes that the delinquent behavior of youth living in "high-risk" settings can be reduced by remodeling and reorganizing the community so that potential offenders can find positive alternatives to delinquent activity. Programs using this approach attempt to deal with significant social institutions which have impact on youth, including legitimate institutions like the school or family and "illegitimate" institutions like gangs, street corner groups, and pool halls. These programs have been characterized by community-wide efforts to offset social and family disorganizations, to mobilize the community and its service providers to meet the needs of youth, and to develop educational programs that will help prepare youth to find their place in society.

Another major class of environmentally based programs was based on the notion of opportunity enhancement, which reached its peak of application in the 1960s. The theoretical underpinnings of these programs were expressed in Cloward and Ohlin's theory of delinquency and opportunity. Cloward and Ohlin developed the thesis that while lower-class youth have internalized conventional goals, these are blocked by their social and economic environment, which produce frustrations which, in turn, lead to nonconformist (and delinquent) behavior. According to this logic, prevention efforts should be targeted toward institutions which could, but do not now, provide youth with opportunities for success in conventional areas. Reflecting these assumptions, the massive Mobilization for Youth project was begun in New York City in 1962. This project attacked conditions believed to cause delinquency; it funneled funds into employment programs, education programs, community organizations, and the provision of services to individuals and families. Although it was intended to "prove opportunity theory" by finding variance in delinquency according to a community's ability to cope with and conquer barriers to mobility, MFY was too long-range, complex, and loosely controlled to establish this correlation.

One of the more recent programs within the same social-institutional framework is the California Youth Authority's Youth Development/Delinquency Prevention Project. This project seeks to increase public tolerance of youthful acting-out behavior, to increase a youth's attachment to social norms through concerted community action, and to reduce opportunities to commit crimes. One demonstration effort, for example, used an existing crisis intervention center to serve as the nucleus for a community development operation aimed at involving both governmental agencies and indigenous groups.

The third theoretical approach, emphasizing the *labeling process*, offers still a different view of delinquency prevention. This position considers most delinquency programs harmful as well as ineffective. It questions the use of the legal system to enforce conformity of behavior to social norms. Fundamental to this approach is the observation that delinquents are frequently not different from nondelinquents. Virtually all youth in the community, it is argued, have at some time been guilty of delinquent misconduct. Singling out only some of those delinquents may contribute to their behavior, however. Prevention activities must avoid the effects of labeling and, instead, strive for a universality of application to all children.

Consistent with this approach is Lemert's contention that criminal careers develop because youth are stigmatized as deviant by social control agencies (the police, the courts, etc.), that this negative experience itself stimulates youth offenses and perpetuates a cycle that frequently carries into adulthood. Advocates of this position favor changes in social policy which would minimize intervention in the lives of so-called delinquents and increase equity in the dispensation of justice. In part, this approach is reflected in current trends of deinstitutionalization and diversion.

Before leaving this overview it would seem appropriate to ask if any of these approaches work? There are two very different answers. First, virtually no prevention program has been able to document its impact on juvenile crime. Second, many programs were nonetheless concerned with filling in gaps and deficiencies in youths' lives which are highly correlated with delinquency. Programs of this sort at least appear to be aimed at the right targets.

The reasons for the lack of demonstrable prevention results are not obscure. One of them is that delinquency is too complex and springs from too many causes to be prevented by any one program. A single program typically engages only a fraction of a youth's time and attention, and it is not surprising that its effects may be overpowered by the other day-to-day forces acting on the child, or by the accumulation of effects that occurred prior to the child's involvement in the program.

A second reason has to do with developmental influences on delinquency. It appears that roughly half of the juveniles who are contacted by the police are not contacted a second time. Further, it has frequently been noted that positive changes in behavior occur independently of a youth's experience in a prevention project. This leads to the view that correction of youthful behavior is more a matter of maturation than of programmatic intervention. Prevention in this context is not measured by the absence of any evidence of criminal behavior, but by a damping of effects to the level of "ordinary" maturational deviance, so that a slide into chronic criminal activity is avoided.

These comments point also to a third important reason for the lack of demonstrable results: the state of the art in evaluation technology. Demonstrating that an event has *not* occurred but would have occurred in the absence of a program is a difficult technical problem. Developing accurate measures and data collection procedures for assessing delinquent behavior is equally difficult, as is the task of isolating the effects of any social action programs from the many other sources of variance. Combined, these obstacles typically demand more from evaluations of prevention programs than available resources or the state of the art can bear. Consequently, the real prevention value of many programs remains essentially untested.

Citizen Action

Citizen involvement in crime prevention efforts is not merely desirable but necessary. The reports of the President's Commission on Law Enforcement and Administration of Justice emphasize the need for direct action to improve law enforcement and for crime prevention to become the business of every American institution and of every American. Police and other specialists alone cannot control crime; they need "all the help the community can give them."[1]

Similarly, a task force of the National Commission on the Causes and Prevention of Violence noted:

> Government programs for the control of crime are unlikely to succeed all alone. Informed private citizens, playing a variety of roles, can make a decisive difference in the prevention, detection and prosecution of crime, the fair administration of justice, and the restoration of offenders to the community.[2]

These and other pleas for citizen action are heeded by too few. Most citizens agree that crime prevention is everybody's business, but too many fail to accept crime prevention as everybody's duty.

The idea that crime prevention is each citizen's duty is not new. In the early days of law enforcement, well over a thousand years ago, the peacekeeping system encouraged the concept of mutual responsibility. Each individual was responsible not only for his actions but for those of his neighbors. A citizen observing a crime had the duty to rouse his neighbors and pursue the criminal. Peace was kept, for the most part, not by officials but by the whole community.

Many crime prevention authorities believe that, for some anticrime programs, the responsibility for planning, decision, and action should be placed at the lowest level consistent with sound decision making—that is, in the neighborhood with the individual citizen.

The typical citizen response to the crime problem is a demand for greater action by the police, courts, correctional institutions, and other government agencies. The citizen asks too infrequently what he can do himself. And when the public does decide to act, its activities often are short-lived, sporadic outbursts in response to a particularly heinous crime or one that occurred too close to home.

Fortunately, this limited and frequently counter-productive type of citizen action shows signs of yielding to more informed citizen involvement in crime prevention efforts.

Other organizations through which citizens can encourage crime prevention efforts include trade associations, educational institutions, political parties, unions, charities, foundations, and professional societies. Several years ago the executive vice president of the American Institute of Certified Public Accountants issued this call to action to his profession:

> There are already cases on record where publicly traded companies have become dominated by hoodlums. A CPA should be watchful of changes in ownership and management of his clients.
>
> If he finds a once solid company taken over or influenced by unsavory elements, he may have to make a difficult decision. He may decide to withdraw from the engagement or he may feel obligated to remain on the scene to protect innocent investors and creditors.
>
> The auditor is expected to have absolute integrity. Any evidence of organized crime coming his way should trigger prompt and drastic action to discharge his professional responsibilities. It should also bring forth cooperation with authorities to discharge his civic duties.[3]

No one is asking an organization to make extraordinary sacrifices on behalf of crime prevention. What is suggested is that decisions relating to daily operations be reviewed in terms of their crime prevention impact as well as other criteria.

Collective efforts by citizens may be directed at strengthening the crime prevention activities of government agencies (e.g., courts, corrections, and law enforcement agencies), or at bolstering anticrime measures undertaken exclusively within the private sector.

Citizens may participate in the crime prevention efforts of government agencies by attending community relations meetings conducted by the local police department, working as volunteers in a probation program administered by the city court, donating time as parole volunteers under the supervision of a state parole commission, or volunteering to help a municipal social or rehabilitative agency improve the delivery of its services.

Important as it is, individual action independent of the efforts of others is not enough. Our society is built upon the premise that each person is responsible for himself and for the general welfare of others. Exclusive reliance on a self- or family-oriented approach to crime prevention causes individuals and family units to become isolated from one another. The result is that the crime prevention effectiveness of the community as a whole becomes considerably less than that of the sum of its parts.

Indeed, with each citizen looking out for himself only, there is no community, no strength in numbers, but rather a fragmentation that can serve only to embolden criminal elements.

Without a sense of community, the crime prevention potential of mutual aid and mutual responsibility is unfulfilled. As noted by one authority on juvenile delinquency:

> Although little systematic research has been done in this area, the reported incidences of communities getting "together" suggest that active "community involvement" in fighting the problems may well be an effective way, and perhaps *the* most effective way, to prevent and reduce crime and delinquency.[4]

Whether frayed by the rise of specialization and professionalism, or eroded by the availability of an overpowering and, perhaps, overprotective institutional structure of urban life, the fibers of mutual assistance and neighborliness that bind citizens to a sense of community have grown precariously thin. Citizen involvement in crime prevention, at all levels, must take care to reinforce, not sever, those fibers.

Attacking Crime's Infrastructure

Citizens can prevent crime by focusing their attention on the social factors that lead to crime, e.g., unemployment, poor education, and lack of recreational opportunities.

Education

Since deviant behavior is the result, in part, of learned socialization processes, the social environment, including the schools, can help to motivate either law-abiding or delinquent behavior.[5, 6]

A great failure of the American educational system is that it has not sufficiently separated its responsibility to provide learning conditions for the development of human beings from its concern with operating schools. It has not seen itself as part of a process providing differential experiences for people maturing into adults. As a consequence, it has found little need to look at itself as an instrument which would contribute to either the prevention or production of crime.

Overemphasis on competition and achievement and insistence that all students constantly struggle for recognition, grades, and scholarships has sometimes resulted in feelings of hostility or hopelessness. In part, this frustration produces rebellion against the society that condones such practices.

The lack of meaningful, parental participation in school programs is another major problem. Even though it is generally recognized that family participation in school affairs influences children's educational success or failure, there has yet been no widespread involvement of parents in the teaching process.

There is also an almost complete absence in school organization and procedures of deliberated examples of justice, respect for privacy, redress of grievance, and other democratic processes.

The rarity of clear learner objectives or of the means for insuring that teachers with demonstrated competencies will help students reach these objectives is also evident. In no state is licensing or tenure dependent upon real proof of ability to impart skills or knowledge to young people. There is practically no consensus on minimum learning goals, what students should experience to reach these goals, or how to evaluate teachers' performances.

Finally, there is an absence of significant cooperation between the schools and other segments of the community. The increasing isolation of the school from the main currents of community life—business, government, church, and social organizations—heightens its irrelevancy in the minds of students, makes its authority suspect, and thus impugns the reasonableness of all authority.

There are doubtless many other aspects of the educational system that bear on the issue of crime prevention, directly or indirectly. Some, like finances and administration, may be as important as those mentioned above.

Many citizens are involved in encouraging school dropouts to complete their education. The "Keep a Child in School" program in Charleston, West Virginia, attempts to meet this objective by working with students on a one-to-one basis and insuring that they have adequate clothes and supplies. This program also provides tutors for students who have fallen behind in their work or need special help.

Other groups have found it is necessary to offer alternative educational opportunities, such as street academies or vocational programs. New York City's Harlem Prep is one of the best known and most successful street academies. It is supported by contributions from foundations and industry and its purpose is to prepare dropouts for college.

Many parents donate their services to schools on an almost daily basis, by preparing instructional materials and assisting teachers in the classroom. Citizen action has contributed to the establishment of community schools and to the formation of neighborhood councils that advise school administrators.

Employment

The average offender, particularly the offender who serves a term of imprisonment, is a loser in the world of work. Characteristics of enrollees in criminal treatment projects uniformly reveal high levels of unemployment and peripheral work patterns. Some of the best available data comes from a comprehensive 1964 survey of males released from federal prisons. This survey shows that 11 percent of the group had never been employed and more than half had been employed a total of less than 2 years before incarceration, even though their median age was 29 years.[7]

Data suggest that for every offender with employment problems there are many nonoffenders in equally serious trouble. Many nonoffenders also have motivational problems, low skills, educational deficiencies, and limited opportunities.

The economically disadvantaged are a minority of the total work force but a majority of the offender population. Statistically, then, they are much more likely to commit crimes than those with greater success in the labor market. Just as the boundaries between legal and illicit activities have become obscured in the subcultures of crime, the distinction between the offender and the nonoffender has become blurred. The losers in the competition for jobs must be regarded as a pool of potential offenders requiring preventive help and attention.

In many core city areas, street life often leads to contact with the law as part of growing up. The late teens, when economic necessity is not usually a prime motivation, are a period of testing and search in the labor market.

Problems can arise when economic opportunities are limited. It has been estimated that between 50 and 90 percent of all inner-city males have a serious encounter with the law before they reach age 25. Arrest records often rule out legitimate employment. An arrest record, which seems almost inevitable for young males in the inner city, often increases the likelihood that these youths will turn to illegal activities.

Businessmen and others are working to place disadvantaged youths in summer and part-time jobs during the school year. The National Alliance of Businessmen's JOBS program is the largest program of this type. They have placed almost 1 million youths in part-time and summer jobs provided by private business and industry.

At the urging of the Urban Coalition and other citizen organizations, some companies have agreed to fill a certain percentage of new jobs with the hard-core unemployed and to set new eligibility standards in this regard. In Riverside, California, a group of employers founded the Job Opportunities Council to recruit the hard-core unemployed and to handle the paperwork involved.

Citizen groups are promoting "hire first, train later" programs, whereby an applicant undergoes a 2-week orientation program prior to being placed with an employer who agrees to provide on-the-job training and other support.

Many citizen organizations provide job counseling and training. Project Bread began in Salem, Massachusetts, as the idea of one individual, who started teaching ex-addicts how to earn a living as cooks. Other groups are active in disseminating job opportunity information to those who live in high unemployment areas.

Recreation

Recreation is common to all peoples and cultures. In its most fundamental sense, the term implies a pastime, a diversion, a respite from labor. Whatever serves to refresh or renew the person's physical or psychic energies is properly termed recreation and answers a completely human need.

Recreation means different things to different people. A definition broad enough to encompass many points of view was used in a recent demonstration project by the California Youth Authority:

> Recreation is the joyful exercise of body, mind and social spirit, of performing and creating skill; that it is to create anew, to restore to good condition the body and the mind, to refresh. Probably the best definition of all is attributed to a little boy, who said that recreation is what you do when you don't have to.
>
> Recreation can be mental, physical, social, or a combination of all three. It may be organized or unorganized, planned or spontaneous, pursued individually or in groups. Recreation provides the opportunity for release and realization of desires for recognition, for adventure, for achievement, for belonging and for self-discovery. Leisure is the time away from work or other necessary activity. Play is the spirit of true recreation. To be truly recreation an activity must involve voluntary participation. While it has no single, universal form, it must be determined by the motivation of the doer. It is serious and purposeful. It is flexible.[8]

Recreation ultimately must be defined by each individual, as one man's recreation may be another man's work. Clear-cut distinctions between work and play are illusory and dangerous; our efforts would be spent better in learning to combine work, leisure, and play in the cause of human enrichment and individual fulfillment.

Recreation is not trivial or inconsequential. It can be a powerful force in fostering an individual's sense of participation and belonging. Many authorities support this view, among them Harold Kennedy:

> Recreation is not, and cannot be expected to be, a panacea for all the antisocial forces of an unplanned society. At its rudimentary worst it can relieve the boredom of aimless leisure hours. At its finest it can illuminate the life of the individual with cultural electricity and solidify the community with the feeling of belonging.[9]

Some of the general principles for youth-oriented recreation programs are worth noting:

1. Recreation is a vital and significant part of life, and it is essential in a democratic society. It can be a positive force in the lives of all, particularly young people.
2. Recreation is a primary responsibility of every community and must be adequately provided to meet the needs of all youth, regardless of race, creed, or economic status.
3. Recreation must receive major attention in planning for the preservation and development of youth and in the prevention and control of delinquency. Government provision for recreation is needed at the local, state, and federal level.
4. Community recreation demands the mobilization and use of all resources—human, physical and fiscal; public, private, and commercial.
5. Youth services must be carefully planned and coordinated.
6. Recreation programs for youth require adequate legislation, funds, facilities, and the leadership of competent paid and volunteer staff.
7. Youth must have both planning and leadership responsibilities in such programs.
8. Recreation has therapeutic values as part of the social treatment of individuals and groups.[10]

A recreation-oriented delinquency prevention program must confront the major influences in the lives of young people. Furthermore, the delinquency prevention recreation activity must be integrated into the total unified delinquency prevention effort.

Special emphasis must be placed on programs that reach out to youths who traditionally reject or avoid established recreation programs, and the effectiveness of such efforts needs to be assessed. Youths whose behavior typically precludes their participation in recreation programs should be permitted to take part in programs designed to deal with disruptive behavior in the recreation setting. Counseling may be necessary to help change that behavior, and thus should be closely associated with the program either as part of it or as a referral option.

Religion

Religious organizations regularly respond to crises in our society. During a natural disaster churches, synagogues, and other religious groups may provide emergency funds and necessary facilities and equipment, or may enlist volunteers to meet the needs of stricken persons and institutions.

The term *crisis* can also be used to describe the nature and extent of crime in American society today. Like the crises created by natural disasters, the problem of crime calls for immediate, mobilized response by large segments of the community.

No one expects the religious community single-handedly to assume the responsibility for crime prevention, but the spiritual centers of the nation can become part of a massive new effort to reduce and prevent crime. The challenge confronts the whole society, not just a part of it. The religious community is a significant part of that society, and has valuable resources to commit to a worthy effort.

According to the Yearbook of American Churches,[11] there are more than 322,000 churches, synagogues, and temples in the United States, with total memberships of more than 128 million persons, or over half the population of this country. The congregations of all faiths, which are included in these statistics, can effectively participate in crime prevention, and their involvement is desperately needed.

The alienation, frustration, and bitterness that can produce illegal behavior often are intensified by apprehension, incarceration, and punishment. Persons convicted of crimes need rehabilitation, but rehabilitation is an after-the-fact effort. Many religious adherents and others believe that concern and assistance provided for troubled individuals before they turn to crime will obviate the need for costly and often ineffective rehabilitative services for convicted offenders. The criminal act makes more difficult the reversal of a person's negative outlook toward society.

Crime reflects the order of society. A rising crime rate is a symptom of disorder that can reach such proportions that only force and coercion can stem it. The police alone cannot be responsible for society's order, for that order depends not only on the law and its enforcement, but upon voluntary adherence to the moral and social principles underlying the law. Adherence helps create a climate of confidence that makes social order possible. A high rate of crime creates a low level of confidence in society. The religious community can address itself to the erosion of trust—between persons, in institutions, and in the government.

Fear may cause people to do the wrong thing; apathy insists that nothing can be done, or that someone else should do it. Many apathetic persons do not want to know about the crime problem or they want to refer it immediately to someone else.

In some cases, apathy may have resulted from an individual's past failures in attempting to find solutions to problems. Whatever its source, the present degree of apathy regarding crime has exempted large elements of the population from direct participation in responsible crime prevention efforts.

Religion can urge the faithful to take responsibility for crime prevention; it can promote empathy rather than apathy. Religious leaders can affirm that the individual is able to contribute toward solving society's problems once he becomes aware of those problems and accepts part of the responsibility for dealing with them.

The religious community could undoubtedly list many other concerns that would reinforce the challenge to its institutions to become directly involved in crime prevention efforts. In responding to that challenge, this community has unique resources that it can dedicate to an effort against crime. In addition to its spiritual resources and moral influence, it has buildings in strategic locations; trained personnel with specific skills; organizations with competency in planning and action; and access to large numbers of volunteers. The religious community also has facilities and equipment for educational and recreational activities; relationships with community organizations and communications networks; and links with state, regional, and national associations.

The religious community can ask its congregations across the nation what they can do to reduce crime and, more specifically, what individual members can do. Such questions can stimulate a flow of ideas and a reassessment of the resources available in the crime prevention effort.

Reduction of Criminal Opportunity

Reduction of the opportunity to commit crime through control and design of the physical environment is an important part of crime prevention. This approach treats crime not as a symptom of other factors that must be corrected but as an act that must be prevented. It attempts to inhibit illegal acts through a controlled physical environment.

Direct controls include only those that reduce environmental opportunities for crime, such as security hardware, street lighting, surveillance, and building design. The environment can be designed so that the individual considering a criminal act thinks that there is a good chance that he will be seen and recognized, that he will be identified immediately as a stranger or an intruder, and that someone will either take action on his own or contact the authorities.

Physical targets can be made so nearly crime-proof that an individual will be deterred from attempting a crime. This approach, often referred to as "target hardening," involves the use of security hardware. Proper use of such hardware can prevent some burglaries, or at least increase the time it takes to complete the criminal act, thereby increasing the chances of the offender's being detected and apprehended.

The fear of crime has caused some disturbing changes in society. It has pushed urban dwellers to the suburbs in ever-increasing numbers; those who stay behind protect themselves behind barred windows and doors and often refuse to go out at night.

In the face of rising crime rates, citizens of the middle and upper economic classes generally could choose between two alternatives: move to the relative safety of the suburbs or buy security in the city. Some who chose to stay in the city have isolated themselves in what has been described as the "fortress apartment." An example of this new life-style was presented by the National Commission on the Causes and Prevention of Violence:

> The entire development will be surrounded by two fences, broken for entry at only two points, both with guardhouses. Residents will be telephoned to approve visitors. The two miles of fencing will be surveyed by a closed circuit television system and fortified by hidden electronic sensors. All residents will carry special credentials for identification.[12]

As the fear of crime keeps people from the streets, parks, and other areas surrounding their homes, the chances that criminal activity will go unnoticed and undetected increase.

The physical design characteristics of residential complexes and housing—for example, architectural features such as the grouping of dwelling units or the design and placement of elevator doors and lobbies—can increase or decrease the probability that crimes will occur.

Oscar Newman, a New York city planner and architect, has identified certain spatial arrangements that promote feelings of proprietorship and increase the sense of community among tenants in public housing, which in turn lead residents to control their own security and encourage their defense of certain areas. Newman's book, *Defensible Space*, discusses the way design and location of housing can provide surveillance opportunities for tenants. For example, he recommends that: (1) semipublic areas such as elevators, halls, lobbies, and fire stairs, in which most crimes occur, be visible to residents and passersby; (2) front entrances be positioned along the street; (3) lobbies be well lit and designed so that all internal activity is visible from the street; (4) semiprivate areas such as paths and hallways be easily seen by tenants from apartment windows; and (5) elevators be monitored with electronic surveillance devices.

A study prepared by the Dillingham Corporation for the Southern California Association of Governments concluded:

> The importance of considering crime prevention in physical planning has not been recognized by other professions, agencies, and activities. A perusal of the planning literature including comprehensive plans for jurisdictions across the country demonstrated that crime prevention is not a crucial factor with planners. Some of the later plans have brief generalities concerning the need to include safety and security in the planning objectives but there is little evidence that the concern has been expressed in specific physical features.[13]

Perhaps this neglect on the part of planners and others involved in physical design stems from a lack of knowledge about crime prevention techniques. Although some research has been done on the relationship of the physical environment to crime, most of it is recent and inconclusive. For example, the effectiveness of lighting as a crime deterrent requires further study before firm conclusions can be drawn.

Designers in the future may have problems balancing crime prevention techniques with existing fire regulations and aesthetic considerations. But as residential crime increases, crime prevention must become one of the primary considerations in physical planning.

There must be effective communication and cooperation between law enforcement agencies, criminal justice planners, and professions involved in building design and physical planning. Such interaction, for example, could facilitate necessary changes in fire codes if it were found that existing regulations block the implementation of essential security measures.

Drug Abuse Treatment and Prevention

During the past decade, the nonmedical use of drugs by increasing numbers of people has emerged as a major national problem.[14] Attempts have been made to control this development through the application of criminal sanctions, through treatment of dysfunctional drug users, and through drug abuse prevention programs.

The multimodality approach to drug treatment should provide a comprehensive range of services to treat all drug users. This approach enables addicts to be treated in a program suited to their individual needs so that they may regain their position as functioning members of society.

Among the recommended elements of comprehensive drug treatment systems are:

- Crisis Intervention and Drug Emergency Centers.
- Facilities and personnel for methadone maintenance treatment programs.
- Facilities and personnel for narcotics antagonist programs.
- Therapeutic community programs staffed entirely or largely by ex-addicts.
- Closed and open residential treatment facilities as well as halfway houses staffed primarily by residents.

It has become clear that there is no one type of addict, but rather a variety of drug users with different degrees of involvement. Further, the great majority of users do not move on to heroin addiction. These points must be understood if treatment and prevention activities are to be rational and responsive to drug-related issues.

There are several different kinds of drug-taking behavior. These do not depend on the substance used or the source from which it is obtained. The following is a description of each type:

1. *Experimental user*. Drugs play no special or regular role in the experimental user's life. Use is episodic and reflects a desire to see what the drugs are like, or to test their effect on other activities ordinarily experienced without drugs.

2. *Social or recreational user*. Drugs are associated with social or recreational activities in which this type of user would take part whether or not drugs were present. Little or no time and effort are devoted to seeking out drugs or making connections to obtain them. The pattern of drug use is occasional and is situationally controlled.

3. *Seeker*. Drugs play a significant role in the seeker's life. Time is dedicated to seeking them out or making connections to obtain them. The user cannot enjoy or cope with some situations without drugs. Use of drugs may range from irregular to regular, controlled, or heavy daily use, although the individual may still remain functional and able to meet primary social and physical needs.

4. *Self-medicating user*. The self-medicator uses legally distributed tranquilizers or stimulants. While this type of use may have beneficial characteristics, it also can become a habitual way of responding to boredom, loneliness, frustration, and stress. The precise incidence of such chemical coping is unknown, but existing data suggest that it is extensive. It is necessary to learn more about the situations and experiences that move the self-medicator to dysfunctional use. At present it is only assumed that some type of emotional difficulty or problem underlies such use.

   Both self-medicators and seekers are attempting to deal with anxiety, depression, or other problems, and both often use drugs as a kind of self-therapy among other reasons.

5. *Dysfunctional drug user*. Drugs begin to dominate the life of the dysfunctional drug user. The process of securing and using them interferes with essential activities.

A conventional view of crime and drug addiction is that the first derives from the second. This view holds that addicts engage in illegal activities to obtain money to support their habits. Another view is that the kind of person most likely to start using drugs is the one also most prone to crime, with or without addiction.

According to some social scientists, for certain individuals both crime and drug abuse may be ways of "acting out" emotional needs for danger, excitement, and self-destructive experiences, or they may offer secondary rewards in terms of a subculture's restricted opportunities for legitimate achievement. Finestone and others have noted that criminality, drug use, and drug selling all may be high status forms of behavior in certain subcultures.[15]

These views may be partially correct, but the link between crime and drugs is too complex to be explained by simple formulas. Because of the criminal definition of the heroin problem, much of the subsequent crime may be related to the drug-seeking behavior. While this is especially true of the "street addict," there are other types of addicts who do not resort to crime and, in fact, may be functioning in conventional ways in other areas of living. The criminal activity, therefore, depends on both the individual and the context in which drug use occurs.

Before a community decides which approach to take in combating drug-related criminal action, it must renounce the prevailing untruths. For example, until recently, Americans saw all drug use as bad or dangerous, leading inevitably to heroin bondage. Marijuana was most often cited as the responsible substance. This imparted a hysterical quality to prevention efforts and often rendered them ineffective.

New prevention strategies based on a better understanding of the various kinds of drug involvement are available. Communities should incorporate this understanding into their planning and take steps to initiate thoughtful prevention activities.

Similarly, treatment strategies today permit a large number of drug users to be engaged constructively. The movement has been to individualize treatment and make it responsive to each drug user's problems. Guidelines for the development of comprehensive programs already exist. Communities are therefore in a position to select those program components that apply to their particular drug problems.

As noted earlier, it is essential to differentiate between the occasional drug experimenter, frequent abuser, and heavily involved dependent. Such distinctions are necessary to sort out the nonopiate drug use that is taking place in a conventional life-style from that associated with sociopathic or maladaptive behavior. These distinctions will encourage the emergence of action programs that reflect the needs of all kinds of drug abusers.

Prevention efforts at present continue to be hampered by a still incomplete understanding of the causes of drug abuse and dependence. The fields of psychology, sociology, and biochemistry provide important insights. However, it is still not possible to explain why many people with the same social, psychological, and biochemical characteristics as known addicts do not become drug users. In short, all of the variables have not yet been identified, nor is it known yet how the identified ones interrelate.

On the other hand, current knowledge permits certain generalizations about which persons are likely to become involved with drugs. It can, for example, be predicted with a high degree of certainty that there will be a greater incidence of heroin abuse among black inner city residents than among white suburbanites, and that the reverse will hold true for antianxiety drugs. Present knowledge also permits differential drug abuse patterns to be anticipated for males, females, adolescents, and adults. Large target populations can thus be identified for certain types of prevention work, even though it is not known with any certainty which particular individuals will become involved in drug abuse.[16]

Preliminary information is similarly available as to how people move toward drug usage—for example, what roles the family and peer groups play, and how knowledge about the potential danger of drug use influences drugs, especially if the providers of that information attempt only to making them afraid to try drugs. Others will choose not to experiment only when given empirical evidence of the physiological damage a particular drug can produce. Still others will simply be made curious by information about drugs, especially if the providers of that information attempt only to frighten them and do not relate drugs to other issues.

Peer group pressure is clearly instrumental in influencing the experimental and social-recreational use of drugs. In addition, family factors, particularly as they relate to personality development, seem to determine whether the individual will become deeply involved with drugs and ultimately addicted. While these are only beginning insights, they can be translated into strategies that should, at the very least, be more effective than prevention efforts that merely provide information. Such efforts must address the emerging personality development of the young and mobilize peer group pressures to support attitudes against drug use.[17]

Drug abuse experts now recognize that it is often necessary to equip youngsters to deal more effectively with life so that they will not resort to dysfunctional drug use. The burden for accomplishing this rests primarily with families and schools. There is need, therefore, to focus on increasing parental child-rearing effectiveness through various kinds of counseling. Where parents themselves have problems, these should be addressed as early as possible, before youngsters have begun school or, better yet, before the child is born.

Similarly, there is need for schools to develop family life curricula that are not focused on drugs alone. The emphasis here should be on enhancing self-understanding, intrafamily relationships, and the role of the family in society. If schools dealt with these subjects from the earliest grades, drug use and abuse would become just one more area to be understood and thereby would be stripped of its more sensational aspects.

Educational emphasis would be placed where it belongs—on the development of at least three essential kinds of skills: (1) intrapersonal skills, or the child's awareness of personal feelings and the ability to deal with them; (2) interpersonal skills, that is, the ability to relate to others and communicate effectively with them; and (3) coping skills, that is, the ability to solve problems without the need to fall back on alternatives such as dysfunctional drug use.

None of these steps can be carried forward easily, but it is clear that they must be pursued. Fortunately, there are a number of programs, designed for use in high schools, colleges, and the general community, that attempt to achieve similar results and are more easily implemented. These lean heavily on the use of peers or specially trained coordinators and staff who can relate to young people on a confidental basis.

The peer group approach requires that selected students be trained in drug abuse prevention work in a way that will enable them to influence their fellow students. Where trained coordinators are utilized, they, too, must be able to maintain rapport with the student body. Rap sessions conducted by counselors after regular school hours provide an opportunity to deal with a wide range of subjects. Staff availability for one-to-one counseling on a drop-in basis also is essential.

Outside the school itself, other groups have sprung up in a number of locations. These bring parents, youngsters, and trained counselors together in an effort to create a counterdrug culture, foster mutual understanding between youngsters and adults, and develop alternative activities. Such organizations go a long way toward developing rational perspectives. They also encourage adults to increase their awareness of their own behavior and thus become better role models for their children.

In the last analysis, the most promising and so the most important method of dealing with crime is by preventing it—by ameliorating the conditions of life that drive people to commit crimes and that undermine the restraining rules and institutions erected by society against antisocial conduct.

Our system of justice holds both juveniles and adults who violate the law responsible for their misconduct and imposes sanctions on them accordingly, even though the level of responsibility may be lower for juveniles than for adults. Society thereby obligates itself to equip juveniles with the means— the educational and social and cultural background, the personal and economic security—to understand and accept responsibility.

Clearly it is with young people that prevention efforts are most needed and hold the greatest promise. It is simply more critical that young people be kept from crime, for they are the nation's future, and their conduct will affect society for a long time to come. They are not yet set in their ways; they are still developing, still subject to the influence of the socializing institutions that structure—however skeletally—their environment: family, school, gang, recreation program, job market. But that influence, to do the most good, must come before the youth has become involved in the formal criminal justice system.[18]

Summary

In controlling delinquent and criminal behavior, prevention is now seen as the hope for the future. The time to come to grips with the delinquency problem is *before* it occurs. This chapter has shown that citizen involvement and citizen action are primary sources of prevention. But to prevent crime at its source, our society must begin by solving unemployment, improving education, and providing outlets and recreational facilities for our youth. Another preventive measure would be to eliminate or reduce within the community the opportunity for criminal behavior.

It is not surprising that drug-related crime constitutes a major problem in the juvenile justice system. The war against drug abuse is also a war against the vast number of crimes that are related to drug use and the constant need for money to purchase drugs. Drug abuse prevention strongly influences the number of crimes and the crime rate. Young people are the most likely targets of the drug pusher, and prevention of drug use through education, knowledge, and understanding offer the most fruitful and effective avenues of action. Prevention is the key to keeping today's juvenile offender from becoming tomorrow's hardened criminal.

REVIEW QUESTIONS

1. List and discuss the three approaches to delinquency prevention. Which, if any, do you feel is the most workable, and why?

2. What reasons can you offer for the lack of demonstrable prevention results? Why?

3. Discuss the concept of "community" involvement in delinquency prevention. What factors do you consider necessary in order to gain full citizen participation in preventing youth crime?

4. What social factors are associated with the infrastructure of juvenile crime and criminality? For example, how has the educational system contributed to either the increase or decrease of delinquent acts?

5. Reduction in criminal opportunities could help in preventing delinquency. What strategies can you suggest to facilitate such a reduction?

6. The authors consider preventing delinquency the key to handling the problem of youth crime. Do you agree? Why or why not?

NOTES

1. President's Commission on Law Enforcement and Administration of Justice; *Task Force Report: The Police* (Washington, D.C.: U.S. Government Printing

Office, 1967), pp. 221, 228. See also the Commission's *The Challenge of Crime in a Free Society* (Washington, D.C.: U.S. Government Printing Office, 1967), p. 288.

2. National Commission on the Causes and Prevention of Violence, *Staff Report: Law and Order Reconsidered* (Washington, D.C.: U.S. Government Printing Office, 1969), p. 278.

3. Leonard M. Savoie, "What Issues Will Challenge CPA's in the 1970's?" (Paper delivered before the convention of the Ohio Society of CPA's, 1969).

4. Ruby B. Yaryan, "The Community Role in Juvenile Delinquency Programs" (Paper presented for the Fourth National Symposium on Law Enforcement, Science and Technology, 1972).

5. F. Zimring and G. Hawkins, "Deterrence and Marginal Groups," *Journal of Research in Crime and Delinquency* (July 1968), pp. 100–14.

6. H. J. Eysenck, *Crime and Personality* (Boston: Houghton-Mifflin, 1964), p. 17.

7. George A. Pownall, *Employment Problems of Released Prisoners* (University of Maryland mimeograph).

8. Robert M. Meyers, Jr., and Cleveland Williams, *Operation Recreation: A Demonstration Project at Two California Youth Authority Institutions* (Sacramento: Institute for the Study of Crime and Delinquency, and the California Youth Authority, 1970), p. 1.

9. Harold W. Kennedy, "The Philosophy and Law of Recreation," prepared for the 39th National Recreation Conference, September 1957, p. 6.

10. Sidney G. Lutzin and R. C. Orem, "Prevention Through Recreation," in William E. Amos and Charles F. Welford, eds., *Delinquency Prevention: Theory and Practice* (Englewood Cliffs, N.J.: Prentice-Hall, 1967), pp. 151–52.

11. Constance H. Jacquet, ed., *Yearbook of American Churches* (Nashville: Abingdon Press, 1972).

12. *Crimes of Violence*, A Staff Report to the National Commission on the Causes and Prevention of Violence (1969) vol. 11, p. xxv.

13. *A Study of Crime Prevention Through Physical Planning*, prepared by the Dillingham Corporation for the Southern California Association of Governments (SUA, 1971), p. 7.

14. See, for example, C. D. Chambers, "An Assessment of Drug Use in the General Population: Special Report No. 1, Drug Use in New York State," New York State Narcotic Addiction Control Commission (May 1971).

15. Harold Finestone, "Narcotics and Criminality," *Law and Contemporary Problems* 22 (Winter, 1957): 69–85; R. K. Merton, *Social Theory and Social Structure* (New York: Free Press, 1949); R. Cloward, "Illegitimate Means, Anomie and Deviant Behavior," *American Sociological Review*, vol. 24, No. 2 (April 1959): 164–76.

16. J. Ball and C. D. Chambers, *The Epidemiology of Opiate Addiction in the United States* (Springfield, Ill.: Thomas, 1970).

17. H. R. Delone, "The Ups and Downs of Drug Abuse Education," *Saturday Review of Education* (November 11, 1972).

18. H. McKay, *Report on the Criminal Careers of Male Delinquents in Chicago* (Washington, D.C.: U.S. Government Printing Office, 1968).

16 Diversions from the System: A New Beginning

By the same token, if the administrator's ideology happens to
conflict with the approach favored by the society he serves,
he may try to resolve the conflict in one of two ways: by
working out a compromise or by trying to sabotage the system
he disagrees with.

HARRY E. ALLEN

As noted in earlier chapters, the juvenile justice system was originally
created in response to the harsh system for adults. Viewed from this
perspective, the juvenile justice system itself is a diversion from the adult
criminal justice system. The adult criminal justice system had so negative an
impact on juvenile offenders that a separate and more compassionate system
was needed. The negative connotations of most diversion programs make
them difficult to examine in proper perspective. Diversion is usually seen as
turning *from*, rather than turning *to*, something. Some of the earliest forms
of diversion, such as forced military service instead of prosecution, resulted
from the broad discretionary powers of the police, the courts, and others
within both the adult and juvenile justice systems.

The first point of discretion in the juvenile justice system is official
contact with the police. The police officer who tells a youth, "Go home and
don't let me catch you doing this again," is responding to personal negative
feelings about the juvenile justice system and about the worth of the
individual offender. If the juvenile justice system is seen by this policeman
as meeting the needs of society, however, he may initiate more formal
proceedings against the offending youth. When the system continues to be
seen as overly oppressive or not doing a good job, informal diversion
increases until the appropriate formal responses are finally provided. This
kind of "street corner justice," while often well-intentioned, does not
provide the kinds of structured responses that are often needed to effect
some change in the juvenile offender. The American Correctional Association offers at least one definition for a diversion program:

A diversion program is a resource which: (1) provides direct services and/or referral assistance to juveniles whose status or conduct makes them subject to the jurisdiction of the juvenile court, but who are referred to the program in lieu of official processing; (2) has a specific program design for diverted juveniles; and (3) produces institutional change by fostering improvement in and new commitments to youth services by existing agencies.

It is the first characteristic that qualifies a program as diversionary and the second which distinguishes it from traditional, informal diversion practices. The second and third characteristics together will determine the extent of the program's impact on the community it serves.[1]

Of course, the police officer is not the only member of the criminal justice team that can use discretion in the handling of juvenile offenders. The juvenile court can, and often does, bend over backward to keep an offending youth out of the formal, institutionalized system. Pretrial diversion is a discretionary power of the court which will be discussed later in the chapter. The institutional workers of the juvenile justice system also use broad discretion in their attempts to direct most juveniles out of the system and into other programs—usually in the community—as quickly as possible.

It has been shown that the *parens patriae* concept was originated as an alternative, albeit woefully inadequate, justice system for the care and treatment of juveniles. Present trends in juvenile justice aimed at providing more rights for juveniles are causing the system to look more and more like the adult system. Because both adult and juvenile correctional systems have failed badly, emphasis is shifting more and more to diversionary programs. Discretionary powers are exercised more and more and it seems that the circular development pattern is underway again, this time aimed at juvenile justice programs in the community as alternatives to and diversions from present institutional programs.

Diversion: A Negative Reaction?

While recidivism among adult and juvenile offenders is not the most reliable yardstick for success, it is often used as a measure of *failure*. The use of diversionary alternatives is usually a response to negativism or dissatisfaction with programs in existence. As a result, juveniles are diverted in programs that are hastily drawn up or not planned at all. As court referrals rise (19.8 cases per 1000 nationwide in 1957, 33.6 in 1972, and up to 34.2 per 1000 in 1976), it becomes more obvious that too much hope has been placed in what juvenile courts can accomplish. The courts are overloaded with cases and are expected to find solutions to multifaceted social problems when they have been poorly trained for this task and are woefully under-financed. The labeling process, which the system tries so hard to minimize, seems to be yet another reason for diversion. (See chapter 4.)

Related to labeling theory is the *social reaction theory*, which focuses on the effects of labeling on a person. Youths who engage in certain behaviors may find themselves labeled "high spirited" in one community and "incorrigible delinquents" in another. The response to the behavior depends on who sees it, who does it, and when and where it occurs. Social reaction theory emphasizes the consequences of stigmatization and the role of formal processing as a factor contributing to future misbehavior. This emphasis, according to such authorities as Lemert,[2] provides strong buttresses for the argument that youths should be diverted from any system that permanently labels them.

Not all arguments for diversion are aimed against the institutions, however. In some cases there are good arguments against the tendency of society to "excommunicate the deviant," as noted by Fant:

> Part of the failure to expand and intensify diversion may well represent an unconscious urge within us as a society to criminalize and excommunicate our social and moral deviants, as well as some trepidation we may have as public officials in bucking the public's clamor for "law and order" at any cost. Yet, we cannot wait for majority public opinion to support or lead us; we may wait indefinitely, for I doubt that there now exists majority support for the concept of diversion or that such will be available immediately ahead.[3]

Clearly, the adult criminal justice system and the juvenile system are victims of the ambivalent philosophical stance of American society, whose attitudes of revenge and retribution are both a major block to, and reason for, effective diversion in both systems.

Diversion from What?

In chapter 12, the problems of juvenile institutions were discussed. It is not necessary here to recount horror stories about incidents in our "prisons for kids." Professional and public reaction against these "training schools for crime" has led to the emergence of diversionary programs around the nation. Again, this approach tends to ignore the need for serious reform and modification of present institutional answers to juvenile crime. The conditions in a house of refuge were described thus in 1848:

> Are children happy in the refuge? There is scarcely any conceivable position in life that would render a human being entirely and uninterruptedly wretched. Complete misery destroys; elasticity of human nature is so great that any state which is endurable, becomes daily more tolerable, until at length it affords intervals of pleasure. Although to children, life in the refuge is dark and stormy, still, in general they know how to avail themselves of all facilities that afford present enjoyment; and do not fail to bask in those rays of sunshine which occasionally light up and warm their dreary path. But nothing short of excessive ignorance can entertain for a moment the idea that the inmates of the refuge are contented. In summer, they are about 14 hours under orders daily. On parade, at table, at their work, and in school, they are not allowed to

converse. They rise at five o'clock in the summer, are hurried into the yard, hurried into the dining room, hurried at their work and at their studies. For every trifling commission or omission which it is deemed wrong to do or to omit to do, they are "cut" with ratan. Every day they experience a series of painful excitements. The endurance of the whip or the loss of a meal—deprivation of play or the solitary cell. On every hand their walk is bounded; while restriction and constraint are their most intimate companions. Are they contented?[4]

In 1972, matters hadn't changed for the better:

"The worst thing you could do to try to get people to live in communities is to put them in institutions. I do not believe in institutionalization for most of the people that have been sent to the girls' school or to the boys' school in the last 50 or 100 years. I am very much in favor of trying to deal with them in the community and trying to deal with their parents and their environments in such a way that they are better able to make it. I think that when you separate them from where they're going to live that you don't do much in the way of reintegration at all. This old rehabilitation concept doesn't make a hell of a lot of sense when it's put into an institutional setting that's totally artificial. . . . [P]robably 60 percent of the girls ever sent to the Girls' School and 50 percent of the boys ever sent to the Boys' School should have never been sent there in the last 50 years; . . . the treatment program does nothing for them—it's a wrong thing—it does them more harm than good."[5]

These two examples, separated by 125 years, illustrate the reasons for diversion programs that prevent youths from being placed in such institutions. When many middle-class youths became more and more involved with the criminal justice systems in the 1960s, an outcry against the oppressive juvenile institutions was heard across the nation. Many, if not most, diversion programs in the 1970s may have been born out of the need to provide alternative punishments for these children, who had not previously been a major part of the institutional population. As mentioned before, when an institutional response is perceived as too harsh, society may provide informal alternatives in the form of discretionary actions at various points of the system. When these informal diversions become too much of an embarrassment to the official system, they tend to be formalized into structured programs.

Diversion to What?

The process of diversion implies "halting or suspending formal criminal or juvenile justice proceedings against a person who has violated a statute, in favor of processing through a noncriminal disposition or means."[6] Diversion should be differentiated from prevention and "minimizing penetration":

Diversion is differentiated from prevention in that the latter refers to efforts to avoid or prevent behavior in violation of statute, while diversion concerns efforts after a legally proscribed action has occurred. For example, programs of character building for youths represent prevention efforts.

Diversion is also differentiated from the concept of "minimizing penetration" in that the latter refers to efforts to utilize less drastic means or alternatives at any point throughout official criminal or juvenile justice processing, while diversion attempts to avoid or halt official processing altogether Probation in lieu of institutionalization represents an example of minimizing penetration.[7]

Under these broad definitions, only those processes that attempt to halt *all* official proceedings in the juvenile justice system should be considered true diversion programs. Pretrial release, increased use of bail, release on recognizance, plea bargaining, and charge reductions are often referred to as diversion, but since these processes are aimed not at halting *all* official actions, but merely at delaying or lessening the impact of some of them, they do not fall within the strict definition of diversion.

The so-called treatment model has answered the need for alternatives to confinement but not without creating its own problems. The search for proper treatment for children to "cure" their delinquent behaviors both fosters expansion of programs and exacerbates the problem:

Perhaps the classic example of this dilemma is in relation to children with delinquent tendencies. At the moment there is considerable doubt in the field of juvenile justice as to whether these children should be subject to "help." Yet, there is a consistent unwillingness to legislatively remove these children and youth from the system until such time as there is some other treatment to provide help. Apparently doing something, no matter how bad, is perceived as being better than doing nothing, even though evidence does not support this position.

Legislative or administrative action that excluded these children and youth from the "help" of the justice system would force development of whatever private or community alternatives were needed. Both indecision and ambivalence enable the field to avoid facing the issue of legislatively excluding from the juvenile justice system juveniles and youths who have not committed acts that would be criminal if committed by adults—a decision that would reduce workloads and offer greater opportunity for constructive work with delinquents remaining within the system.[8]

Goffman calls this "ritual maintenance," meaning that an action of which society disapproves must be met by some activity in response. *What* happens is not as important as the fact that *something* happens. "Society must act in some visible way against behavior that is considered illegal. Action is a necessity; treatment is not—not necessarily."[9]

In the case of diversion, a number of models have arisen from this new name for an old practice. School diversion programs are one of the oldest alternatives to referral to official agencies of the criminal justice system. While most school officials would not consider themselves as operating diversionary programs, they do so almost daily. Counseling, in-house disciplinary actions (even spanking of students, which has been upheld by the Supreme Court), family conferences, special classes, and special schools are all programs familiar to the school administrator. When behaviors such as vandalism, truancy, and incorrigibility are dealt with in this manner, without referral to the police, the actions comprise a true diversionary program. In this case the diversion is back to the school with the order and authority it *might* provide.

Another type of diversion is a program called the Comprehensive Youth Service Delivery System. This program focuses on the enhanced provision of needed services to a 2 to 3 percent per year diversion group in selected juvenile justice systems across the nation. There are some specific ingredients to these programs:

> (1) Diversion of youth from the juvenile justice system within a given target area by 2 to 3 percent per year; (2) development of an integrative, jointly funded youth service system containing programs and services that enhance both prevention and diversion activities; (3) involvement of youth themselves in the planning, development, and execution of the programs and service delivery systems.
>
> As designed, the programs are intended to eliminate the need to label children as delinquent before rendering service. Units of State and local government traditionally have been constrained in their delinquency prevention and diversion efforts because they had no jurisdiction to intervene with a juvenile or his family until the youth committed one or a series of delinquent acts. The basic idea of this project is to provide a broad range of services, preventive, rehabilitative, health, tutorial, etc., to all youths, delinquent and nondelinquent, in a narrowly restricted target area containing large percentages of children and families at risk without regard to traditional eligibility requirements.[10]

This program diverts a small percentage of juvenile offenders back to the community for enhanced service and a chance for change before commitment to the formal system.

Among the many programs of the 1960s and 1970s that were given great hopes for success was the concept of the Youth Service Bureau. One of the most promising recommendations of the President's Crime Commission in 1967, the Youth Service Bureau concept, had spread to 150 jurisdictions by the time of the National Advisory Commission Reports in 1973 and is still growing, but very slowly. This relatively simple but comprehensive concept is described as follows:

The Youth Service Bureau was intended to be a community agency to provide those necessary services to youth that would permit law enforcement and the courts to divert youthful offenders from the justice system. It was intended to involve the entire community, its agencies and resources in effective programs of crime prevention, diversion, rehabilitation, care, and control.

Today, the future of Youth Service Bureaus appears to be financially uncertain, and those bureaus that are surviving tend to be related to established agencies. Those related to the police, probation, or the courts are expanding and show the greatest evidence of being able to offer acceptable alternatives to justice system processing. Some may be incorporated with comprehensive youth service delivery systems.[11]

Although the bureaus that were established seem to have had a relatively good record of success, the procedure for returning the offending youths to their community does not seem to be destined for broad support. These programs are expensive and, in a time of shrinking government budgets and tight money, not the most feasible.

Who Should Be Diverted?

A major reason for diversion from the juvenile justice system, besides the public belief that the official system is inherently bad, is to provide services not available in the formal institutional system. A major issue of the 1970s, in both the adult and juvenile justice systems, is what is generally called the *right to treatment,** which revolves around the medical model that is generally applied to correctional intervention in the United States, both adult and juvenile.

Correctional professionals generally agree that the main goal of adult prisons, and the entire correctional system as well, is rehabilitation of the inmate. The medical model of criminals implies that something is wrong with them that would be "cured" if only the right treatment were available. Unfortunately, few states have the resources needed to provide the treatment promised by many statutes. The conflict between the stated goals of the system and the realistic chances of accomplishing them forms the core of a rapidly growing controversy. As Justice Bazelon has stated:

> The rationale for the right to treatment is clear. If society confines a man for the benevolent purpose of helping him . . . then its right to so withhold his freedom depends entirely upon whether help is in fact provided.
>
> . . .
>
> When the legislature justifies confinement by a promise of treatment, it thereby commits the community to provide the resources necessary to fulfill the promise.[12]

*A complete discussion of right to treatment in a juvenile institution is contained in chapters 7 and 12. The case of *Morales* v. *Turman,* in chapter 12, is especially applicable.

The right to treatment is especially critical when the offender has been removed from the correctional setting and placed in the mental health system. Gaver has defined active treatment and the right to treatment:

Active Treatment is:

1. A written and individualized plan.
2. Based on diagnoses.
3. Based on goals relative to arrest, reversal or amelioration of the disease process and aimed at restoring the individual's adaptive capacity to the maximal extent possible.
4. Based upon objectives related to the goals.
5. Comprised of defined services, activities, or programs related to the objectives.
6. Specific as to the responsibilities for the conduct of such services or activities.
7. Specific as to the means to measure the progress or outcome.
8. Clear as to periodic review and revision of the plan.

Recent court decisions have also dealt with the personal rights of the patient, the legal right to conduct business, the right to retain mental competency, the right to freedom from work without pay, and a host of other rights. While these rights seem almost inextricably entangled with the right to treatment, it is, however, the right to treatment which bears the greatest importance for the provider. And by extension it bears the most importance not only for the treating physician and the hospital, but also for the superintendent of the hospital, for the state commissioner of mental health and even for the legislative assembly. For the right to treatment has great potential significance for the budget of the hospital and, as well, for the budget of state mental health agency.[13]

Because of the diversity of medical programs and the qualifications of medical personnel, the quality of medical aid varies. Many times the federal courts have been forced to overlook the issue of federal rights in order to correct flagrant violations in the provision of medical service. This is a problem that has produced prison riots over the years. It is also one of the critical issues that will be involved in right to treatment legal cases over the next decade.

It is argued that if society accepts treatment as a right and still fails to treat adequately, commitment may be unjustified. But many questions arise from this complex issue. Does the inmate have the right to accept or the right to refuse all treatment? Does he have the right to choose punishment instead? Can he waive his right? Is he competent to do so? Can a guardian accept or refuse treatment in his stead? In the case of the juvenile, who is theoretically being incarcerated for his or her own ''protection,'' these questions are even more perplexing to those who believe the medical model is the answer to delinquency.

While many still believe that the medical model is a viable explanation for deviant behavior and advocate the use of institutional programs to "cure" such behaviors, others see it as a dead issue. Allen and Gatz point out several criticisms of the medical model:

Researchers

The failure of the medical model can be readily documented. Martinson, for example, examined 231 treatment projects and found that very few were significantly or consistently successful.[14] Indeed, he calls rehabilitation a myth.[15]

. . .

Inmates

Another source of discontent with the existing rehabilitation model is the inmate population, some of whom are fond of misquoting R. D. Laing:

> If you don't admit that you're sick—
> You're really sick,
> If you admit that you're sick—
> You're obviously right.

. . .

Prisoners, as correctional administrators are increasingly realizing, are acquiring a sizable body politic. Through demonstrations, work stoppages, riots, and other manifestations of discontent, they have won sizable concessions from grudging prison administrators. These concessions include inmate councils, grievance procedures, an elimination of censorship, and, in some jurisdictions, even union demands.[16]

. . .

Inmates are increasingly perceiving rehabilitation as a game to be played and that, in exchange for minimal conformity to prison rules, the system can be corrupted. The demands for concessions are, in part, an outgrowth of that recognition.

Courts

The courts, in abandoning the "hands off" philosophy of Felix Frankfurter, have begun to express dismay over and disagreement with correctional practices. In one state (Arkansas), the courts threatened to close down the system. In others, courts have forced prison administrators to institute due-process and humane practices. In some cases (*Sostre* v. *Rockefeller*), the courts have ruled against prison administrators and awarded punitive damages. Courts are paying increasing attention to an escalating number of inmate briefs. For example, the number of inmate briefs filed annually has increased from 2,000 in 1960 to 16,000 in 1970.[17] They constitute one out of every six civil findings.

. . . Unless some highly effective "treatments" for criminal behavior are found which withstand the test of basic rights *and* are backed by solid evaluations, these programs and the medical model are in serious trouble.

Economists

Economists too are looking at our correctional model with some dismay. Only in recent years, when state money is increasingly in short supply, has it become evident that criminal justice and corrections are very expensive. Total spending on federal, state, and local levels for police, prosecutors, courts, and prisons has shot up from $3.5 billion in 1969 to $14.6 billion in 1972. The police spent $3.2 billion; the courts spend $2.8 billion; and the penal system spent $3.2 billion.[18]

While replacing the medical model with the more appropriate process model is the current vogue, it is still important to review the keys to the diversion decision:

Others, who would legitimately be left within the scope and application of criminal law, could then be given a preliminary screening and diagnosis after arrest and, if found not to require criminal processing, could be diverted with maintenance of reasonable controls to potential community-based treatment resources and services. The key to diversion decisions might very well then rest on (1) the degree of potential risk to society which the person's immediate release portends, (2) the person's potential for accepting and using help and (3) the availability and accessibility of the resources needed.[19]

The pressures for right to treatment in the juvenile justice system, the growing list of procedural rights for juveniles, and the urge for more humane treatment of juvenile offenders all lead to selection of a range of options for diversion. The more specific the need of the offender, the more formalized and specific the program. A few of the more promising programs are outlined next.

Some Promising Diversion Programs

While the range of diversion programs has been broad and diverse, there are some programs that stand out as more effective or more innovative than others. Some of these programs have been singled out as "exemplary projects" by the Law Enforcement Assistance Administration (LEAA). The first of these is the Philadelphia Neighborhood Youth Resources Center.[20]

Neighborhood Youth Resources Center

The Neighborhood Youth Resources Center (NYRC) answers youths' need for support by offering direct assistance as well as referrals to related community agencies. It is a neighborhood project, accessible to young people and committed to the task of making community resources available to youths who need them.

By pooling the skills and talents of a number of specialists, the center is able to provide a new approach to delinquency prevention and help for young people already involved with the juvenile system. NYRC does more than link youngsters with services: the center makes these services work.

When the first store-front Youth Service Center was established in 1971, HEW's Office of Youth Development underwrote most of the funding. After a one-year trial run in offices that used to be the waiting room of a railroad commuter station, the center relocated in facilities shared with the Boy's Club. Today, they not only share facilities but integrate staffs and complement each other's programs and services.

This kind of cooperation is characteristic of the center's success in linking a variety of official and community-based service programs. During the first year of operation, the Model Cities Program acted as the sponsoring agency, and the Crime Prevention Association of Philadelphia acted as the delegate agency. Consequently, the center was able to enlist the support of a number of related agencies. Encouraged by its progress, HEW now sponsors the NYRC project independent of Model Cities.

NYRC's target population includes 4,000 boys and girls between the ages of 10 and 17 living in two police districts of North Philadelphia where unemployment and gang warfare are at their highest. Most are poor and many have high truancy records, a result of peer or gang pressure, family instability, or substandard reading and writing skills.

In 1973 the project served over 1,000 youth who had problems ranging from landlord-tenant disputes to minor disorderly conduct, burglary, and status offenses. Many of the young people simply needed an advocate, a strong friend who cared about their problems enough to do something that gave them some control over the events that shape their lives.

While the bulk of NYRC's cases are referred by the schools and courts, the center has an "open door" policy. Neighborhood kids frequently come in on their own for help. Perhaps the most persuasive referral is through a friend.

NYRC is demonstrating that a Youth Services Center should operate within the context of a community services center. It does this by offering five kinds of services:

1. Crisis intervention, or immediate short-term aid.

2. Casework, or the development of individualized service plans leading to long-term comprehensive assistance.

3. Groupwork, involving counseling and educational assistance to groups of youths.

4. Referrals to cooperating agencies and a careful system of agency monitoring and follow-up.

5. Legal representation.

The center is open more than 13 hours each day. All cases, whether referrals or "walk-in" cases, are scheduled for an interview with a service coordinator. After an initial assessment, the youth meets with his or her community Resource Worker. Home visits are always conducted to provide additional insight into the youth's problems and to determine the need for any immediate crisis intervention.

Once this preliminary assessment is completed, a case team is assembled to determine an appropriate service plan. The youth and the team agree on both short-term and long-term goals. Each youth must be able to identify his or her problem, understand the goals of the service strategy, and be willing to cooperate. Although a few youths are released to the project in lieu of incarceration—or as a condition of probation—project staff stress the noncoercive nature of NYRC's service policies. Voluntary participation is one part of the attempt to provide each youth with personal growth incentives.

Immediate goals may involve untangling a youth from the law or school authorities, providing medical services, or coping with family food needs. Longer-term goals may involve placement in an alternative school or providing job-training or job placement services.

In some cases, the kids begin "doing it on their own" because they can feel that NYRC is there, ready to support them when they need it.

If a youth's program includes referrals to outside agencies, a center staff member accompanies the youth to the first agency, which has been prepared for this visit by the staff member. The results are followed up by the caseworker and recorded in the youth's files. The followup not only ensures that the youth takes full advantage of the services; it provides an ongoing quality check on each referral agency.

Sometimes a youth's problem will be resolved immediately. But as far as the NYRC project is concerned, the case is not closed. Community workers follow up each case to ensure that the youth's needs continue to be met. Street work is an unending process in the project's target area.

The staff is drawn largely from Model Cities neighborhoods. There exists an exceptionally strong commitment to creating better lives for NYRC clients and a better environment within the neighborhood. A full-time project director, two youth services coordinators, a social worker, and six community resource workers assist specialists in youth problems to develop the best possible service plan for each youth. Moreover, the youngsters themselves contribute to the success of the program. The shared experiences, the support of new friends, and the feeling that NYRC is a "family" gets them working together for each other and for the whole community.

One feature of the project that enables it to provide comprehensive help to young people is its purchase-of-services arrangements. This system has brought to the staff:

- A lawyer from the Defenders Association of Philadelphia
- A psychiatric social worker from the State Department of Welfare

- Two area "gang" workers from the Youth Conservation Service of the City Department of Welfare
- A juvenile court "liaison" probation officer

The quality and variety of NYRC resources makes *direct* services a reality for each client.

- The center's core staff provides sex and drug education, vocational counseling, career development, group and educational counseling, and individual social casework.
- The juvenile court liaison officer regularly informs NYRC of any target area youth referred to court and counsels the youth on probation.
- Working out of the NYRC office, the attorney from the Defenders Association assists in securing the release of youths detained at the police station, provides legal representation in any proceedings against juveniles who use the center, and fulfills an important legal education role in the neighborhood.
- Gang work is the primary responsibility of the two area youth workers who work on the street to identify gang members, "cool out" potential conflicts, and link members to the services of NYRC and other projects.

Outside resources are used to enhance the project's own direct service capabilities. Through the exchange of understanding, 240 other agencies and projects have formally pledged their cooperation and commitment to NYRC clients. Many more offer services to clients on an informal basis.

A four-month study, which compared target and nontarget area youths within two precincts, indicated that arrest rates for boys in the target group were significantly lower in the felony and status offense categories. In one district, target boys had a significantly lower arrest rate for lesser misdemeanors as well.

In 1973 the project delivered direct services and referrals to 535 youngsters at a direct cost of $285,342, an average cost per client of $533. An additional 492 boys and girls received referral services without project counseling and evaluation assistance. NYRC estimates that approximately $568,060 in cash and services was expended by public agencies on NYRC-referred clients, some of whom also received direct project assistance. Thus, for a total outlay of $853,402, services were provided to a total of 1,027 youths of an average cost per client of $831.

The Neighborhood Youth Resources Center is designed to fill youth service needs that are often uniformly missing in many urban communities. For many youths, NYRC provides an opportunity for personal triumph over overwhelming odds. It is a program that provides the hope that one more juvenile will not become an adult criminal offender.

Although modeled along the lines of the Youth Service Bureau concept, which, it was noted, was not catching on to any great degree, the NYRC program is reason enough to rethink attitudes toward youth service programs.

Juvenile Diversion Through Family Counseling

Another LEAA exemplary project is the *Juvenile Diversion Through Family Counseling* program in Sacramento, California.[21]

A teenage girl has an argument with her mother over restrictions imposed by her father. Later in the day she hitchhikes out of town in an attempt to get away from her family. On the other side of town, a 16-year-old youth cuts classes from his high school for the fifth straight day. His mother, with whom he lives in a fatherless home, calls the police, saying he is totally beyond her control.

As in thousands of similar cases across the country, the youths involved are brought to the attention of local law enforcement officials—with likely consequences of detention overnight in juvenile hall, appearance in juvenile court, and probation for six months to a year. In California's Sacramento County, however, there is a new approach to this problem.

Called the Sacramento Diversion Project, this approach mobilizes the whole family in coping with the juvenile's problem and keeping the case out of the court. Specially trained probation officers meet with the family as soon as possible for crisis counseling and seek to return the youth to the home with a commitment by all family members to work out the problem.

The Sacramento Diversion Project, which began handling cases in the fall of 1970, is a joint effort of the Sacramento County Probation Department and the Center on Administration of Criminal Justice, a University of California, Davis, research group. The project sought to test whether juveniles charged with such status offenses as runaway and incorrigibility could be handled better through short-term family crisis therapy at the time of referral than through the traditional procedures of the juvenile court. The project hoped to achieve four main goals:

1. To reduce the number of cases going to court.
2. To reduce the number of repeat offenses.
3. To decrease overnight detentions.
4. To accomplish these goals at a cost no greater than that required for regular processing of cases.

Referrals to the Probation Department may come from the police, the schools, or the family itself. Most come from the police and are made shortly after the event which precipitates the crisis. When a referral is received by the project counselor, he immediately seeks to arrange a family session, generally to be held within the first hour or two after referral.

Through family counseling techniques, the counselor presents the problem as a family matter to be solved by the whole family. He emphasizes the importance of avoiding sending the youth to jail. If underlying emotions are too strong to permit the youth's return home immediately, a temporary alternative home is sought for the youth. This is a voluntary procedure which requires consent of both the parents and the youth.

Families are encouraged to return for additional sessions, with the maximum number usually five. Sessions last more than one hour and often over two hours. In many cases, counselors are in contact with the family by phone whether or not there is a followup visit.

The technique of crisis intervention and family crisis counseling is crucial to the concept of the project. Counseling is based on two premises: (1) problems should be dealt with immediately as they occur, and (2) problems are best dealt with by the whole family rather than by the child alone. These techniques seek to unblock communication between family members and to help the family achieve both the desire and the ability to deal with the problems itself.

The project is organized to provide counseling at the earliest possible point after referral. Regular intake procedures do not allow sufficient time for this. In addition, intake personnel are generally not trained in family crisis counseling techniques.

A major accomplishment of this project has been to prove that with proper training, probation officers can competently handle these cases. Initial project training included demonstrations of actual family counseling and intensive discussion of and role-playing in the kinds of situations counselors were expected to face. Ongoing training, considered essential, is built around weekly meetings with experienced family counselors (a psychologist and a psychiatrist).

The project staff consisted of a supervisor and six deputy probation officers. The experience of the counselors (three male and three female deputies) in a probation setting ranged from none to approximately 10 years of experience. The three deputies without probation experience all had some previous experience in a social service agency. All staff members were volunteers, chosen on the basis of interest and aptitude.

The Sacramento Diversion Project has had substantial success in meeting its major project goals. To evaluate the effects of the diversion procedures, approximately half of the referrals to the Probation Department were handled by the project staff. The other half served as control cases and were handled by regular intake procedures. Each group handled over 1000 cases during the two-year experiment.

In the first year only 3.7 percent of the project cases went to court as a result of petitions filed, as compared with 19.8 percent of the control cases.

Based on a 12-month followup of the first-year cases, there was a substantial difference in the number of project cases rebooked for any kind of offense (including criminal offenses) as compared to control cases—46.3 percent versus 54.2 percent. Looking only at offenses which involved criminal conduct, the relative improvement of the project group over the control group was also significant—22.4 percent versus 29.8 percent.

At the end of the first year, 13.9 percent of the project youths had spent at least one night in juvenile hall; 69.4 percent of the control youths had done so. The average number of nights spent for project youths was 0.5; for control youths it was 4.6.

For all cases during the first year and for a one-year followup period, the average total handling time for each of the 674 project youths was 14.2 hours; for the 526 control youths, the average time was 23.7 hours. The average cost for handling, detention, and placement was $284 for each project youth and $562 for each control youth. These costs included the expenses of training the diversion unit over a one-year period.

The family counseling approach to handling predelinquency and minor delinquency cases is supported and approved by many probation and diversion professionals, as well as juvenile justice administrators.

California Youth Authority's Intensive Treatment Program

A third example of a program that seems to be a useful alternative to traditional institutional programs for specialized problem juveniles is the California Youth Authority's Intensive Treatment Program in Norwalk, California.

The Intensive Treatment Program (ITP) was proposed on March 1, 1973, to meet the needs of emotionally disturbed juvenile offenders who could not be adequately treated in existing youth authority institutional programs. The ITP was designed to provide treatment for:

1. Psychotics
   a. Who were chronic escapees or too disruptive or assaultive for the Department of Mental Hygiene.
   b. Who had been treated by the Department of Mental Hygiene but returned to the Youth Authority as improved yet sill too disturbed for regular institutional programming.
   c. With organic brain syndromes.
2. Borderline personalities who are unable to adapt to existing regular programs.
3. Chronic self-destructive youth requiring constant supervision.

The intensive treatment program was set up to serve a total youth population of 40. Of these, 50 percent were black, 40 percent were white, and 10 percent were Chicano. The average age of these wards was 18 years,

9 months at the program's inception. Thirty of the 40 youths are placed at any one time in the Long-Term Residential Treatment Program and five in the Crisis Intervention Program which handles acutely disturbed wards from other institutions who are in need of short-term intensive therapy in a secure setting. The remaining five are in the Transitional Program which offers specialized programming during the last 90 days of the treatment program.

The ITP has a number of treatment components: a residential treatment program, crisis intervention, transitional program, educational program, recreational program, and vocational program. The treatment philosophy for the overall program is based largely on a social learning model. There is a token economy system within which each of the treatment components operate. Major programs are supplemented by individual and group psychotherapy, chemotherapy, behavioral therapy, assertion training, empathy training, bio-feedback training, and any other specific components or treatments that are necessary to specialized problems. A specific individualized treatment program is worked out by the treatment staff to meet the specific needs of each ward.

The staff for the intensive treatment program was initially suggested by an individual in the California Youth Authority who was familiar with the treatment staffs in various institutions. The individuals finally selected were handpicked from other institutions. They were chosen for their compassion, their stamina, and their enthusiasm. Additional staff members, as well as replacement staff, were chosen by a committee made up of members of the existing ITP staff. The staff-patient ratio in this treatment program could hardly be better, but even more impressive was the quality of the staff. All 16 of the youth counselors are between BA and Master's level in terms of school credits.

Each component of the ITP has its own evaluation criterion. Although there is no randomly assigned control group, the California Youth Authority (CYA) ward population was large enough so that comparison groups could be selected on the basis of all relevant variables.

The most important success/failure criterion for a corrections program involves comparisons of recidivism rates between the special treatment program and a comparable group. The recidivism of the ITP wards was recorded over a 21-month period between July 1, 1973, and April 1, 1975. During this time, 48 ITP wards were paroled—34 from the residential program and 14 from the crisis program. Of those paroled, 8 wards had violated their parole and subsequently had their parole revoked. The recidivism rate was 16.6 percent. Table 16–1 on page 392 presents a comparison between the recidivism rates of ITP wards and other CYA wards.

Besides reduced recidivism rates for the ITP graduates, there was a highly significant reduction in the frequency of both major and minor acting out behavior within the treatment program. There were also significantly fewer AWOLs and escapees among ITP wards as compared to CYA wards placed in Department of Health facilities.

TABLE 16–1. PAROLE REVOCATIONS FOR ITP GRADUATE COMPARED WITH OTHER Y.A. PAROLES BY THREE-MONTH PERIODS

TIME ON PAROLE PRIOR TO REVOCATION	ITP WARDS (N = 48)		OTHER CYA WARDS	
	Number	Cumulative	Number	Cumulative
3 months or less	4	8.3	458	10.5
6 months	4	8.3	865	19.8
9 months	4	8.3	1184	26.9
12 months	6	12.5	1385	32.0
TOTAL—15 months or more	8	16.6	1577	36.1

Source: From G. Kougleman, "Visit to California Youth Authority: Intensive Treatment Program, Norwalk, California."

One of the goals of the ITP was to upgrade the basic reading and computation skills of its wards so that they could successfully compete in the job market. Comparisons showed that ITP wards made significantly greater gains than wards from the Fred C. Nelles School in arithmetic comprehension, reading vocabulary, and reading comprehension, as well as arithmetic application.

Post-treatment integration of ITP wards into the community was compared with a randomly selected group of CYA wards released from other institutions at approximately the same time. This study, which compared the two populations on academic as well as vocational involvement, showed that a significantly greater number of ITP wards were involved in academic and vocational pursuits than were the group from other CYA institutions.

In a comparative cost analysis of the Intensive Treatment Program with other CYA programs as well as with the Department of Health programs, the ITP costs were 46 percent higher than other CYA programs and 15 percent higher than DOH programs. But the cost factor of the reduced recidivism over the longrun showed the program to be more economical. It is clear that at least this specialized population was able to receive great benefit from a diversion project aimed at meeting their special needs.

These have been but three examples of the more successful models for diversion of different types of juvenile clients. They are not the only models that have worked well, but they are representative of the range of possibilities.

The Future of Diversion

The future of juvenile diversion programs seems to be one of solid growth and development. Now that many informal diversion programs have become more specialized and institutionalized, they will be more permanent. Behavior is the key to judging the effectiveness of programs, because behavior is where awareness and attitudes are translated into action. Most diversion programs seem to depend upon community involvement whose goal is to affect the behavior of the "primary" (family and individual) and "secondary" (potential neighborhood community) groups in the neighborhood. Specific needs and consequent behaviors will have to be defined ultimately in the neighborhood. There are, however, some broad goals that most neighborhoods would likely agree on in any crime and delinquency prevention and reduction efforts:

1. How can the functioning of the family unit be enhanced, so that delinquency can be effectively prevented through the dynamic socializing processes that occur within the family unit?

2. What roles can the adolescent peer group have both (a) on the prevention and reduction of delinquency among its members, and (b) on the development of positive, responsible behaviors or "positive citizenship" among its members?

3. How can neighborhood residents be motivated to *help* their neighbors, both during the time a neighbor is being victimized and after the neighbor has been victimized?

4. How can individuals and neighborhood groups be motivated and mobilized to be more concerned and more realistic about their own safety and the safety of their neighbors? How can these concerns be translated into effective actions?

5. How can the primary and secondary groups in a neighborhood be motivated and mobilized to participate more responsibly and more effectively in the criminal and/or juvenile justice process? How can neighborhood trust in the criminal justice process be restored, so that broader segments of the neighborhood will support the law and principles of justice?[23]

If each neighborhood could develop and implement strategies to answer these broad questions more effectively, the neighborhood could have an immediate and significant impact on preventing and reducing the crime on its streets. To the extent that the individuals and groups at the neighborhood level have a real sense of importance, participation, individuation and dignity, complemented by a sense of competence, usefulness, belongingness, and power, the neighborhood can function effectively as a positive social force, using legitimate means to attain the desired goals of prevention and reduction in crime and delinquency. That is to say, they can convert attitudes into actions.

In contrast, if the primary and secondary groups of potential neighborhood communities are ignored by social planners, negative consequences might well be anticipated. These consequences would include greater social isolation and anomie and higher rates of crime and delinquency. A growing territorial effect could be anticipated, where individuals transform their residences into stronger and stronger "fortresses," further increasing the social isolation and anomie of the people. As anomie and social isolation are increased, the distrust of law, the justice process, the political and other leadership, and basic social institutions will grow. When distrust of basic social processes is high, people, both individually and collectively, will likely take extra-legal means to meet their needs and to reduce their fears, both real and imagined.[24]

Pretrial Diversion: Another Approach

While pretrial diversion does not meet the rigid definition of true diversion, it does reduce the penetration into the criminal justice and juvenile justice systems. For this reason, it is worth examination. Figure 16–1 shows how the paths of diversion for adults from the criminal justice pretrial process are aimed at reducing the system's impact. Although the juvenile justice process is somewhat different, the principles are similar. The pretrial diversion concept was examined in detail in *Cost Analysis of Correctional Standards: Pretrial Diversion:*

> Diversion provides an alternative to the traditional criminal pretrial process. Diversion occurs either prior to official police processing (arrest) or prior to official court processing. Among the reasons for promoting diversion is that it redistributes criminal justice system resources. By screening out less serious offenders, resources can be devoted to serious cases; if all offenses were handled officially, the costs would be prohibitive. "Diversion" is not a new concept; it has occurred informally and unofficially at all stages of the criminal justice system in the past. Without it the system would have collapsed.
>
> The Commission's argument for diversion, however, is not to keep a poorly functioning system in operation. Instead, *formalized* diversion is advocated for two reasons. First, it is an opportunity to make society more conscious and sensitive to the deficiencies of the present system, thus forcing needed changes. Second, diversion is to be a systematic, equitable, and logical alternative in an improved criminal justice system excluding "individuals who truly do not need the services and resources of the justice system, even though they may need forms of help outside the justice system." Diversion provides the vehicle for referring individuals in their contact with the law to those outside services and resources.[25]

Cost-benefit analysis of diversion programs is difficult to accomplish in most cases. Project Crossroads in Washington, D.C., was most sophisticated in regard to system costs and benefits, so figures are available:

> When Project Crossroads clients were matched with a control group, the 1969 judicial system costs were estimated to be reduced by $34,000, correctional system costs by $82,000. While the type of control group chosen (and thus these averted costs) have been questioned, the estimated costs of various types of criminal justice processes prepared for the Crossroads study (adjusted to 1974 dollars) are useful in establishing the approximate magnitude of criminal justice resources potentially available for reallocation:

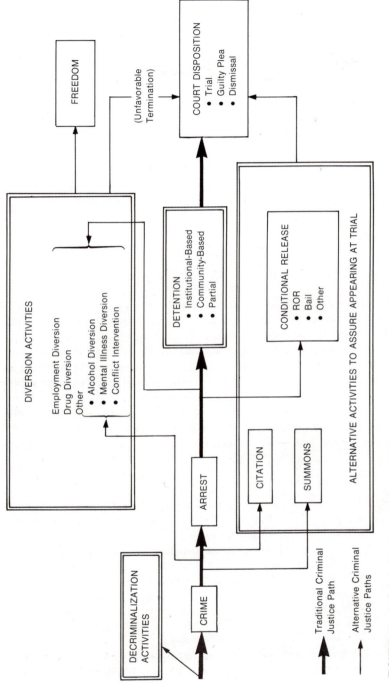

FIGURE 16–1. Criminal justice process: pretrial.

Source: National Institute of Law Enforcement and Criminal Justice, *Cost Analysis of Correctional Standards: Pretrial Diversion*, vol. 2 (Washington, D.C.: U.S. Government Printing Office, 1975), p. 2.

- Grand jury hearing, $37.10
- Jury trial, U.S. District Court, $3,096.66
- Nonjury trial, U.S. District Court, $1,151.36
- Plea, U.S. District Court, $130.35
- Jury trial, local court, $756.00
- Nonjury trial, local court, $197.82
- Parole, marginal daily cost per parolee, $1.36
- Probation, marginal daily cost per case, $0.53–$0.91
- Incarceration, $5.78 per day[26]

Pretrial diversion in the adult system is one process that has produced actual dollar savings. In the juvenile justice system, similar savings can also be found in preadjudicatory diversion, used to the maximum extent.

Summary

Diversion is nothing new. It is merely another label for a practice that has been in use for centuries. The basis for diversion decisions still resides in the broad powers of discretion held by many members of the juvenile justice system. Since most diversion efforts are directed toward leading the juvenile offender back to the community and/or home, however, they need the support of these primary and secondary social groups to be productive. It is an unfortunate indictment of the juvenile justice system that diversion programs are diversions *from* something that seems to be failing. It would be to everyone's benefit if they were to become, instead, diversions *to* something that was at least no *worse* and less expensive.

In its program rationale for research projects in the area of juvenile diversion, the LEAA's Office of Juvenile Justice and Delinquency Prevention outlines 12 logical points to consider in the development of diversion programs. It seems appropriate to end this chapter with an examination of these points.

1. Delinquent offenders constitute a disparate group of youths, ranging from youngsters involved in petty, transitory, and isolated acts of misbehavior to youths who represent "hard core" recidivists.

2. Hard core offenders are the most appropriate cases for official juvenile court attention, while less serious juvenile lawbreakers can often be better dealt with outside the framework of the juvenile court.

3. Juvenile misconduct is often a manifestation or product of problems encountered by juveniles within major institutional areas or life arenas, such as schools or the world of work and is less frequently a symptom of individual psychological maladjustment.

4. Diversion programs are often ineffective because they focus upon youth whose misconduct is minor and a reflection of normal maturational stress;

or, because they are inadequately funded, not coordinated and fragmented in their approaches.

5. The number of juveniles entering the juvenile justice system is more a function of police arrest patterns and community tolerance of youth behavior than of the nature or seriousness of juvenile misconduct.

6. Diversion must mean the referral of youth to programs outside of the auspices of the juvenile justice system in order to reduce the likelihood of expansion of control by juvenile justice agencies over an increased number of youth.

7. The process for diverting youth is often not identified or is confused with diversion programs and therefore does not become subject to systematic and deliberate efforts directed toward its improvement.

8. Diversion must limit penetration of youth into the juvenile justice system. Diversion can occur at any point between apprehension and adjudication.

9. Attempts to reduce delinquency through diversion programs must do more than simply remove youths from the juvenile justice system. Diverted youngsters should be provided positive life experiences through diversion programs that provide meaningful and viable roles for youth.

10. Diversion of less serious cases from the juvenile court should allow the courts to deal more effectively with the more serious lawbreakers, for diversion would relieve some of the present congestion of cases within the official juvenile justice system.

11. The programs developed will vary from community to community, providing various program models which can be compared through evaluation to determine the relative utility of alternative approaches.

12. Although there are plausible arguments that can be advanced in favor of diversion programs which provide positive experiences and services for youths, this is still a relatively untested assumption. The program design requirement of assignment either to diversion with services or diversion without services will provide for the assessment of the gains, if any, to be achieved through diversion to services.[27]

REVIEW QUESTIONS

1. Define what is meant by *diversion,* giving examples of programs that are not true diversion from the juvenile justice system.

2. Explain how diversion is different from the concepts of prevention and minimization of penetration.

3. What is the essential aspect of a true diversion program?

4. How will the right to treatment issue cause more and more diversion programs to be developed?

5. Does the emergence of legal rights for juvenile offenders in the juvenile justice system have an effect on diversion program growth? Explain.

NOTES

1. American Correctional Association, *Juvenile Diversion: A Perspective* (College Park, Md.: ACA, 1972), p. 7.

2. Edwin M. Lemert, *Human Deviance, Social Problems, and Social Control,* 2nd ed. (Englewood Cliffs, N.J.: Prentice-Hall, 1972).

3. Fred D. Fant, "How Do We Divert More Offenders from the Criminal Justice System?", *Proceedings of the National Conference on Corrections* (Williamsburg, Va.: U.S. Government Printing Office, 1971), p. 138.

4. Larry Cole, *Our Children's Keepers* (New York: Grossman, 1972), pp. xix–xx.

5. Ibid., p. 73.

6. National Advisory Commission on Criminal Justice Standards and Goals, *Corrections* (Washington, D.C.: U.S. Government Printing Office, 1973), p. 73.

7. Ibid., p. 73.

8. Ibid., p. 76.

9. E. Goffman, *Asylums* (Garden City, N.Y.: Doubleday, 1961), p. 34.

10. National Advisory Commission, *Corrections,* p. 78.

11. Ibid., p. 79.

12. D. Bazelon, "Implementing the Right to Treatment," *University of Chicago Law Review* 36 (1969), pp. 742–49.

13. K. Gaver, *The Right to Treatment: Ramifications for Providers,* Unpublished paper presented to the 19th annual conference of the AMA Mental Health Representatives, Chicago, 1973.

14. *Criminal Justice Digest* 3 (May 1974), p. 1.

15. R. Martinson, "What Works: Questions and Answers about Prison Reform, *Public Interest,* Spring 1974, pp. 22–55.

16. R. Huff, "Unionization Behind the Walls," *Criminology* 12 (August 1974): 175–94. Quotation from pp. 176–77.

17. National Advisory Commission on Criminal Justice Standards and Goals, *A National Strategy to Reduce Crime* (Washington, D.C.: U.S. Government Printing Office, 1973), p. 115.

18. "The Losing Battle Against Crime in America," *U.S. News and World Report,* December 16, 1974, p. 20.

19. Fant, "How Do We Divert More Offenders from the Criminal Justice System," p. 139.

20. National Institute of Law Enforcement and Criminal Justice, *The Philadelphia Neighborhood Youth Resources Center: An Exemplary Project* (Washington, D.C.: U.S. Government Printing Office, 1977). This material used in the text has been taken from the synopsis document that describes this project.

21. National Institute of Law Enforcement and Criminal Justice, *Juvenile Diversion Through Family Counseling: An Exemplary Project* (Washington, D.C.: U.S. Government Printing Office, 1977). This material appears here in essentially the same form as in the synopsis document.

22. G. Konzelman, ''Visit to California Youth Authority: Intensive Treatment Program, Norwalk, California.'' Unpublished trip report, Bureau of Juvenile Rehabilitation, Department of Social and Health Services, State of Washington (August 1976). This material is repeated in the text with slight editing.

23. R. Yaryan, ''The Community Role in Juvenile Delinquency Programs,'' in *New Approaches to Diversion and Treatment of Juvenile Offenders* (Washington, D.C.: U.S. Government Printing Office, 1973), p. 169.

24. Ibid., pp. 169–70.

26. National Institute of Law Enforcement and Criminal Justice, *Cost Analysis of Correctional Standards: Pretrial Diversion,* vol. 2 (Washington, D.C.: U.S. Government Printing Office, 1975), p. 1.

26. Ibid., vol. 1, p. 20.

27. Law Enforcement Assistance Administration, *Diversion of Youth from the Juvenile Justice System* (Washington, D.C.: U.S. Government Printing Office, 1976), pp. 24–25.

17 Summary and Overview of Juvenile Justice

Every profession has its own myths, totems, and taboos. In the legal profession these serve to camouflage the dependency of the legal status quo on the established power systems.

RALPH NADER

In previous chapters, we have sought to describe the procedures, processes, and people that make up the juvenile justice system. This final chapter attempts to integrate descriptions of some of the forces at work in the system and point out important areas where change is occurring.

Juvenile Justice: The Model Muddle

Humphry Osmond first applied the term "model muddle"[1] to the situation in the field of mental illness; the term applies equally well to the juvenile justice system, each member of which seems to have a different view of what the juvenile justice system is and what it is supposed to accomplish. Juvenile judges, probation officers, police, juvenile correctional personnel, and parole staff are far from agreeing on which "model" to use in processing juvenile offenders.

Two of the most prevalent models have been discussed in several previous chapters. The *treatment* model assumes that delinquent behavior has some root cause in a physical, mental, educational, or occupational handicap of the offender. If the underlying problem can be identified and a liberal dose of corrective medicine, (e.g., therapy, training, education, or surgery) applied, the patient will be *cured* of any further deviant behavior. This model is under heavy attack at both the adult and juvenile levels of criminal justice, for its efficacy has never been proved. The medical model has been attacked as a failure because many jurisdictions do not follow up recommendations by providing the financial and professional resources needed to administer those "treatments" for which the individual was confined. Without treatment, there is no justification for confinement, and the model has no validity.

The original philosophy behind the juvenile justice system was the model of *parens patriae*. While the rhetoric behind these high-sounding words claims *protection* of youths from the harsh realities of broken homes, criminal companions and other evils, the setting that developed to implement this "protection" has often been worse than the conditions from which youths were being protected. The state has seldom proven to be a *better* parent for juveniles in trouble, only a harsher and stricter one, so the incarceration of juveniles has had to be justified on the basis of a model other than *parens patriae*.

Deterrence whose literal meaning is "that which frightens away from," may be either *individual* and *general*. It might be argued that some individual deterrence does take place at various points in the juvenile justice system, but there is little evidence of success with general deterrence. Juvenile crime rates continued to rise, despite the deterrence efforts of the harsh reform schools of the 1930s and 1940s and the work camps or treatment centers of the 1960s and 1970s. It is generally conceded that deterrence is most effective when punishment is swift, sure, and universally applied, but in the juvenile justice system it is often delayed, capricious, and applied mainly to the poor and the powerless. Such a model seems doomed to failure.

Reform or *corrections* are different terms for the same model. As noted by Sommer:

> Literally, to reform is "to reshape, form again, or change into a new and improved condition." Its concrete realization, the reformatory, had as its goal the reshaping of a young person's character. Although the term has rather archaic overtones, this is what most advocates of rehabilitation really want. Rather than restoring a person to a former status, either as someone desperately in need of money or full of hatred, the goal of the reformer is to reshape the offender into a new and improved form.
>
> This model is the logical antecedent of today's emphasis on *corrections*, literally "a setting right or on a straight path." John Augustus, the first probation officer, wrote in 1852 that "the object of the law is to reform criminals, and to prevent crime and not to punish maliciously, or from a spirit of revenge." This eminently sensible view led Augustus to bail offenders out of prison and keep them in his home. Unfortunately, the term *reform* subsequently became associated with such brutal institutions as the reform school and state reformatory, so it became lost to the criminal justice system and a less useful term (rehabilitation) was substituted. However, the attempt at euphemism was only partial. We still talk about reforming prisons when we want to change them. To rehabilitate prisons, at least in common speech, would mean refurbishing or modernizing older facilities. Both reform and

corrections emphasize a reshaping, and corrections has the additional connotation of a standard to guide the process of change—setting the person not just on a different path, but on the right path. Most inmates will acknowledge the legitimacy of reform as a social objective, whereas rehabilitation makes no sense to them. Their criticism concerns the practicability of accomplishing positive character change through immersion in a total criminal society; any reforming or reshaping under such circumstances would probably be in a negative direction. Ironically, *reform* today is more often applied to efforts to change institutions than to programs to change prisoners.[2]

This warning seems especially applicable to a juvenile justice system that calls its institutions "reform schools" and "reformatories" while inmates and critics refer to them as *schools of crime,* where children learn to be tough and aggressive in order to survive.

The *punishment* model is one that American society finds hard to accept in principle even though it seems to be the most common in practice. Punishment is another form of the *retribution* or *vengeance* model which seeks an "eye for an eye and a tooth for a tooth." The manner in which much of our institutional "protection" of juvenile offenders is carried out makes it clear that the punishment model, however rejected in principle, is the basis for a great deal of juvenile justice practice. The following description of conditions in a juvenile institution of the 1970s illustrates this point.

> Wallace had already prepared me for the worst. The place was jammed. The majority of kids locked up in the place weren't allowed to attend school. Many were being kept months after their sentencing to other institutions, and their months of waiting at Youth House did not count toward their 'time.' Psychotic kids were mingled with lost kids, kids with sexual problems mingled with truants. Big kids awaiting trial for murder sat confined with little kids awaiting trial for glue-sniffing. The windows were still stuck closed. For the perversely nostalgic, Youth House has remained free from the surrounding currents of change . . . the New York *Daily News* began another expose series on the Youth House, calling it by its new name—Spofford Juvenile Center—and headlining drug traffic, sadism and "unnatural sex acts." Two state legislators promised a legislative hearing and the carousel music began again.[3]

It would be difficult to justify these conditions, typical of many jurisdictions today, under the rubric of *parens patriae.* Until society decides what it really wants to do *to* or *for* juveniles, the model muddle, the lack of direction or purpose, will continue to strangle any progress.

The current trend toward the provision of more *rights* for juveniles constitutes an improvement but poses a new dilemma. This movement attempts to provide at least some of the protections of due process that have become an integral part of the adult criminal system. When one examines the adult system, however, it becomes doubtful that society really wants to inflict a similar monstrosity on its juveniles! Torn between the need for more structural and legal safeguards for youth while attempting to maintain the informal atmosphere of *parens patriae,* the juvenile justice system reaches out in every direction for a model to cling to. It will be a long time before the vast gaps between the rhetoric and reality of this haphazard *non-*system close enough so that it may be described as having a "model."

Fragmentation: A Major Problem

Juvenile justice is meted out at every level of government in America, but their differing standards, procedures, and alternatives make these juvenile justice systems a fragmented hodge-podge of contradictory programs which compete for the same limited resources. Under these circumstances, it is less surprising to the authors that juvenile justice is as *bad* as it is than that it is as *good* as it is!

From the garbage heap detention centers that may be found in major metropolitan areas to the campus-like cottages in some of the more affluent areas, juvenile justice can be described as *inconsistent.* Fragmentation of resources in the corrections sector of the criminal justice system has been described as a major problem:

> It should now be apparent that the segment of the criminal justice system we call *corrections* is actually a poorly connected network of many other subsystems, most of them directed to a specific kind of clientele. Probation and parole are often not in tune with institutional programs; juvenile courts, adult institutions, and community programs often vie with each other for resources and personnel. Women's institutions and special-category offender programs are pushed into the background, while operation of the larger correctional units gets top priority. These various programs all compete for the same limited dollars in state and local correctional budgets, often resulting in an attempt by administrators to distribute shortages equitably, rather than making a coordinated and effective use of whatever funds are available. The fragmentation of the criminal justice system as a whole is one of the major problems in developing effective rehabilitative programs; disorganization at the correctional level only aggravates an already critical situation.[4]

The fragmentation problems of the juvenile justice system are further exacerbated by the broad discretionary powers of the juvenile court. When the juvenile correctional system does not seem to meet the needs of the court, it uses one of a number of available alternatives which include private placement at public expense.

An almost endless chain of federal, state, and local commissions, panels, ad hoc committees, etc., have commented on the fragmentation problem. In 1973, yet another problem was noted by the National Advisory Commission on Criminal Justice Standards and Goals:

The structure of juvenile court systems varies widely. In some jurisdictions, the juvenile court is a separate court—or a distinct division of a trial court with a broader jurisdiction—that hears nothing but juvenile cases. Judges of these courts do not divide their efforts between juvenile and other cases, and they consequently have an opportunity to develop expertise in juvenile matters. In other jurisdictions, courts hearing juvenile matters also have other judicial duties; often the probate court is given jurisdiction over juvenile matters. Judges on these courts focus less of their attention and efforts on juvenile matters, and therefore have fewer opportunities to develop the specialized skills that juvenile matters require.[5]

Whether or not the gigantic effort of this commission becomes yet another set of dusty volumes on practitioners' bookshelves or a rallying cry for action remains to be seen.

Status Offenders: An Attempt to Clarify the System

The umbrella of *parens patriae* has been used to cover juveniles in a number of categories. Recently, there has been pressure to eliminate from the system those juveniles whose only offense is a "status" that requires protection by the state. It has been urged that only juveniles whose acts would result in criminal prosecution if they were adults be handled in the juvenile justice system and that status offenders should be kept from contact with the juvenile justice system and cared for by alternative agencies.

Washington has developed a piece of model legislation in this regard. In the essence, it states:

> **Handling of Status Offenders.** Probably the most comprehensive change in the juvenile court system suggested by this legislation is the method of dealing with status offenders—young people whose offenses are running away, incorrigibility, truancy, etc.; offenses which are not crimes for adults.
>
> 1. *Repeal of Current Definition of Dependency* (§1). The current definition of dependency provides for juvenile court jurisdiction over various oblique status offense categories. Among these: children who are "in danger of being brought up to lead an idle, dissolute or immoral life," "who wander about in the nighttime without being on any lawful business or occupation," who are "incorrigible, that is, beyond the control and power of his parents, guardian, or custodian by reason of the conduct or nature of said child," etc.
>
>   With the repeal of that section, juvenile court jurisdiction over all status offenders is eliminated. §14–35 of the bill, however, provide for a new method of handling certain kinds of status offenders.
>
> 2. *Limited Law Enforcement Authority to Arrest Runaway Youth* (§14–18). The first new provisions regarding status offenders are codified in a new

RCW chapter which establishes the ''Washington State Runaway Youth Act.'' This act authorizes a law enforcement officer to take a runaway child into custody for not more than six hours; requires him to take the juvenile home *if he consents* and if at all possible; if the child cannot be returned home the law enforcement officer may release the child to a relative or other responsible person and if that is not possible must take the child to a temporary residential facility licensed by the Department of Social and Health Services.

3. *Responsibility of DSHS for Runaways and Families in Conflict* (§19–20). The child welfare services law which currently places responsibility with DSHS for homeless, dependent, incorrigible, and neglected children and children in danger of becoming delinquent is amended: references to ''incorrigible as defined in RCW 13.04.010 (7)'' are repealed since that category has been repealed in §1 of the proposed bill; and, a responsibility for families in conflict who request services is substituted. These services are primarily crisis intervention and alternative residential care.

4. *Limited Juvenile Court Responsibility for Status Offenders* (§21–26). The juvenile court becomes involved in a family conflict situation under this bill only if the child or his parents file a special petition in the juvenile court asking the court to resolve a conflict over where the child is going to reside. The court can issue an order approving or disapproving the child's placement, can remove a child from a situation if a preponderance of the evidence shows the situation ''imperils'' the child, and can order alternative placement. A six-month review of any order is required. Legal counsel is appointed at no cost to the child or parent in these cases.

5. *No Detention or Institutionalization of Status Offenders* (§20 [4] [e] and §60). A runaway or child in conflict with his family cannot be detained under this proposal. The 1976 law (SB 3116), permitting a 30-day commitment of incorrigibles, is also repealed.

6. *Provision for Emancipation of a Child* (§27–34). Under this bill a juvenile could petition a court to be emancipated. The child would have to show that he or she could manage his or her own affairs, could be self-sufficient, and that his or her emancipation is in the best interests of the child, the parents, and the state. On order declaring a child an emancipated minor terminates all parental rights and obligations and makes the child an adult for purposes of Washington State law.

7. *Repeal of Juvenile Court Responsibility for Truants* (§35). The section of the compulsory school attendance law which authorizes any law enforcement officer to take a child into custody without a warrant if he or she is truant from school and requires the officer to take the child to his or her parent or teacher; or, if school officials think the child is ''an habitual or incorrigible truant'' the officer is authorized to refer the child to juvenile court. This change is consistent with Section 1 of the proposed bill which, in repealing the current definition of dependency, repealed the juvenile court's jurisdiction over any child ''who is an habitual truant, as defined in the school laws of the State of Washington.''

The section of the compulsory school law which authorizes an attendance officer to take a child into custody and return the child to school and to arrange for conference with parents, etc., is not repealed (RCW 28A.27.040).[6]

This elimination of such a large portion of the juvenile population from the juvenile justice system *should* result in a better focus on the problems of those remaining. This legislation appears, at least, to be a move in the right direction and one that is here to stay.

Alternatives to the System: One Solution

Diversion, discussed in chapter 16, has usually been a turning away from a system that is dysfunctional to satisfy the needs of the juvenile court for some categories of juveniles. Status offenders may be treated by a completely separate system, and other offenders have also been singled out for special programs.

Many alternative programs have been developed by communities to handle specific problems in that particular community. Placing an inner-city juvenile drug addict in a rural juvenile institution, for example, can result in serious problems for the institution and for the juvenile when he returns to the urban setting. Community treatment centers for juvenile drug abusers are one alternative response to this specific problem.

While alternatives to the juvenile justice system are necessary and helpful, they cannot proliferate indefinitely. At some point it is necessary to look for better alternatives *within* the juvenile justice system itself, to satisfy the needs of juveniles within the institutional system. The state of Washington has developed and is testing specific procedures to accomplish this goal, which, when combined with the removal of *status offenders* from the juvenile justice system may prove to be models for others to follow.

Florida has chosen to meet the problem of status offenders head on, refusing to believe that there is no other place to house them except juvenile institutions. As noted by Latina and Schembera:[7]

> Florida's search for detention alternatives began early in 1974. At that time, detention conditions in the Sunshine State were about as bleak as anywhere else. Dangerous overcrowding, inadequate staffing, lack of therapeutic programming and indiscriminate mixing of status offenders with delinquents was common throughout the State. In a 1-day detention survey conducted in 1974, it was found that 22.8 percent of all children detained in security facilities were status offenders.
>
> Concerned with the results of this survey, Florida Youth Services officials began a determined search for alternative ways of housing the hundreds of status offenders who had to be temporarily removed from their own homes but did not really require security facilities. There were few options. The economic recession meant that new State tax dollars for any alternative detention

programs were unlikely. Finally, in March 1975 Youth Services officials settled on the one option available to them throughout the state: *Volunteer Homes*. This innovative approach rejected the traditional stand that volunteers do not replace paid services. A national consultant on volunteerism doubted the volunteer bed program would work effectively but administration made the decision to "go."

The decision to go with the volunteer concept was not pulled out of the air. It was based on a highly successful pilot project that had been operating in the Tampa area for over a year.

The Tampa Volunteer Detention Project was born in January of 1974 out of an attempt by State Youth Services officials to relieve overcrowding at the Hillsborough County Detention Center, one of the State's largest facilities. To avoid a potential crisis, State administrators resolved to place, on an emergency basis, 30 of the least dangerous detained youngsters with families in and around the Tampa area.

Essentially, the structure of the Tampa volunteer program evolved over several months through trial and error. The concept was to place in the volunteer homes status offenders whose circumstances required a temporary stay and who were not considered serious security risks. Since this was as an emergency measure, there was little opportunity to systematically plan the volunteer program. Only the barest of procedures were in place when the first group of 30 volunteer families were recruited from the Tampa community, screened, trained, and certified to receive children.

Surprisingly, there were few major problems and most of the children housed in the volunteer homes adjusted exceedingly well. Division officials were so pleased with the initial results of the project, that it was continued as a regular component of the Tampa detention program. Thus, a project initially begun as an emergency measure to relieve dangerous overcrowding in one of the State's detention centers, was maintained on a regular basis.

This innovative alternative to the incarceration of status offenders underscores the need for better diversions to programs that work.

One of the dangers of a proliferation of diversion programs is that it gives rise to a search for dollars instead of answers to the juvenile justice problems. This is outlined in *Hard Cores Don't Come from Apples:*

Diversion, like therapy and counseling, is fast becoming a catchall term to describe various programs for the purpose of obtaining funds. Rossi objects strongly to those people and programs which act under the guise of diversion. Some people are quick to catch onto semantics and use a new term when it's popular and can be used to their monetary advantage. Those who would labor under the mistaken thought that they can be successful and obtain funds by adding a program like ceramics to their appeals, are sadly misinformed. They aren't truly exercising a diversion program. Diversion is a total commitment. It is dedication that requires a 24-hour job . . . those misdirected imitative programs that go under the title of diversion must be separated from those programs which are purely diversion.

. . .

The tragedies of diversion and the economics of its success form an interesting eye-opening parallel. This strange brotherhood of opposite magnetic poles can be exemplified through the near awesome fact that neither force is well known. By-and-large, hardly a respectable percentage of the population is familiar with diversion. Certainly, a large percentage of the people who should be aware of it are not. Therefore, they are totally unaware of the ramifications of diversion.

It is also disastrous that not enough funds have been extended to expand diversionary programs into private agencies within the communities of the United States. Who can debate the fact that most communities, large and small, could use diversion programs? But that presents another area of insufficient planning. Not enough people have been trained for diversion. Its study is an entirely new field, as it were, and its new perspective of criminal justice needs to be explored and cultivated. Perhaps, it's realistic to say that not enough people care about our youth. Or, it could be that not enough parents care about their own children. There are several methods of dealing with juveniles, but diversion is *the one* coming area which our city, county, and country fathers cannot afford to overlook.[8]

Juvenile Rights: A Solution or Part of the Problem?

In re Gault opened the door for procedural rights in juvenile justice. Since that decision there has been a continuing re-examination of procedures resulting in the provision of juvenile rights similar to those of adults in most areas. Guaranteeing these rights, however, has been a mixed blessing. The provision of procedural safeguards has not yet transformed the juvenile justice system into a copy of the adult system. Thus far it seems to have combined some of the less desirable aspects of *both* systems, not a very desirable outcome.

The informal nature of juvenile justice was originally predicated on the belief that protective and reformative procedures would follow which would be good for the juvenile. As the juvenile correctional system became less and less *reformative,* and more and more *punitive,* the need for greater procedural safeguards became apparent. It took action by the Supreme Court in the Gault decision to bring about action, however. This has been a pattern in both the adult and juvenile systems—to wait until the judiciary makes a major decision before taking action to remedy the ill.

As each of the procedural rights have been provided, the juvenile justice process has undergone great change, which has been positive by legalistic standards, but hard to measure in human terms. One major change has been from the informal proceeding of the past to the advocacy proceedings of the present.

Advocacy: A New Meaning Since Gault

The Gault decision has provided new strength to juvenile justice advocacy. The advocacy process between the prosecution and defense was previously conducted without the participation of the juvenile, and sometimes without the juvenile's presence. Mistakes and bad decisions in the juvenile court could not be corrected by the juvenile's representative in the courtroom or later on appeal prior to the Gault decision.

Advocacy is aimed at the decision-maker, in this case the juvenile court judge, to get him to adopt the advocate's view of the case. Through this process, facts are brought to light that might otherwise have remained undiscovered. The purposes of the advocate system, often misunderstood by the public, are legitimate and functional. Without this system of attack and counterattack, unidimensional decisions would be made and the system (and the accused) would suffer and flounder.

Advocacy is not limited to attorneys for the defense or for the prosecution in the juvenile justice system. At each step of the process someone is trying to sway decision makers to a different view of the situation. All participants in the process seem to adopt a ''side'' and generally stick to it in attempting to influence the outcome. The policeman who wants to get a ''rotten'' juvenile off the streets will adopt the prosecution ''side.'' Friends and concerned parents may adopt the defense ''side'' as their own. While the practice of providing a specific prosecution and defense in juvenile proceedings was not the rule until after Gault, they have existed as rough categories all along.

Prosecutors have had a very small part in juvenile proceedings in the past, for most of the process was relatively relaxed and the rules of evidence were seldom adhered to. Petitioners (complainants) were seldom in need of representation in this informal atmosphere. The court was there to *protect* the juvenile, and the role of prosecutor seemed to violate this concept. But, as more and more juveniles were being represented by *defense* counsel, the scales of justice tipped too far in the direction of the defense. Pre-trial investigation and preparation by a strong defense advocate caused many otherwise provable cases to be dismissed.

The function of the judge is to be a referee. Assuming the prosecution role obviously results in bias on the part of the judge, closing a mind that should be open, Besharov notes:

> The judge should be ''the only disinterested lawyer connected with the proceeding. He has no interest except to see that justice is done, and he has no more important duty than to see that the facts are properly developed and that their bearing upon the question at issue are clearly understood by the jury.'' He can intervene in a proceeding only in situations where counsel is inadequately examining a witness, the witness is reluctant, an expert is inarticulate or less than candid, the facts are insufficiently elucidated in a long trial, an issue needs to be clarified or when justice or the orderly progress of the trial requires it.[9]

Attorneys for the petitioners, therefore, have had to become real prosecutors, ready to fight for the rights of their clients instead of assuming a *parens patriae* relationship with the court and the juvenile accused. After proof of their case, they can look toward nonjudicial handling of the case and the use of diversion and other alternatives. Above all it is the prosecutor advocate's job to seek the truth and do *justice;* anything less is unethical and probably illegal.

The defense advocate's role in the juvenile process grew during the press for similar advocacy in the adult system during the 1950s and 1960s. *In re Gault* made this role a right and regular representation of juveniles is now the rule. Juvenile advocates seek to keep their clients from any further contact with the juvenile justice system, if possible. They have generally shown great energy toward getting their clients "off." The lack of proof that treatment, offered under *parens patriae,* is effective spurs many juvenile defense advocates to use all their skills to keep clients out of the clutches of the system. The defense advocate must be prepared to fight as hard as the prosecution and leave *parens patriae* to the judge.

Advocacy, since Gault, has turned the juvenile court proceeding into a true legal proceeding. The advocates on both sides have had problems in developing protocols and procedures in a system that had not previously been a legal battleground. Many of the same tactics—motions, delays, obfuscation and bluster—that have slowed down the adult system are creeping into juvenile proceedings, for advocacy, like rights for juveniles, is a two-edged sword. As the practice grows, the system becomes more and more cumbersome. Unfortunately, the juveniles are the ones who often suffer by either being denied the treatment needed for their problems (defense wins) or by being placed into a system that doesn't work (prosecution wins). It is still too early to make judgments on advocacy, but it appears to be leading to another adult system at the juvenile level.

Youth in Juvenile Justice: Offenders or Victims?

Virtually all the experts in the field of juvenile justice agree that the most effective way to help children in trouble is keep them *out of the system entirely.* The juvenile institutions of America, from the worst detention center to the finest cottage facility, create two sets of victims: first, the juvenile offender, who is victimized by the other residents, the staff, the guards, and the shame of institutionalization; second, society, which is victimized by the creation of yet another bitter, angry, and well-trained young criminal who will take out the frustration of his experience on the society that inflicted it upon him.

There is yet another victim in this process, the victim of the offense itself. The victims of crimes which bring juveniles into the institutions of America have their rights as well, but any movement toward a juvenile justice system that more closely approximates the adult criminal justice system, while satisfying the desire of the victims for punishment and vengeance, will only exacerbate the victimization of the youths.

Children are doubly victimized by a system that seems to punish them for crimes of which they are the victims. In cases of child abuse and incest, for example, it is often only the child/victim who is removed from the family setting and institutionalized. Granted, the motive for removing the child from an environment which exposes him to danger may be protection. Being placed in a detention center or juvenile institution, however, has the same impact on the juvenile *victim* as the juvenile *offender*. As juveniles try to understand why they have been institutionalized while abusing or incestuous family members remain free, they also begin to learn the tricks of the trade so that they can victimize society.

Yet another kind of victim is the juvenile exploited by the adult world. Boy prostitutes, children in pornographic films and publications, runaways used for sexual exploitation and even for ritual murder, are all described in a fascinating book by Robin Lloyd, *For Money or Love: Boy Prostitution in America*. Children who are mere victims of adults who prey upon their weakness are arrested and further victimized by the system. As noted by Lloyd:

> The theory behind institutionalization is that if a boy cannot learn to live within society's rules, then he must be locked up so that society is protected from him—all this done, of course, in the best interest of the child.
>
> The sheer madness of the theory must surely be obvious. Put in simplistic terms the cycle is as follows: A boy is having a problem in school. The parents go to the juvenile authorities and complain they can no longer handle the boy and ask for help; they have given up. Even if there are alternatives, the parents rarely know what they are. So the hapless parents and the helpless boy stand before a juvenile judge, often unqualified, who sets the judicial process in motion by bringing the boy into the juvenile justice pipeline—that grim, inept system so stoutly supported by the grim, inept people who administer it.
>
> Once in the juvenile justice maze, the boy joins the half million other children being held annually in juvenile facilities, many of them for such "crimes" as truancy, talking back, petty theft, running away, and a litany of other inconsequential incidents that have been foisted off on the public as juvenile crimes. The boy will be thrown into contact with others committed for murder, rape, arson, drug abuse, drug dealing, burglary, mayhem, and manslaughter.
>
> Dr. Korn put it this way: "We persist in these activities in the face of incontrovertible evidence that we are failing. Even so, this failure does not result in the loss of our exclusive confession, our monopoly we defend against all competition, especially from the private citizens. Our field is almost unique in that failure is a virtual guarantee of greater prestige, power—and more money. I can think of no other business in which the failure of the product has been so successfully used as an argument for more of the same operations that produced it . . . In spite of all the trouble we take, and all the suffering we inflict, the security and peace of the citizenry—who are the victims of crime—continues in jeopardy. And that jeopardy appears to be growing."[10]

Screening and Classification: Some Hope

Juveniles whose needs are best met outside the juvenile justice system by more effective school counseling programs and family therapy should be screened out as early as possible. In many jurisdictions screening is combined with classification in an attempt to match juvenile problems with effective solutions.

As noted in chapter 7, the promise of treatment has been largely unfulfilled because of society's lack of financial support. The newer movement attempts to provide a more effective match between the juvenile's specific custody/treatment combination of needs to protect society while helping the juvenile to cope. Identification of the deficiencies in the juvenile's ability to handle behavioral problems has become a specific goal of current projects aimed at classification for treatment.

Many classification typologies have been attempted in past juvenile justice systems. The failures of these typologies are more the result of *omission* than of *commission*. Too often, the classification diagnostics were ignored or modified by institutional personnel with a vested interest in perpetuation of the status quo. New attempts at classification seem to have promise.

Some Modest Proposals for "Justice" for Juveniles

American society has always attempted to classify its problems in simplistic terms—good guys and bad guys, success and failure. One thing that research in juvenile delinquency has proved is that none of our juvenile offenders are all *bad* or all *good* either. Programs aimed at the worst characteristics of our problem juveniles sometimes eliminate whatever was good in those juveniles as well.

It seems time to examine the possibility of a *social justice* model for the juvenile offenders of America. The social justice model would be aimed at the specific needs and problems of the individual juvenile, without regard to the offense that brought them into the system.

The social justice model shown in Figure 17–1 provides for alternatives and screening points at all points of the process that are programmed, not diversionary. Alternative routes in the process would be chosen because of identified needs rather than the hesitancy of those within the system to use its procedures. Major problems, such as mental illness and physical deficiencies, are addressed by an appropriate system.

Because so many juveniles are removed from the social justice system soon after initial contact (i.e., status offenders), the remainder will be able to receive financial and personnel resource support adequate to meeting their needs.

While the social justice model is at present only a flow chart, it could be a reality within the limits of current resources and facilities. The most significant problem that faces the implementation of such a system is the

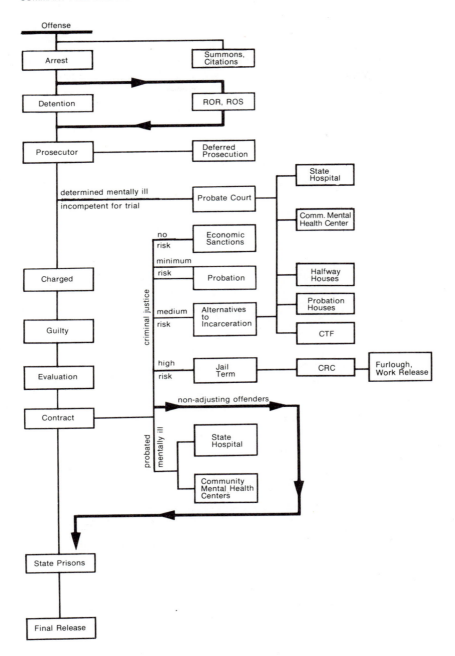

FIGURE 17—1. A model for a social justice system

Source: Harry E. Allen and Clifford E. Simonsen, *Corrections in America* (Encino, Ca.: Glencoe Publishing Co., Inc. 1975), p. 490.

fragmentation that stymies efforts to create anything approaching a juvenile justice "system." Consolidation of juvenile justice administration at the state level would be an important start toward a solution to this problem. So long as juvenile justice creates jobs and patronage at all levels of the political process, however, it is unlikely that we shall see the proposed model of social justice except in brief glimpses.

Where Next?

In this somewhat lengthy text on juvenile justice, we have often accentuated the negative, perhaps because there is so much of it to accentuate. Perhaps we have often attempted to apply principles that have failed in other systems to the juvenile justice system, describing intervention strategies and detailing processes for their implementation. Perhaps it is time to reaccess our priorities.

If intervention, under whatever model, has been such an abject failure, perhaps we should consider active *non*intervention as a model for a juvenile justice system of the future. Edwin Schur, in *Radical Non-Intervention: Rethinking the Delinquency Problem*, suggests some broad guidelines for priorities:

1. *There is need for a thorough reassessment of the dominant ways of thinking about youth "problems."*
   We can no longer afford the comforting illusion that these problems are completely attributable to identifiable individuals—whether we label them "bad," "sick," or "socially disadvantaged." The behavior patterns in question are part and parcel of our social and cultural system, and any efforts to change them must take that centrally into account. Youthful "misconduct," like misconduct generally, is inevitable under any form of social order. There is some leeway to influence the extent and forms of misconduct that prevail under a particular set of social conditions, but this influence can only operate as a consequence of efforts to shape the broader sociocultural and definitional contexts that the behavior reflects. From this standpoint the specific youth "problems" we now experience have to be recognized as one of the prices we pay for maintaining a particular kind of social structure and dominant value system. We have to consider whether it is worth paying the price. We may conclude on sober reflection that we have greatly and unnecessarily exaggerated the price; that we accept some of this behavior instead of considering it socially problematic and trying to "solve" it by legal methods. In some instances, we may feel that the price paid is so high and so alarming that major changes in our social and cultural systems are necessary.

2. *Some of the most valuable policies for dealing with delinquency are not necessarily those designated as delinquency policies.*
   This follows from the fact that delinquency reflects more general sociocultural conditions. Yet . . . we "compartmentalize" crime and delinquency

phenomena. Somehow, when we try to remake our socioeconomic order and reshape our dominant cultural values, we do not feel that we are confronting the specifically disturbing behavior we call delinquency. The impact of such efforts must be indirect, and perhaps incomplete, but we would do well to heed the following recent comment: ''the construction of a just system of criminal justice in an unjust society is a contradiction in terms.'' Since delinquency and juvenile justice are in some degree inherently political phenomena, major changes in this area necessarily require broad political decisions.

3. *We must take young people more seriously if we are to eradicate injustice to juveniles.*

   There is some evidence that the most potent deterrent to delinquency lies in bonds of attachment to conventional society. Perhaps we should concentrate more on strengthening those bonds than on combating ''criminogenic'' forces that supposedly have a hold on our children. This, in turn, implies not only the creation of a more just and egalitarian society, but also a legal system that young people can respect, and above all, a sense among young people that the society respects them. It is not necessary that we all join the counterculture. But our acceptance of cultural pluralism (as in racial and ethnic matters) must also govern our attitudes and policies toward youth. Our traditional reactions to youth and our definitions of youth problems have been very ambivalent—fear and envy mixed with admiration and fond concern. Indeed, the fact that adults see youth as a ''problem'' reflects this outlook. Sane youth policies will have to be based on greater acceptance of young people on their own terms, a willingness to live with a variety of life styles, and a recognition of the fact that the young people of our society are not necessarily confused, troubled, sick, or vicious. These attitudes cannot emerge within the context of the present juvenile justice system, with its paternalistic, patronizing, even hostile philosophy.

4. *The juvenile justice system should concern itself less with the problems of so-called ''delinquents,'' and more with dispensing justice.*

   A major first step in this direction would be to greatly narrow the present jurisdiction of the juvenile court. It is significant that even the President's Crime Commission, a far from ''radical'' body, has made such a recommendation: ''in view of the serious stigma and the uncertain gain accompanying official action, serious consideration should be given complete elimination from the court's jurisdiction of conduct illegal only for a child.'' But beyond this, the entire conception of ''individualized justice'' requires reassessment. In combination with the vagueness of delinquency statutes, the enormous amount of discretion vested in officials at the various stages of delinquency-processing invites uncertainty and confusion and sets the stage for discriminatory practices. Nor does the basic notion of ''treating'' the child's broad problems, rather than reacting to a specific law violation, appear to further the aim of ''rehabilitation'' in any meaningful way. In fact the sense of injustice to which this approach gives rise may, as we have seen, actively reinforce attitudes that breed delinquency.

   . . .

Individualized justice must necessarily give way to a *return to the rule of law*. This means that while fewer types of youthful behavior will be considered legal offenses, in cases of really serious misconduct such traditional guidelines as *specificity, uniformity,* and *nonretroactivity* ought apply. Juvenile statues should spell out very clearly just what kinds of behavior are legally proscribed, and should set explicit penalties for such violations (with perhaps some limited range of alternatives available to sentencing judges). This is quite consistent with what research has told us about the nature of delinquency causation and the efficacy of treatment, and carries the great advantage that it would increase clarity, ensure more equitable administration of justice, and would probably generate among young people greater respect for the legal system. Such measures would not constitute a "get tough" policy so much as a "deal evenly" one, and—it should again be emphasized—they would apply to a much narrower range of "offenses" than now exists. For those kinds of behavior that society is reluctant to simply "do nothing about," but for which a stern legal approach seems inappropriate, various "diversion" schemes such as those cited earlier could be developed.

These policies would squarely face up to the euphemistic evasions that have characterized much of juvenile "justice" in the past, and they would state premises and goals candidly and decisively. It is not heartlessly conservative to recognize that there may be certain actions we wish to punish, provided the range of offenses is carefully circumscribed and the rules equitably administered. But most of the stern measures taken against young people have not been in their "best interests." Continuing to delude ourselves on that score can only impede the development of sane delinquency policy.

5. *As juvenile justice moves in new directions, a variety of approaches will continue to be useful.*

Even if enough people with the power to effect legislative and judicial change become convinced that an entirely new approach along the lines I have indicated is needed, it will take time to reach that goal. While the system is moving in that direction (and I have tried to show that it already is), certain understandings that already are beginning to be part of the "conventional wisdom" in the delinquency field might well guide policy. With respect to prevention programs those with a collective or community focus should be preferred to those that single out and possibly stigmatize particular individuals. Programs that employ "indigenous" personnel (local community people such as older youths who have been gang members) should be preferred to those that employ only outside professionals. As regards treatment, noninstitutional and voluntary programs should be preferred over institutional and compulsory ones, and most likely the ultimate goal should be the abolition of treatment institutions as such. In the meantime, available evidence favors emphasizing relatively unstructured group sessions more than intensive individual psychotherapy. Bureaucratic and identity-destroying features should be eliminated in existing institutions, and practical training that can be useful on return to the outside world should be stressed.[11]

These noble principles, combined with a greater emphasis on developing a true juvenile justice *system* of integrated and articulated alternatives will perhaps finally begin to provide a picture less grim than that described by Mark Green:

> Youth are today's paternalized and oppressed group. They are considered undisciplined spirits, marginal citizens, in need of training and social control. Schools, therefore, exercise *in loco parentis* dominion over them, courts exercise *parens patriae* command over them, and the family leverage of economic support binds them to the home. Yet, like predecessor groups protected for their own benefit, the young do not passively accept their predetermined roles. Boxed in by these three insensitive institutions, they often fight to break out.[12]

NOTES

1. M. Siegler and H. Osmond, *Models of Madness, Models of Medicine* (New York: Macmillan, 1974).

2. R. Sommer, *The End of Imprisonment* (New York: Oxford Press, 1976), pp. 24–25.

3. L. Cole, *Our Children's Keepers* (New York: Grossman, 1972), pp. 26–27.

4. H. Allen and C. Simonsen, *Corrections in America: An Introduction* (Beverly Hills, Calif.: Glencoe Press, 1975), p. 361.

5. National Advisory Commission on Criminal Justice Standards and Goals, *Courts* (Washington, D.C.: U.S. Government Printing Office, 1973), p. 289.

6. J. Van Ravenhorst, "Proposed Juvenile Code Revision—Discussion Draft for February 7, 1977," Unpublished memorandum, Judiciary Committee, Forty-fifth Legislature, State of Washington, Olympia, Washington (February 4, 1977), pp. 3–5.

7. J. Latina and J. Schembera, "Volunteer Homes for Status Offenders: An Alternative to Detention," *Federal Probation*, December 1976, pp. 45–46.

8. J. Rossi, *Hard Cores Don't Come From Apples* (Pasadena, Calif.: Ward Ritchie Press, 1976), pp. 124–25.

9. D. Besharov, *Juvenile Justice Advocacy Practice in a Unique Court* (New York: Practicing Law Institute, 1974), p. 42.

10. R. Lloyd, *For Money or Love: Boy Prostitutes in America* (New York: Vanguard Press, 1976), pp. 118–19.

11. E. Schur, *Radical Non-Intervention: Rethinking the Delinquency Problem* (Englewood Cliffs, N.J.: Prentice-Hall, 1973), pp. 166–70.

12. M. Green, "The Law of the Young," in *With Justice for Some* (Boston: Beacon Press, 1970), pp. 1–2.

Index